MILTON'S PECULIAR GRACE

This book is dedicated to
Joan
Sam, Claire, and Dan
Anna and Martin

Copyright © 2007 by Cornell University

All rights reserved. Except for brief quotations in a review, this book, or parts thereof, must not be reproduced in any form without permission in writing from the publisher. For information, address Cornell University Press, Sage House, 512 East State Street, Ithaca, New York 14850.

First published 2007 by Cornell University Press

Printed in the United States of America

Library of Congress Cataloging-in-Publication Data

Fallon, Stephen M.
  Milton's peculiar grace: self-representation and authority / Stephen M. Fallon.
    p. cm.
  Includes bibliographical references and index.
  ISBN-13: 978-0-8014-4516-3 (cloth : alk. paper)
  ISBN-10: 0-8014-4516-7 (cloth : alk. paper)
  1. Milton, John, 1608-1674—Criticism and interpretation. 2. Self in literature. 3. Autobiography in literature. 4. Authority in literature. I. Title.
PR3592.S38F35   2006
821'.4—dc22   2006023312

Cornell University Press strives to use environmentally responsible suppliers and materials to the fullest extent possible in the publishing of its books. Such materials include vegetable-based, low-VOC inks and acid-free papers that are recycled, totally chlorine-free, or partly composed of nonwood fibers. For further information, visit our website at www.cornellpress.cornell.edu.

Cloth printing   10 9 8 7 6 5 4 3 2 1

MILTON'S PECULIAR GRACE

Self-Representation and Authority

STEPHEN M. FALLON

CORNELL UNIVERSITY PRESS
ITHACA AND LONDON

Contents

Preface: The Anomalous Milton	ix
Acknowledgments	xv
Texts and Abbreviations	xix
1. Self-Representation, Intention, and Authority	1
Interlude: The 1633 "Letter to a Friend"	14
2. The Least of Sinners: Milton in Context	21
3. "Himself before Himself": The Early Works	45
4. "Kingdom of Free Spirits": The Anti-Prelatical Works	79
5. "The Spur of Self-Concernment": The Works on Domestic Liberty	110
Interlude: Interregnum Poetry	146
6. "It Was I and No Other": Interregnum Prose	150
7. "Elect above the Rest": *De Doctrina Christiana* and *Paradise Lost*	182
8. "If All Be Mine": Confidence and Anxiety in *Paradise Lost*	203
9. "I as All Others": *Paradise Regained* and *Samson Agonistes*	237
Epilogue	265
Index	271

Preface: The Anomalous Milton

John Milton found it difficult to resist writing about himself. Whether speaking in his own person as author of controversial prose works, in the partially mediated voice of lyric speaker or epic narrator, or in the displaced form of narrative or dramatic characters who uncannily resemble him, Milton gives us Milton. John Diekhoff found enough explicitly autobiographical passages to fill a substantial volume, *Milton on Himself,* a title Milton might well have liked. Northrop Frye remarked that Shakespeare despite his bawdry is the chastest of writers, in that he does not write about himself.[1] By that measure, the autobiographically promiscuous Milton, to borrow Hamlet's simile, unpacks his heart like a whore.

   Milton's penchant for autobiography fits his cultural context, in which spiritual autobiographies and conversion narratives proliferated. It is, on the other hand, a striking anomaly that Milton, in many ways the archetypal Puritan author, studiously avoided the all but compulsory script of Puritan autobiography. According to this script, derived from the examples of Paul's letters and Augustine's *Confessions,* one describes a trajectory from youthful, often grotesque, sinfulness, through conviction of sin, reception of the Word, regeneration of the spirit, and sanctification, with each step from conviction onward attended by enabling grace. Milton did not turn his hand, either right or left, to this story. Instead, and astonishingly, he often writes as if untouched by human frailty. Diekhoff could not possibly have titled his

---

   1. Northrop Frye, *A Natural Perspective: The Development of Shakespearean Comedy and Romance* (New York: Columbia University Press, 1965), p. 43.

collocation of autobiographical passages *Confessions,* to say nothing of *Grace Abounding to the Chief of Sinners.* It is to this anomaly that my study owes its genesis. Why did Milton write about himself so compulsively? Why did he avoid the otherwise universal story? Why did he substitute a story of precocious and continued virtue, even at times, it seems, of sinlessness? What pressures resulted from his going so directly against the grain?

One answer to all but the last of these questions suggests itself. Milton avoids one tradition, the Augustinian confessional, for another, the Aristotelian ethical proof. One purchases authority by demonstrating one's own gravity and virtue. Clearly many of Milton's self-representations are essays in the ethical proof. But this answer complicates rather than settles the question. In Milton's time and place, paradoxically but not surprisingly, an admission of sinfulness had become part of the ethical proof. Not to acknowledge one's sinfulness is a sign of pride, just as to recapitulate Augustine's story is a sign of Christian humility and godliness. In the language of the Son in Milton's *Paradise Regained,* condemning the classical wisdom in which the ethical proof had its origin, those ignorant of "how man fell / Degraded by himself, on grace depending" are "Ignorant of themselves" (*PR* 4.311–12, 310).[2] Milton himself may not have been immune from the infirmity diagnosed here.[3]

I take my title from an anomalous moment in *Paradise Lost,* when the Father explains to his Son and the angels his disposition of grace and his plan of election: "Some I have chosen of peculiar grace / Elect above the rest; so is my will: / The rest shall hear me call, and oft be warned / Their sinful state" (*PL* 3.183–86). The rest who hear the call, the Father goes on to explain, are given sufficient grace to pray, repent, obey, and be saved, a process, as Milton insists elsewhere in the epic and at length in his theological treatise, available to all fallen human beings. The anomalous category, those "chosen of peculiar grace," is a momentary Calvinist eruption in an otherwise Arminian epic, but it may be more than this. It may mark Milton's inchoate perception of blamelessness and perfection, a peculiar grace indeed given Milton's endorsement elsewhere of the universality of the fall.

One thesis of this book is that while Milton is a theological poet, he is not a religious poet. The Augustinian theology of fall, grace, and regeneration that he endorses seems to have little or no effect on the way he thinks about himself. While he shares the doctrine that led his contemporaries to follow anxiously in the scripts of their own lives a drama of alienation, grace, and justification, Milton seems oblivious to the effects of the fall in himself, or at

---

2. For citation abbreviations of Milton's works, see abbreviations, p. xix.
3. Richard Strier argues that Milton was more comfortable with the classical ideal of magnanimity than with the Christian ideal of humility. See "Milton against Humility," in *Religion and Culture in Renaissance England,* ed. Claire McEachern and Debora Shuger (Cambridge: Cambridge University Press, 1997), 258–86.

least in his representations of himself. There is nothing like the wrestling with sin that one finds in contemporaries across the theological spectrum, from Donne to Herbert to Bunyan.

The story I tell traces the implications of the story Milton tells of himself. The acknowledgment of sin and weakness repressed in his self-representations returns inevitably, in representations of an alternate self not owned by the author but clearly resembling him. Despite the theme of the return of the repressed, this book will not attempt the kind of global psychoanalytic reading of Milton mounted by John Shawcross.[4] While informed by the insights of William Kerrigan's *Sacred Complex*—most notably concerning the subtle Miltonic dialectic between "the bliss of unfallen existence" and "the narrowed horizons and implacable sorrows of fallen existence"—this book's aim is different.[5] Rather than commenting on Milton's life outside his texts, I examine the construction of a life through his self-representations. I am interested in the development of, and the tensions generated by, these self-representations, as well as their disabling and enabling effect on Milton's thinking and his art. *Peculiar Grace* attempts a *literary* biography of the *autobiographical* Milton.

Addressing Milton's self-representations will bring me hard up against the anomalous place of Milton in contemporary literary studies. Milton represents himself mainly to establish his authority in the world and in his texts. In more than one case, Milton supports his interpretation of a text by pointing to the character of the author and his presumed intention. He manifestly wishes to embed himself in his own texts in order to gain immortality for himself, authority for his arguments, and control over his readers' interpretations. His insistent presence in his texts thus has implications for the relation of intention and meaning. No wonder, then, that Milton and Milton studies have been scandals in the contemporary academy. If Roland Barthes famously announced three decades ago the "death of the author," Milton is one author who has resolutely refused to die. The tension between Milton's practice and recent theory is played out within the work of a scholar who is both a leading Miltonist and leading theorist, and whose name and fame have been serendipitously and proleptically yoked by Milton in his phrase "that noted Fish" (*YP* 2:642).[6]

In the first of two introductory chapters, I define what I mean by the terms self-representation, intention, and authority and consider their implications.

---

4. John Shawcross, *John Milton: The Self and the World* (Lexington: University of Kentucky Press, 1993).

5. Kerrigan, The *Sacred Complex: On the Psychogenesis of "Paradise Lost"* (Cambridge, Mass.: Harvard University Press, 1983); I quote from p. 295.

6. Here and elsewhere, I quote Milton's English prose from the *Complete Prose Works of John Milton,* ed. Don M. Wolfe et al., 8 vols. (New Haven, 1953–82); references to this edition are cited in the text as *YP.*

For a poet virtually all of whose characters are versions of the author, the definition of the first term is crucial. The second chapter surveys the forms of self-representation that Milton might have been expected to echo but did not. Between these introductory chapters, I pause to examine the 1633 "Letter to a Friend," in the hope that this concentrated specimen of Milton's practice of self-representation will ground the discussion of Milton's relation to theories of intention and provide an initial Miltonic foil to the contrasting autobiographical practice of his contemporaries. The body chapters are arranged chronologically. The alternative would have been to organize the discussion by the central themes of Miltonic self-representation (the writer as prophet, the writer as exceptionally virtuous, the writer as the refined product of progressive moral and intellectual sifting) or the central strategies (turning defense into offense, identification with heroes or God, projecting anxieties and self-criticism onto nameless third persons or adversaries). Organization by theme and strategy has its advantages, but it exaggerates the static, Milton's so-called unchanging mind. The chronological method will allow me to foreground the trajectory of Milton's self-representations, from early, relatively naïve, uncomplicated, and univocal assertions of preternatural virtue, through the unsettling of this idealized self-construction, to the more conflicted and chastened self-representations of the mature Milton.

If the typical Puritan autobiography strives to show the meeting between the particular texture of one life and the applicability of that life's trajectory to every (godly) man or woman, Milton's entirely atypical self-representation attempts to purchase authority for a singular prophetic voice suspended above the rest. The perfectionism implicit in his self-representations suggests an affinity with the Quakers,[7] but his own theological perspective, and particularly his Augustinian conception of the fall and original sin, is not congenial to perfectionism. Milton, I will argue, at times implicitly treats himself as a member of what must be for him a null set, the set of the unfallen. Ultimately, the strain of standing on this lonely and godlike pinnacle leaves its mark on Milton's self-representations in displaced, implicit, and apparently unintentional self-representations, which register the frailty and common humanity studiously avoided in the explicit self-representations. In the uneasy balance between the two sets of self-representations one can look for the creative energy and the perspective informing Milton's greatest works.

I have come to see Milton, then, as a creatively divided figure. The divisions run between acknowledged and unacknowledged self-representations, between arguments designed to apply to all and those designed to apply to the few who resemble Milton, and between the Olympian perspective of the epic

---

7. For Milton's relation to the Quakers, see David Loewenstein, *Representing Revolution in Milton and His Contemporaries* (Cambridge: Cambridge University Press, 2001), pp. 242–68.

narrator and the empathetic perspective of a son of Adam. Peter Herman's opposition to reading Milton as monolithic does not go far enough, for in the place of the real disjunctions in Milton's texts Herman provides a catalogue of the pervasive binaries and alternatives composing what has been called Milton's poetics of choice. Perhaps shying away from the implications of his argument, Herman finds consistency even in Milton's treatment of gender, with *Paradise Lost* resolving the antinomies of the divorce tracts and emerging as "possibly the most thorough critique of misogyny in the English language," a judgment that will startle many readers who see Milton as tensely divided between patriarchalism and something approaching egalitarianism.[8]

Two caveats may be necessary before beginning. First, because my topic will be Milton's self-representations, my readings will perforce be partial; I realize that more is going on in the works that I examine than the self-representing that I discuss. Second, while describing Milton's self-representations as at times self-aggrandizing, as strained and defensive, and as marshaled for special pleading, and while arguing that the imperative of self-representation can sometimes distort Milton's arguments, I do so within the context of an immense respect for Milton's art, mind, and character. I cast a bright light on his practice of self-representation in the hope of understanding better one of the figures in the Western literary tradition most worth knowing. The self revealed, and the manner of that revelation, are endlessly fascinating, as Coleridge has testified: "it is a sense of [his] intense egotism that gives me the greatest pleasure in reading Milton's works. The egotism of such a man is a revelation of spirit."[9] This praise is arresting because egotism has for so long been a term of reproach. This study shares Coleridge's perspective, even at those moments when it locates and highlights tensions in Milton's self-representations.

---

8. Herman, *Destabilizing Milton: "Paradise Lost" and the Poetics of Incertitude* (New York: Palgrave Macmillan, 2005), p. 154.

9. From *Specimens of the Table Talk of the Late Samuel Taylor Coleridge*, ed. Henry Nelson Coleridge, 2 vols. (London, 1835), 2:241.

Acknowledgments

To list all of the debts incurred in the making of this book would be, like the task imposed on Psyche, an "incessant labor." Because of limitations of memory and space, some are sure to be left out, and for that I apologize. Among Milton scholars, I owe my greatest debts to John Rumrich and William Kerrigan; we have shared ideas and friendship, as well as the welcome labor of editing Milton for Modern Library. For support and encouragement, I am deeply grateful to Michael Lieb, David Loewenstein, Regina Schwartz, and to my other colleagues in the Newberry Milton Seminar, especially Achsah Guibbory, Alan Hager, Janel Mueller, Stella Revard, and Richard Strier. I have drawn inspiration and encouragement from countless Milton scholars further afield—a necessarily partial list includes Sharon Achinstein, Joan Bennett, Thomas Corns, Dennis Danielson, Stephen Dobranski, Richard DuRocher, J. Martin Evans, Stanley Fish, Laura Knoppers, John Leonard, Paula Loscocco, Thomas Luxon, Diane McColley, Annabel Patterson, John Rogers, Jason Rosenblatt, Alan Rudrum, Ashraf Rushdy, John Shawcross, Nigel Smith, Paul Stevens, John Tanner, James Grantham Turner, and Joseph Wittreich.

For their contributions to my writing and thinking, I am thankful to my colleagues at Notre Dame, and in particular to Henry Weinfield, Ted Cachey, Julia Marvin, Clark Power, and Graham Hammill. The book has benefited from exchanges with graduate students, notably Hong Won Suh, Jennifer Nichols, Sara Crosby, Mike Tomko, and Joel Dodson, and also with the many undergraduate students with whom I have read *Paradise Lost*. Jeffrey Speaks, Jennifer Nichols, Emily Husted, Gina Cora, Stephanie Thomas, Samuel

Fallon, Natalie Tenner, Claire Fallon, and Jack Calcutt provided diligent and able research assistance.

I have circulated sections of the book to various readers and audiences, and their responses have made the book better. John Rumrich, Henry Weinfield, and the anonymous reader for Cornell University Press read the entire manuscript and improved it greatly with their insights. The faults that remain are my own.

Research for this book has been supported by a Senior Fellowship for University Teachers from the National Endowment for the Humanities (1995–1996) and a special research leave from Notre Dame's College of Arts and Letters (2003–2004).

This book contains material originally included in four previously published essays; I thank the publishers for allowing me to draw upon my earlier work. A portion of chapter 5 is adapted from "'The Spur of Self-concernment': Milton in His Divorce Tracts," from *Milton Studies* 38, ed. Albert C. Labriola, © 2000 by University of Pittsburgh Press, reprinted by permission of the University of Pittsburgh Press. The section on the *Defences* in chapter 6 includes material from "Alexander More Reads Milton: Self-Representation and Anxiety in Milton's *Defences*," in *Milton and the Terms of Liberty*, ed. Graham Parry and Joad Raymond (D. S. Brewer, 2002): 111–24. A version of chapter 7 originally appeared as "'Elect above the Rest': Theology as Self-representation in Milton," in *Milton and Heresy*, ed. Stephen B. Dobranski and John P. Rumrich (Cambridge University Press, 1998), 93–116; © 1998 by the Syndics of Cambridge University Press. Chapter 8 incorporates material from "Intention and Its Limits in *Paradise Lost:* The Case of Bellerophon," published in *Literary Milton: Text, Pretext, Context,* ed. Diana Treviño Benet and Michael Lieb (Duquesne University Press, 1994), 161–79, 246–49. I also thank Random House for granting me permission to quote Milton's poetry from *The Complete Poetry and Essential Prose of John Milton,* ed. William Kerrigan, John Rumrich, and Stephen M. Fallon (New York: Modern Library, 2007).

It has been a pleasure working with Cornell University Press, and in particular with Roger Haydon, the Executive Editor, with Candace Akins, who oversaw the editing of the manuscript, and with everyone in the editorial and design departments.

This book has been some time in the making. As I wrestled with the question of how Milton thought and wrote about himself, events in my own life prompted self-reflection and change. When I took up the project there was no way of knowing that I would be widowed and spend five years as a single parent. Nancy Hungarland Fallon, my late wife, has left her mark on this book in many ways, as have our children, Sam, Claire, and Dan, in whom indeed "nature seems fulfilled in all her ends." As I completed the book, I found myself surprised by joy in the form of my wife, Joan Wulff Fallon, and my stepchildren, Anna and Martin Duchossois. I am grateful to Joan, "my latest found, my ever new delight," for her help, support, and encouragement as I finished the book, and for so much else.

Texts and Abbreviations

KJV — The Bible is quoted from the King James Version.

Works — *The Works of John Milton.* Edited by F. A. Patterson. 18 vols. New York: Columbia University Press, 1931–38. Milton's Latin prose is quoted from this edition.

YP — *Complete Prose Works of John Milton.* Edited by Don M. Wolfe et al. 8 vols. in 10. New Haven: Yale University Press, 1953–82. Milton's English prose and his Latin prose in translation are quoted from this edition.

The Complete Poetry and Essential Prose of John Milton. Edited by William Kerrigan, John Rumrich, and Stephen M. Fallon. New York: Modern Library, 2007. Milton's poems, including new translations of the Latin poetry by Gordon Braden, are quoted from this edition.

Abbreviations and Short Titles of Milton's Works

1673 Poems — *Poems, &c., upon Several Occasions*

Animadversions — *Animadversions upon the Remonstrants Defence against Smectymnuus*

Apology	*An Apology against a Pamphlet Call'd A Modest Confutation of the Animadversions upon the Remonstrant against Smectymnuus*
Civil Power	*A Treatise of Civil Power in Ecclesiastical Causes*
DDD	*The Doctrine and Discipline of Divorce*
De Doctrina	*De Doctrina Christiana*
Defensio	*Pro Populo Anglicano Defensio (Defence of the English People)*
Defensio Secunda	*Pro Populo Anglicano Defensio Secunda (Second Defence of the English People)*
Hirelings	*Considerations Touching the Likeliest Means to Remove Hirelings from the Church*
A Mask	*A Mask Presented at Ludlow Castle*
Of True Religion	*Of True Religion, Hæresie, Schism, Toleration*
Of Reformation	*Of Reformation Touching Church-Discipline in England*
PL	*Paradise Lost*
Poems 1645	*Poems of Mr. John Milton, Both English and Latin, Composed at several times*
PR	*Paradise Regained*
The Readie and Easie Way	*The Readie and Easie Way to Establish a Free Commonwealth*
The Reason of Church-Government	*The Reason of Church-Government Urg'd against Prelaty*
SA	*Samson Agonistes*
Tetra.	*Tetrachordon*

MILTON'S PECULIAR GRACE

Chapter 1

Self-Representation, Intention, and Authority

Contemplating self-representation, the hyphenated word itself, can like Keats' urn tease us out of thought. What is being represented, a self prior to the representation or a self constructed in the act of representation? Who is representing, the self as revealed in the literary artifact or the forever inaccessible author? What is the relation between the represented self and the historical figure of the author? In short, is the "self" in "self-representation" the self representing as well as the self represented, or is it merely the latter? Does it matter what the author thinks about the representation, or should we regard authorial claims for the authenticity of the self-representation as naïve?

Approaching self-representation in Milton, one confronts another set of questions. What counts as self-representation in this apparently most self-revelatory of authors? Or, one might ask, what does *not* count as self-representation? Coleridge says of *Paradise Lost* that "John Milton himself is in every line"; he "is himself before himself in every thing he writes."[1] Himself before himself. Coleridge's reflexive construction voices the involutions of self-representation. Milton is before himself in the quasi-spatial sense that he is to himself an object of contemplation. In the temporal sense he is the precursor; the story of John Milton precedes and occupies the center of his diverse works. Milton proliferates in his texts, as again Coleridge notes: "In the Paradise Lost— indeed in every one of his poems—it is Milton himself whom you see; his Satan,

---

1. From *Specimens of the Table Talk of the Late Samuel Taylor Coleridge,* ed. Henry Nelson Coleridge, 2 vols. (London, 1835), 1:129–30.

his Adam, his Raphael, almost his Eve—are all John Milton."[2] If Milton is everywhere in his texts, can he be anywhere in particular?

Varieties of Self-Representation

In this book, *self-representation* denotes writing in which the author provides, or appears to provide, an image of himself outside of and/or prior to the text. The qualification ("appears to provide") is indispensable, for my definition encompasses not merely intentional acts by which the historical author attempts to describe himself, but also moments when the author assimilates his image to conventional literary (and particularly generic) roles as well as when he reveals himself unintentionally. No account of Milton's self-representations can leave out those passages in the controversial prose and the familiar letters when Milton writes explicitly about himself. Notwithstanding his assertion in *The Reason of Church-Government* that "a Poet soaring in the high region of his fancies with his garland and singing robes about him might without apology speak more of himself then I mean to do . . . sitting here below in the cool element of prose" (*YP* 1:808), in the controversial works and the letters Milton claims to write in his own person about himself. That self is a construction, of course, a "self-representation," but it is unambiguously an attempted representation of the historical writer Milton, without the additional mediated layer of the poetic speaker or narrator. The largest share, at least in terms of volume, of the great set-pieces of Miltonic self-representation fall into this category, notably the extensive autobiographical excursions of *The Reason of Church-Government*, *An Apology for Smectymnuus*, the *Defensio Secunda*, and almost the entirety of the *Pro Se Defensio*.

The many and close resemblances between the self-representations in the prose and the characterization of Milton's speakers and narrators suggest that here at least we might relax the literary critic's customary caution against identifying the voice of the author with the voice of the work. In "Lycidas," for example, the speaker's anxious comments about immortality, prematurity, and belatedness echo and foreshadow passages in which Milton, in the prose, writes about Milton. The same is true for the voice of the narrator in *Paradise Lost*, whose moving evocation of blindness both places the speaker in the line of blind visionary poets and carries the conviction of the lived experience of a blind man.[3] However much we may need to remind ourselves that narrators are not in any simple and uncomplicated manner identical to authors, Milton

---

2. Ibid., 2:240–41.
3. Stella Revard rightly insists on the calculated literary and political resonance of moments in Milton's epic invocations that some readers have taken as merely autobiographical, but she does not deny that Milton uses his own biography even as he employs and inflects traditional pictures

constructs his narrator as a public face for himself.⁴ He invests his narrators with words and experiences that we recognize from the self-representing author of the prose.

Asserting that identifying the epic narrator with Milton implies "an author who is certain in his convictions," John Mulder views that narrator as a *persona* constructed by an author who is far less certain.⁵ While agreeing that Milton is not always certain, and that in the narrator we witness "Milton's simultaneous avowal and disavowal of his character, his aims, and his achievements" (147), I will maintain that this is all the more reason to identify the narrator with Milton. While one might argue, for example, that the intimations of overreaching surrounding the narrator's voicing of epic aspirations constitute signs of Milton's maintaining distance from that narrator, I will suggest that at these moments we see the ground shaking under Milton's feet as well as the narrator's. The aspirations remain Milton's aspirations, and the anxiety is the price he pays.⁶

Identifying self-representation is most difficult when considering characters in the poetry other than speaker or narrator. Milton himself speaks on both sides of the question of whether characters should be taken as proxies for their authors. He notes in 1642, albeit in a satiric and polemical context, that "the author is ever distinguisht from the person he introduces" (*YP* 1:880). But he also writes nearly a decade later in *Pro Populo Anglicano Defensio* that "it is the custom of poets to place their own opinions in the mouths of their great characters" (*YP* 4.1:446). Milton's poems can seem like halls of mirrors, with aspects of the poet peering back from virtually every character. Milton is always arguing, and his arguments are ventriloquized in his characters. In *Paradise Lost,* Milton speaks through Adam, Satan, Raphael, Eve, Abdiel, the Son, and the Father, in addition to the narrator. Here one could enter mazes of self-representation and find no end. To separate self-representation from mere ventriloquism, one might simply exclude all passages in which Milton

---

of the epic narrator ("Milton and the Progress of the Epic Proemium," in *John Milton: The Author in His Works,* ed. Albert C. Labriola and Michael Lieb, *Milton Studies* 38, [Pittsburgh: University of Pittsburgh Press, 2000], pp. 122–40).

4. Victoria Silver's argument that Milton keeps an ironic distance from his narrator in *Paradise Lost* is undermined by its fundamental dependence on a curious assertion that Milton's basic stance in the poem is Lutheran (*Imperfect Sense: The Predicament of Milton's Irony* [Princeton: Princeton University Press, 2001]). John Guillory is more persuasive in his claim that "Milton does not admit any distance between himself and the poet in the poem" (*Poetic Authority: Spenser, Milton, and Literary History* [New York: Columbia University Press, 1983], p. 104).

5. Mulder, "The Lyric Dimension of *Paradise Lost,*" *Milton Studies* 23 (1987): 146.

6. Joseph Wittreich has extended Mulder's arguments in interesting directions in "'Reading' Milton: The Death (and Survival) of the Author," in *John Milton: The Writer in His Works,* ed. Albert C. Labriola and Michael Lieb, *Milton Studies* 38 (Pittsburgh: University of Pittsburgh Press, 2000), pp. 10–46. Wittreich is a subtle guide to the kind of phenomena upon which I focus.

or the character of the narrator or speaker is not speaking. Making too hard and fast a distinction on this point, however, would imply a closer identification between the historical Milton and the narrator than even I would want to admit. Narrators and speakers, even if in many ways similar to Milton, are constructed characters. Milton nevertheless does speak in, and represent himself through, other characters.

I will begin with the assumption that the lines given to Milton's lyric speakers and epic narrators are the most likely sites of self-representation in his poetry. I will distinguish between those characters who voice sentiments that can reasonably be ascribed to Milton (e.g., the Father or Raphael in *Paradise Lost*) and those to whom Milton ascribes lived experiences that reconstitute in significant detail his own, for example the blind Samson of the tragedy and the precociously studious Son of the brief epic. Selecting these characters is a matter of relative judgment. Lacking an articulated life, Abdiel cannot resemble Milton in as many points as Samson, but his lone and courageous stand against Satan ("Among the faithless, faithful only he" [*PL* 5.897]) echoes Milton's single opposition to massed error in, for example, his suicidally principled opposition to the Restoration. Narrators' and other characters' relative potential for authorial self-representation can be viewed in two ways. On the one hand, because all characters, including narrators, are constructs, and because Milton patently draws on his own biographical experience as he creates characters, Milton can represent himself in any character and not only in the voice of "Milton" as speaker or narrator. On the other hand, in the autobiographical digressions in his prose or in the speakers and narrators in his poetry, Milton constructs public representations of the writing self, expecting his readers to accept the figure of the writer as the image of John Milton. These figures are in this way privileged or authorized self-representations.

Another way of saying this is that Milton intends the figures of speaker and narrator in his poems to be self-representations, much as he intends as self-representations those passages in the prose in which he makes a show of digressing from his argument to talk about his own upbringing, experience, character, and aspirations. The convergence between Milton's acknowledged depiction of his thoughts and inner life and the actions and words of some of his characters I will treat as self-representations in the wider sense; in the absence of self-representation in the more limited sense, this other manner of self-representation takes on greater weight, as in the cases of the brief epic and the biblical tragedy. One must be wary of circular argument (the character represents Milton because he or she says things that are characteristic of the author, which we know from the fact that he has characters say these things); a good test is consonance with passages in which Milton apparently intends to be taken as speaking in his own voice.

Intentional self-representations comprise the largest but not necessarily the most interesting part of the spectrum of literary phenomena that this book addresses. I am equally interested in unintended self-representations, those moments in which the text becomes a window into that which Milton neither chooses to share with his audience nor acknowledges as self-representation. Such passages might be labeled self-revelations or self-betrayals rather than self-representations. In *An Apology* Milton, having suffered a personal attack, prefaces his defense by autobiography with a comment that is revealing in more than one sense: "With me it fares now, as with him whose outward garment hath bin injur'd and ill bedighted; for having no other shift, what helpe but to turn the inside outwards, especially if the lining be of the same, or, as it is sometimes, much better" (*YP* 1:888–89). This strikingly apt figure, to which I will return, suggests how writing can simultaneously reveal and conceal the author. Milton means to signal his intention to share with his readers what is innermost and normally secret. As he turns not only his garment but himself inside out in this work and in others, it is not surprising that he reveals to us what was hidden from himself.

The Battle over Intention

Those who deny that authors can be present in texts, that authorial intentions can be discovered, or that such intentions even if discoverable can be relevant to interpretation and criticism, will turn from what I have been saying as from an impending train wreck. My method is on a collision course with a way of looking at the relation of authors to texts epitomized in a familiar assertion, now virtually a truism, in Roland Barthes's essay "The Death of the Author": "Writing is the destruction of every voice, of every point of origin. Writing is that neutral, composite, oblique space where our subject slips away, the negative where all identity is lost, starting with the very identity of the body writing."[7] The subject and his or her identity slip away because, in Barthes's eyes, literary writing, or at least fictional writing, is *intransitive*. Actions in literary texts are not performed with a view on affecting reality, but narrated. As a result, they have a function within the symbolic order of the text but no function outside the text. Barthes argues that in "ethnographic" or primitive societies, narratives were the responsibility of "a mediator, shaman or relator whose 'performance'—the mastery of the narrative code—may possibly be admired but never his 'genius'" (168). The author is a modern invention, which Barthes traces to the discovery of the "prestige

---

7. Barthes, "The Death of the Author" (1968), in *Image-Music-Text*, trans. Stephen Heath (London: Fontana, 1987), p. 142; subsequent quotations from Barthes are from this essay.

of the individual" fostered by "English empiricism, French rationalism, and the personal faith of the Reformation." (The swift leap from the shamanistic societies to the early modern period should raise some doubts at this point, as should the linking of shamanistic narrative and intransitivity.) It was left to the modern period, and particularly Stephane Mallarmé, to debunk the fetishization of the author, and to see that "it is language that speaks, not the author" (168).[8] With the formerly lionized author and his (authoritative) intentions dethroned, the text is left open to the play of meanings inherent in language: "Once the Author is removed, the claim to decipher a text becomes quite futile. To give a text an Author is to impose a limit on that text, to furnish it with a final signified, to close the writing. . . . In the multiplicity of writing, everything is to be *disentangled,* nothing *deciphered*" (171). Barthes celebrates the kind of reading possible only when the text is wrested from the illusory grip of the author and cleared of the fixed meanings tied to his or her intentions. The text becomes a space for the play of language, which is foreclosed by tyrannizing belief in rigid authorial intention. The freedom of the text bestows freedom on the critic.[9]

My approach will appear naïve from this perspective, but it has the virtue of taking Milton on his own terms. He insists on being present in his texts, on leaving something "doctrinal and exemplary to a Nation" in works marked by a distinctive style that is tied at least figuratively to what is banished by Barthes: "the very identity of the body writing." Those who read Milton's early work judged that "the stile by *certain vital signes* it had, was likely to *live*" (*YP* 1:815,809; my emphasis). This figure from *The Reason of Church-Government* anticipates the claim in *Areopagitica* nearly three years later that "Books are not absolutely dead things, but doe contain a potencie of life in them to be as active as that soule was whose progeny they are" (*YP* 2:492). For Milton, writing and the writer are continuous and inseparable; immortality gained by the writing will guarantee the immortality of the writer. The next moment, even as he gestures toward the death of the physical author, he reasserts that author's immortality: "a good Booke is the pretious life-blood of a

---

8. Barthes's reading of Mallarmé is tendentious. For a more nuanced sense of what Mallarmé means when he says in "Crise de Vers" that the poet's voice must *"cede l'initiative aux mots"* (cede the initiative to words), see Henry Weinfield, "Ceding the Initiative to Words: Mallarmé, Lyric Poetry, and the Problem of Translation," *Talisman: A Journal of Contemporary Poetry and Poetics* 20 (1999): 3–7.

9. Barthes argues, ironically (from my perspective), that the illusion of authorial intention gives the "victory to the critic" (presumably, victory over the text); if one can find the author and ascribe an intention, then "the work is 'explained' " (171). It is at least as plausible to say that it is the postmodern critic, freed from the responsibility of ascertaining intention, ranging only within the zodiac of his own or her wit in flying over the freely playing, endlessly signifying text, who enjoys an illusory victory over the text.

master spirit, *imbalm'd* and treasur'd up on purpose to a *life beyond life*" (*YP* 2:493; my emphasis).

Milton makes his bid for immortality not only as author but also as subject of his works (or, in other terms, as object as well as subject). The speaker in Shakespeare's *Sonnets* promises continuing, breathing life to the young man and the dark lady ("So long as men can breathe or eyes can see, / So long lives this, and this gives life to thee"; "You still shall live—such virtue hath my pen—/ Where breath most breathes, even in the mouths of men"[10]), but Shakespeare suppresses the fact that the first breather of the lines is the poet, not the young man. Milton takes the place both of the writer of the text and the subject embodied in the text. The distinction between the author who drops out and the text that survives evaporates when Milton claims that one who "hope[s] to write well hereafter in laudable things, ought him selfe to bee a true Poem" (*YP* 1:890). Milton here anticipates claims that the author like the text is a construct, but he insists that the construction or composition of the author is carried out by and inseparable from the living person who writes.

Milton's insistence on the author's immortality and on the continuity between historical author and the written texts does not by itself falsify the argument that the author dies in and into writing. Barthes does not require that authors know that they are dying. But Milton's practice does call into question Barthes's assertion of the intransitivity of the literary text. Barthes's literary texts represent rather than perform actions.[11] Michel Foucault argues along the same line when he says of modern literary texts that "without being restricted to the confines of its interiority, writing is identified with its own unfolded exteriority."[12] There are texts from Milton's time that may fit more closely Barthes's and Foucault's models of hermetic isolation from action. Andrew Marvell's "To His Coy Mistress," for example, with the skewed syllogism at its heart, is no less effective as a poem for its dubiousness as a piece of seduction. But Milton's texts are more transitive than Marvell's poem. The sonnet "On the Late Massacre at Piedmont," for example, is a sustained performative utterance. Milton's epic does not merely represent the act of justifying the ways of God to men. The poem is, among other things, the attempted justification announced at the beginning.

---

10. Sonnets 18 and 81, quoted from *The Sonnets,* ed. William Burto, rev. ed. (Harmondsworth: Signet, 1988).
11. Monroe C. Beardsley makes a point similar to Barthes' in "Intentions and Interpretations: A Fallacy Revived," in *The Aesthetic Point of View,* ed. Michael J. Wreen and Donald M. Callen (Ithaca: Cornell University Press, 1982), p. 190. According to Beardsley, literary authors represent illocutionary acts rather than perform them.
12. Foucault, "What Is an Author," in *Modern Criticism and Theory,* ed. David Lodge (London: Longman, 1988), pp. 197–98.

If Barthes and Foucault clearly assert that the author is dead, they are less clear on the time of death. Is the author always already dead, and is the celebrated birth of the author in the early modern period merely the rise of an illusion? Or is the modern writer a new animal, whose works must be read in ways different from those appropriate for older works? I alluded above to Barthes's foreshortened history of authorship, with the invention of the author in early modern European civilization following hard upon shamanistic, ethnographic societies. After a few centuries of literary dominance, this author is demystified by Mallarmé, who "was doubtless the first to see and to foresee in its full extent the necessity to substitute language itself for the person who until then had been supposed to be its owner. For him [Mallarmé], for us too, it is language which speaks, not the author" (168). Even here, where he makes his argument, it is ambiguous whether Mallarmé inaugurates a new line of writer, whom Barthes terms "scriptors," or whether he articulates what has always been true of all writers. Do scriptors replace authors, or have all authors been scriptors all along? Barthes gestures toward the former answer:

> The Author is thought to *nourish* the book, which is to say that he exists before it, thinks, suffers, lives for it, is in the same relation of antecedence to his work as a father to his child. In complete contrast, the modern scriptor is born simultaneously with the text, is in no way equipped with a being preceding or exceeding the writing, is not the subject with the book as predicate; there is no other time than that of the enunciation and every text is eternally written *here and now*. (170)

While his own historical survey makes the more modest claim that Mallarmé and his successors write a new kind of literature deliberately in tension with author-centered works, Barthes tips the discussion toward the other alternative: "The author *is thought* to nourish the book" (my emphasis). Barthes stretches beyond its limits a plausible historical argument on how and why some modern texts differ from premodern texts. When he concludes, "*We know now* that a text is not a line of words releasing a single 'theological' meaning (the 'message' of the Author-God) but a multi-dimensional space in which a variety of writings, none of them original, blend and clash" (170; my emphasis), he suggests that the kind of authorship that many Milton scholars find in Milton is not so much antiquated as illusory. Foucault also moves from historical argument to a blanket conclusion in "What Is an Author." When he writes that in "today's writing" the "point is not to manifest or exalt the act of writing, nor is it to pin a subject within language; it is rather a question of creating a space into which the writing subject constantly disappears,"[13] he seems to say that

---

13. Ibid., p. 198.

the modern period has seen the death of the author, but he goes on to argue that Aristotle and Shakespeare are no more present than modern authors.

Barthes moves swiftly from the rise of the author to his demise, and he ends his seminal essay with the arresting claim that "the birth of the reader must be at the cost of the death of the Author" (172). Milton as author proves from this perspective to be something like a group hallucination, now transcended. Catherine Belsey articulates a Barthesian truism when she argues that Milton would not have acknowledged her reading of his texts:

> Intention is not—cannot be—an activity of reconstructing an intended meaning which preceded the writing process. This traditional quarry of criticism is always a phantom—not merely elusive and probably illusory, but also dead. The author's intended meaning died in the moment that the texts came into being, and the text is necessarily more than the author conceived or knew."[14]

If the text is freed from the author at the moment of writing, then the author's intentions become irrelevant even if decipherable. It is undeniable that a text can mean more than the author knew, and it can needlessly straiten our reading to rule out any meanings not demonstrably arising from an author's conscious intention. But that is far short of the dubious claims that intention "*cannot* be" a matter of "reconstructing intended meaning" or that the "traditional quarry of criticism is *always* a phantom." It makes little sense to look, as we do, for intention behind what our contemporaries say and write, and then to deny that intention is relevant to a construal of what our predecessors said and wrote. We normally and appropriately read literary texts as carrying meaning, and meaning in ordinary language situations is understood to be generated by an intending speaker with the purpose of communicating to an audience. It is precisely the intending speaker who makes a word sequence that yields meaning as opposed to a random series of sounds.[15] In the absence of a principle for banishing intention more convincing than Barthes's intransitivity, we are free to continue reading literary texts as intentional constructions.

Milton and Intention

To read texts in this way has the significant advantage of aligning our assumptions with those of Milton's and his time. Marvell records the centrality of

---

14. Catherine Belsey, *John Milton: Language, Gender, Power* (Oxford: Basil Blackwell, 1988), p. 6.
15. This is true even of computer-generated sentences, which express at one or more removes the intentions of programmers.

author's intention to *Paradise Lost* when he worries aloud in his encomiastic poem,

> the Argument
> Held me a while misdoubting his Intent,
> That he would ruine (for I saw him strong)
> The sacred Truths to Fable and old Song,
> (So *Sampson* groap'd the Temples Posts in spight)
> The World o'rewhelming to revenge his Sight.[16]

For Marvell, intention is not merely decipherable in a literary work, it has the power to burst beyond the limits of the text and to overwhelm the world.

For his part, Milton simply assumed that one should read texts, notably but not only scriptural texts, according to the intention of the author.[17] In the divorce tracts, Milton tackles the difficult task of reversing Christ's apparently definitive proscription of divorce by pointing to a set of reconstructed intentions that, first, would not allow that proscription, and, second, would explain the ironic function of the apparent prohibition. Because God intended the new covenant to be milder and more merciful than the old, as He makes clear often enough in the New Testament, we know that it would run counter to His intention for Jesus to substitute a harsh law of divorce for Moses' mild one. His apparent violation of his merciful intention is itself explicable in terms of the Son's situationally specific intention to thwart the tempting Pharisees,

> which he could not more effectually doe, then by a countersway of restraint, curbing their wild exorbitance almost into the other extreme; as when we bow things the contrary way, to make them come to thir naturall straitnes. And *that this was the only intention of Christ is most evident* [my emphasis]; if we attend but to his own words and protestation made in the same Sermon not many verses before he treats of divorcing, that he came not to abrogate from the Law *one jot or tittle.*(*YP* 2:283)

Milton moves from what is to him an anomalous (or embarrassing) moment in the text to the intention of the speaker (in this case, the speaker not only in

---

16. Andrew Marvell, "On Mr. Milton's Paradise Lost," ll.5–10. *The Poems and Letters of Andrew Marvell*, ed. H. M. Margoliouth, 2nd ed., 2 vols. (Oxford: Clarendon, 1952), 1:131–32.

17. Addressing Parliament at the opening of *The Judgement of Martin Bucer concerning Divorce*, Milton writes, "I find it cleer to be the authors intention that this point of divorcement should be held and receav'd as a most necessary and prime part of discipline in every Christian government" (*YP* 2:432).

but, by way of the evangelist's mediation, of the text), and finds that intention authoritative even though it contradicts the apparent sense. Knowledge of the speaker and a grasp of his intention is the key to interpretation. His own efforts at self-representation, accordingly, are directed in large part at securing the interpretive control of his texts.

Milton's success in this gambit, if not universal, has been impressive. It is thrown into silhouette in the criticism of Stanley Fish, who straddles skillfully but uneasily the sometimes antagonistic worlds of Milton studies and postmodern theory. This is the Fish who both sees meaning as a construction of interpretive communities, who goes so far as to say that we "write" the texts that we read, and who at the same time says that "I *do* think that meaning is a function of what a particular speaker in a specific set of circumstances was intending to say. . . . To put the matter baldly, the act of construing meaning is ipso facto the act of assigning intention within a specific set of circumstances; you cannot do one without the other."[18] If in Fish's "Interpreting the Variorum," Milton can seem at times like a cipher who produced series of words with little awareness or calculation of the effect of, for example, line endings and enjambments, in *Surprised by Sin: The Reader in "Paradise Lost"* Milton appears as the nearly omniscient and omnipotent creator and controller of our reading.[19] The tension between these positions is not a function of Fish's development over time; it is a constant throughout his career.[20] Recently, in the preface to the second edition of *Surprised by Sin,* Fish in quick succession asserts that interpretations are created and validated by interpretive communities and that a reading by a Miltonist with whom he disagrees is mistaken. It is difficult to see by what criteria, except for authorial intention or internal incoherence, the judgment could be based. By the criteria of interpretive communities, that judgment would always be open, awaiting the specification of an interpretive community that would find it valid. The extraordinary gravitational pull of the intending Milton is evidenced by the manner in which it pulls Fish from the premises of his own theory of interpretive community. It may in part be a result of Fish's immersion in Milton's works that the theorist

---

18. Fish, "Biography and Intention," in *Contesting the Subject: Essays in the Postmodern Theory and Practice of Biography and Biographical Criticism,* ed. William H. Epstein (West Lafayette: Purdue University Press, 1991), p. 11. Fish adds that one cannot "read independently of biography, of some specification of what kind of person—and with what abilities, concerns, goals, purposes, and so on—is the source of the words you are reading. . . . [D]isputes about meaning are always disputes about biography, whether or not they are explicitly so labeled" (p. 12).

19. Fish, "Interpreting the Variorum," *Critical Inquiry* 2 (1976): 465–85; *Surprised by Sin: The Reader in "Paradise Lost"* 2nd ed. (Cambridge, Mass.: Harvard University Press, 1997).

20. On disjunctions between Fish's theoretical commitments and his readings of Milton, see Peter Herman, *Destabilizing Milton* (New York: Palgrave Macmillan, 2005), pp. 16–19.

of reader response and of interpretive communities is also the theorist of authorial intention, as he is at least implicitly in *Surprised by Sin* and *How Milton Works* and explicitly here:

> Biography will always be the winner, because we will always be reading [the author's] words as the intentional product of the person or nonperson we understand him to be. I repeat: this is not a recommendation or even a prediction, but a declaration of necessity. There remain many things we can do with texts, many ways in which we can construe them, but we cannot at the same time construe them and free ourselves from the considerations of biography.[21]

If Fish looks in two theoretical directions, his readings of Milton are virtually all relentlessly author-centered. Early and late, Fish elucidates what he sees as the response carefully and deliberately elicited by an intending author.

To read as I do with intention in mind is not to restrict oneself either to the explicitly stated intentions or even to consciously intended meanings of an author. Even those skeptical of imposed biographical intentionalism allow for intentions discernible *within* texts. Texts, as Paul de Man has argued, can exhibit "structural intentionality," an aim decipherable in the text as opposed to applied to the text a priori.[22] This structural intentionality and operative mind may or may not be identical to the conscious intention of the historical author. If, for example, Shelley is right that Milton's Satan is superior to Milton's God as a moral being, then the structural intention of the poem is presumably different from the historical Milton's intention. The distance between structural intention and what the author would offer as his or her intention might arise from the author's ineptness or, more interestingly, from unresolved tensions in the author that emerge in the work. It is the latter possibility that interests me in this study. The self-representing Milton is a tense, divided Milton. Milton intends his self-representations in large part to control response to and guide the interpretation of his works. Milton's conscious project is complicated by the fragmentation of his carefully planned self-representation, as an alternative and unacknowledged self-representation disrupts the surface of his texts, in a version of the return of the repressed. As

---

21. Fish, "Biography and Intention," p. 15.
22. On "structural intentionality," see Paul de Man, "Form and Intent in the American New Criticism," in *Blindness and Insight: Essays in the Rhetoric of Contemporary Criticism*, rev. ed (Minneapolis: University of Minnesota Press, 1983), p. 31. DeMan's "structural intentionality" resembles the intention admitted to literary interpretation by one of the leading anti-intentionalists, W. K. Wimsatt, who speaks of "*effective* intention or *operative* mind as it appears in the work itself and can be read from the work" ("Genesis: A Fallacy Revisited," in *On Literary Intention*, ed. D. Newton-de Molina [Edinburgh: University of Edinburgh Press, 1976], p. 136).

Colin Lyas observes, "The words I use may have a meaning independent of my will, but in using them I can display myself."[23]

Living with Milton's works has made me more rather than less convinced that intending authors can be present in texts. In Milton, that presence takes a particularly salient form. The author writes about himself, composing autobiographical narratives or micronarratives, commenting on the scene or purpose of writing, directing future readers or predicting their responses to the work and to himself. Through the surface of the texts, with their intentional self-representations, erupt now and then unintended and displaced self-representations, allowing us to view a Milton normally hidden from us and, I will argue, from Milton himself.[24] In the tension between intended and unacknowledged self-representations one can follow a fascinating drama of chosen-ness and exclusion, perfectionism and error, confidence and despair. The explicit and intended self-representations are easy to discern. A key for identifying the others will most often be a disturbance in the surface of the text, a contradiction, an elision, or a syntactic crux (think of the many moments when Milton resorts to complex and knotted double and triple negative passages, where the text seems to be trying to say two things at once as the subject hits close to home). Disturbances in the surfaces of texts that Milton worked so strenuously to organize point us to a hidden story as compelling as any of his narratives.

---

23. Lyas, "Wittgensteinian Intentions," in *Intention and Interpretation*, ed. Gary Iseminger (Philadelphia: Temple University Press, 1992), p. 146.

24. The obvious problem with claims for unconscious self-representation is that the historical Milton is unavailable for analysis. In talking about repressed self-representations, I follow the lead of Francesco Orlando, who in *Toward a Freudian Theory of Literature*, trans. Charmaine Lee (Baltimore: Johns Hopkins University Press, 1978) argues that we should not busy ourselves with the impossible task of psychoanalyzing the dead author and tracing textual phenomena to the author's early life. Orlando's Freud is not the interpreter of dreams and neuroses but the interpreter of jokes and parapraxes. Here Freud does not depend on talking to a patient to discover and verify interpretations; he considered jokes as structures bearing marks of repression and transference, marks explicable without recourse to analysis of an absent author. Like a joke, a text, including its self-representations, is an object that we can scrutinize.

Interlude

The 1633 "Letter to a Friend"

Early in 1633 Milton rehearsed several characteristic strategies of self-representation in a remarkable draft letter. The so-called Letter to a Friend records Milton's defensive response to an older friend who, it appeared, had questioned his belatedness in taking up a career.[1] The letter survives in the Trinity manuscript in two drafts, neither of which is a fair copy. The drafts, with their many revisions, provide at least the illusion of intimacy with their author. The convoluted sentences and significant changes reveal Milton moving from the defensiveness triggering the letter to the assertiveness typical of most of his self-representations. The brief space of the letter is crowded with characteristic rhetorical and thematic elements of Milton's later self-representations: a concern with timeliness and belatedness, a combination of pugnacity and defensive anxiety, a readiness to entertain alternative provisional self-conceptions, and a division of the self into both subject and object. It also is marked by the syntactic tortuousness typical in Milton's self-representations.

The twenty-four-year-old Milton, having reached the age at which he would have been expected to take holy orders, was instead pursuing in Hammersmith a self-directed course of independent reading. Milton acknowledges those expectations and his friend's pointed question at the beginning of the letter:

> Besides that in sundry other respects I must acknowledge me to profit by you when ever wee meet, you are often to me, & were yesterday

---

[1]. The addressee is probably Thomas Young, formerly Milton's tutor. William Riley Parker has argued persuasively for a date of early 1633, in *Milton: A Biography*, 2 vols. (Oxford: Clarendon,

especially, as a good watch man to admonish that the howres of the night pass on (for so I call my life as yet obscure, & unserviceable to mankind) & that the day wth me is at hand wherin Christ comands all to Labour while there is light. (*YP* 1:319)

Parables idiosyncratically interpreted, beginning with this one, will be the vertebrae of Milton's self-representation in the letter. In the second sentence, a seemingly anxious young man offers a (characteristically) tortuous prologue to the self-representation that will constitute the body of the letter:

wch because I am persuaded you doe to no other purpose then out of a true desire that god should be honourd in every one; I therfore thinke my selfe bound though unask't, to give you account, as oft as occasion is, of this my tardie moving; according to the præcept of my conscience, wch I firmely trust is not w^thout god. Yet now I will not streine for any set apologie, but only referre my selfe to what my mynd shall have at any tyme to declare her selfe at her best ease.

He briefly considers and then rejects the possibility that the friend's motives are themselves suspect. The reversals and staccato syntax suggest that the suspicion is directed inward, that Milton is struggling to resist being what he will later term "too inquisitive, or suspitious of my self and mine own doings" (*YP* 1:804). As is often the case when Milton, writing about himself, contemplates the possibility of error, he falls into knotted, uneasy double negatives. He has acted "according to the præcept of my conscience, wch I firmly trust is not w^thout god." The strain is evident even as he claims that he "will not streine for any set apologie" (in the first copy of the letter, "not" is inserted late, above the line) and as he describes his justification as a drama of fragmented or nested selves. He will refer himself to what his mind shall declare her self at her ease. The best view of Milton, he suggests, is that presented by Milton's mind or soul to Milton himself, a view that can then be shared with the friend.

The body of the letter responds to the friend's suggestion, the day before, that Milton's "too much love of Learning is in fault" for his "tardie moving" to take up the office of minister (*YP* 1:319). Framed by allusions to Christ's parables of the wise and foolish virgins, the talents, and the laborers in the

---

1968), 2:786–87. William Hunter places it at the end of 1631 (*The Descent of Urania: Studies in Milton, 1946–1988* (Lewisburg, PA: Bucknell University Press, 1989), 179–83. The "Letter to a Friend" appears in *YP* 1:319–21.

vineyard, Milton offers two provisional and canceled self-representations, and then one authorized version.[2]

An excessive love of learning, were he to have it, would spring, Milton suggests, from a principle either "bad, good, or naturall." He proceeds to argue in logically strained but elegant form why none of these principles would be proof against stronger incentives to leave solitary study.[3] He asks, rhetorically, "if it be bad why should *not* all the fond hopes that forward Youth & Vanitie are fledge with together wth Gaine, pride, & ambition call me forward more powerfully, then a poore regardlesse & unprofitable sin of curiosity should be able to with hold me" (my emphasis). The italicized "not" is added to the draft above the line, a graphic indication that the convoluted sentence slipped beyond Milton's control at first, and that the sentence looks in two directions at once. Even more significant is another emendation: "if it be bad" was originally "if it be evil in me." Milton cancels the more univocally moral *evil* for the wider latitude of *bad*. The resistance to contemplating evil in himself, anomalous for a Puritan, will become a Miltonic signature. By the sin of curiosity, Milton continues, "a man cutts himselfe off from all action & becomes the most helplesse, pusilanimous & unweapon'd creature in the *word*, the most unfit & unable to doe that wch all mortals most aspire to [,] either to defend & be usefull to his freinds, or to offend his enimies"(my emphasis).[4] The Yale editor suggests sensibly that by "word" Milton evidently meant "world." At the same time, the slip of the pen, or the failure to slip the l-shaped letter *l* into "word," could be a signifying parapraxis. Taken in one sense, as philological and literary learning, the "word" is that gained by the kind of ostensibly self-indulgent study reproved by the friend; taken as knowledge and championing of the "Word" or the Scripture, the term points

---

2. It is significant, given the Christian purpose, that Milton does not here as so often elsewhere mingle classical and Christian allusions. He suppresses in the later draft a simile comparing his studious retirement to the wearing of "Pluto's helmet." Christopher Grose notes that the one remaining classical reference, that to "Endymion wth the Moone," is attributed to the friend (*Milton and the Sense of Tradition* [New Haven: Yale University Press, 1988], p. 31).

3. The body of the letter revises the announced sequence, moving from bad through natural to good, an ascending trajectory complementing Milton's self-construction. This clear sequencing is one of the main differences from the first draft, which is chaotic in its handling of these alternative motivations. The first draft concludes its middle section with the claim that, if it were merely excessive love of learning that motivated his failure to take orders, "it had by this bin round about begirt, & over master'd whether it had proceeded from vertue, vice, or nature in me" (*John Milton: Poems*, Reproduced in Facsimile from the Manuscript in Trinity College, Cambridge [Menston: Scolar Press, 1972], p. 6.)

4. Milton may have had in mind here a passage that his favorite ancient playwright, Euripides, places in the mouth of his ambiguous heroine Medea: "Let no one think me a weak one, feeble-spirited, / A stay-at-home, but rather just the opposite, / One who can hurt my enemies and help my friends; / For the lives of such persons are most remembered" (*Medea*, trans. Rex Warner [London: John Lane, 1944], ll. 791–94).

ironically toward that which the friend rebukes Milton for neglecting and that which Milton in a moment will claim to be the object of his labors.

Of the three principles possibly motivating Milton's "studious retirement," the second or "natural" is the most straightforwardly handled. A mere natural proneness to learning could not hold out against the stronger natural inclination to start a family and make one's way in the world. He does add as a revision to the second draft that in addition to this desire for a household "yet there is to this another act if not of pure, yet of refined nature no lesse available to dissuade prolonged obscurity, a desire of honour & repute, & immortal fame seated in the brest of every true scholar wch all make hast to by the readiest ways of publishing & divulging conceived merits as well those that shall as those that never shall obtaine it" (*YP* 1:319–20). The gesture foreshadows the tagging of fame in "Lycidas" as "That last infirmity of noble mind" (71). At the same time it prepares for the move to the "good" or third principle.

The logic of Milton's argument to this point would suggest that he would offer some end that would prevail over a mere love of learning based even on a good principle ("whether it proceed from a principle bad, good, or naturall it could not have held out thus Long"), but he does not. The extraordinary passage is worth quoting at length:

> Lastly this Love of Learning as it is ye pursuit of somthing good, it would sooner follow the more excellent & supreme good knowne & præsented and so be quickly diverted from the emptie & fantastick chase of shadows & notions to the solid good flowing from due & tymely obedience to that comand in the gospell set out by the terrible seasing of him that hid the talent. It is more probable therfore that not the endlesse delight of speculation but this very consideration of that great comandment does not presse forward as soone as may be to underg[o] but keeps off wth a sacred reverence & religious advisement how best to undergoe [,] not taking thought of beeing late so it give advantage to be more fit, for those that were latest lost nothing when the maister of the vinyard came to give each one his hire. (*YP* 1:320)

At the outset there is a significant revision, from "If this Love of Learning be the pursuit of somthing good" to "this Love of Learning as it is ye pursuit of somthing good." The simple indicative voice replaces the subjunctive voice that has governed the discourse to this point, and even as far as the canceled draft of this passage. It is clear that Milton loves learning, and it is as clear that this must be based on a good principle. This assured good principle is then quickly attached to the *summum bonum,* the good as God. Any straying from this love of learning, which a moment ago was entertained as a potential threat to godly occupation, would itself be disobedience to the (parabolic)

Gospel command against hiding the talent.[5] In another of his strained negative constructions ("*not* the endlesse delight ... but ... that great commandment does *not* press forward") Milton completes the reversal. It is *not* this *but* that that does *not* move him forward; again we are left to sort out the actions and elements of the sentence. Milton switches from defending tardy movement to claiming an urgent divine command to forgo hasty motion.[6]

The surprising use of the parable of the talents redirects the reader's attention to the implicit argument by way of a Gospel allusion that unifies the letter (also pointing in this direction is the copied sonnet "How Soon Hath Time," with its centrally important allusion to, again, the parable of the talents). At the outset, Milton is grateful that the friend has been a been a vigilant watchman in admonishing him "to Labour while there is light." Milton alludes here to John 9:

> 1 And as Jesus passed by, he saw a man which was blind from his birth. 2 And his disciples asked him, saying, Master, who did sin, this man, or his parents, that he was born blind? 3 Jesus answered, Neither hath this man sinned, nor his parents: but that the works of God should be made manifest in him. 4 I must work the works of him that sent me, while it is day: the night cometh, when no man can work.

This is proleptic of a later period when Milton will dispute arguments that his blindness is a mark of divine disfavor. In 1633, though, blindness in the allusive context points indirectly to Milton's obscurity. The "command" to which Milton refers is a statement by Jesus about his own practice, and only indirectly a command to his followers, and Milton thus compares Jesus' labor to the labor on which he is obscurely embarked. There is another, more significant inversion. John 9:4 speaks of the need to do one's work before night; Milton places himself in the night (as a metaphor for his obscurity), and places the time of work in the future, precisely reversing the burden of the passage. By an adroit set of reversals, Milton relates himself to Christ, and in the process he paradoxically justifies inaction by alluding to a parable that counsels timely action.

This prefatory reversal prepares the way for the reversal in the allusion to the parable of the talents. Now the public labors and honors of those who

---

5. On the talent of the parable as a traditional figure for possession and dissemination of the divine word, see Dayton Haskin's lucid analysis in *Milton's Burden of Interpretation* (Philadelphia: University of Pennsylvania Press, 1994), pp. 29–53.

6. For the dialectic between belatedness and prematurity in Milton here and elsewhere, see Hong Won Suh, "Haste and Delay in the Works of John Milton" (PhD diss., University of Notre Dame, 1998).

have made their way in the world (presumably including those who have made their way as ministers of the Word) are claimed counterintuitively to be evidence, in terms of the famous parable from Matthew 25:14–30, of the hiding of the talent. Milton's continued obscurity, equally counterintuitively, now exemplifies the investment of the talents.

Just when we think our heads cannot spin (or be spun) faster, Milton offers a dizzying, surprising retrospective justification of his delay by way of an interpretation of the parable of the workers in the vineyard (Matthew 20:1–16). In the parable, the vineyard master contracts with workers in the morning for a day's labor, and then goes on to hire more laborers at the third, sixth, ninth, and eleventh hours; when the day ends he pays all the workers equally, which strikes those who have worked all day as unfair. This apparent injustice calls for parabolic interpretation, the burden of which seems to be a rebuke to the self-righteous who think they deserve more from God than others and a demonstration of the mercy of God, who saves even those who come late. (Inasmuch as all are unworthy of salvation, consideration of the parable should ultimately comfort all.) Milton reads the parable, however, as if the workers hired in the eleventh hour are less the objects of particular indulgence than particularly meritorious by reason of their having spent the earlier hours diligently preparing to serve well.[7] There is nothing in the parable that would lead to this conclusion, but everything in Milton's situation would make this an attractive reading. This letter, and particularly its wresting of the parables of the talents and of the vineyard, provides striking evidence of the self-valorizing imperative in Milton, which leads him to a counterintuitive reading of the Gospel. The letter sets a pattern for Milton's later self-representations.

There is one additional, ingeniously implicit element in Milton's argument by parable allusion. A watchman appears in the passage alluding to John 9 on the imperative to work while it is light ("you are often to me . . . as a good watch man to admonish that the howres of the night passe on"), but there is no watchman in the source text. The watchman does appear prominently in Matthew 24 and 25, framing the parable of the wise and foolish virgins of Matthew 25:1–13, the parable immediately preceding the parable of the talents. The foolish virgins waste their oil, or their resources, and thus cannot attend the bridegroom to the wedding, unlike the wise virgins, who have carefully husbanded their resources. Jesus ends the parable by exhorting his listeners, "Watch therefore, for ye know neither the day nor the hour

---

7. David Urban traces Milton's repeated yoking of the parables of the talents and of the workers in the vineyard ("The Talented Mr. Milton: A Parabolic Laborer and His Identity," *Milton Studies* 43 [2004]: 1–18). I agree with Urban that Milton deploys the vineyard parable to neutralize his fear that he may be, in terms of the parable of the talents, the unprofitable servant; unlike Urban, I argue that Milton reverses the burden of the vineyard parable as part of a self-valorizing strategy.

wherein the Son of man cometh" (25:13). The same listeners are told in the preceding story to watch for the Lord, who will come like a thief in the middle of the night. By allusion and argument, then, Milton justifies his present obscurity both as preparation for the future and as the work of watching for the lord. He is both preparing to work and he is working now.

In the parabolic discourse Milton turns defense into offense, a justification of his actions as not particularly tardy or guilty into an assertion of the timeliness and virtue of those actions. He is not content to be blameless; he must be virtuous. Something similar is happening in the manner in which he gradually redefines ambition in the letter of 1633. He moves from the general "Ambition" of "Youth & Vanitie" in the first movement, to the "refined" if not "pure" "desire of honour & repute" among more noble souls in the second. This refined desire, as I noted above, foreshadows the distinguished ambition of noble minds in "Lycidas." In the third movement, as in the last movement in "Lycidas," even this noble infirmity is left behind for the sacred distinction of those specially dedicated to God and willing to put off worldly ambitions. As the group narrows in size, the distinction aimed for and earned becomes more rarefied and exalted, an early enactment of yet another of Milton's strategies of self-representation, the move to cut himself off from others and place himself in a charmed and small circle. In the course of a lifetime of writings, Milton's self-representations will repeat the patterns foreshadowed in this early letter, although the pressure of lived experience will make it harder to suppress anxiety and uneasiness as he writes and rewrites his life.

Chapter 2

The Least of Sinners

Milton in Context

"To read Milton is to know what it was to be a Puritan."[1] For the most part, N. H. Keeble's judgment is on target. Milton embodies the extreme development of Puritan belief and practice: a suspicion of institution and hierarchy, a passionate belief in the priesthood of all believers, a reliance on the indwelling Spirit as guide to action and to the proper interpretation of Scripture, an aversion to set prayer, and a commitment to toleration among Protestants. When it comes to self-representation, however, Milton's writings are anything but representative of Puritan practice and perspective, or for that matter of seventeenth-century Protestant or even generally Christian practice and perspective. Where anxious self-examination and conviction of sin is a Protestant norm enforced by Lutheran and Calvinist theology, Milton writes instead of his blamelessness and heroic virtue. Even those contemporaries who write from the conviction of their election publish the sins of youth. Milton's accounts of his youth, on the other hand, reveal a boy who is godly and dutiful without benefit of the conversion experience obligatory in Christian autobiography. The "Letter to a Friend" embodies a recurrent pattern in Milton's writing, one in which the author scrutinizes himself, finds nothing

---

1. N. H. Keeble, "Milton and Puritanism," in *A Companion to Milton*, ed. Thomas N. Corns (Oxford: Blackwell, 2001), p. 126. Keeble, an acute student of Nonconformist literary culture, labels Milton "a central figure in the cultural history of Puritanism." See also his *The Literary Culture of Nonconformity in Later Seventeenth-Century England* (Athens, Ga.: University of Georgia Press, 1987). For Milton's views as the logical culmination of the imperatives driving Puritanism, see Geoffrey R. Nuttall, *The Holy Spirit in Puritan Faith and Experience* (1946; repr. Chicago: University of Chicago Press, 1992).

amiss, and asserts his innocence. Despite the claim in the Letter of searching introspection ("I am something suspicio[us] of my selfe" [*YP* 1:320]), and its echo nearly a decade later in *The Reason of Church-Government* ("if I be either by disposition, or what other cause too inquisitive, or suspicious of my self and mine own doings, who can help it? [*YP* 1:804]), in neither the letter nor tract does he find anything to blame.[2] Instead, we read repeatedly a story of singular virtue. Although writing about the Quakers, the Presbyterian Richard Baxter (1615–1691) could be describing Milton when he scornfully asks, "Is it possible that any man in this life, that is not mad with spiritual pride, can indeed believe that he has no sin?"[3] By this measure Milton is worse than the Quakers, for they normally did admit their youthful errors.

The survey of the varieties of contemporary self-representation in this chapter will throw into silhouette the idiosyncratic quality of Milton's self-representations. Autobiographical writing was rare in England as the seventeenth century began, but by the end it was common.[4] It came in many forms, including journals and autobiographies, normally but not always religious in emphasis and purpose; autobiographical digressions inserted in polemical works and designed to establish the author's probity; and essays that, while not offering a life narrative, communicate the author's temperament, character, and principles of action, as do Sir Thomas Browne's *Religio Medici* and George Herbert's *A Priest to the Temple*. The lines between these categories are not always clearly drawn. Paul Delaney, for example, excludes Milton from his study of seventeenth-century British autobiography in part because "Milton always used his self-revelations as aids to the fulfillment of some other aesthetic or controversial end."[5] But on Delaney's own account most religious autobiography, by far the most common kind, served controversial ends in the denominational wars of the period.

Religious autobiographical writing reflected the doctrinal commitments and historical circumstances of their authors' denominations. Presbyterians, for example, true to the corporate nature of their denomination,

---

2. In the Letter, Milton's suspicion of himself issues in a remarkable sonnet, "How Soon Hath Time," in which Milton exonerates rather than convicts himself (*YP* 1:320).

3. Baxter, *The Quakers' Catechism or the Quakers Questioned* (1655), p. C', reprinted in Hugh Barbour and Arthur O. Roberts, eds., *Early Quaker Writings: 1650–1700* (Grand Rapids: Eerdmans, 1973), pp. 267–68.

4. See Paul Delaney, *British Autobiography in the Seventeenth Century* (London: Routledge & Kegan Paul, 1969); Michael Mascuch, *Origins of the Individualist Self: Autobiography and Self-Identity in England, 1591–1791* (Stanford: Stanford University Press, 1996); David Booy, ed., *Personal Disclosures: An Anthology of Self-Writings from the Seventeenth Century* (Aldershot, England: Ashgate, 2002); N. H. Keeble, *The Literary Culture of Nonconformity*, chap. 6, "'A paradise within': Internalization, Introspection and Individualism in Nonconformist Writing," pp. 187–214.

5. Delaney, *British Autobiography*, p. 2. Delaney's other criterion, if more valid, is less interesting theoretically: Milton did not compose a freestanding autobiography.

wrote accounts not of their own characters but of the characteristics they shared with their fellow Presbyterians. In almost every case, Presbyterians wrote about themselves only late in life and did not publish their autobiographies during their lifetimes.[6] Staunch Calvinists, they acknowledged their sinfulness and attributed any good they had done to God's grace. Calvinist Independents composed many of the immediately published spiritual autobiographies of the period, and their stories, designed as exempla for others and as advertisements for their theological and ecclesial principles, followed a script as rigidly determined as a romance novel's, with a plot following a trajectory from sin through grace, conviction, conversion, regeneration, and sanctification. But if Calvinist authors vied with each other for the title of "chief of sinners," even libertarian, anti-Calvinist autobiographers acknowledged their early waywardness (were it not for the Quakers, for whom spiritual autobiographies and journals became a powerful tool to recruit members and raise the spirits of those already in the fold, there would be relatively little of such writing). The "vulgar prophets" wrote about their experiences in an ecstatic manner, testifying to the miracles wrought by the Spirit that brought them the gift of prophecy. Antinomian sectarians offered lurid descriptions of their lives, often of their sexual lives, that served to demonstrate the manner in which, to the pure, all things are pure (Titus 1:15). These accounts offer a kind of photographic negative to accounts of similar sins lamented and left behind by their non-antinomian sectarian contemporaries. Against this landscape Milton's autobiographical writings stand out, not only for their literary qualities but also for the idiosyncratic and audacious story they tell.

The Chief of Sinners

Everywhere one looks in seventeenth-century religious autobiography, one finds admissions of sin. The Presbyterian Richard Baxter observes of the life that he records, "I humbly lament it, and beg pardon of it, as sinful and too unequal and unprofitable. And I warn the reader to amend that in his own which he findeth to have been amiss in mine."[7] Baxter holds up his flawed life as both a comfort and a warning to fellow Christians. Earlier in the century, the Presbyterian adventurer and explorer Richard Norwood (1590–1675) described "the mass of sin and folly" that marked his youth. In his school years only the "seeds of religion" kept him "from divers enormous

---

6. Ibid., p. 57.
7. *The Autobiography of Richard Baxter*, ed. J. M. Lloyd Thomas (London: Dent, 1931), p. 129. Originally published in *Reliquiae Baxterianae* (London, 1696).

sins whereof I was in danger." After a crisis he relapsed, and "for many years next ensuing I so grievously stained my life and lived so dissolutely that I even abhor the remembrance of those times."[8] Guilt engendered by masturbation issued in the lurid nightmares recorded in his journal. Like many others, Norwood explicitly lays claim to the title of chief of sinners; his manuscript, which he did not publish, is headed "Jesus Christ came into the world to save sinners, of whom I am chief."[9] Vavasor Powell (1617–1670) confesses that he devoted his youth to "the pleasures and vanities of this wicked world."[10] The Presbyterian Oliver Heywood (1630–1702) writes at the beginning of the 1660s of his childhood depravity:

> I remember how proud I was of any little coveted excellency, . . . how forward to sinful practices, how tractable to follow bad examples; . . . the time was when with children in playing I vented my selfe in many barbarous ways, yea undoubted oathes; . . . so foolish was I and ignorant even as a beast before god . . . —when I was a child I spake as a child, yea rather like a devil incarnate, of the desparate wickedness of my deceitful hart.[11]

John Bunyan's (1628–1688) account of his immoral childhood in *Grace Abounding to the Chief of Sinners* (1666) is more familiar than most other accounts and more caustic than some, but otherwise it is typical: "from a child, . . . I had but few equals, especially considering my years, which were tender, being few, both for cursing, swearing, lying, and blaspheming the holy name of God."[12]

In dwelling on their sinfulness before the reception of enabling grace, these writers reflect the Reformation emphasis on Paul's theology. Paul laments the distance between his intention to do good and his flawed actions: "For the good that I would, I do not: but the evil which I would not, that I do. . . . O wretched man that I am! who will deliver me from the body of this death" (Romans 7:19, 24). Martin Luther in *The Bondage of the Will* teaches that, left to our own devices, we will do evil, that virtues are divine gifts, and that good

---

8. *The Journal of Richard Norwood* (composed 1639), intro. Wesley Frank Craven and Walter B. Hayward, published for the Bermuda Historical Monuments Trust (New York: Scholars' Facsimiles and Reprints, 1945), pp. 4–5.

9. Ibid., p. 4.

10. *The Life and Death of Vavasor Powell* (1671), in *The Library of Christian Biography*, ed. T. Jackson, vol. 12 (London, 1840), p. 2.

11. Oliver Heywood, *His Autobiography*, ed. J. H. Turner (London: Brighouse, 1882), pp. 153–54.

12. John Bunyan, *Grace Abounding to the Chief of Sinners* (1666; London: Everyman, 1928), p. 8. For ease of reference to other editions, I will hereafter identify citations from this work by paragraph number. The present passage can be found in ¶4.

acts are performed not by the individual but by God working in us. Even more than Luther, though, John Calvin influenced the seventeenth-century English understanding of sin, grace, and conversion. The conventional narrative of sinfulness and conversion owes much to the shared Calvinist, predestinarian view of most of Milton's British contemporaries, including but not limited to Presbyterians and many Independents. Calvin's God predestines individuals to salvation or damnation prior to and regardless of any choices they might make, which are themselves the product of God's choices either to grant or withhold irresistible saving grace. With this grace, the sinner chooses God, becomes regenerate (i.e., no longer bound to sin), and is sanctified (i.e., saved or justified). Without this grace, the sinner is left in bondage to sin and is condemned.

Reformation teaching inevitably led to introspection. If one's eternal bliss or anguish depends on an irreversible foreordination, then one could hardly avoid anxious introspection for signs of election. If works flow inevitably from the faith made possible only by particular and irresistible grace,[13] one would naturally look inside for signs of faith and for the concomitant works. It is no accident that Augustine, from whom Calvin and other reformers adapted their understanding of predestination, gives us our first great introspective autobiography.[14] The Calvinist perspective does not merely account for the popularity of the genre in Milton's time, it gives the narratives their characteristic shape of conviction, repentance, and regeneration. In retrospect, the preconversion protagonist can do no good; all that issues from the human being is corruption. Autobiographical accounts differ in the extent to which the protagonist is subject to temptation and relapse after conversion. Calvinist theology precludes the permanent relapse or nonperseverance of the elect saint, but not the reprobate individual's illusion of saving grace.

Calvin thought of the teaching of predestination as a counsel of mercy; if one is elect, there is no need for anxious accounting of sins and good works. Inevitably, however, the anxiety was transferred to the search for signs of election or reprobation. God may do all, but how does one know if one has received grace or not? Calvin's teaching left many followers a legacy of despair rather than comfort, as individuals became convinced that they had not been chosen for the elect minority. The germ of this despair lies just beneath

---

13. For the manner in which good works flow spontaneously from those justified by faith, see Luther, "The Freedom of a Christian," in *Martin Luther: Three Treatises* (Philadelphia: Fortress Press, 1970), pp. 295–98.

14. Augustine is a complicated figure, whose arguments on free will and predestination are often adapted to their polemical contexts. Even within one work, he can seem an advocate and opponent of predestination; compare, e.g., the *City of God* 15.1 and 22.1. During the predestination versus free will controversies of the sixteenth and seventeenth centuries, both sides could and did cite him.

the surface of the opening pages of Calvin's *Institutes*. Introspection, Calvin argues, reveals a gulf between God's goodness and our corruption:

> The miserable ruin, into which the rebellion of the first man cast us, especially compels us to look upward. Thus, not only will we, in fasting and hungering, seek thence what we lack; but, in being aroused by fear, we shall learn humility. For, as a veritable world of miseries is to be found in mankind, and we are thereby despoiled of divine raiment, our shameful nakedness exposes a teeming horde of infamies. . . . [N]othing appears within or around us that has not been contaminated by great immorality.[15]

In Calvin's optimistic intention, the vision of corruption has the salutary effect of throwing into silhouette divine goodness and mercy and eliciting the gratitude of the elect who, for no merit of their own, are rescued from the mass of corruption. But the converse is the despair of the reprobate, whom no effort or accumulated merit can save.[16]

Searching for signs of saving grace, some autobiographers became convinced that they had been left among the reprobate. Upon reading Matthew 5:20 ("except your righteousness shall exceed the righteousness of the scribes and Pharisees, ye shall in no case enter into the kingdom of heaven"), John Rogers (1627–1670) breaks down: "the more I *read* the more I *roar'd* in the *black gulf* of *despair.*"[17] The black hole of despair, even suicidal despair, is a common feature of Puritan autobiography, appearing, for example, in Vavasor Powell and Anna Trapnel (1622?–).[18] In his *Autobiography,* Thomas Shepard (1605–1649) records his brush with a despair that is not merely a psychological condition but the unpardonable sin against the Holy Spirit:

> I fell to doubt whether I had not committed the impardonable sin. . . . For three quarters of a year this temptation did last, and I had some strong temptations to run my head against walls and brain and kill myself. And so I did see, as I thought, God's eternal reprobation of me, a fruit of which was this dereliction to these doubts and darkness, and I did see

---

15. Calvin, *Institutes of the Christian Religion* 1–2 (1559), ed. John T. McNeill and trans. Ford Lewis Battles, 2 vols., The Library of Christian Classics (Philadelphia: Library of Christian Classics, 1960), 2:36, 38.

16. For an astute study of the literary effects of Calvinist despair, see John Stachniewski, *The Persecutory Imagination: English Puritanism and the Literature of Religious Despair* (Oxford: Clarendon, 1991).

17. John Rogers, *Ohel or Beth-shemesh. A tabernacle for the sun: or irenicum evangelicum. An idea of church discipline, in the theorick and practick parts* (London, 1653), p. 426.

18. Owen Watkins, *The Puritan Experience: Studies in Spiritual Autobiography* (New York: Schocken, 1972), p. 96.

God like a consuming fire and an everlasting burning, and myself like a poor prisoner leading to that fire, and the thought of eternal reprobation and torment did amaze my spirits.[19]

Bunyan's swinging between despair and intimations of God's grace and salvation resembles a grim and frenetic tennis match:

> I was more loathsome in my own eyes than was a toad; and I thought I was so in God's eyes too; sin and corruption, I said, would as naturally bubble out of my heart, as water would bubble out of a fountain. I thought now that everyone had a better heart than I had; I could have changed heart with anybody; I thought none but the devil himself could equalise me for inward wickedness and pollution of mind. I fell, therefore, at the sight of my own vileness, deeply into despair; for I concluded that this condition that I was in could not stand with a state of grace. Sure, thought I, I am forsaken of God; sure I am given up to the devil, and to a reprobate mind; and thus I continued a long while, even for some years together.[20]

The chilling final phrase, "even for some years together," opens bleak vistas of internal suffering. The ensuing pages of *Grace Abounding* tell a pathetic story of brief moments of assurance of grace, with their attendant happiness, alternating with long bouts of agonized despair. The stark contrast between Shepard's and Bunyan's anguished soul-searching and anything in Milton undermines Keeble's claim that Milton exhibits the "experiential immediacy" that marks Puritan individualism.[21]

Behind Calvin lie the teachings of Paul and Augustine, who also left Puritan autobiographers their most important narrative models. The example of Paul would have been generally available, even to the illiterate. Paul left in Acts 22–27 an example of Christian apology or self-defense, beginning with the famous story of his conversion on the road to Damascus. Setting a pattern familiar in seventeenth-century English religious autobiography, Paul begins with an acknowledgment of sin, followed by the intervention of the divine, conviction, and regeneration.

If Paul, directly and by way of Calvin, supplies the doctrine behind and a narrative model for much of seventeenth-century English religious autobiography, Augustine is the genre's great progenitor. A celebrated leader

---

19. Shepard's *Autobiography*, as reprinted in *God's Plot: The Paradoxes of Puritan Piety, Being the Autobiography and Journal of Thomas Shepard*, ed. Michael McGiffert (Amherst: University of Massachusetts Press, 1972), p. 43.
20. Bunyan, *Grace Abounding*, ¶84.
21. Keeble, "Milton and Puritanism," p. 129.

of the Christian community, Augustine represents himself as a guilty and reluctant servant of God. If he is elect, as his references to his mother Monica's inevitably successful prayers suggest, he is a reluctant saint, who delays, backslides, and rationalizes before he succumbs to grace. He deals unsparingly with his vices of pride and lust. His retrospective view of his depravity embraces not only his lustful burning in Carthage but even what we would consider the most innocent of childlike preferences; remembering moments in his boyhood when he would rather have played than studied, he concludes, "I was a great sinner for so small a boy."[22] Augustine extends this extraordinary singularity back to his infancy:

> Who can recall to me the sins I committed as a baby? . . . It can hardly be right for a child, even at that age, to cry for everything, including things which would harm him; to work himself into a tantrum against people older than himself and not required to obey him; and to try his best to strike and hurt others who know better than he does, including his own parents, when they do not give in to him and refuse to pander to whims which would only do him harm.[23]

Milton's contemporaries echoed Augustine's *Confessions* closely and extensively. Richard Norwood signals his debt in the title of his autobiographical *Confessions*. Robert Blair (1593–1666) recounts in 1663 that when he read the *Confessions* in his early twenties, it led him to reflect on the sinfulness of his own youth.[24] Several autobiographers found Augustine's story of stolen pears as irresistible as Augustine found the pears themselves. Richard Baxter repeats the sin itself:

> 2. I was much addicted to the excessive gluttonous eating of apples and pears; which I think laid the foundation of that imbecility and flatulency of my stomach which caused the bodily calamities of my life.
> 3. To this end, and to concur with naughty boys that gloried in evil, I have oft gone into other men's orchards and stolen their fruit, when I had enough at home.[25]

Paul Delany has observed that "Calvinist autobiographers . . . compete[d] with each other in confessions of precocious wickedness, with the result that

---

22. Augustine, *Confessions* I.xii, trans. R. S. Pine-Coffin (Harmondsworth: Penguin, 1961), p. 33.
23. Ibid., I.vii, pp. 27–28.
24. Robert Blair, *Autobiography*, in *The Life of Mr. Robert Blair*, ed. T. McCrie (Edinburgh, 1848), p. 6.
25. Baxter, *Autobiography*, p. 5.

their histories blur together in the reader's mind, and individual reminiscences can scarcely be distinguished from each other."[26]

Delaney argues nevertheless that Augustine paled as a model next to Paul, on the plausible sociological grounds that those who knew Augustine best were literate men who gravitated to conservative religious expression rather than to Augustine's more enthusiastic style, while those closer to Augustine in spirit, the radical sectarians, were as a group less educated and in many cases ignorant of Augustine. But the repeated stories of childhood wickedness, and the frequent stories of gradual and struggling conversion recall Augustine rather than Paul. And knowledge of Augustine's confessions may have been more common than we would think. Bunyan's familiarity with the *Confessions,* for example, suggests that the Catholic Sir Tobie Matthew's 1620 English translation of the *Confessions* may have made its way into the hands of Protestants as well as Catholics.[27] Augustine's influence in many cases most likely spread at second and third hand, as less-educated autobiographers copied the impression of Augustine's story as it appeared in the work of their well-read contemporaries.

Milton certainly knew the *Confessions,* but he conspicuously avoids the standard story. Unlike the contemporary Puritans who recalled early lives of compulsive sin, and unlike Augustine who upbraided himself for being distracted from study, Milton was a dutiful child and pupil: "My father destined me in early childhood for the study of literature, for which I had so keen an appetite that from my twelfth year scarcely ever did I leave my studies for my bed before the hour of midnight" (*YP* 4.1:612). The picture of virtuous youth is an apt prelude to his representation of the rest of his life. Unlike Bunyan, Milton does not treat himself as the chief of sinners. Far from expressing bouts of despair, Milton's autobiographical excursions are marked by an apparently serene confidence in his righteousness, an attitude starkly at odds with the religious culture surrounding him.

The influence of Augustine and Paul and the acknowledgment of sinfulness in autobiographical writing were not confined to the subculture of Calvinist Puritans; the narrative of reclaimed sinner cuts across denominational and theological boundaries. The 1619 autobiography of an Anglican Bishop, William Cowper (1568–1619), is one of the earliest British spiritual autobiographies to follow the Augustinian model of sin, conviction, and conversion.[28] The Roman Catholic priest John Gerard (1542–1612) recalls that at fifteen he "first heard God in His infinite mercy and goodness call me from

---

26. Delaney, *British Autobiography,* p. 89.
27. For Matthew's translation of Augustine, see ibid., p. 45.
28. Delaney, *British Autobiography,* p. 47. The full title is *The Life and Death of William Cowper* (London, 1619).

the crooked paths of the world to the straight road." He acknowledged his weakness and his nearly succumbing to temptation (albeit under torture) in his 1609 Latin autobiography.[29] If Gerard does not agonize over the state of his soul like his Calvinist compatriots, neither does he claim with Milton to have never strayed from the straight path. Sir Tobie Matthew (1575–1655), the Catholic translator of Augustine's *Confessions,* admits to youthful wickedness: "I frequented plays, and worse places. I went equally to the mountebanks and to preachers. I read also books of all kinds, and very often such as were of the lightest air."[30] Matthew does not attempt, like Milton in the nearly contemporary *Apology for Smectymnuus,* to assert the blamelessness of his playgoing. In these and other similar texts, the admissions of youthful error are often brief and formulaic. But this is significant in itself, revealing that confession is an expected element of the genre that must be served up to readers.

The culturally dominant narrative of conviction and confession could be expected to exert a powerful drag on claims of righteousness such as Milton's. In the following chapters I will trace the reemergence of conviction and despair in Milton's texts, like the river Arethuse, from subterranean depths.

One might argue that his failure to retell the standard Puritan story is explicable in terms of his anti-Calvinist soteriology. An Arminian, Milton believed that grace sufficient for salvation is given to all, and that human beings are left with freedom to accept or reject this grace (and thus to accept or reject God and obedience to his commands).[31] If one's salvation or damnation is not predetermined, then there may be less reason to search oneself anxiously for signs of election or reprobation. Richard Strier, who has commented perceptively on Milton's rejection of a Calvinist ethic of humility in favor of a classical ethic of magnanimity, argues that Milton's Arminianism is important because

> it allowed Milton to accept classical ethics as fully and directly relevant to Christian soteriology. The will of man, after the Fall, was

---

29. John Gerard, *The Autobiography of a Hunted Priest,* trans. Philip Caraman (1952; repr. New York, Image Books, 1955), p. 28. Delaney discusses this work in *British Autobiography,* pp. 40–43.

30. Tobie Matthew, *A True Historical Relation of the Conversion of Sir Tobie Matthew to the Holy Catholic Faith,* ed. A. H. Matthew (London, 1904), p. 35.

31. For Milton's Arminianism, see Maurice Kelley, *This Great Argument: A Study of De Doctrina Christiana as a Gloss upon Paradise Lost* (Princeton: Princeton University Press, 1941), pp. 14–20; Dennis Danielson, *Milton's Good God: A Study in Literary Theodicy* (Cambridge: Cambridge University Press, 1982), pp. 75–82 and passim; and my "Milton's Arminianism and the Authorship of De Doctrina Christiana," *Texas Studies in Literature and Language* 41 (1999): 103–27.

not (as Luther and Calvin thought) bound to sin.... Milton holds that even in the post-lapsarian world, "everyone is provided with a sufficient degree of innate reason to be able to resist evil desires *by his own effort.*"[32]

While Strier is right that Milton does not emphasize depravity as strongly as Calvin does, it is also true that Milton acknowledges in the *De Doctrina Christiana (Christian Doctrine)* the universal effects of sin and the weakness of free will, particularly in the chapter "Of the Punishment of Sin." Milton argues that the fall has resulted in the "extensive darkening of that right reason, whose function it was to discern the chief good" (*YP* 6:395). While the freedom of the will has

> not quite disappeared even where good works are concerned, or at least good attempts, at any rate after God has called us and given us grace, . . . it is so weak and of such little moment, that it only takes away any excuse we might have for doing nothing, and does not give us the slightest reason for being proud of ourselves. (*YP* 6:396)

Despite his emphasis on freedom of the will, Milton steers clear of Pelagianism, with its belief that we can do good without grace. Arminius for his part insists that the free will must be assisted by grace, and that, despite the charges of his enemies, he is adamantly opposed to Pelagianism.[33] Thus Milton's anti-Calvinist, Arminian soteriology alone is insufficient to account for his refusal to acknowledge sinfulness in his self-representations. If there is, in other words, a theological reason for Calvinist autobiographers to dwell almost morbidly on their sins in a way Arminians might not, there is at the same time no theological reason for an Arminian to ignore sinfulness when he or she turns to self-examination. Moreover, Milton's habit of ignoring his

---

32. Richard Strier, "Milton against Humility," in *Religion and Culture in Renaissance England,* ed. Claire McEachern and Debora Shuger (Cambridge: Cambridge University Press, 1997), p. 269 (the embedded quotation is from the chapter "Of Predestination" in *De Doctrina* [*YP* 6:186]; emphasis Strier's).

33. Arminius writes in his *Letter to Hippolytus* IV:

> Concerning grace and free will, this is what I teach according to the Scriptures and orthodox consent: Free will is unable to begin or to perfect any true and spiritual good, without grace. That I may not be said, like Pelagius, to practice delusion with regard to the word "grace," I mean by it that which is the grace of Christ and which belongs to regeneration. I affirm, therefore, that this grace is simply and absolutely necessary for the illumination of the mind, the due ordering of the affections, and the inclination of the will to that which is good (*Writings of James Arminius,* trans. James Nichols and W. R. Bagnall, 3 vols. [Grand Rapids: Baker Book House, 1956], 2:472).

own sinfulness in his self-representations predates his adoption of Arminian ideas.[34]

There were, however, perfectionists in Milton's England, both Quakers and those whom Owen Watkins has termed "vulgar prophets."[35] The Society of Friends was of course a self-identified group, unusually well-organized among Nonconformist sects by means of an itinerant leadership. Milton thought highly of Quakers, including the prominent Quaker leader Isaac Pennington. The Quaker connection is most familiar in the person of his student and friend Thomas Ellwood (1639–1713), who left in his autobiography an account of a conversation with Milton that, from Ellwood's perspective at least, led to the composition of *Paradise Regained*.[36] The vulgar prophets, on the other hand, were a miscellaneous group of uneducated enthusiasts, who shared claims of direct inspiration from God. They ranged from antinomian Ranters such as Abiezer Coppe (1619–1672) to more moderate figures such as Richard Coppin (dates unknown) and the ecstatic Anna Trapnel. At the beginning of the movement, Quakers were often confused with Ranters, apparently with some justification, but by the late 1650s and 1660s the Quakers had clearly separated themselves from sensational antinomian claims and behavior. Nevertheless, the Quakers shared with the Ranters and other vulgar prophets an assertion of immediate divine guidance and the possibility of the perfection of saintly life on earth.

Despite this shared perfectionism, the writings of neither of these groups provide an analogue for Milton's anomalous self-representations. Milton asserted that sinfulness is a universal condition after the fall but wrote about himself as if he had never sinned, whereas the Quakers, who wrote that perfection is possible, acknowledge their sinfulness, at least before conversion. The explicit claims to sinlessness by the antinomian vulgar prophets, such as Abiezer Coppe and Laurence Clarkson (1615–1667), bear no resemblance to Milton's implicitly perfectionist accounts of his own blameless life. These sectarian enthusiasts presented their participation in what virtually all Christians would consider lurid sins as paradoxical confirmation of their status as saints, inasmuch as, according to Titus 1:15, "Unto the pure *all things* are pure."

Quoting Titus, Clarkson in *The Lost Sheep Found* (1660) seems to claim that the innocent performance of actions considered sinful is a prerequisite

---

34. Milton's autobiographical digressions on his virtuous youth in *An Apology for Smectymnuus* precede his opposition to Arminian teaching in *Areopagitica*.

35. Watkins, *The Puritan Experience: Studies in Spiritual Autobiography* (New York: Schocken, 1972), pp. 144–59.

36. Thomas Ellwood, *History of the Life of Thomas Ellwood*, ed. C. G. Crump (London, 1900), pp. 144–45; the work was first published in 1714, the year after Ellwood's death. William Riley Parker retells Ellwood's story in *Milton: A Biography*, 2 vols. (Oxford: Clarendon, 1968), 1:597.

of sainthood. There is, he writes, "no sin, but as man esteemed it sin, and therefore none can be free from sin, till in purity it be acted as no sin, for I judged that pure to me, which to a dark understanding was impure, for to the pure all things, yea all acts were pure."[37] Until one acts against the letter of the law, he seems to assert, one cannot be pure: "till you can lie with all women as one woman, and not judge it sin, you can do nothing but sin." Clarkson and his fellow sectarians acted on this principle. In this same text he tells the story of a meeting he attended with a Mrs. Star, another man's wife, with whom he was living: "they improved their liberty, where Doctor *Pagets* [i.e., Milton's friend Nathan Paget] maid stripped her self naked, and skipped among them, but being in a Cooks shop, there was no hunger, so that I kept my self to Mrs. *Star,* pleading the lawfulness of our doings as aforesaid" (p. 183). The plenty of the cook's shop notwithstanding, it could be argued that by his principles Clarkson should not have stopped with Mrs. Star. Coppe in *A Fiery Flying Roll* (1649) resembles Clarkson in his dependence on Titus and his paradoxical assertion of the purity made possible by gross breaches of the moral law: "To the pure all things are pure. God hath so cleared cursing, swearing, in some, that that which goes for swearing and cursing in them, is more glorious then praying and preaching in others."[38] Anticipating Clarkson, Coppe favors the luridly sexual; in *A Second Fiery Flying Roule* (1649–50) he relates how he ate and drank with

> Gypseys, and clip't, hug'd and kiss'd them, putting my hand in their bosomes, loving the she-Gipsies dearly. . . . [S]o I can for a need, if it be my will, and that in the height of honor and majesty, without sin. But at that time when I was hugging the Gipsies, I abhorred the thoughts of Ladies, their beauty could not . . . intangle my hands in their bosomes; yet I can if it be my will, kiss and hug Ladies, and *love my neighbors wife as my self, without sin.*[39]

Audaciously and ingeniously, Coppe appropriates and recasts the second of the two great commandments to which Christ reduces the decalogue as a rebuke to the censorious Pharisees: "Thou shalt love thy neighbor as thyself." By substituting in this allusive context his neighbor's wife for his neighbor, Coppe presents his unconventional sexual practices as not merely blameless but as a mark of special fidelity to divine command. His "kisses, have been

---

37. Laurence Clarkson, *The Lost Sheep Found,* excerpted in Nigel Smith, *A Collection of Ranter Writings* (London: Junction Books, 1983), p. 180.
38. Coppe, *A Fiery Flying Roll* (1649), as reprinted in Smith, *Ranter Writings,* p. 92.
39. Coppe, *A Second Fiery Flying Roule* (1649–50), in Smith, *Ranter Writings,* pp. 106–7 (my emphasis).

made the fiery chariots, to mount me swiftly into the bosome," and he concludes that "through BASE things I have been lifted up."[40]

Coppe's and Clarkson's claims of exemption from sin differ fundamentally from Milton's implicit one. Milton considers himself above the kind of actions the Ranters point to as paradoxical proof of their purity. When Milton in *Areopagitica* takes Titus 1:15 as a watchword, he refers to the use by the godly of things indifferent, not licensed transgressions of the moral law. Milton has in mind the precursors of the Ranters when he scornfully dismisses in 1645 those who misunderstood his arguments on divorce: "Licence they mean when they cry liberty; / For who loves that, must first be wise and good" (Sonnet 12). It is significant that, when forced to recant his teachings, Coppe assigns to himself the same phrase as Norwood and Bunyan, "the chief of sinners."[41]

The group to which Milton was closest is the Quakers. Without the lurid sensational antinomianism of the vulgar prophets, they like Milton placed the Spirit above law, letter, and tradition. They shared his opposition to a paid clergy and institutionalized liturgical forms that place mediators between the creature and God. Most significantly in this context, they argued for moral perfectibility in this life. James Nayler argues for perfectibility on earth in *Love to the Lost:* "By receiving and joyning to that which is perfect [the gifts of God] is the creature made perfect."[42] When joined to God, one can retrieve on earth a state of prelapsarian purity: "where the Seed is born and rules, that creature is not under the law, letter, not tradition, nor bondage, but led by the Spirit, and born of that Nature which was before transgression was."[43]

George Fox, the leader of the Quakers, also taught that the godly could be more perfect while still on earth than even Adam in his prelapsarian state. In his *Journal,* he describes the effects of his conversion:

> Now I was come up in spirit through the flaming sword, into the paradise of God.... I knew nothing but pureness, and innocency, and

---

40. Ibid., pp. 108, 109.
41. Coppe, *Copps Return to the Wayes of Truth* (1651), in Smith, p. 135. The surrounding passage makes a litany of orthodox Calvinist self-examination:

> O Sin! Sin! Sin!
> There is Sin.
> Murther, Theft, Adultery, Drunkenness, Swearing, Cursing, Uncleanness, Uncleanness [sic], Covetousness, Pride, Cruelty, Oppression, Hypocrisie, Hatred, Envy, Malice, Evil surmising is sin.
> Nothing but villany, sin, and transgression in me, the chief of sinners.
> In man—
> In every man.
> There is none righteous; no, not one.
> None that doth good; no, not one.

42. *Love to the Lost,* 2nd. ed. (London, 1656), p. 28.
43. Nayler, *A Door Opened for the Imprison'd Seed in the World* (London, 1667), p. 35.

righteousness; being renewed into the image of God by Christ Jesus, to the state of Adam, which he was in before he fell. The creation was opened to me; and it was showed me how all things had their names given them according to their nature and virtue. . . . I was immediately taken up in spirit to see into another or more steadfast state than Adam's innocency, even into a state in Christ Jesus that should never fall. And the Lord showed me that such as were faithful to Him, in the power and light of Christ, should come up into that state in which Adam was before he fell.[44]

Fox is explicit that this Adamic state involves sinlessness: "For of all the sects in Christendom (so called) that I discoursed with, I found none could bear to be told that any should come to Adam's perfection,—into the image of God, that righteousness and holiness, that Adam was in before he fell; to be clean and pure, without sin, as he was" (p. 101).

Fox met ferocious resistance from those who shared the general Christian understanding of the fall, to say nothing of Calvin's strong emphasis on depravity. He observes that "the professors [i.e., conventional Christians] were in a rage, all pleading for sin and imperfection, and could not endure to hear talk of perfection, and of a holy and sinless life" (p. 85).[45] Richard Baxter, as we have seen, calls the Quakers "mad with spiritual pride" for their claims of sinlessness.[46] Just as Milton felt compelled to distinguish himself from libertines after the publication of the divorce tracts, so the Quakers felt compelled to distinguish themselves from the Ranters with whom they were sometimes confused (or to whom they were tied by hostile observers) because of their teaching of perfectibility.[47]

Milton shares with the Quakers an affirmation of universal grace and free will, and hostility toward Calvinist predestination. Nayler, for example, writes that "God's gift is free in Christ Jesus, and his tender is to all men; who would

---

44. Fox, *The Journal of George Fox,* ed. Rufus M. Jones (New York: Capricorn, 1963), p. 97.

45. Francis Higginson complains of the Quakers in *A Brief Relation of the Irreligion of the Northern Quakers* (1653), "I could never see, or hear, or learn, that they speak almost anything of the miserable estate of all men by nature," p. 15 (Barbour and Roberts, *Early Quaker Writings,* p. 72). Higginson also levels the Miltonic charge that Quakers are advocates of libertinage rather than liberty (p. 1; Barbour and Roberts, p. 65).

46. Baxter, *The Quakers' Catechism,* p. C^r (see note 3 above).

47. James Nayler, for example, attacks "those unclean ranting Spirits" in *Having Heard that Some Have Wronged . . . ,* (London, 1671), p. 4; George Fox records an interrogation in Derby in 1650, where he attempts to clear himself from the charge of Ranterism, in *The Journal of George Fox,* pp. 120–21. The anonymous author of *From the Sweet-Singers of Israel, or the Family of Love* (London, 1678) distinguishes between Quaker perfectionism and the sensational antinomianism of another group, the Familists:

> For not withstanding they, under these pretences [of religion], give themselves over to all Excess and Ryot, yet they have the impudence to boast they are Immaculate as the Angels themselves, and whereas the frantick Quaker holds a temporal perfection or a possibility of

have all men to be saved, and come to the knowledge of the Truth . . . if you receive it."[48] Fox is as impatient as Milton with the aspersion cast on God's goodness by particular and absolute predestination:

> the priests had frightened the people with the doctrine of election and reprobation, telling them that God had ordained the greatest part of men and women for hell; and that, let them pray, or preach, or sing, or do what they would, it was all to no purpose, if they were ordained for hell. . . . So the priests said the fault was not at all in the creature, less or more, but that God had ordained it so.
>
> I was led to open to the people the falseness and folly of their priests' doctrines, and showed how they, the priests, had abused those Scriptures they quoted. Now all that believe in the Light of Christ as He commands, are in the election, and sit under the teaching of the grace of God, which brings their salvation.[49]

From the Calvinist perspective, this libertarian or Arminian assertion of the creature's significant participation in his or her salvation or damnation insults God's omnipotence and divine prerogative, and is thus a symptom of pride.

Even more galling to the Calvinist was the claim of perfection on earth. And, if anything, Baxter's charge that the Quakers are "mad with spiritual pride" is even more applicable to Milton. The Quakers Nayler and Fox, however much they stress their achievement of prelapsarian purity, acknowledge their sinful pasts. For Nayler, freedom from sin is impossible without conviction of sin: "Before you can judge of this Freedom, . . . you must own the Judgement of Him that condemns the man of sin in you."[50] Even Fox's *Journal*, despite Henry Cadbury's claim that it lacks "a single confession of sin or guilt or prayer for forgiveness in the name of Jesus," contains several accounts of Fox's near despair and at least one acknowledgment of sin: "*For all are concluded under sin, and shut up in unbelief, as I had been* [Fox's emphasis]; that Jesus Christ might have the pre-eminence, who enlightens, and gives grace,

---

> living without Sin, these men, (because they will out doe all the impudence that ever went before them) hold that they cannot Sin in the world, not but they are liable to the same temptations with other Men; but that the property of the Act alters by their doing of it. Which in effect is as much as to say they may Steal, and not Sin; murder, and not Sin; and in short for that certainly was the bottom of him who invented it, be Trayters and not sin; . . . they are indeed no other than a company of Debaucht viciated Atheists. (pp. 3–5)

48. Nayler, *A Door Opened*, p. 31.
49. Fox, *Journal*, pp. 299–300. The radical sectarian Richard Coppin also attacked predestination (*Divine Teachings*, p. 50).
50. Nayler, *A Door Opened*, p. 36.

and faith, and power. Thus when God doth work, who shall hinder it? and *this I knew experimentally.*"⁵¹

The admission of sin as necessary before conversion and regeneration cuts across all theological and sectarian boundaries in mid-seventeenth-century England, embracing everyone from Quaker perfectionists to hard-line Calvinists. The Calvinist Thomas Shepard terms the saving value of sin and consciousness of sin "God's deep plot."⁵² The prophetic Anna Trapnel acknowledges her sin when she writes of being "conscious to herself of the deceitfulness of her own heart."⁵³ The sectarian Richard Coppin, often accused of Ranterism, argues that "God suffers his dearest children to sin that thereby he might show unto us the weakness of ourselves in not forbearing of them, the evil and cursed effects in acting of them, and the richness of his love in pardoning of them."⁵⁴ The perfectionist Gerrard Winstanley, who opposed predestination and argues that all will be saved, treated the fall allegorically: each person goes through prelapsarian innocence, the fall into sin, and regeneration. Winstanley's God "lets innocent man fall so that He may raise him up again."⁵⁵

Milton himself endorses what appears, except for the Ranters, to be a universal position. Regeneration and conversion, he explains in *De Doctrina Christiana,* cannot take place until one is delivered from the spiritual death that follows from original sin (*YP* 6:395). In *Paradise Lost,* Michael tells Adam that the Law will be given to his descendants "to evince / Their natural pravity, by stirring up / Sin against law to fight" (12.287–89); when they see that they are unequal to fight sin, they will turn to the sacrifice of Christ.

Yet, despite this endorsement, Milton nowhere in his autobiographical writings acknowledges his own sinfulness, in the way that even the perfectionist Quakers do. He thus would seem to open himself up to the diagnosis of religious enthusiasm in Robert Burton's discussion of "Religious Melancholy" in *The Anatomy of Melancholy* (1628), a discussion that seems remarkably prescient of the sectarian enthusiasm of the mid-century:

> Some of us again are too dear, as we think, more divine and sanctified than others, of a better metal, greater gifts, and with that proud Pharisee,

---

51. Fox, *Journal,* p. 82. For Cadbury's argument, see his essay on "The Influence of *The Journal of George Fox,*" prefacing Jones's edition, p. 17. Fox, in the Derby interrogation alluded to above, acknowledges that "Christ my Savior has taken away my sin; and in Him there is no sin" (p. 121).

52. Shepard, *Journal,* in *God's Plot,* p. 141.

53. Trapnel, *Strange and Wonderful Newes from Whitehall, or the Mighty visions proceeding from Mistress Anna Trapnel* (London, 1654), p. 4.

54. Coppin, *Divine Teachings,* p. 97.

55. Winstanley, *Fire in the Bush: The Spirit Burning, Not Consuming, but Purging Mankind* (London, 1650), reprinted in Gerrard Winstanley, *The Law of Freedom and Other Writings,* ed. Christopher Hill (Cambridge: Cambridge University Press, 1983), p. 255. For Winstanley's anti-predestinarianism and universalism, see in the same volume *A New Year's Gift Sent to the Parliament and the Army* (London, 1650), p. 193.

contemn others in respect of ourselves, we are better Christians, better learned, choice spirits, inspired, know more, have special revelation, perceive God's secrets, and thereupon presume, say and do many times which is not fitting to be said or done. Of this number are all superstitious Idolaters, Ethnicks, Mahometans, Jews, Hereticks, Enthusiasts, Divinators, Prophets, Sectaries, and Schismaticks.[56]

Milton would not relish being lumped in such suspect company. In one respect Milton cannot be tarred with the same brush. For all his claims that he is one of the "selected heralds of peace, and dispensers of treasure inestimable without price to them that have no pence," that his lips have been touched "with the hallow'd fire" of Isaiah 6,[57] Milton never sounds like an enthusiast claiming a personal and ecstatic vision of God. One cannot imagine his sharing Coppe's putative experience with angels of vengeance descended from heaven, or saying with Coppe "Some of these Angels I have been acquainted withall."[58] He is not given to visions like Trapnel's. It is the experimental knowledge of God, so important to Fox, that seems lacking in Milton.

The absence of a narrative of an overwhelming inner experience of light or of God's presence, as opposed to an abstract assertion of fidelity to the Spirit, distinguishes Milton's self-representations from those in the spiritual autobiographies of Puritans and Nonconformists with whom he otherwise shares so much. It may be true that, as William Kerrigan suggests, "Quintessentially a Protestant, Milton experienced his God in the heart," but if he shares the Protestant doctrine of indwelling, he refrains at least in his prose from any vivid narrative of the experience.[59] As John Spencer Hill puts it, "Milton never experienced the sudden, blinding infusion of divine grace described by so many of his Puritan contemporaries in their spiritual autobiographies and records of religious conversion."[60] The dispensibility of this infusion of grace is a function of the apparent absence of a conviction of sin. From this perspective, Milton, though very much a theological writer, is hardly a religious writer at all.

The Ironies of the Ethical Proof

If the Puritan Milton's self-representations fail to fit the Pauline and Augustinian models of conviction and self-abasement, they are more at home

---

56. Burton, *The Anatomy of Melancholy* (III.4.i.1), ed. Floyd Dell and Paul Jordan-Smith (London: George Routledge & Sons, 1931), p. 873.
57. *The Reason of Church-Government, YP* 1:802,821.
58. Coppe, *A Fiery Flying Roll*, in Smith, *Collection*, p. 91.
59. William Kerrigan, *The Prophetic Milton* (Charlottesville: University Press of Virginia, 1974), p. 11.
60. John Spencer Hill, *John Milton: Poet, Priest, and Prophet* (Totowa, NJ: Rowman and Littlefield, 1979), p. 103.

in the context of two other traditions. One is the Christian tradition of the singularly virtuous prophet. Kerrigan observes that patristic authors "insisted on the exemplary character of the prophets. Yahweh was mysterious, not random, and there was nothing arbitrary about His selection of mortal vessels."[61] Kerrigan quotes Origen's *Contra Celsum* (VII.7) on the exemplary character of the prophets: "They were chosen by providence to be intrusted with the divine Spirit and with the utterances that He inspired on account of the quality of their lives, which was of unexampled courage and freedom; for in the face of death they were entirely without terror. And reason demands that the prophets of the supreme God should be such people." In this model of prophecy, unblemished virtue gave individuals selected by God the serenity and clarity necessary for prophetic vision along with the courage to face persecution for prophesying.[62] This understanding of prophetic selection accounts for much of the tension in the prophetic role Milton claims. If all is his, rather than God's, then he is presumptuous and in mortal danger, but if he does not make himself stand out for virtue, his election as prophet is all the more doubtful. The prophet must merit election by virtue, but the prophetic virtue itself must be God's gift and possession. Nigel Smith observes that when Milton's contemporaries wanted to exhibit their credentials as prophets, they wrote about themselves on the model of Old Testament prophets, with an emphasis on divinely inspired madness. In the conversion and prophetic narratives, Smith writes, "The prophet's self-presentation is crucial for the communication of inspired authority. . . . [T]he specific qualities of pseudepigraphic writing include details of the prophet's life, his background, birth, and habits which make him special, apart from other people, and so enhance his authority."[63] These sectarian prophets, including Coppe, Joseph Salmon, and Thomas Tany, adopted a pose of prophetic madness and zeal.

While willing and even eager to cast himself in the roles of Hebrew prophets such as Jeremiah and Isaiah, and while partial to self-representation as one burning with zeal, Milton, however "smit with the love of sacred song," never presented himself as mad. Instead, his self-representations as virtuous prophet are inflected through a secular, classical prism. His self-representations as exemplary recall the mode of ethical proof in ancient rhetoric. Aristotle, Quintilian, and Cicero, mindful of the persuasive value of an audience's belief in a speaker's virtue and probity, encouraged orators to present themselves as virtuous. Aristotle elaborates on the "ethical proof" in his *Rhetoric*:

---

61. Kerrigan, *Prophetic Milton*, p. 29.
62. There is another model, the classical *furor poeticus,* the divine frenzy that Socrates relates to both poetry and prophecy (and love) in *Phaedrus*. On the *furor poeticus* in the Renaissance, see Kerrigan, *Prophetic Milton*, pp. 38–82.
63. Nigel Smith, *Perfection Proclaimed: Language and Literature in English Radical Religion, 1640–1660* (Oxford: Clarendon, 1989), p. 55.

> Persuasion is achieved by the speaker's personal character when the speech is so spoken as to make us think him credible. We believe good men more fully and more readily than others. . . . It is not true, as some writers assume in their treatises on rhetoric, that the personal goodness revealed by the speaker contributes nothing to his power of persuasion; on the contrary, his character may almost be called the most effective means of persuasion he possesses.[64]

Aristotle adds later that while an orator must make the argument demonstrative, "he must also make his own character look right and put his hearers, who are to decide, into the right frame of mind" (1377b23–24). The orator establishes good character by demonstrating "good sense, good moral character, and goodwill" (1378a9).

But if the classical ethical proof bears a family resemblance to the patristic understanding of the role of virtue in prophets, the context could hardly be more different. By virtuous life one might make oneself eligible for prophetic election, but the choice, and the resulting prophecy, are God's. The proper stance of the prophet is humility. From both the Aristotelian and Ciceronian perspectives, the acquired virtue is in part a demonstration of personal excellence, and this excellence is itself source of the value of actions. The proper stance of the subject of ethical proof is justified pride in personal abilities and accomplishments.

As Milton contemplated how to represent himself in his works, and particularly in his polemical works, he faced a choice between the Pauline and Augustinian models so influential among fellow Puritans and the Aristotelian and Ciceronian humanist model of ethical proof. He repeatedly chose the classical model of self-justification. Joan Webber proposes a Milton who does not need to make a choice, for whom the clash of ethos is reconcilable. Webber's Milton tells the typical Puritan story, but transposes it into literary terms. Gifts of the spirit become the gifts of poetry; doubts about the reception of saving grace become doubts about prematurity or belatedness.[65] Webber uncovers a formal mirroring, but the heart of the Puritan experience, with its anguish, anxiety, and conviction, is missing. Where Webber finds a seamless fusion of religious and literary motives in Milton's self-representations, Paul Stevens finds discontinuity. In a contest between the Puritan stance of humility and the humanist stance of worthiness, the humanist stance wins out, as Stevens observes of one of Milton's most significant autobiographical

---

64. Aristotle, *Rhetoric* 1356a4–13, in *The Basic Works of Aristotle*, ed. Richard McKeon (New York: Random House, 1941), p. 1329. Further quotations from Aristotle are from this edition and indicated in the text by marginal numbers.
65. Webber, *The Eloquent "I"* (Madison: University of Wisconsin Press, 1968), p. 217.

digressions: "At the very moment Milton announces his calling by the Word in *The Reason of Church-Government,* decorum, the general style of the pamphlet, demands that the scriptural rhetoric be enclosed within the personal digression of a Ciceronian orator. His words dissolve just as much into those of *De oratore* as they do into those of scripture."[66]

Given the discontinuity and even contradiction that Stevens uncovers, Milton's humanist-tinged self-representations are inherently unstable. Cicero's audiences did not require the orator to admit to failures; they would have been surprised were he to do so. Calvinist and Puritan audiences would have reason to suspect those who failed to do so. One self-representing author who meets this expectation is the Calvinist, though not Puritan, Sir Thomas Browne. In *Religio Medici,* Browne resembles Milton in his elitist disdain for the vulgar and his numbering himself in a natural aristocracy, "a Nobility without Heraldry, a naturall dignity, whereby one man is ranked with another, another Filed before him, according to the quality of his desert, and preheminence of his good parts."[67] Again like Milton, he sees his membership in this aristocracy as inseparable from his virtue. After professing his powerful and faithful love for a friend, he adds, "This noble affection fals not on vulgar and common constitutions, but on such as are mark'd for vertue; he that can love his friend with this noble ardour, will in a competent degree affect all" (II.6, p. 143). Nevertheless, Browne on several occasions acknowledges his errors and his sinful nature. He writes, "I finde in my confirmed age the same sinnes I discovered in my youth" (I.42, p. 113), and "I feele sometimes a hell within my selfe, *Lucifer* keeps his court in my brest, *Legion* is revived in me" (I.51; p. 125). Browne, observing himself coolly and with some ironic detachment, is closer to Montaigne than to Bunyan, but he nevertheless admits his sinfulness. This admission is itself ironic evidence of his trustworthiness and part of the ethical proof.

Milton addresses the dilemma facing one who would rely on the ethical proof in religious polemic at the beginning of *An Apology for Smectymnuus,* where he considers himself "forc't" by the "rancor of an evil tongue" to examine himself and "to give a more true account of my selfe abroad then this modest Confuter . . . hath given of me" (*YP* 1:869–70). Milton admits that as a result he might be "thought too much a party in mine owne cause," especially as "the best apology against false accusers is silence and sufferance, and honest deeds set against dishonest words" (*YP* 1:870). He concludes, however, that to omit a defense of himself would be to leave exposed to opprobrium

---

66. Paul Stevens, "Discontinuities in Milton's Early Public Self-Representation," *Huntington Library Quarterly* 51 (1988): 274.
67. *Religio Medici* (II.1), in *Sir Thomas Browne: The Major Works,* ed. C. A. Patrides (Harmondsworth: Penguin, 1977), p. 134; further references will be cited by section and page number from this edition.

the truth that he has defended, "[l]est those disgraces which I ought to suffer, if it so befall me, for my religion, through my default religion be made liable to suffer for me" (*YP* 1:871).

With this defense of his defense out of the way, Milton plunges into a self-laudatory set piece. The example of several contemporaries who chose a different route is instructive. The Presbyterian John Bastwick (1593–1648?), who suffered with William Prynne the mutilating knife of the prelates, devotes a fifty-page appendix in his *The Utter Routing of the whole Army of all the Independents and Sectaries* (1646) to a defense against a personal attack by Henry Burton.[68] All but absent from this personal defense, despite its protracted length, is any autobiography, or indeed any particular defense of himself. Instead, Bastwick offers brief portraits of Presbyterian worthies (something Milton will do for Independent worthies in the *Defensio Secunda*). Bastwick betrays irritation with those who "daily brag of their gifts and graces, and of the singularity of their parts, and priviledges, and so of their familiarity with Jesus Christ, and of their holinesse and piety, appropriating all those prerogatives to themselves."[69]

The example of Thomas Edwards (1599–1647), the Presbyterian heresy hunter who attacks Milton on divorce in his *Gangraena* (1646), illustrates the dilemma facing Milton when he turns to the ethical proof. In his *Antapologia* (1644), Edwards relates that he considered composing a vindication of himself:

> I had many thoughts and purposes in my Epistle, *to have given the Reader an accompe of my especiall call to the making this Answer,* as also to have laid down the Principles and Rules I more especially went by in the studying of these controversies, and then to have Apologized for my self and my Book, by answering some objections and clearing aspersions cast abroad in this mistaking age, and by representing to the Reader my many sufferings, constant labours, &c.[70]

Like Milton, Edwards perceives a need to indicate what authorizes him to enter public debate, but he reaches a very different conclusion:

> but conceiving the danger of this way in comparing with the Apologists, least I might become a foole in glorying, and runne into the same fault

---

68. Bastwick, *THE UTTER ROUTING of the whole Army of all the INDEPENDENTS & SECTARIES, with the Totall overthrow of their Hierarchy that New Babel, more groundless than that of the Prelates, or 'INDEPENDENCY not gods ORDINANCE'* (London, 1646), pp. 611–62.
69. Ibid., F3^v ("Epistle to the Reader").
70. Thomas Edwards, *Antapologia: Or, A Full Answer to the Apologeticall Narration of Mr Goodwin, Mr Nye, Mr Sympson, Mr Burroughs, Mr Bridge, Members of the Assembly of Divines* (London, 1644), A1^r(my emphasis).

I charge upon the Apologists, and least it might be thought I sought to commend my Answer by such wayes rather then by the strength of the discourse it selfe, I resolved to forbeare all those comparisons and vindications of my selfe, and to refer all to God.

The clear implication is that the kind of defense offered by Milton is a foolish glorying and a failure "to refer all to God."

Alexander More (1616–1670) in his *Fides Publica* will attack Milton for such foolish glorying. He fulfills the Pauline and Augustinian expectations that Milton frustrates. The main purpose of the work is to clear his name from Milton's violent aspersions. On the last page of the *Fides Publica,* More, in the midst of a prayer like those with which Milton ends many of his tracts, confesses his guilt:

A suppliant, I venerate the will of Thy providence which justly permits that I be falsely accused among men because of so many hidden faults of which in Thy sight I am truly guilty. . . . There is great sin to be observed here in my soul, which I confess before the whole world. I have never served Thee according to my strength. That little talent of Thy grace which Thou has designed to bestow upon me I have not yet multiplied, whether because I have followed too much the pleasures of study, or because I have consumed too much time and effort in refuting the curses of malevolent men, to whom, so does it please Thee, I have been a constant target. . . . I confess that I have sinned against Thee.[71]

While elsewhere More busies himself with self-defense, here he offers a clear admission of sinfulness, unlike anything in Milton's works. He invokes the parable of the talent, as does Milton in the "Letter to a Friend," but to self-convicting rather than self-exonerating ends. The difference between More and Milton does not necessarily mean that More is more sincere than Milton; it does show that he is more careful to employ the paradoxical Protestant version of the ethical proof. Recognition of sinfulness is a mark of progress in the Spirit, and thus witnesses ironically to virtue. In *Pilgrim's Progress,* failure to acknowledge sinfulness is the distinguishing trait of the character Ignorance.[72] Milton makes the same connection in his attack in *Paradise Regained* on the pride of self-sufficiency that links otherwise disparate ancient ethical systems (4.301–15).

---

71. The passage is from More's *Supplementum Fidei Publicæ* (1655), which completes the unfinished *Fides Publica* (1654). The passage, translated by Paul W. Blackford, appears in *YP* 4.2:1128.

72. John Bunyan, *Pilgrim's Progress,* ed. Roger Sharrock (Harmondsworth: Penguin, 1987), p 127.

Milton makes just enough gestures toward the convention of conviction and conversion to indicate that he knows what is expected of him. The retraction appended to the last of his Latin elegies (examined at the end of chapter 3), in which Protestant and poetic conventions merge, is an example of such a gesture. Another of these moments comes late in the "Letter to a Friend," but only after Milton has dismissed the possibility of suspect motives and turned to conventional and humorous self-deprecation:

> & heere I am come to a streame head copious enough to disburden it selfe like Nilus at seven mouthes into an ocean, but then I should also run into a reciprocall contradiction of ebbing & flowing at once & doe that wch I excuse myselfe for not doing [,] preach & not preach. *Yet that you may see that I am something suspicio[us] of my selfe,* & doe take notice of a certaine belatednesse in me I am the bolder to send you some of my nightward thoughts some while since . . . made up in a Petrarchian stanza [Sonnet 7, "How soon hath time"]. (*YP* 1:320; my emphasis)

If there is self-suspicion in the letter, it does not issue in the kind of conviction that More, however conventionally, displays; instead, it is overwhelmed in self-justificatory claims for the writer's alignment with divine will. The suspicion enters the letter only after the business of the letter is done. In the sonnet as well, momentary unease about a possible failing that is at least as much literary and careerist as it is moral is laid to rest with reassertion of union with the will of God. Milton may be aware of the part of doubt and conviction he is supposed to play, but his heart is not in it.

Chapter 3

"Himself before Himself"

The Early Works

Intimations of later self-representations punctuate Milton's early writings. Already in his Prolusions, or Cambridge academic exercises, he rehearses defining roles. In the 1628 "Vacation Exercise" verses with which he concludes the Sixth Prolusion, Milton projects a future in which as an epic singer he will "look in" at "Heav'n's door." In the Seventh Prolusion the young speaker, having elaborately identified himself with learning, imagines the appearance of a learned individual who will be "a great gift of God, . . . sufficient to lead a whole state to righteousness (*magnum Dei munus toti Reipub. satis esse possit ad bonam frugem*)" (*YP* 1:292; *Works* 12:258). Milton represents himself to his friend Charles Diodati, in the Latin verse of Elegy 6 in 1629 and in a familiar letter eight years later, as a godly and God-inspired epic poet, at least in aspiration. Biographers are tempted to read back into youth an anticipation of the accomplishments of age; Milton treats his own unfolding youth in the same fashion. Autobiography usually invites retrospection and introspection; Milton, toward the beginning of his writing life, is focused on prospect.[1]

In his proleptic self-representations or fragmentary autobiographies, Milton reverses a schema according to which, in John Sturrock's words,

> The autobiographer already has a proper name that is known to others as a result of the public achievements that entitle him to come forward

---

1. For the convergence of introspection and retrospection in autobiography, and thus its resemblance to psychoanalysis, see Paul Jay, *Being in the Text: Self-Representation from Wordsworth to Roland Barthes* (Ithaca: Cornell University Press, 1984).

as an autobiographer; he is singular to start with. . . . In reflecting on his life, the autobiographer traces the purposeful, seemingly anticipated course of his own separation out from others, his escape from among the great mass of the anonymous.[2]

The motivation behind Milton's early self-representations (or, in the case of the "Letter to a Friend," its subject) is the lack of "public achievements" and the handicap of anonymity. The singularity is promised rather than achieved, as Milton attempts to purchase authority on credit against future deeds.[3]

Sturrock highlights the tense relationship between autobiography and theory. The genre in his view assumes precisely what contemporary theory places under suspicion, the presence of the author and the text's direct reference to an extra- or pretextual ground. Milton's proleptic self-representations, however, anticipate theoretical insistence on the textuality of the "self." The congruence between Milton's early prospective and later retrospective self-representations says as much about the textuality of the self as it says about his consistency and foresight. Paul de Man writes that "We assume that life *produces* the autobiography as an act produces its consequences, but can we not suggest, with equal justice, that the autobiographical project may itself produce and determine the life . . . ?"[4] With Milton, there is at least the illusion that the life outside the text is produced or determined by the self-representation. As if illustrating Oscar Wilde's dictum that life imitates art,[5] Milton's life imitates the proleptic self-representation in the early works.

Milton focuses so intently on prospect and retrospect that the present moment is swallowed up. In narrating moments of crisis in his profoundly retrospective *Confessions,* Augustine creates the illusion of suspense even when we know the general shape of the outcome. We are absorbed in the remembered present when he asks that his will be amended, but not yet, or when he hears the child's voice saying, "*Tolle et lege.*" As Milton habitually looks forward to a state of heroic completion, the present moment of crisis is elided and obscured. Thus in the *Reason of Church-Government,* as we will see, Milton comes to a crossroad and immediately projects upon it a future from which he can look

---

2. John Sturrock, "Theory Versus Autobiography," in *The Culture of Autobiography: Constructions of Self-Representation,* ed. Robert Folkenflik (Stanford: Stanford University Press, 1993), p. 27.

3. John Guillory has argued that Milton attempts to project "a sense of authority *prior* to any actual achievement as a writer" (*Poetic Authority: Spenser, Milton, and Literary History* [New York: Columbia University Press, 1983], p. 97).

4. Paul de Man, "Autobiography as De-facement," *Modern Language Notes* 94 (1979): 920.

5. In "The Decay of Lying," Wilde claims that "Literature always anticipates life. It does not copy it, but molds it to his purpose" (*Critical Theory since Plato,* ed. Hazard Adams [New York: Harcourt Brace Jovanovich, 1971], p. 681).

back at the present.⁶ One implication of this habitual move is the eclipsing of the temporal site of conversion, the moment of direct confrontation with one's own sinfulness and with a redeeming God.⁷

Anticipating a Role in the 1620s

As soon as Milton writes of his own accord, as opposed to prescribed schoolboy exercises, he begins to write about himself and, inaugurating a familiar pattern, to defend his character and actions. In Elegy I, written at seventeen while rusticated from Cambridge in the spring of 1626, Milton is determined to elevate himself above those who have wronged him:

> *Iam nec arundiferum mihi cura revisere Camum,*
> . . . .
> *Quam male Phoebicolis convenit ille locus!*
> *Nec duri libet usque minas perferre magistri*
> Caeteraque ingenio non subeunda meo.
> *Si sit hoc exilium, patrios adiisse penates,*
> *Et vacuum curis otia grata sequi,*
> *Non ego vel profugi nomen sortemve recuso,*
> *Laetus et exilii conditione fruor.*
> (El I, 11-20; my emphasis)

Nor do I now have any interest in returning to the reedy Cam. . . . How badly that place suits Phoebus's followers. It is not pleasing to keep bearing the threats of a harsh master *and other things intolerable to my talent.* If this is exile—to have returned to my homeland gods and pursue a welcome leisure free from worries, I have not shunned the name, nor do I refuse the fate, and I am happy to rejoice in the condition of exile.⁸

---

6. Milton, Richard Halpern writes, "tends to view himself from the projected point of later reckoning" ("The Great Instauration: Imaginary Narratives in Milton's 'Nativity Ode,'" in *Remembering Milton: Essays on the Texts and Traditions,* ed. Mary Nyquist and Margaret W. Ferguson [New York: Methuen, 1987], p. 3); Joan Webber observes that Milton provides for himself "an audience for both present and future" (*The Eloquent "I"* [Madison: University of Wisconsin Press, 1968], p. 198).

7. On this point I will differ with a reading that in other respects I find exemplary, J. Martin Evans's *The Miltonic Moment* (Lexington: University of Kentucky Press, 1998). Evans finds in Milton's early poems an "intense *presentness*" (p. 4), wherein can be found a Miltonic version of Christian conversion. I will argue, on the contrary, that the occlusion of the present is tied to the absence of a conviction of sin, a crucial element in conversion.

8. Here and elsewhere, I quote Milton's poetry from *The Complete Poetry and Essential Prose of John Milton,* ed. William Kerrigan, John Rumrich, and Stephen M. Fallon (New York: Modern Library, 2007); the translations, from the same edition, are by Gordon Braden.

Feeling defensive about having been disciplined, Milton responds by turning defense into offense and claiming membership in a select society. One of "Phoebus' followers," he finds his tutor's threats unbearable to his *ingenium* (his "spirit" or "talent").[9] As the poem proceeds, the society becomes more rarefied. Milton compares his exile to Ovid's; had Ovid's been as pleasant, he would have surpassed Homer and Virgil. Milton does not claim equality with these poets, but the form of the later self-representations, in which he will lay claim to fellowship with the greatest poets, is already in place. Although writing to his closest friend, Charles Diodati, Milton pays attention to a larger public and to his reputation. The multiple audience helps to account for an awkward reversal: the young man who opens with condescending disdain for Cambridge ends with eager preparations to return to Cambridge.

The young Milton goes out of his way to style himself in prospect an inspired heroic poet. As a nineteen year old in 1628, he violates precedent by adding to a Latin academic exercise English verses about his own poetic ambition. Looking ahead from the present occasion toward future achievement, he searches for a "graver subject" for English verse (30),

> Such where the deep transported mind may soar
> Above the wheeling poles, and at Heav'n's door
> Look in, and see each blissful deity
> How he before the thunderous throne doth lie,
> Listening to what unshorn Apollo sings
> . . . .
> Then passing through the spheres of watchful fire,
> And misty regions of wide air next under,
> And hills of snow and lofts of pilèd thunder,
> May tell at length how green-eyed Neptune raves,
> In Heav'n's defiance mustering all his waves.
>   (33–44)

The lines augur Milton's tendency to treat himself as subject as well as singer: to sing and to be worthy of song will become two sides of the same coin. The ability to fly to Olympian heights narrows the distance between the singer and the heroic (and divine) subjects of graver poetry. Even given the ludic and combative setting of the "Vacation Exercise" verses, Milton's soaring self-representation stretches propriety, as he acknowledges indirectly in the poem ("I have some naked thoughts that rove about / And loudly knock to have their passage out" [23–24]), even as the end of the Prolusion acknowledges

---

9. On Milton's use of *ingenium* to refer to his poetic gift, see Dayton Haskin, *Milton and the Burden of Interpretation* (Philadelphia: University of Pennsylvania Press, 1994), pp. 41–42.

the impropriety of the poem itself: "Now I will overleap the University Statutes as if they were the wall of Romulus and run off from Latin into English" (*YP* 1:286).

Milton had earlier placed himself in the position of the soaring poet, but through words placed in the mouth of the deceased Bishop of Ely. Milton has Felton compare himself to Elijah, that "old prophet" (*Vates . . . senex*) who was "rapt to heaven" (*raptus ad coelum*) (49), much as Milton will be "rapt above the pole" nearly four decades later in *Paradise Lost* (7.23). In choosing *vates* over *propheta* here, Milton gestures toward the divine madness or *furor poeticus* of the inspired poet.[10] Henry John Todd, early in the nineteenth century, heard an echo of lines from Sylvester's *Du Bartas,* a work known well by Milton, lines in which the poet asks the Holy Spirit to guide him through the heavens.[11] Felton was not a poet, and the intrusion of the term *vates* suggests that in this poem of mourning, as in "Lycidas" a decade later, Milton contemplates himself more than the nominal subject.

The rapt *vates* Bishop Felton flies through the heavens until he arrives at Olympus:

> *Erraticorum syderum per ordines,*
> *Per lacteas vehor plagas,*
> *Velocitatem saepe miratus novam,*
> *Donec nitentes ad fores*
> *Ventum est Olympi, et regiam Chrystallinam, et*
> *Stratum smaragdis Atrium.*
>
> (59–64)

I am carried through the ranks of the wandering stars, through the Milky Way, often marvelling at my new speed, until I have come to the shining gates of Olympus and the crystalline palace and the forecourt paved with emerald.

In the course of the long speech, taking up more than half the poem, the first person address of Felton becomes less and less distinct from the first person of the poetic speaker, an effect emphasized at the end when Felton voices a formula typical of the poet speaking of things forbidden or invisible to mortal

---

10. On *vates, propheta,* and the *furor poeticus,* see William Kerrigan, *The Prophetic Milton* (Charlottesville: University Press of Virginia, 1974), pp. 17–82.

11. *The Poetical Works of John Milton with Notes of Various Authors,* ed. H. J. Todd, 3rd ed., 6 vols. (London, 1826), 6:321. Todd points to these lines of Sylvester's *Divine Weekes,* his translation of du Bartas's *Semaines:* "Pure Spirit, that rapt'st aboue the firmest sphear, / In fiery coach, thy fruitful messenger.—/ O! take me vp; that, far from earth, I may, / From sphear to sphear, see th'azure heav'ns to-day."

sight: "*Sed hic tacebo, nam quis effari queat / Oriundus humano patre / Amoenitates illius loci?*" ("But here I fall silent, for who born of a human father could speak the pleasures of that place?") (65–67). Who falls silent, the ostensible speaker or the poet? The ambiguity underlines the difficulty Milton has in keeping himself out of the center of things. And as the voices of the elder bishop and youthful poet coalesce, Milton looks forward to a time when he can look back on heroic and prophetic accomplishment. The prospective and retrospective take the place of present accomplishment. Even into his early thirties, as is evident in "Ad Salsilli" and "Manso," Milton continues to represent (and authorize) himself as an epic poet in prospect.

In the Prolusions Milton speaks before many who know him well, and the premium on in-jokes invites self-representation.[12] Milton's self-representation is shaped also by the agonistic ethos of the academic disputation. He paints a picture of an embattled self, joined by the pure and right-thinking few and opposed by the promiscuous many. Ethical proof alternates with *ad hominem* attack on opponents, as in this passage from the First Prolusion:

> [H]ow can I hope for your good-will, when in all this great assembly I encounter none but hostile glances? . . . Yet to prevent complete despair, I see here and there, if I do not mistake, some who without a word show clearly by their looks how well they wish me. The approval of these, few though they be, is more precious to me than that of the countless hosts of the ignorant, who lack all intelligence, reasoning power, and sound judgment, and who pride themselves on the ridiculous effervescing froth of their verbiage. (*YP* 1:219–20)

Ignorance and folly is not the worst of the unfit audience; it is accompanied by moral depravity. Who would speak in opposition to his defense of day over night except for "a son of darkness, a robber, a gamester, or one whose wont it is to spend his nights in the company of harlots" (*YP* 1:232). The jests anticipate the weapons of insult and character assassination that Milton would wield in earnest in later polemics.

In the Seventh Prolusion, Milton, as champion for learning over ignorance, associates learning with moral purity, with a commitment "to live modestly and temperately, and to tame the first impulses of headstrong youth by reason and steady devotion to study, keeping the divine vigour of our minds unstained and uncontaminated by any impurity or pollution" (*cœlestem animi vigorem ab omni contagione & inquinamento purum & intactum servantes*) (*YP* 1:300; *Works* 12:274). Here Milton first associates purity, learning, and

---

12. The dates of most of the Prolusions are not known; see Gordon Campbell, *A Milton Chronology* (New York: St. Martin's, 1997), pp. 31–41.

heroic speech, the complement and perhaps the full substitute for heroic action,[13] a combination integral to later self-constructions.

Invested with virtue and learning, the lover of learning becomes, like the Milton of the *Defences* two decades and more later, an oracle to nations: "I pass over a pleasure with which none can compare—to be the oracle of many nations, to find one's home regarded as a kind of temple, to be a man whom kings and states invite to come to them, whom men from near and far flock to visit, while to others it is a matter for pride if they have but set eyes on him once" (*YP* 1:297). While learning is the shared pursuit of the university, Milton's imagination is fired by desire to be a lone individual eminent in learning and wisdom, who becomes a savior to the nation: "a single household, even a single individual, endowed with the gifts of Art and Wisdom, may often prove to be a great gift of God, and sufficient to lead a whole state to righteousness" (*YP* 1:292). Like Socrates in Plato's *Apology* (30d), Milton imagines himself a divine gift to his compatriots. The vision again is proleptic. An undergraduate of high ideals and a present need to authorize himself, he draws on the future capital of anticipated achievement.

For a young man of vast ambition and confidence in future achievement, crossing the threshold of adulthood could hardly fail to spur reflection. Would he prove worthy of inspiration, and would that inspiration come if he were to prove worthy? Milton elaborates on the relation between virtue and poetic inspiration in Elegy 6, written around his twenty-first birthday, after Christmas of 1629. He contrasts the life of the graceful elegist Diodati with the more rigorous life of the heroic poet,[14]

> *qui bella refert, et adulto sub Iove caelum,*
> *Heroasque pios, semideosque duces,*
> *Et nunc sancta canit superum consulta deorum,*
> *Nunc latrata fero regna profunda cane.*
>
> (55–58)

who tells of wars, and of heaven under the rule of Jove in his maturity, and reverent heroes and semidivine leaders, and sings now of the sacred deliberations of the supreme gods, now of the deep realm where the fierce dog barks.

---

13. In the Third Prolusion Milton refers to "two things which most enrich and adorn our country: eloquent speech and noble action" (*YP* 1:246).

14. For an excellent discussion of the relation in Elegy 6 between the manner of a poet's life and the nature of his poetry, see Stella Revard, *Milton and the Tangles of Neaera's Hair: The Making of the 1645 Poems* (Columbia: University of Missouri Press, 1997), pp. 121–23.

Milton teases Diodati, who has been feasting in the country, by emphasizing the role of Bacchus, wine, and feasting in the inspiration of elegy: "*Massica fecundam despumant pocula venam, / Fundis et ex ipso condita metra cado*" (Cups of Massic wine foam out a fertile vein, and you pour out verses stored in the bottle itself) (31–32). The heroic poet must live frugally, abstaining from wine and rich food:

> *Stet prope fagineo pellucida lympha catillo,*
> *Sobriaque e puro pocula fonte bibat.*
> *Additur huic scelerisque vacans et* casta iuventus,
> *Et* rigidi mores, *et* sine labe manus.
> (61–64; my emphasis)

let the clearest water stand nearby in a beechwood vessel, and let him drink sober draughts from a pure spring. Add to this a *youth* free of crime and *chaste,* and *strict morals,* and a *hand free from stain.*

Living like this will allow the young poet to join the prophet Tiresias, Linus (Orpheus's teacher), and Homer. Milton credits Homer, on the strength of his chaste and frugal life, with the power to guide Odysseus safely through the palace of Circe and the shallows of the Sirens.

The aspirant to heroic verse must be more than chaste and pure, he must also be as courageous as the heroes he describes. He will be blessed on the basis of his life with special intimacy with and access to the divine: "*Diis etenim sacer est* vates, *divumque sacerdos, / Spirat et occultam pectus, et ora Iovem*" (For a *bard* is sacred to the gods, and a priest to the gods, and both his hidden heart and his mouth breathe forth Jove) (77–78; my emphasis).[15]

The reward reserved for the one devoted to learning, poetry, and chaste virtue will be rapt flight, an image traceable through Milton's career from the poem on Ely all the way through *Paradise Lost.* In turn, that rapt flight will evoke the anxiety of one who may have overreached in his claims for both his poetry and his unspotted life. The dialectic of flight as reward for virtue and flight as dangerous overreaching gives rise to a drama of self-assertion and self-occlusion in many of Milton's major works. In the rest of this chapter I will examine how Milton writes about himself in a series of major poems of

---

15. The relation between Milton and Diodati echoes that between the speakers of "L'Allegro" and "Il Penseroso," poems that again raise the question of the fit between manner of life and poetic vision. Countering the view that the poems represent Milton's repudiation of Mirth, Revard argues that the companion poems, like Elegy 6, are descriptive rather than prescriptive; they contribute to Milton's meditation on the proper life for a heroic poet, without suggesting that the alternative to heroic virtue is depravity (*Milton and the Tangles*, pp. 126–27).

his early period, before he sets aside verse to contribute to the prose battles of the 1640s. In the "Nativity Ode," Sonnet 7, *A Mask,* "Lycidas," "Ad Patrem," and "Epitaphium Damonis" Milton wrestles, sometimes implicitly, with his identity as a poet and as a man.

Coming of Age in the "Nativity Ode" and Sonnet 7

In pointing to the remarkable continuity in Milton's self-construction in this period and from this period to his maturity, I differ with William Riley Parker, who warns against identifying the mature Milton with, for example, the epic poet of Elegy 6:

> Because he later wrote an epic, we have no excuse for reading his determination to do so into every piece of verse or prose that mentions epic material. Because he had an orderly mind and a penchant for autobiography, we must not find autobiography where none exists and mistake occasional reflection for statements of programme.[16]

But Milton's "occasional reflection" matches precisely his statements on his chastity and on his epic aspirations later. Elegy 6 foreshadows the explicit self-representations in the *Apology* and the *Reason of Church-Government.* Milton may not be firmly settled on his path in December of 1629, as Parker suggests, but in the Elegy he is, nevertheless, trying on a self-construction. The occasion, an exchange between serious young men and close friends, is ripe for earnest reflection on future plans and the trying on of potential roles. If de Man is right that "the autobiographical project may itself produce and determine the life," the provisional construction in Elegy 6 may summon the life.

At the end of Elegy 6, Milton offers to Diodati his "Nativity Ode," in which, he somewhat misleadingly says, he sings "*Vagitum . . . Dei, et stabulantem paupere tecto*" (the baby cries of God, and the stabling under a poor roof) (83). For Louis Martz, who echoes Parker's skepticism that the figure of the epic poet in Elegy 6 constitutes self-representation, the Ode as described here "makes a clean break with the previous discussion of elegy and epic."[17] But one can see the coda of the Elegy not merely as continuous with the praise of the epic singer but as raising the ante. Milton, after all, has sung "*caelesti semine regem* (the king of heavenly seed)." His subject is "*Qui suprema suo cum patre regna colit. / Stelliparumque polum, modulantesque aethere turmas, / Et subito elisos ad sua fana deos*" (him who inhabits the highest kingdom with his father,

---

16. William Riley Parker, *Milton: A Biography,* 2 vols. (Oxford: Clarendon, 1968), 1:70.
17. Louis Martz, *Milton: Poet of Exile,* 2nd ed. (New Haven: Yale University Press, 1986), p. 52.

and the star-spawning sky, and the hosts making music in the air, and the gods suddenly shattered in their own shrines) (84–86). His poem is epic in scope; if anything, the substitution of the true God for the pagan gods strengthens the ascetic imperative, the call to chaste purity. The distance between the Diodati figure and the Milton figure now measures the space between the sacred and secular as well as that between epic and lyric.

The "Nativity Ode," like the elegy to which it is attached, explores the role of the poet through reflection on the oppositions between the sacred and profane and between the chaste and erotic. In Milton's own backward view, the poem would be a primary exhibit in his self-construction and self-representation as a poet. He placed it first in both the *Poems of Mr. John Milton* (1645) and *Poems, &c. Upon Several Occasions* (1673). Milton appears in the poem in several guises, in the figures within the narrative as well as in the frame.

J. Martin Evans has argued recently against reading the "Nativity Ode" "as a kind of confessional autobiography," in which, as Patrick Cullen and I. S. MacLaren had claimed, the speaker and poet are transformed through grace.[18] According to Evans, the poem "is the most rigorously depersonalized of all Milton's nondramatic works" (12). Evans's Milton erases himself from the poem and omits any reference to the effect of the Nativity on himself, leaving the reader to experience the conversion directly. Thus, despite the absence of the subjective presence of the writer familiar in Puritan autobiography, the poem is quintessentially Puritan, in that it removes all mediation between the individual reader and the experience of the divine (13–16). Evans is persuasive in arguing that the poem cannot be viewed as Milton's conversion narrative, but he is less persuasive in suggesting that Milton reserves the subject position for the reader. Milton's presence is palpable in the poem, not as the sinner requiring conversion but as poet coming of age. Nowhere in his works does Milton acknowledge the need for a conversion experience. The idea of a conversion experience is not resituated in terms of the reader; it is simply absent from Milton's vocabulary. The theological and Puritan poet is in this way, paradoxically, not a religious poet; he lacked the conviction of sin that is both a prerequisite to and a component of conversion. Arthur Barker and A. S. P. Woodhouse, whom Evans also cites, are closer to the truth when they suggest that the poem enacts an experience analogous to Puritan conversion.[19] The "I" of the "Nativity Ode" engages in a minute introspection of the soul, but in the process it becomes

---

18. Evans, *Miltonic Moment*, pp. 11–12; he refers to Cullen's "Imitation and Metamorphosis: The Golden Age Eclogue in Spenser, Milton, and Marvell," *PMLA* 84 (1969): 1559–70, and to MacLaren's "Milton's 'Nativity Ode': The Function of Poetry and Structures of Response in 1629," *Milton Studies* 15 (1981): 181–200.

19. Barker, "The Pattern of Milton's 'Nativity Ode,'" *University of Toronto Quarterly* 10 (1941): 170; Woodhouse, "Notes on Milton's Early Development," *University of Toronto Quarterly* 13 (1943): 73.

convinced not of its sinfulness and its need for grace but of its extraordinary gifts and poetic election.

The shifting of temporal perspectives in the poem, so often noted, is not only theologically significant, in that it allows Milton to figure the intersection of the eternal with time, it also participates in a characteristic strategy in Milton's self-representations, the emphasis on prospect and retrospect. As December of 1629 merges with the beginning and the end of time, Milton moves backward and forward in time through a process of identification with other prophets and singers, both human and angelic. Even the vividly imagined present moment in the proem quickly dissolves into a paradoxical vision of Milton's imminent future, a merging with the Magi. The connection between the collapsing of time and the collapsing of poet with his subjects is established in the opening lines:

> This is the month, and this the happy morn
> Wherein the Son of Heav'n's eternal King,
> Of wedded maid, and virgin mother born,
> Our great redemption from above did bring;
> For so the holy sages once did sing.
> ("Nativity Ode," 1–5)

There are several intersections here: two days more than sixteen hundred years apart, earth and heaven, and poet and prophet. Milton tells Diodati in the elegy that he is singing the heaven-born king to commemorate the day centuries before. Mirroring him are the prophets, the "holy sages," who centuries before the birth also, significantly, sing. Wisdom, prophetic power, and song are intertwined in line 5 as they have been intertwined in Milton's self-representations.

In the third and fourth stanzas of the prologue, the relationship between muse and poet is complex and shifting. Milton first asks the "Heav'nly Muse" (15) if she will contribute a song to celebrate the birth: "shall not thy sacred vein / Afford a present to the infant God? / Hast thou no verse, no hymn, or solemn strain, / To welcome him to this his new abode" (15–18). Does Milton ask the muse to sing her own song or to inspire his song? The third stanza invites the first alternative. The displacement of the song from poet to heavenly figure might provide cover for Milton's ambition to "prevent them ["the star-led wizards"] with thy humble ode" (24). Through the agency of the timeless heavenly muse, Milton wants this song to be there first, to beat the Magi to a place they reached sixteen centuries before. But the next several lines mark a shift, suggesting that it is Milton as well as the muse who prevents or comes before the Magi: "Have thou the honor first, thy Lord to greet, / And join thy voice unto the angel choir, / From out his secret altar touched with hallowed fire" (26–28). The "hallowed fire," like the same "hallow'd fire of [God's] Altar" carried by seraphim to the poet-prophet in *The Reason of Church-Government* (*YP* 1:821), is what raises a man to the status of prophet, allowing him to see what, presumably, a heavenly muse already sees. Now it is the poet, or Milton, who arrives with his song before the Magi. The song will be a "humble ode," a paradoxical animal, for, as Paul Fry has shown, the ode is an assertive rather than a humble genre; humility pertains rather to the hymn.[20] The hymn is always choral, and the ode only sometimes so. Milton, while hoping to merge with the angel choir, also gestures toward the uniqueness of his song.[21] Although the proem promises an ode, Milton heads the body of the poem "The Hymn." The tension between labels recapitulates and gives generic force to the interplay of assertion and self-effacement in Milton's use of the muse.

The momentary confusion between heavenly song and the poet's song returns on a larger scale in the "Hymn." Song lies at the center of the poem, literally and figuratively. In the opening stanzas of the "Hymn" an exquisite silence descends, leaving the world so quiet that one can hear in the distance shepherds "simply chatting in a rustic row" (87), their murmurs heightening rather than disturbing the illusion of silence. Music then fills this silence: "such music sweet / Their hearts and ears did greet, / As never was by mortal finger struck" (93–95). The celestial music is defined precisely as that which human beings cannot produce, and thus could exclude the poet's song. But the poet will find a way to reenter.

The song ties together the disparate times of the "Hymn." It is the same that attended the Creation:

> Such music (as 'tis said)
> Before was never made,
>   But when of old the sons of morning sung,
> While the Creator great
> His constellations set,
>   And the well-balanced world on hinges hung,
> And cast the dark foundations deep,
> And bid the welt'ring waves their oozy channel keep.
>   (117–24)

---

20. Paul H. Fry, *The Poet's Calling in the English Ode* (New Haven: Yale University Press, 1980).

21. The complex stanza form of the hymn, with its intricate rhyming and patterns of trimeters, tetrameters, pentameters, and hexameters (a3a3b5c3c3b5d4d6), calls attention to craftsmanship and thus to the human poet as opposed to the divine muse, as do such salient musical effects as are found in ll.64–66: "The *W*inds with wonder *whist,* / Smoothly the waters *kissed,* / *Whis*pering new joys to the mild Ocean.

It accompanies now (or then) the Incarnation. And it will sound again at the Last Judgment:

> For if such holy song
> Enwrap our fancy long,
>   Time will run back, and fetch the age of gold,
> And speckled Vanity
> Will sicken soon and die,
>   And lep'rous Sin will melt from earthly mold,
> And Hell itself will pass away,
> And leave her dolorous mansions to the peering day.
>   (133–40)

The song binds together, inaugurates, redeems, and ends history. Standing precisely in the middle of the "Hymn," the "holy song" stanza foregrounds the singer. Although specifying that it was no mortal song, Milton places himself in a line of inspired singers, the "holy sages" who also collapsed time in their prophecies of the Messiah. The promotion of the singer, and thus of Milton, culminates in a moment when he ceases merely to report action and enters the action. Discarding the indicative for the imperative, the singer summons and conducts the celestial music: "Ring out ye crystal spheres, / Once bless our human ears, / (If ye have power to touch our senses so)" (125–27). Despite his earlier stance as humble spectator, Milton steps onto the timeless stage of the poem. The parenthesis implies an arresting reversal, asking not whether our ears have power to hear celestial music, but whether the celestial music has power to reach our ears. The prophetic poet, enjoying access to the divine along with the power to reach human senses, possibly surpasses the music his poem at first seeks only to shadow.

    Having come this far, he can only retreat, as he does immediately in specifying the unique role to be played by the Son of God. After toying with the idea of song redeeming us and ushering in a new Golden Age, Milton catches himself up short:

> But wisest Fate says no,
> This must not yet be so,
>   The babe lies yet in smiling infancy,
> That on the bitter cross
> Must redeem our loss;
>   So both himself and us to glorify.
>   (149–54)

The irreducibility and uniqueness of the Son's passion, and the necessity of waiting for it, breaks the seamless convergence of place and time (and of celestial music and poet's song), though the fact that in 1629 the passion has occurred qualifies the absolute difference suggested here. The distance between what song can do and what the Son must do recalls the interplay between self-assertion and self-effacement from the beginning of the poem. Milton as singer is close to the heart of the divine mystery; Milton as singer is only a distant recorder of the divine mystery. It is as if, having made as salient a claim as he can for song and for himself as singer, Milton must step back into a humbler role.

This thematic logic continues in the next section, devoted to the banishment of the pagan gods. The exquisite beauty of the lines describing the discredited and fleeing gods, language that inspired Keats in his "Ode to Psyche," serves as a kind of poetic self-assertion. Milton's song, having celebrated divine mysteries and having perhaps claimed too much for itself, now celebrates the pagan gods even as they are banished:

> From haunted spring, and dale
> Edged with poplar pale,
>   The parting Genius is with sighing sent;
> With flow'r-inwoven tresses torn,
> The Nymphs in twilight shade of tangled thickets mourn.
>   (184–88)

> The Libyc Hammon shrinks his horn;
> In vain the Tyrian maids their wounded Thammuz mourn.
>   (203–4)

The beauty of the poetry betrays Milton's love for the myths of classical literature. But, in the association of beautiful song with the defeated gods, we may also see a kind of penance for overreaching. If the young Milton had claimed too much for song, mixing it with the divine prerogative, his song now serves the cause of the gods whom Christ alone can banish. The song, a moment before hardly distinguishable from the music of the spheres, is now, as the poem ends, "tedious":

> But see the virgin blest
> Hath laid her babe to rest.
>   Time is our tedious song should here have ending:
> Heav'n's youngest-teemèd star,
> Hath fixed her polished car,
>   Her sleeping Lord with handmaid lamp attending:
> And all about the courtly stable,
> Bright-harnessed angels sit in order serviceable.
>   (237–44)

This is an extraordinary gesture of self-effacement for Milton, in light not only of later heroic self-representations but also of what we have already seen of his youthful writings. There will be a similar moment in "Lycidas," in which Milton allows his voice to be overtaken and silenced by other voices. Nevertheless, the description of the poem as "tedious" is jarring. We don't need to imagine an access of humility here, however; the gesture is rhetorically necessary and thematically effective. The overreaching claims for song in the middle of the poem need to be balanced by a return to humility. And the description of the song as "tedious" is balanced against the merging of poet's song and the timeless celestial music that binds all of time into one moment. The tedious song unfolds serially within time from a beginning to an end. Acknowledgment of a loss of immediacy and timeliness serves as an expiation for exaggerated claims for timelessness.

Thus from the shifting temporal perspectives of the "Nativity Ode" Milton constructs a dialectical self-representation with two poles: a singer in concert with the prophets and with the divine and a mortal who reminds himself and us of his earth-boundedness and humility. The dialectic behind the self-representation also informs personification in the poem. The drama of the female Nature who "wanton[s] with the sun her lusty paramour" (36) contributes to Milton's self-regarding meditation on chastity and erotic license central in the Elegy to which the poem is appended. Nature reacts with shame to the advent of the divine; just as Milton tells Diodati in the Elegy that the heroic singer must be chaste and ascetic, so Nature in the Ode wishes, however paradoxically, to return to virginity:

> Only with speeches fair
> She woos the gentle air
>   To hide her guilty front with innocent snow,
> And on her naked shame,
> Pollute with sinful blame,
>   The saintly veil of maiden white to throw.
>   (37–42)

The erotic attachment of earth and sun goes back to the erotic Elegy 5, from which Milton attempts to distance himself in Elegy 6. In the earlier poem, Earth "luxuriant . . . bares her all-nurturing breasts [*Pandit ut omniferos luxuriosa sinus*]" to Phoebus (58). Earth in the "Nativity Ode" reacts with shame, as does night (111). The sun is ashamed as well, though not because of his lusty wantoning with the Earth, but because he is not as great as the Son: he "hid his head for shame, / As his inferior flame, / The new-enlightened world no more should need" (80–82). The abashedness of the sun, the Phoebus or poet figure, foreshadows the enforced humility of the poet at the end of the poem, after he had risen to a zenith in the middle. And Milton's representation of his invulnerability to sexual error as a prerequisite for poetic achievement may account for the sun's lack of sexual shame that narrative continuity would lead one to expect.

Essential to the poem's implicit self-portrait of the poet is a dialectic of self-assertion and self-effacement, a succession of advances and retreats. Michael Lieb characterizes the self-effacement as humility: "through the humility of his posture and through the humble nature of his gift, he desires metaphorically to take upon himself the form of a servant."[22] Richard Halpern follows Lieb in comparing Milton's humbling himself in the poem to Christ's self-emptying or *kenosis*.[23] Ironically, however, the humbling or self-effacement is a constituent element in a drama that places the poet squarely at the heart of the poem. For in elaborate gestures of humility, the poet points to himself, and these gestures are interwoven with gestures of self-assertion.

While the oscillation between self-assertion and humility will be a constant in Milton's representations of himself as inspired poet-prophet all the way through *Paradise Lost*, gestures toward humility are naturally more pronounced in the early works, before Milton can look back on a body of significant achievements. The gap between aspiration and accomplishment results in the anxiety marking Sonnet 7 ("How soon hath time"). The sonnet reflects its original context, the 1633 "Letter to a Friend," in addressing potential criticism of, and perhaps Milton's own anxiety about, his failure to take his place in the world, whether as a minister or as a poet. The second quatrain's tortuous and syntactically ambiguous language addressing the gap between seeming and being betrays defensiveness and anxiety:

> Perhaps my semblance might deceive the truth,
> That I to manhood am arrived so near,
> And inward ripeness doth much less appear,
> That some more timely-happy spirits endu'th.
>
> (5–8)

These lines do not yield their meaning without strenuous effort. The speaker seems to suggest that his appearance misrepresents the truth that he is a man rather than a boy, and that inner maturity is not as visible as that apparent maturity that clothes his more fortunate-seeming contemporaries. But the fact that the lines must be carefully sorted out is as significant as the sorted meaning. Milton can make plain sense when he wants to. His language invites

---

22. Lieb, "Milton and Kenotic Christology: Its Literary Bearing," *ELH* 37 (1970): 352.
23. Halpern, "The Great Instauration," p. 7.

opposing readings. "Perhaps my semblance might deceive the truth" might also be taken to disclose the speaker's dissimulation. The following lines could be taken, however briefly, to mean that the "timely-happy spirits," as opposed to the speaker, are endowed with "inward ripeness." Milton has so composed his lines that these meanings are held in suspension with the primary meanings. The suggestion of agency and deception picks up on the opening image of "Time the subtle thief of youth" (1). Syntactic ambiguity betrays the defensiveness and anxiety that the poem shares with the letter in which it was inscribed.

The sestet of this Petrarchan sonnet is if anything even more unsettled than the octave. Where earlier a clearly dominant sense is held in suspension with a fugitive countersense, now the lines become hard to construe at all, and competing senses run headlong into each other:

> Yet be it less or more, or soon or slow,
>   It shall be still in strictest measure even
>   To that same lot, however mean, or high,
> Toward which Time leads me, and the will of Heaven;
>   All is, if I have grace to use it so,
>   As ever in my great Taskmaster's eye.
>   (9–14)

"It" in lines nine and ten refers apparently to the "inward ripeness" of line seven. The "strictest measure," while it denotes congruity between providential plan and Milton's unfolding ripeness, suggests gravity and deliberation, tipping the scale perhaps from "soon" to "slow." If the general sense of the final lines is discernible, it is difficult to pin down a determinate specific sense. Is the "all" of line thirteen, for example, the "inward ripeness" or the implied "all [that matters]"? Louis Martz, who sees in the poem a "severe Calvinist view of life," locates that sense firmly in the last two lines: "The meaning of these lines, I think, is clarified if we take the word 'grace' in a strict Calvinist sense: the speaker's future lies completely in the hands of God."[24] But if the poem were written from a strict Calvinist perspective, one would expect to see an acknowledgment of failing rather than, as in the "Letter to a Friend," ingenious essays at self-justification. Martz's language ("strict . . . sense," "completely") belies the studied indefiniteness and ambiguity of the final lines. The clause "All is . . . / As ever in my great Taskmaster's eye," which seems to assign all to God's omnipotence, is interrupted by the (in this context) puzzling "*if* I have grace to use it so" (my emphasis). The vatic "All is," with its potential

---

24. Martz, *Milton: Poet of Exile*, p. 44.

conflict between what God does and what Milton claims for himself, recalls a turning point in the "Nativity Ode": "And then at last our bliss / Full and perfect is, / But now begins" (165–67). By their indeterminacy the final lines, far from confirming a Calvinist sense, open a space for Milton's agency otherwise foreclosed by Calvin. The theology of the poem does not simply fit the orthodox Calvinism of the letter's recipient any more than does the letter itself.

Although Sonnet 8, "Captain or Colonel," was written a decade later, as Milton's next sonnet it follows "How Soon Hath Time" in the 1645 *Poems.* It is a happy placement. In the earlier poem Milton foregrounds his belatedness, and in the later poem he speaks confidently of himself as not merely accomplished but eminent. In the opening quatrain, the poet, apparently, addresses an invading officer imagined as arriving at the poet's doors. By the fourth line, however, the poet begins to occupy the third rather than the first person: "him within protect from harms" (4). It becomes apparent in retrospect that what is apparently the poet's voice in the opening lines of the poem is actually the "voice" of his lines, which now have speaking force. If the late spring showed no bud or blossom in Sonnet 7, now the poetic blossoms speak forcefully. By the sestet the poet who once offered defenses of his silence now claims kinship with Pindar and Euripides, whose biographies share the disarming of conquerors by poetic reputation.

Versions of the Self in *A Mask*

As in his late masterpiece in dramatic form, *Samson Agonistes,* Milton finds a way to write about himself in *A Mask Presented at Ludlow Castle* of 1634 despite the absence of a narrator or speaker, but with a crucial difference. Blinded and defeated like the protagonist of his biblical drama, the mature Milton could have expected to be identified with Samson, into whom Milton pours his frustration with the English who, like the subjected Israelites, preferred bondage with ease to strenuous liberty. Milton's presence in *A Mask,* on the other hand, is diffuse and veiled. While the characters can tell us much about him, they do so more by voicing his preoccupations than by sharing his experience. I will therefore look only briefly at *A Mask*.

In an influential reading, William Kerrigan argues that "Milton inscribed three images of himself in the Ludlow masque."[25] The "Shepherd lad" who gives haemony to the Attendant Spirit (618–41) represents in his leisured study of medicinal herbs Milton's period of studious retirement between Cambridge and his Italian journey. The Elder Brother, occupying like Milton

---

25. *The Sacred Complex: On the Psychogenesis of Paradise Lost* (Cambridge, Mass.: Harvard University Press, 1983), p. 37.

a middle place between an older sister and younger brother, praises chastity in a manner foreshadowing Milton's retrospective self-construction in *An Apology* nearly a decade later. The Lady resembles Milton in her enthusiastic and idealistic reliance upon chastity. The inscription of Milton in both brother and sister foreshadows Milton's investment in *An Apology* both in the chaste virgin or matron and in the knight who defends her. Kerrigan concludes that "The double identification with knight and lady that structured Milton's reading of romances has been projected onto the plot of *A Mask* in the kinship of Elder Brother and Lady. They are vested in each other: the armed brother says that his chaste sister has the arms and honor of a knight, while the sister announces a high mystery that the brother expounds."[26]

The investment of Milton, the "Lady of Christ's," in the Lady is particularly plausible. Her celebration of chastity parallels Milton's self-construction as a poet. The connection is thrown into silhouette by the excision of many of the verses addressing chastity and virginity in the Bridgewater manuscript, presumably the text most closely resembling the version acted by the Earl of Bridgewater's children.[27] Milton freighted the Lady with his own ideals and sexual self-understanding to an extent inappropriate for the entertainment he had been solicited to write.

The Lady completes Kerrigan's triangle with the Elder Brother and the shepherd boy. She also completes another self-referential triangle with the Attendant Spirit and Comus. Milton is, at least in aspiration, the Attendant Spirit, who "will tell ye now / What never yet was heard in tale or song / From old or modern bard" (43–45). The Attendant Spirit, like Milton in the "Vacation Exercise" verses, travels between heaven and earth, though in the opposite direction, descending from the "regions mild of calm and serene air" at "the starry threshold of Jove's court" (1–4). He is a gift to mortal men in the manner of the later prophetic Milton, and he will stage-manage the action of the masque, disposing characters where he wants them and directing their actions, though not always successfully. When, to disguise himself, he appears and functions as a pastoral singer, he further bridges the distance between himself and Milton.

He falls silent, to be replaced by his foil Comus, another demigod who disguises himself in humble form, as a "harmless villager" (166), to appear to the human actors. But where the Attendant Spirit assumes a disguise in order to clear a space for the brothers to exercise choice, Comus is predatory. He resembles the Attendant Spirit in taking on the role of the poet, who works by "charms" (150), though now "to cheat the eye with blear illusion, / And give it false presentments" (155–56). He wrestles for the role of playwright with the

---

26. Ibid., p. 44.
27. See *A Mask* 195–224, 737–55, 779–806.

Attendant Spirit, making elaborate sets and blocking the role to be played by the Lady.

The Attendant Spirit resembles Milton in his aspirations. In his negative mirroring of the Spirit, Comus represents the antithesis of those aspirations. Puritan anti-theatricalists charged dramatists with cheating with illusions and with debasing the audience by appealing to their passions; in writing this masque (and *Arcades* some time in the preceding two years), Milton for the first time made himself liable to these charges. In Comus Milton attempts to exorcize the specter of the falsifying and morally pernicious poetry and drama.

The figure of Milton is also inflected through Sabrina, another exemplar of chastity and another charming and charmed singer. Milton populates a world in *A Mask*. The proliferation of Miltons points toward a habit of involuntary and unintentional self-representation. Normally the "I" of the poetic speaker refers to John Milton directly. As John Guillory writes of the poet's typical practice, "Milton does not admit any distance between himself and the poet in the poem, and we can sense in the refusal to admit this distance a hunger for the nonfigurative ground of the poetic act."[28] There is no poet's "I" in *A Mask,* so Milton inhabits the I of all the characters. Shakespeare disappears into his characters; Milton's characters mirror Milton. In *A Mask* we might speak more accurately of self-discovery or betrayal than of self-representation, as Milton ventriloquizes his preoccupations and fears through a series of characters.

Humility and Assertion in "Lycidas" and "Ad Patrem"

In November of 1637, the month in which he composed "Lycidas," nearly eight years after his Elegy 6, the Latin verse letter to Diodati that announced his dedication to heroic poetry and presented his first great English poem, Milton again wrote to his close friend, in two Latin prose letters. In the second, rising to a level of seriousness not found in the letters from Diodati, Milton makes a confession of Platonic faith:

> For though I do not know what else God may have decreed for me, this certainly is true: *He has instilled into me, if into anyone, a vehement love of the beautiful.* Not so diligently is Ceres, according to the Fables, said to have sought her daughter Proserpina, as I seek for this *idea of the beautiful,* as if for some glorious image, throughout all the shapes and forms of

---

28. Guillory, *Poetic Authority,* p. 104.

things ("*for many are the shapes of things divine*"); day and night I search and follow its lead eagerly as if by certain clear traces. Whence it happens that if I find anywhere one who, despising the warped judgment of the public, dares to feel and speak and be that which the greatest wisdom throughout all ages has taught to be best, I shall cling to him immediately from a kind of necessity. (*YP* 1:326–27; italicized passages translate Milton's Greek)

Milton dramatizes his position by representing himself as in conflict with the vulgar ("despising the warped judgment of the public"). He recasts himself as the Socrates of *The Apology,* single-mindedly focused on the one and the beautiful, clinging to anyone who loves the beautiful and the true and suffering the enmity and misconstruction of the many. In Elegy 6 Milton had yoked serious poetry and divine philosophy, an idea echoed in *A Mask* ("How charming is divine philosophy," the Younger Brother exclaims, "musical as is Apollo's lute" [476, 478]). Now he follows his Platonic profession of *philosophia* or love of wisdom with an announcement of poetic achievement and aspiration: "You ask what I am thinking of? So help me God, an immortality of fame. What am I doing? *Growing my wings and practising flight.* But my Pegasus still raises himself on very tender wings. Let me be wise on my humble level" (*YP* 1:327; italics indicate original Greek). Milton catches himself at the end, claiming wisdom only on a humble level with tender wings. The phrase epitomizes the dual movement of confident assertion and modest withdrawal familiar in the self-representations in the early poetry. The wings themselves have genealogical roots in Plato's *Phaedrus,* where they figure philosophic ascent; at the same time they evoke the "viewless wing" of poetry in Milton's early poem "The Passion" (50), a phrase picked up in Keats's Nightingale ode. The wings carry Milton upward, but they are yet young and weak. The humility, then, is an ascending humility. The confident aspiration is for immortality. And with good reason, for Milton is now writing "Lycidas."

In "Lycidas" questions concerning the author's identity, his representation of himself, and his tendency to reveal and occlude himself at the same time rise to the surface. The poem's reception history is crowded with identity puzzles. Who is speaking? How many are speaking? Is the author *in* this supposed "monody" as the "uncouth swain" or the anonymous singer of the ottava rima? Are the intrusions and confusions of voice flaws or excellences? Is Milton in control of his poem, in two senses? First, thematically and immanently, is the figure of the poet imagined in the poem represented as being in control of that poem? Second, in aesthetic terms, has the poem gotten away from Milton? How "sincere," finally, is the poem's grief? Is it focused on fulfilling generic conventions rather than on a contemporary's death? Decades ago E. M. W. Tillyard advanced discussion of "Lycidas" by observing that the poem makes more sense when we realize that it is about Milton.[29] Stanley Fish has argued that the poet engineers his own disappearance in the poem, and that the poem is "finally anonymous."[30] Tillyard and Fish only seem to be at loggerheads. The care with which Fish's Milton orchestrates his own disappearance paradoxically foregrounds the centrality and presence of the author, and the rise and eclipse of the poet replay Milton's signature dialectical self-representation.

Samuel Johnson, who liked Milton's poetry but not Milton, objected vigorously to "Lycidas." Johnson could forgive Milton no more for claiming that Edward King and he "drove afield . . . Batt'ning our flocks" than for taking the wrong side in the Civil War: "We know that they never drove a field, and that they had no flocks to batten; and though it be allowed that the representation may be allegorical, the true meaning is so uncertain and remote, that it is never sought because it cannot be known when it is found."[31] Johnson finds the fiction that King and Milton were companion shepherds repellent. His animus ostensibly reaches to all pastoral: "In this poem there is no nature, for there is no truth; there is no art, for there is nothing new. Its form is that of a pastoral, easy, vulgar, and therefore disgusting: whatever images it can supply, are long ago exhausted; and its inherent improbability always forces dissatisfaction on the mind."[32] Johnson's approving comments on Pope's pastorals demonstrate that he was not always so hostile to pastoral. The crucial difference, beyond party animus against Milton, may be the disjunction between the conventional artifice of the genre and the urgency of the poem's realism. Johnson might have reacted better to the fictionalized shepherd Milton if Milton the man were not so palpably present.

In the harshly urgent opening lines the poet's distress for having to write before sober preparation mingles with sorrow for the dead friend:

> Yet once more, O ye laurels, and once more
> Ye myrtles brown, with ivy never sere,
> I come to pluck your berries harsh and crude,
> And with forced fingers rude,
> Shatter your leaves before the mellowing year.
> Bitter constraint, and sad occasion dear,
> Compels me to disturb your season due:
> For Lycidas is dead, dead ere his prime.
>
> (1–8)

---

29. Tillyard, *Milton* (London: Chatto & Windus, 1930), pp. 80–85.
30. Fish, "'Lycidas': A Poem Finally Anonymous," in *Lycidas: The Tradition and the Poem*, ed. C.A. Patrides (Columbia: University of Missouri Press, 1983), 319–40.
31. Johnson, "Life of Milton," excerpted in *Milton: Poetry and Prose*, ed. A.M.D. Hughes (Oxford: Clarendon, 1920), p. 3.
32. Ibid., p. 2.

Before coming to the death that occasions the poem, Milton fixes on the invasion of symbols of poetic excellence, the laurel and ivy leaves "shattered" by his own "forced fingers rude." The adjective-noun-adjective construction characteristic of Milton is particularly expressive here, as Milton is sandwiched in a chain of action. The occasion forces his hand before his time, a situation from which—in his self-representation, at least—he recoils, and his fingers in turn rudely disturb the leaves. The horticultural violence mimics the violence suffered by Lycidas/King. The premature poetic expression into which King's death forces Milton threatens violence to Milton's own poetic aspirations; the leaves shattered now might have been reserved for Milton's laureate crown. The poem betrays anxiety about a more visceral threat to Milton's poetic plans, the threat of premature death. If King, with his own poetic pretensions, could be killed before their fruition, why not Milton? This fear leads Milton to lament the fate of Orpheus, the mythic singer killed by a different kind of violence (58–63). Orpheus will become a touchstone for Milton's fear both of premature death and of the violation of poetic harmony by the vulgar crowd.

Milton continues to focus on himself as he turns to invoke the muses. He expresses the hope that "some gentle muse / With lucky words [will] favor my destined urn, / And as he passes turn / And bid fair peace be to my sable shroud" (19–22). Milton sings as he would be sung for. Like the speaker in Shakespeare's *Sonnets,* Milton stands to gain the immortality both of the singer and of the singer's subject. Unlike the *Sonnets,* "Lycidas" exhibits Milton's recurrent dialectic of self-representation and self-occlusion. The self-occlusion is the product of the fragmentation of voice in the poem familiar since the reading of John Crowe Ransom.[33] This fragmentation is unmistakable first in the interruption by Apollo of the imminent action of the blind Fury's mortal shears:

> But the fair guerdon when we hope to find,
> And think to burst out into sudden blaze,
> Comes the blind Fury with th' abhorr'd shears,
> And slits the thin-spun life. "But not the praise,"
> Phoebus replied, and touched my trembling ears.
> (73–77)

But the fragmentation has begun more subtly in the earlier Orpheus passage. When Milton challenges the nymphs for not saving Lycidas, he interrupts himself: "Ay me, I fondly dream! / Had ye been there—for what could that

---

33. Ransom, "A Poem Nearly Anonymous," in *Lycidas: The Tradition and the Poem,* ed. C. A. Patrides (Columbia: University of Missouri Press, 1983), 68–85.

have done?" (56–57). J. Martin Evans argues that "the second thoughts . . . open up a tiny fissure in the mourner's consciousness, a fissure that widens dramatically with the intervention of the god of poetry."[34] The interruption by external voices objectifies the division of internal voices increasingly important in the poem.

In short order the voices proliferate and crowd the poem. If it is clear when Apollo's voice begins, it is not clear when it ends. Within the fiction of the poem, is it the poet or Apollo who speaks the discourse on fame in lines 78–84? It seems to be the poet, but the next verse paragraph ("That strain I heard was of a higher mood" [87]) suggests, though not conclusively, that the discourse on fame is Apollo's. After the interlude, the poet again summons the pastoral muse, but, as Fish observes,[35] as soon as he announces that he will resume, he is silenced: "But now my oat proceeds, / And *listens* to the herald of the sea" (88–89; my emphasis). Seeking the cause of the drowning, the herald interrogates the waves and winds. A conclusion is imposed on the inconclusive line of questioning by an oracular voice of uncertain origin: "It was that fatal and perfidious bark, / Built in th' eclipse, and rigged with curses dark, / That sunk so low that sacred head of thine" (100–2). This unspecified voice is followed by the brief cameo appearance of Camus and then by St. Peter's violent attack on false shepherds, spoken to the true shepherd Lycidas. The apparent poet's voice, seemingly relieved by the departure of Peter's "dread voice," once again invokes the gentler pastoral muse (132). He establishes his elegiac credentials with an arrestingly beautiful flower catalogue ("Bring the rathe primrose that forsaken dies, / The tufted crow-toe, and pale jessamine, / The white pink, and the pansy freaked with jet, / The glowing violet" [142–45]). In this, the first section of the poem not shared with another voice since the questioning of the nymphs, he again interrupts *himself* ("Ay me, I fondly dream" [56]). He ends a final lament for the desecration of the body with an exhortation to St. Michael and the dolphins to carry the singer home. Then, in a voice that may be the poet's but that some see as a new voice,[36] the shepherds are told to "Weep no more" (165), for Lycidas has risen from the dead, and is now, like Michael himself at St. Michael's Mount, "genius of the shore" (183). Finally, in perhaps the most puzzling of the interruptions, an ottava rima stanza at the end frames the first-person speaker of the poem retrospectively as the third person "uncouth swain."

Given the poem's many and severe dislocations, the range of critical response to the question of authorial presence is natural. For James Holly Hanford,

---

34. Evans, *Miltonic Moment*, p. 109.
35. Fish, "'Lycidas': A Poem Finally Anonymous," p. 332.
36. See, e.g., W. B. Madsen ("The Dread Voice in 'Lycidas,'" *Milton Studies* 9 [1976]: 238), who assigns the lines to Michael the archangel.

"Lycidas," despite its apparent anguish, is an impersonal exercise in the genre of funeral elegy, and therefore we need not look for the author in it.[37] Ransom agrees that "Lycidas" begins with the impersonality of generic imitation, but argues that it is unsettled by the unique and irrepressible personality of the poet, who inserts "errors" and anomalies to announce his idiosyncratic presence. Fish, on the other hand, sees the poem as a triumph of anonymity, as the poet gives up his voice, engineers his own disappearance, and thus reveals an alternative to his familiar egotism. Evans reads in "Lycidas" the eclipse of one speaker and the birth of a new one, who is announced in the heroic ottava rima; for Evans, the poem records the death throes of Milton's early persona as a poet empowered and protected by chaste retirement, and his subsequent turning toward heroic action (Milton would write little poetry for the next twenty years).

In all of these readings except for Hanford's, the poem is about Milton; even Fish's "Lycidas" foregrounds the question of Milton's presence by its carefully calibrated drama of his disappearance. That Milton has not yielded the center of the stage becomes clearer when we note that the proliferation of voices and the apparent disintegration or disappearance of the poet's voice, while salient in "Lycidas," are not unique to the poem. These elements contribute to the poem's Miltonic, self-representational signature. The poem, like the "Nativity Ode" before it and *Paradise Lost* long after, is marked by an egotism that is not eclipsed but expressed through gestures of self-occlusion. "Lycidas" is about inspiration, and the paradoxes that attend inspiration in the early ode and the great epic inform "Lycidas" as well, generating the play of voices and the apparent disappearance of the poet's. If it is not always clear in "Lycidas" who is speaking, it is no clearer in the "Nativity Ode." Is the "Hymn" the muse's or Milton's? Who is to run and prevent the Magi with the ode? As I argued above, in the "Nativity Ode" there is a tension and interpenetration between the young poet's song, the muse's, and the angels'. Much of the drama of the poem lies in Milton's learning to join his voice humbly (and, paradoxically, boldly) with the angel choir's. In *Paradise Lost* again, the song is divided and then united. Is it the muse who sings or Milton? On the one hand Milton assigns the song to another: "Sing Heav'nly Muse." On the other hand he asks guidance so that he himself "may assert eternal providence, / And justify the ways of God to men." In *Paradise Lost* the either/or becomes a both/and. Milton goes out of his way to highlight an ambiguity already built in to epic invocation.[38]

---

37. James Holly Hanford, "The Pastoral Elegy and Milton's 'Lycidas,'" in *Lycidas: The Tradition and the Poem,* ed. C.A. Patrides (Columbia: University of Missouri Press, 1983), pp. 31–59.

38. On the question of shared and ambiguous voices in Milton's poetry, see Evans, "The Birth of the Author: Milton's Poetic Self-Construction" in *John Milton: The Writer in His Works,* ed. Albert C. Labriola and Michael Lieb, *Milton Studies* 38 (Pittsburgh: University of Pittsburgh Press, 2000): 47–65.

In "Lycidas," the lesser muses of pastoral elegy (the "fountain Arethuse" and the "Sicilian muses") run up against sacred muses, first the pagan Apollo and ultimately St. Peter and the angelic choir. As in the companion poems, Elegy 6, and the prose letters to Diodati, Milton weighs the alternatives of elegiac poetry versus heroic or sacred poetry. As in the "Nativity Ode," Milton both tries his own voice and joins his voice to the angel choir. The subject of inspiration is a largely implicit but central theme in St. Peter's speech. The attack on false shepherds as "Blind mouths" (119) foreshadows in a terse and reversed form the later self-description of the prophetic Milton, who will "see and tell / Of things invisible to mortal sight" (*PL* 3.54–55). Without inspiration, the songs of the blind-mouthed shepherds are "lean and flashy," discordant and empty. Their hungry sheep are not fed by inspired words, but "swoll'n with wind" (126), a phrase that ironically foreshadows Hobbes's dismissive view of inspiration.[39]

The poet's voice at this point in the poem still resists the "dread voice," seeking a doomed refuge in the Sicilian muse and consolation in the flower catalogue. The voice then changes dramatically and abruptly:

> Weep no more, woeful shepherds, weep no more,
> For Lycidas your sorrow is not dead,
> Sunk though he be beneath the wat'ry floor,
> So sinks the day-star in the ocean bed,
> And yet anon repairs his drooping head,
> And tricks his beams, and with new-spangled ore,
> Flames in the forehead of the morning sky.
>
> (165–71)

It is not necessary to posit a new voice, Michael's or anyone else's, here. To do so is to further complicate the closing stanza that comments most immediately on this speech, if also on the poem as a whole ("Thus sang the uncouth swain"). It is the voice of a dramatically transformed Milton, no longer resisting the sacred muse and the influence of the divine, no longer holding tenaciously to the erotic and elegiac muses. This is an authorial voice that again makes the choice of Elegy 6, and now speaks with divine authority. In letting that inspiration take him over, he does not disappear. As in Elegy 6, the poet and the divine speak as one: "*Spirat et occultum pectus, et ora Iovem*" (both his hidden heart and his mouth breathe forth Jove) (78). He finds his authentic voice in merging with the divine voice.

---

39. "INSPIRATION . . . is nothing but the blowing into a man some thin and subtile aire, or wind, in such manner as a man filleth a bladder with his breath," *Leviathan,* ed. C. B. Macpherson (Harmondsworth: Penguin, 1968), p. 440 (chap. 34).

The change in tone and ethos in the voice at line 165 is a key to the more abrupt and puzzling change of voice itself at line 186 ("Thus sang the uncouth swain to th' oaks and rills"). The poem presents a puzzle here: why a closing frame when it lacks an opening frame. Is the poet's voice the one inside the frame—the uncouth swain's—or the one outside? The puzzle resolves itself if one thinks of Milton's voice having undergone a change in the course of the poem, a change like the one I have outlined above. A secular poet, dedicated to craft, is taken over by inspiration, after early and repeated resistance. The swain is "uncouth," that is to say, unknown. The fear of anonymity is itself a theme in "Lycidas." The reflective voice of the ottava rima is informed by the confidence earned by the process described in the poem, but more importantly by the achievement of the poem. By the end, the swain is no longer uncouth in the older or in our modern sense, and thus the voice can look back retrospectively at himself as at someone else. The dual figure of the swain has roots in *A Mask,* where uncouth (in both senses) swains celebrate with dancing at the end of the masque (951–53), and where on the other hand the Attendant Spirit takes the form of a swain (84) and the swain Meliboeus is most likely a figure for Spenser and/or Virgil. The poems work by transformations: ontological, as the spirit becomes a swain; allegorical, as a former poet is figured as a swain; and existential, as an uncouth swain becomes both refined and known. This helps account for the paradox of "Lycidas," for it is no more satisfying to think of the opening and closing voices of the poem as simply identical than it is to think of either as belonging to someone besides Milton.

We may, moreover, have been too quick to conclude that the poem is framed only at the end, for the headnote in the Cambridge manuscript ("In this Monodie the author bewails a lerned freind unfortunatly drownd in his passage from Chester on the Irish Seas 1637"), to say nothing of the addition in *Poems . . . 1645* ("And by occasion foretells the ruin of our corrupted clergy then in their height"), frames the opening of the poem. The headnote's reference to "the Author" balances the final ottava rima. Its implicit role as comment on the poem just completed (a role confirmed by the fact that it is crowded into the small space between the title and the poem in the Trinity manuscript) links the closing voice with the author's. The maturity, understatement, and restraint of the closing stanza comments on the agitation of the poem's opening and measures the distance the poet has traveled.

The movements and countermovements of self-assertion and self-occlusion that mark the poem as Milton's are encoded in the repetition of the ejaculation "Ay me." Milton dismisses his vain and outdated hopes that the nymphs might have saved Lycidas ("Ay me, I fondly dream!") and that flowers might console him for his loss ("our frail thoughts dally with false surmise. / Ay me!") (56, 153–54). "Ay me" sounds as "I me." At precisely the points at which Milton demotes himself by suggesting the inadequacy of his responses and of the poetic resources that inform them, he names himself as both maker and object of his poem.

A similar dialectic of assertion and humility marks "Ad Patrem," a poem that has been dated as early as 1631 and as late as 1645.[40] "Ad Patrem" is full of surprises, beginning with the genre. Why an ode to a father that follows the form of an epideictic ode to a god? Trying to make sense of Milton's genre choice, scholars have debated whether the tone is grave or light and parodic. Is Milton mixing high (the praise of the divine) with low (intimate family matters) for comic effect, or is he seriously dedicating himself, by way of genealogy, to divine poetry?[41] These questions do not demand either/or answers. There is intimacy and sly humor in the poem: what better way to disarm fatherly fears about the dedication of one's life to poetry than to speak of poetry as a divine gift mediated through the father? Nonetheless, this same mediation makes the high form appropriate; a claim of real access to the divine calls for the gravity of hexameters and the ritual structure of epideictic ode.

Milton asks the muse to inspire him with fitting words of gratitude to his father for nurturing a gift for poetry that the father ostensibly does not value. Milton reminds his father of poetry's divine origins and powers, before alluding to his father's musical accomplishments and suggesting that Apollo divided his gifts between father and son. He thanks his father for the education that has prepared him not for base gain but for poetry and that has ushered him along with his father into the company of the learned.

Milton interweaves assertion and humility (and defensiveness and aggression) as he often has when writing of himself. Claiming exalted status for the *vates,* the poet/prophet (and thus for himself), Milton risks overreaching. His choice of mythical precedents betrays his awareness of the risk. He compares his own good fortune in the gifts of his father with Phaeton's:

> *Non potiora dedit, quamvis et tuta fuissent,*
> *Publica qui iuveni commisit lumina nato*
> *Atque Hyperionios currus, et frena diei,*
> *Et circum undantem radiata luce tiaram.*
>
> (97–100; my emphasis)

---

40. See the *Variorum Commentary* 1:232–40 and Parker's *Life* 2:788–89. In tentatively placing the poem around 1638 I choose the midpoint of scholarly speculation and follow the dating of John Shawcross in *John Milton: The Self and the World* (Lexington: University of Kentucky Press, 1993), p. 68.

41. For the view that the poem is whimsical, see Marguerite Little, "Milton's 'Ad Patrem' and the Younger Gill's 'In Natalem Mei Parentis,'" *Journal of English and Germanic Philology* 49 (1950): 345–51, and William J. Kennedy, "The Audiences of 'Ad Patrem,'" *Milton Studies* 19 (1984): 73–86. For "Ad Patrem" as a serious defense of and dedication to the role of inspired poet, see Revard, *Milton and the Tangles,* pp. 208–15.

He did not give more precious gifts, even if they had been given safely, who entrusted to his young son the common light and Hyperion's chariot and the reins of day and the tiara billowing with radiant light.

If his father's gift is the gift of Phoebus, Milton may be a second Phaeton, in danger of a fiery descent. Phaeton appears implicitly earlier in the poem as well, where the divine music soothes and makes harmless the constellations that threatened Phaeton in his ill-fated journey (38–40). Earlier still, Milton praises divine song as "*Prometheae . . . vestigia flammae*" (traces of Promethean fire) (20). Prometheus is credited with the origin of wisdom among mortals, but his theft of fire was punished by the jealous gods.

Milton attempts to neutralize the danger in two ways. The first is the simpler, as he counters potential arrogant overreaching with a display of humility. His first reference to his verbal powers, which the poem will celebrate, is to "*gratia . . . vacuis . . . arida verbis*" (arid thanks which is given in vain words) (10–11). The barrenness or aridity of words is contrasted with the fluid torrent of inspiration from the "*Pierios . . . fontes*" (Pierian fountains) of the opening line. The second strategy takes us to the heart of the poem. Milton addresses his father in such a way that the distinguishing and potentially dangerous connection to the divine is located in him. Milton need not claim to have forged a connection with the divine; he can claim it as an inheritance under the protection of filial piety.[42] If Milton runs the risk of placing himself with Prometheus or Phaeton in a vulnerable position above the level of others, in dangerous proximity to the divine, he enlists the protecting presence of his senior.

This move is itself provisional, for Milton dismantles the relationship of subsidiarity even as he constructs it. Although his words are "empty" early in the poem, soon afterward it is words that distinguish human art, in pointed contrast to the music in which his father excels:

> *Denique quid vocis modulamen inane iuvabit,*
> *Verborum sensusque vacans, numerique loquacis?*
> *Silvestres decet iste choros, non Orphea, cantus,*
> *Qui tenuit fluvios et quercubus addidit aures*
> *Carmine, non cithara, simulacraque functa canendo*
> *Compulit in lacrimas.*
>
> (50–55)

---

42. I follow here Sara Crosby, who writes that Milton "does not address John Milton Sr. the scrivener, but the divine poet within him." He does so, Crosby suggests, to "avoid illegitimate exaltation" ("'Ad Patrem': Milton's Argument for the Legitimacy of His Poetic Project," unpublished essay).

> In the end, what good is an empty modulation of the voice, lacking words and sense and expressive meter? That is fitting for woodland choruses, not for Orphic music, which entranced streams and gave ears to oaktrees with his song, not with his lyre, and brought dead phantoms to tears with his singing.[43]

Words, significantly, are the son's contribution to family song, the divided inheritance of the divided God (64–66); their presence distinguishes divine song from low or common song. If before his words are empty ("*vacuis . . . verbis*"), now song is empty without words and sense ("*Verborum sensusque vacans*").

With this distinction, Milton sets himself above the father under whose shadow or wing he simultaneously protects himself. While displaying warm human feeling for his father, the poem also argues for the superiority of the son's gift. The select society in which Milton places himself at the end is the "*doctae . . . catervae*" (ranks of the learned) (101), a group to which he belongs more surely than his father. From the perspective of the insider, Milton then looks with disdain on the vulgar without: "*Iamque nec obscurus populo miscebor inerti, / Vitabuntque oculos vestigia nostra profanos*" (I will no longer mingle in obscurity with the witless mob, and our footsteps will shun profane eyes) (103–4). From defensiveness and humility, Milton has moved to superiority and disdain. In the final verse paragraph, as we saw above, Milton claims to have immortalized "*parentis / Nomen*" (the father's name) (119–20). Curiously, however, he has not named his father in the poem. The one name explicitly attached to the poem is the name of the author.

Renunciation and Dedication in "Epitaphium Damonis" and the "Retraction"

The "Epitaphium Damonis," the most ambitious and the last of the poems in the "Sylvarum Liber," is like and unlike "Lycidas." Both are pastoral elegies, but the "Epitaphium Damonis" responds to the death of a close friend, Charles Diodati. The poem complements "Lycidas" in its half-frame; the "Epitaphium" has an opening frame but not an ending one, balancing the ending frame of "Lycidas." In the frame, Milton states explicitly that Damon is to be understood as Diodati ("*Damonis autem sub persona hic intelligitur Carolus Deodatus*"), which strongly implies that Thyrsis is to be understood as Milton. The opening verse paragraph treats Thyrsis in the third person, much as the last stanza in "Lycidas" treats the swain. What disturbed Johnson about "Lycidas," the fiction that King and Milton were shepherds, is even

---

43. Orpheus is another divine singer who came to a bad end; he thus participates in the submerged cautionary function of Prometheus and Phaeton.

more pronounced in the Latin poems. Thyrsis is an unusually well-traveled shepherd, who leaves his flock in England to take in foreign sights (14–15). Thyrsis-Milton recalls the times when with Damon-Diodati he braved lions and wolves to protect the sheepfold (41–42).

The poem is built on the same themes as "Lycidas," the choice of love or sacred verse, the elusiveness of fame, and the outgrowing of the pastoral form in which the poems are cast. It is now the chorus of nymphs, not the figure representing Milton, who make the case for carelessness and erotic indulgence that Milton had made in "Lycidas" ("Alas! What boots it with uncessant care / To tend the homely slighted shepherd's trade" [64–65]):

> *Quid tibi vis? aiunt, non haec solet esse iuventae*
> *Nubila frons, oculique truces, vultusque severi;*
> *Illa choros, lususque leves, et semper amorem*
> *Iure petit; bis ille miser qui serus amavit.*
>
> (83–86)

What do you want? The forehead of youth is not usually cloudy like this, or the eyes angry, or the looks severe; by rights it seeks out dances and easy-going games and, always, love; he is twice as wretched who loves too late.

Thyrsis answers the nymphs indirectly by dedicating himself to heroic poetry, as he plays variations on the promise in "Manso" to compose epic poetry on the matter of Britain (162–68).

Milton-Thyrsis at this point lays aside the pastoral pipe, something he had done implicitly in "Lycidas":

> *O mihi tum si vita supersit,*
> *Tu procul annosa pendebis fistula pinu*
> *Multum oblita mihi, aut patriis mutata Camenis*
> *Brittonicum strides.*
>
> (168–71)

O, if life then is left to me, you, pipe, will hang far off on an aged pine-tree, all forgotten by me; or, changed to homeland muses, you will whistle a British theme.

This is a complex moment of self-representation. Announcing a new direction, Milton wants to be viewed as a heroic as opposed to a pastoral or an elegiac poet. But he is also alluding to Virgil's own pastoral practice. As John Carey notes in his edition, Milton is both "renouncing pastoral verse and echoing

Vergil, *Eclogues* vii.24, '*pendebit fistula pinu.*'" Thus at the same time that he establishes himself in the line of great pastoral poets, Milton walks away from pastoral, following in the footsteps of his great pastoral predecessor.

Admission to the higher rank of heroic poet again requires inspiration and the self-denial that prepares one for it. Sexual abstinence, lamented by the nymphs earlier in the poem and celebrated and rewarded in heavenly erotic orgies at the end of the poem, is compensated by Damon's (and the poet's) becoming targets for the heavenly Cupid.

> *Parte alia polus omnipatens, et magnus Olympus,*
> *Quis putet? hic quoque Amor, pictæque in nube pharetræ,*
> *Arma corusca, faces, et spicula tincta pyropo;*
> *Nec tenues animas, pectusque ignobile vulgi*
> *Hinc ferit, at circum flammantia lumina torquens,*
> *Semper in erectum spargit sua tela per orbes*
> *Impiger, et pronos nunquam collimat ad ictus;*
> *Hinc mentes ardere sacræ, formæque deorum.*
>
> (190–97)

In another part, the unbounded sky and great Olympus—who would have thought?—here also Love, and in a cloud his colorful quivers, his gleaming arms, his torches, and his arrows coated with golden bronze. From here he does not strike at frivolous souls or the ignoble heart of the mob, but turning his flaming eye about, he always, tirelessly, casts his weapons upward into the spheres, and never aims a downward blow. From this source sacred minds catch fire, and the forms of the gods.

After being kindled by the holy fire, secular in form but otherwise the complement of Isaiah's burning coal in the "Nativity Ode," Thyrsis like the reformed speaker in "Lycidas" becomes the source rather than the object of consolation:

> *Nec tibi conveniunt lacrymæ, nec flebimus ultra;*
> *Ite procul lacrymæ, purum colit æthera Damon,*
> *Æthera purus habet, pluvium pede reppulit arcum;*
> *Heroumque animas inter, divosque perennes,*
> *Æthereos haurit latices et gaudia potat*
> *Ore sacro. Quin tu coeli post iura recepta*
> *Dexter ades, placidusque fave quicunque vocaris,*
> *Seu tu noster eris Damon, sive æquior audis*
> *Diodatus.*
>
> (202–10)

nor are tears fitting for you, and we will weep no longer. Be gone far away, tears. Damon inhabits the pure heavens; in his purity he possess the heavens, he spurns the rainbow with his foot. Among the souls of heroes and the eternal gods he drinks heavenly liquid and downs its joys with his holy mouth. So now, after receiving your due in heaven, you are at my right hand; favor me also in your kindness, however you are called: whether you will be our Damon, or whether you prefer Diodati.

The self-representation that has emerged in the 1630s is complete here. The speaker is chaste, articulate, skilled in the ways of poetry, chosen by the divine, and the conduit for telling of things invisible to mortal sight.

Advancement to this elect, religio-poetic status comes by way of a set of choices, disciplines, and renunciations that runs parallel to but never embraces Puritan conversion narratives. Milton's resistance to admitting weakness, much less sinfulness, separates his self-representation from those conversion stories. The closest one comes to such a narrative is in the brief retraction, of uncertain date, appended to Elegy 7 in *Poems 1645*. The retraction assigns the elegiac verses to youthful foolishness and error:

> *Haec ego mente olim laeva, studioque supino*
> *Nequitiae posui vana trophaea meae.*
> *Scilicet abreptum sic me malus impulit error,*
> *Indocilisque aetas prava magistra fuit.*
> *Donec Socraticos umbrosa Academia rivos*
> *Praebuit, admissum dedocuitque iugum.*
> *Protinus extinctis ex illo tempore flammis,*
> *Cincta rigent multo pectora nostra gelu.*
> *Unde suis frigus metuit puer ipse sagittis,*
> *Et Diomedeam vim timet ipsa Venus.*

These empty trophies to my wantonness I once made with a frivolous mind and perverse enthusiasm. Clearly malign error drove me when I was abducted this way, and untaught youth was my depraved teacher—until shady Academia offered its Socratic streams, and made me unlearn the burden which I had taken up. With my flames quenched immediately from that time on, our heart stiffens, encased in thick ice. Whence the boy himself fears the cold on his arrows, and Venus herself dreads the strength of Diomedes.

It is not clear whether the ten lines refer to all the elegies or to the seventh only. The plural of "*vana trophaea*" (empty trophies) suggests the former, but the rest of the epilogue fits so well with the seventh and so ill with most of the others that Milton may have had in mind the seventh only. This retraction hardly fits the poem of mourning for Andrews (Elegy 3) or the earnest elegiac letter to Thomas Young (Elegy 4), although Milton may allude to the tribute to English girls in Elegy 1, or the ardent and erotic Elegy 5 to Spring ("*Tellus lasciva suos suspirat amores*" (lascivious Earth breathes out her love) (95). The retraction ultimately may have less to do with the body of the elegies than with convention, the signaling of the moment for ascent of the genre ladder, from lyric grace to epic gravity. But the language suggests another set of conventions as well. Vanity, wantonness, foolishness, and laziness have led him astray. The ignorance of youth fed perversity. Here as nowhere else in Milton we get an apparently straightforward confession of youthful error, followed by the resolve of conversion, which has extinguished the flames of passion. For once, Milton represents himself in something like the plot of Puritan conversion narrative. Two crucial differences, however, separate Milton's "confession" from Augustine's or Bunyan's. The first is the stylization and indebtedness to lyric tradition. This is the expected gesture of the rising poet, not the Pauline Christian. The second and more important difference is the identification of the "master text." The young poet was reclaimed by Plato rather than Christ. If, at the inaugurating moment of Christian spiritual autobiography, Augustine credits Platonic teaching with greater closeness to the Gospel than other pagan philosophies, he must repudiate untransmuted Platonism as part of the process of his conversion to Christianity.[44] It is significant that at the moment when Milton offers something most closely approximating the narrative we might expect from a Puritan of his time, it is entirely secularized. His aspiration to the status of divine poet depends more on his cultivation as a poet than on his conversion as a Christian. But this may be, as I have suggested, owing to Milton's unusual and audacious sense of his own freedom from sin. This sense of freedom would be sorely tested in the following decades.

---

44. The Augustinian perspective is embodied in the notorious dismissal of Greek wisdom in *Paradise Regained*.

Chapter 4

"Kingdom of Free Spirits"

The Anti-Prelatical Works

By his own account, Milton's turn to polemical prose in the 1640s narrowed his opportunities to write about himself. Sir Philip Sidney observed that the poet is free to range "only within the zodiac of his own wit."[1] In *The Reason of Church-Government* Milton suggests that this freedom extends to the poet writing about himself: "For although a Poet soaring in the high region of his fancies with his garland and singing robes about him might without apology speak more of himself then I mean to do, yet for me sitting here below in the cool element of prose, a mortall thing among many readers of no Empyreall conceit, to venture and divulge unusual things of my selfe, I shall petition to the gentler sort, it may not be envy to me" (*YP* 1:808). It is not immediately clear why poets are freer than others to write about themselves. Whatever the reason, Milton does not observe it. He liberally salts his prose with autobiographical digressions. Even his programmatic statement in *The Reason of Church-Government* ends with Milton's petition for a waiver from the prohibition against self-representation in prose.

Of the five anti-prelatical tracts published in less than a year bridging 1641 and 1642, Milton puts his name only to the fourth, *The Reason of Church-Government*.[2] In the "Nativity Ode" Milton told a story of the silencing of

---

1. Sidney, *An Apology for Poetry*, in *Critical Theory Since Plato*, ed. Hazard Adams (New York: Harcourt, Brace, Jovanovich, 1971), 157.
2. The influence of Joan Webber's chapter on the anti-prelatical tracts will be obvious in this chapter, even when I disagree with her (*The Eloquent "I"* [Madison: University of Wisconsin Press, 1968], pp. 184–217). On the anti-prelatical tracts, see also Thomas Kranidas, *The Fierce Equation: A Study of Milton's Decorum* (The Hague: Mouton, 1965), and *Milton and the Rhetoric of Zeal* (Pittsburgh: Duquesne University Press, 2005).

his individual voice and of his joining a chorus; in the anti-prelatical tracts, on the other hand, he gradually emerges from anonymity. The last works in the series contain two of his most revealing autobiographical set-pieces. But if one can make a case for a chiastic structure, from assertion to anonymity in "Nativity Ode" and "Lycidas," and from anonymity to self-assertion in the anti-prelatical tracts, one can also argue that the anti-prelatical tracts are constant in their assertion of singularity. Beginning with *Of Reformation*, the authorial voice claims for itself the elected prophetic status informing the early poetry.

For the first time Milton would publish his ambitions to a wide audience, protected in the early anti-prelatical tracts by a veil of anonymity that may have been more apparent than real. He treats writing style in *Of Prelatical Episcopacy* as a marker and warrant of identity: "In the midst therfore of so many forgeries where shall we fixe to dare say this is *Ignatius?* as for his stile who knows it? so disfigur'd and interrupted as it is" (*YP* 1:639). Three years later, in the *Judgement of Martin Bucer*, he claims that the style of the anonymous *Doctrine and Discipline of Divorce* gave away his identity:

> My name I did not publish, as not willing it should sway the reader either for me or against me. But when I was told, that the stile, which what it ailes to be so soon distinguishable, I cannot tell, was known by most men, and that some of the Clergie began to inveigh and exclaim on what I was credibly inform'd they had not read, I took it then for my proper season both to shew them a name that could easily contemn such an indiscreet kind of censure, and to reinforce the question with a more accurat diligence. (*YP* 2:434)

Milton's pride in his style is discernible behind the pose of modesty. As he writes in 1642, from his youth observers judged that his style "in English, or other tongue, prosing or versing, . . . by certain vital signes it had, was likely to live" (*YP* 1:809). And amidst the throng of anti-episcopal polemics of the early 1640s, which makes Milton's claims of forwardness and courage somewhat tenuous, it is a distinctive style that Milton has to offer. Part of the work of the anti-prelatical tracts is to establish a voice that will lend authority to his arguments even as he makes those arguments. The anonymity is provisional and partial, deployed to be seen through. Contributing to the play of the proleptic and the retrospective marking his self-representations, Milton in his early polemical prose works extends promissory notes on future achievement, looking forward to a time when he can look back on those accomplishments. In the earliest works, he banks on a name not yet earned; in the later works he claims authority from his earlier polemic efforts.

Of Reformation: "Some One Perhaps May Bee Heard"

Of Reformation is as close to an anonymous work of persuasive prose as Milton ever wrote. He does not put his name to it, and the speaking voice rarely points to itself. The work is cast as a letter to an unnamed friend, which gives it a hint of intimacy that paradoxically highlights the impersonality of the work. John Diekhoff found only eight lines suitable for his collection of Milton's autobiographical writings.[3] Nevertheless, even in this pamphlet Milton finds occasion, though implicitly, to talk about himself. When, significantly, after recalling the heroes of the Reformation, he first refers to himself, he does so in a curious construction in which he inhabits both the agent and object positions:

> The pleasing pursuit of these thoughts hath oft-times led mee into a serious question and debatement with my selfe, how it should come to passe that *England* (having had this *grace* and *honour* from GOD to bee the first that should set up a Standard for the recovery of *lost Truth,* and blow the first *Evangelick Trumpet* to the *Nations,* holding up, as from a Hill, the new Lampe of *saving light* to all Christendome) should now be last, and most unsettl'd in the enjoyment of that *Peace,* whereof she taught the way to others. (*YP* 1:525)

Milton seems to objectify himself in this vignette of engaging himself in contemplation and speculation. The distance glimpsed here between Milton and Milton parallels the distance between the author and his public self, and for a moment we see him contemplating that self as an object.[4]

This moment of objectification sets the stage for Milton's practice in the rest of the work of writing about himself in the third person. In the single departure from this practice, Milton employs the first person in his defense of his use of vehement language:

> And heerewithall I invoke the *Immortal* DEITIE *Reveler* and *Judge* of Secrets, That wherever I have in this BOOKE plainely and roundly (though

---

3. Diekhoff, *Milton on Himself* (New York: Oxford University Press, 1939), p. 191.
4. At the same relative position in *Of Prelatical Episcopacy,* Milton repeats the gesture. After an opening consideration of the episcopal party's burying of biblical authority under the testimony of antiquity, Milton observes that "*it came into my thoughts to perswade my selfe,* setting all distances, and nice respects aside, that I could do Religion, and my Country no better service for the time then doing my utmost endeavour to recall the people of GOD from this vaine forraging after straw, and to reduce them to their firme stations under the standard of the Gospell" (*YP* 1:627; my emphasis). Not surprisingly, given its vigorous attacks on human authority, this work is unusually free of self-representation.

worthily and truly) laid open the faults and blemishes of *Fathers, Martyrs,* or Christian *Emperors;* or have otherwise inveighed against Error and Superstition with vehement Expressions: I have done it, neither out of malice, nor list to speak evill, nor any vaine-glory; but of meere necessity, to vindicate the spotlesse *Truth* from an ignominious bondage. (*YP* 1:535)

Milton acquits himself here of indecorousness, faulty judgment, ill will, and pride. But the last, vainglory, is a temptation for Milton, and in third-person implicit self-representations Milton wrestles with and adopts a more assertive and exalted position. Early in the second book he refers to "Poets" as if they were a separate breed: "O Sir, if we could but see the shape of our deare Mother *England,* as Poets are wont to give a personal form to what they please, how would she appeare, think ye, but in a mourning weed, with ashes upon her head, and teares abundantly flowing from her eyes" (*YP* 1:585). If these images are conventional, elsewhere in the tract the imagery is vivid, urgent, and affective, demonstrating that Milton is a poet and not merely an observer of poets, nowhere more so than in the digression on the greedy wen on the body politic, adapted from Livy, that immediately precedes the passage quoted (*YP* 1:583–84). Milton likewise betrays himself as a poet when he writes of "purg[ing] with sovrain eyesalve that intellectual ray which *God* hath planted in us" (*YP* 1:566), of the prelates' "canary-sucking, and swan-eating palat[s]," and of the "surfeted Priest" who "scruples not to paw, and mammock the sacramentall bread, as familiarly as his Tavern Bisket" (*YP* 1:549,548). Lana Cable has shown that much of the argument of *Of Reformation* is carried not in logical argument but in affective imagery.[5] Milton speaks of poets in the third person, but the work shows him to be one.

And the poet-writer, even in this relatively anonymous work, emerges by the end as the unique hero. In his peroration, Milton prays confidently to a God who will destroy his episcopal enemies and reward the righteous. But even as the prayer unfolds, agency is transferred from God to human beings, and particularly to the poet-singer who is indistinguishable in voice from Milton himself: "Yet will I not insist on that which may seeme to be the cause on GODS part; as his judgement on our sinnes, the tryall of his owne, the unmasking of Hypocrites. . . . But I shall cheifly indeavour to declare those Causes that hinder the forwarding of *true Discipline,* which are among our selves" (*YP* 1:527–28). Janel Mueller comments, "I know of no analogue for such a summary dismissal of 'GODS part' in the interrelation of prophecy and

---

5. Cable, *Carnal Rhetoric: Milton's Iconoclasm and the Poetics of Desire* (Durham, NC: Duke University Press, 1995), pp. 52–89.

history, although Milton has company enough in his activism and polemics."[6] In the peroration, Milton moves seamlessly from what God will do to what man, and specifically Milton, can and will do. As God crushes his enemies in apocalyptic retribution,

> Then amidst the *Hymns,* and *Halleluiahs* of *Saints* some one may perhaps bee heard offering at high *strains* in new and lofty *Measures* to sing and celebrate thy *divine Mercies,* and *marvelous Judgements* in this Land throughout all AGES; whereby this great and Warlike Nation instructed and inur'd to the fervent and continuall practice of *Truth* and *Righteousnesse,* and casting farre from her the *rags* of her old *vices* may presse on hard to that *high* and *happy* emulation to be found the *soberest, wisest,* and *most Christian People* at that day when thou the Eternall and shortly-expected King shalt open the Clouds to judge the severall Kingdomes of the World, and distributing *Nationall Honours* and *Rewards* to Religious and just *Commonwealths,* shalt put an end to all Earthly *Tyrannies,* proclaiming thy universal and milde *Monarchy* through Heaven and Earth. (*YP* 1:616)

The first controversial prose work reverses the arc of the "Nativity Ode," in which an initial pose of singularity modulates into membership in a choir. This transformation, as we saw in chapter 3, accounts for much of the drama of the poem. Now the poet's voice emerges from the chorus of saints to sing its own song. The third-person casting of that voice, "some one may perhaps bee heard," does not disguise that this is a proleptic self-representation, another promissory note of future achievement.[7]

The self-representation is assertively heroic. Hong Won Suh has related the song imagined here as signaling the millennium to the song described in the "Nativity Ode" as being heard three times, at Creation, Incarnation, and Last Judgment.[8] The end of *Of Reformation* recalls that poem in another way as well, as the pamphlet places its author in the position of potential overreacher, apparently vying for the office and power of the Son of God. The heroic singer is responsible for the national reformation auguring the Son of God's returning for his millennial reign. The blessing and curse at the end of the work, pronounced just after the introduction of the singer, come at

---

6. Mueller, "Embodying Glory: The Apocalyptic Strain in Milton's *Of Reformation,*" in *Politics, Poetics, and Hermeneutics in Milton's Prose,* ed. David Loewenstein and James Grantham Turner (Cambridge: Cambridge University Press, 1990), p. 23; Mueller demonstrates the tract's uniqueness in its emphasis on human over divine agency.

7. On this strategy, see Christopher Grose, *Milton and the Sense of Tradition* (New Haven: Yale University Press, 1988), p. 75.

8. Hong Won Suh, "'They Also Serve': Haste and Delay in the Works of John Milton" (PhD diss., University of Notre Dame, 1998), p. 91.

least as much from the Miltonic singer as they do from the "shortly-expected King." The closing curse is savagely eloquent:

> But they contrary that by the impairing and diminution of the true *Faith,* the distresses and servitude of their *Countrey* aspire to high *Dignity, Rule* and *Promotion* here, after a shamefull end in this *Life* (which *God* grant them) shall be thrown downe eternally into the *darkest* and *deepest Gulfe* of HELL, where under the *despightfull controule,* the trample and spurne of all the other *Damned,* that in the anguish of their *Torture* shall have no other ease then to exercise a *Raving* and *Bestiall Tyranny* over them as their *Slaves* and *Negro's,* they shall remaine in that plight for ever, the *basest,* the *lowermost,* the *most dejected,* most *underfoot* and *downe-trodden Vassals* of *Perdition.* (YP 1:616–17)

It seems that it is as much Milton as God who pronounces the curse that will send Milton's enemies to perdition.[9] A claim to the prerogative of weighing and separating is implicit in the balanced and paired constructions of the passage on the singer, an effect emphasized by the printer's italics: "*Hymns,* and *Halleluiahs,*" "*strains*" and "*Measures,*" "*divine Mercies,* and *marvelous Judgements,*" "*Truth* and *Righteousnesse*" opposed to "*rags*" and "*vices,*" "just *Common-wealths*" opposed to "Earthly *Tyrannies.*"

In the "Nativity Ode," Milton had inserted himself into the play of timelessness and time, into the eternal now of the providential plan. His song aspired to the glory of celestial music. But in that poem Milton withdrew from the brink of overreaching, and his song merged with the deferential and celebratory song of the angels. In *Of Reformation,* he does not step back. In the poem, he gets ahead of himself and of providential time even as he attempts to get ahead of the Magi, and he must bow to that time. But in the pamphlet, he presses forward into providential time, and in the process makes it stand still, an action only God can perform in the "Nativity Ode." The unique and audacious role for human agency extends even to the moment of apocalypse. At the Second Coming, Milton is still there as heroic agent, as a singer emerging even as Christ descends. As Suh argues, the "stretching of a time even beyond time allows Milton to wedge himself into the process, significantly, not simply as a participant, but as the one clear voice that leads the hymns of the saints."[10] The self-representation requires a distortion of time,

---

9. See Mueller, "Embodying Glory," pp. 34–35; James Grantham Turner, "The Poetics of Engagement," in *Politics, Poetics, and Hermeneutics in Milton's Prose,* ed. David Loewenstein and James Grantham Turner (Cambridge: Cambridge University Press, 1990), pp. 268–69. On the rhetoric of violence in Milton's peroration, see David Loewenstein, *Milton and the Drama of History: Historical Vision, Iconoclasm, and the Literary Imagination* (Cambridge: Cambridge University Press, 1990), pp. 28–31.

10. Suh, "'They Also Serve,'" p. 91.

as Milton operates in the newly levered space between Christ's descending and the reformation of the godly nation.

Animadversions: "In One Man, as Well as in a Thousand"

After the relative reticence of *Of Prelatical Episcopacy,* Milton in *Animadversions upon the Remonstrant's Defence against Smectymnuus* (July 1641) again presents himself, in the third person, as a specially chosen and specially gifted spokesman of God. His self-representation, moreover, is marked by the anxiety springing from a questionable rhetorical strategy, the savage attack on Bishop Joseph Hall. Milton acknowledges in the opening lines "something in this booke, which to some men perhaps may seeme offensive" (*YP* 1:662). The language is vague, in sharp contrast to the "something" for which he begs indulgence, the concrete savagery of his handling of Hall. The qualifiers ("some," "perhaps") along with the most tenuous of verb forms ("may seem") address Milton's strategy as delicately as that strategy addresses Hall roughly. That roughness, he claims, is warranted by the danger posed by Hall and his fellow self-interested advocates for episcopacy:

> I suppose and more then suppose, it will be nothing disagreeing from Christian meeknesse to handle such a one in a rougher accent, and to send home his haughtinesse well bespurted with his owne holy-water. Nor to do thus are we unautoritied either from the morall precept of SALOMON to answer him thereafter that prides him in his folly; nor from the example of Christ, and all his followers in all Ages, who in the refuting of those that resisted sound Doctrine, and by subtile dissimulations corrupted the minds of men, have wroght up their zealous souls into such vehemencies, as nothing could be more killingly spoken. (*YP* 1:662–63)

The bullying in the phrase "I suppose and more then suppose," which brooks no contradiction, suggests unease, an effect underlined by the double negative immediately following ("it will be nothing disagreeing from Christian meeknesse") and even more so by the one opening the next sentence ("Nor to do thus are we unautoritied"). Milton had defended vehemence in *Of Reformation,* but without the elaborate and knotted sentences and the anxiety evident here. Still relatively young and uncredentialed, he is searching for authority, and the syntactic tortuousness reveals the strain.

He attempts to purchase authority by representing himself as a singular and heroic figure. He argues that religious authority is not tied to office in the church: "a man shall commonly find more savoury knowledge in one Lay-man, then in a dozen of Cathedrall *Prelates*" (*YP* 1:690). The distinction between single and many is as important here as that between lay and clerical; it picks up on a claim in his own voice a few pages earlier, "I shall be bold to say that reason is the gift of God in one man, as well as in a thousand" (*YP* 1:684–85). While Milton will grant, with unusual (and rhetorically calculated) generosity that "a plaine unlearned man that lives well by that light which he has, is better, and wiser, and edifies others more towards a godly and happy life" than a "learned Hypocrite" (*YP* 1:720), the single layperson and single reasonable man resemble the learned Milton.

Milton reacts sharply to Hall's charge that attacks on the bishops are libelous. It is unreasonable to ask men to be silent now, after a long period of restraint between Parliaments; Hall's request is "something pinching in a Kingdome of free spirits" (*YP* 1:669). Milton's meaning is clear; Hall's position is an insult to the many serious and searching spirits in the kingdom of England. At the same time, the phrase suggests a paradox. The free spirits are plural, but the head of a kingdom is single. Behind Milton's simply patriotic and enthusiastic endorsement of shared inquiry we glimpse the wish for precedence, for a world in which a free spirit can take on the self-determining power of a king. The phrase recasts the tension between the one and the many introduced in Milton's assertion of the wisdom of the single figure. This context suggests a second reading of Milton's "I suppose and more then suppose." The phrase implies not only anxiety but also aggressive assertiveness. Milton's supposing, like that of an authoritative party or even a king, counts for more than supposing. Milton claims magisterial power to make his supposing stick.

The tension between the one and the many also informs the language of procreation central in Milton's imagery from this pamphlet on. The collective wisdom and learning of the bishops finally does not equal that of a single and learned godly man. That one can then multiply into the many by spiritual procreation. As he had in *Of Reformation,* Milton describes his function and power as continuous with God's:

> He [God] can stirre up rich Fathers to bestow exquisite education upon their Children, and so dedicate them to the service of the Gospell; he can make the sons of Nobles his Ministers, and Princes to be his Nazarites; for certainly there is no imployment more honourable, more worthy to take up a great spirit, more requiring a generous and free nurture, then to be the messenger, and Herald of heavenly truth from God to man, and by the faithfull worke of holy doctrine, to procreate a number of faithfull men, making a kind of creation like to Gods, by infusing his spirit and likenesse into them, to their salvation, as God did into him. (*YP* 1:721)

Milton, who has received an exquisite education from his father and who consistently views himself as a divine messenger, represents himself here, as he does a moment later when he contrasts his spiritual fertility with the bishops' barren lechery, or "darksome barrennesse" (*YP* 1:721). While he has spiritual children, and earns from his grateful children the "title of Father," the bishops "keep back their sordid sperm begotten in the lustinesse of their avarice" (*YP* 1:722). Milton heaps scorn on the idea of what Hall calls "your Mother the Church of *England*" (*YP* 1:727). To accept that mother is to "make ourselves rather the Bastards, or the Centaurs of [the bishops'] spirituall fornications" (*YP* 1:728). In claiming for himself the title of father and contrasting his fruitfulness with the bishops' vicious barrenness, Milton, the young man challenging age, turns the table on Hall and the other bishops. Now they are the immature and impotent ones, while Milton is the figure of gravity and patriarchy. Significantly, Milton reduces the number of procreation itself to one; like God, he procreates without a partner.

Milton also defines himself against the ordained clerics, and particularly the bishops, who work for hire. He echoes "Ad Patrem" in its contempt for work done for money:

> he is not esteem'd to deserve the name of a compleat Architect, an excellent Painter, or the like, that beares not a generous mind above the peasantly regard of wages, and hire; much more must we thinke him a most imperfect, and incompleate Divine, who is so farre from being a contemner of filthy lucre; . . . it is justly expected that they should bring forth a baseborn issue of Divinity like that of those imperfect, and putrid creatures that receive a crawling life from two most unlike procreants the Sun, and mudde. (*YP* 1:720)

Sexual irregularity and money-grubbing help define by contrast the image of the author. Milton defines himself by a kind of economic chastity.

As in the first two tracts, Milton addresses himself ("I shall adresse my self in few words" [*YP* 1:662]), and the momentary objectification prepares the ground for the development of his self-portrait in the third person. While most of the work engages in staccato quotation and response, in one of several more florid set pieces, Milton echoes the third-person self-representation of the singer at the end of time in *Of Reformation:*

> When thou [God] hast settl'd peace in the Church, and righteous judgement in the Kingdome, then shall all thy Saints address their voyces of joy, and triumph to thee, standing on the shoare of that red Sea into which our enemies had almost driven us. And he that now for haste snatches up a plain ungarnish't present as a thanke-offering to thee, which could not bee deferr'd in regard of thy so many late deliverances

wrought for us one upon another, may then perhaps take up a Harp, and sing thee an elaborate Song to Generations. (*YP* 1:706)

Once again, the single voice's emergence from a choir reveals Milton's desire to be outstanding. Even the self-deprecation that seems to ground the self-assertion ("he that now for haste snatches up a plain ungarnish't present") disappears in retrospect. As James Grantham Turner observes, from the perspective of *An Apology for Smectymnuus* the "ungarnish't present" of *Animadversions* is recast as a "a fully-realized 'hymne in prose,' an even higher genre than prayer."[11]

Milton in the early prose works, as in the early poetry, assembles a proleptic self-representation as singular, heroic, and godly. The rhetorical challenge at an early stage is clear—how does one who is not merely young but also a late bloomer claim the authority to speak and to teach? Already by *Animadversions,* Milton has elaborated a self-representation that, more than merely qualifying him to speak, sets him on a rarefied plane. The vatic Milton so attractive to the Romantics surfaces in these early works. When Milton asks, "would he tugge for a Barony to sit and vote in Parliament, knowing that no man can take from him the gift of wisedome, and sound doctrine which leaves him free, though not to be a member, yet a teacher, and perswader of the Parliament?" (*YP* 1:722), and when in the next breath he suggests that he is above the legislator as Christ is above Moses, he anticipates Shelley's poet as unacknowledged legislator. The Milton whose passing Wordsworth laments ("Milton, thou should'st be living at this hour") comes to birth in the self-representations of the 1630s and 1640s.

The Reason of Church-Government: "to Venture and Divulge Unusual Things of My Selfe"

With *The Reason of Church-Government* (January–February 1642), the first of his prose works to appear under his name, Milton's self-representation enters a new phase. Previously, self-representation had been veiled, either allegorized under a poetic persona, partially obscured by third-person frames, or distanced by anonymous publication. In his fourth anti-prelatical tract, Milton for the first time writes in English directly and explicitly about himself. Self-representation is literally the centerpiece of the work: a literary autobiography takes up the lengthy Preface to Book Two. Describing his learning and his literary goals, Milton seems far from being what he, perhaps inadvertently, called himself in the "Letter to a Friend," the "most . . . unwepon'd creature

---

11. Turner, "Poetics of Engagement," p. 269 (quoting *YP* 1:930).

in the word" (*YP* 1:319). This literary self-representation is flanked in the first and last body chapters by ethical self-representations (in *An Apology for Smectymnuus* these two functions will be integrated). The personal digressions serve the purpose of the ethical proof.[12] If the audience is predisposed against a young, unknown challenger of learned and celebrated bishops, Milton describes a life that will lend weight to his words. His preoccupation, as so often in his early works, is with gaining the authority of age for the works of youth.

The work itself, however, leaves no room for authority. Scripture makes God's disposition of church government clear and unambiguous, rendering human authority irrelevant. Because God would not have left his church without direction, and because it is almost beyond learned and wise men's capacity to mold even civil discipline, why should we expect human reason to settle church discipline? Framing civil laws, Milton argues,

> if it be at all the worke of man, . . . *must be of such a one as is a true knower of himselfe,* and himselfe in whom contemplation and practice, wit, prudence, fortitude, and eloquence must be rarely met, both to comprehend the hidden causes of things, and span in his thoughts all the various effects that passion or complexion can worke in mans nature; and hereto must his hand be at defiance with gaine, and *his heart in all vertues heroick.* (*YP* 1:753; my emphasis)

Ostensibly surveying the qualifications of the lawgiver, Milton surveys himself; the heroic lawgiver resembles the image of himself in the rest of this tract and even more the one that will inform *An Apology*. In this opening body chapter as in the last, Milton advances implicitly the ethical proof. We are asked to trust a man of virtue, as we will be asked to respect a man of learning in the long preface. Learning and rhetorical skill give force to Milton's prophetic vocation, but moral virtue qualifies him for that vocation in the first place. His image for the church in need of divine discipline in this first chapter of Book One is the virgin, and Milton's own claims for the power of virginity in *Comus* and soon in *An Apology* suggest a link between the church and the inspired figure who will settle its discipline. Armed with virtue, and despite his earlier distinction, Milton now returns to religious discipline: "And therefore all the ancient lawgivers were either truly inspir'd as *Moses,* or were such men as with authority anough might give it out to be so, as *Minos, Lycurgus, Numa,* because they wisely forethought that men would never quietly submit to such a discipline as had not more of Gods hand in it then mans" (*YP* 1:753–54). The possibility of inspiration opens a door in the blank wall of human inadequacy for legislating

---

12. See John Diekhoff, "The Function of the Prologues in *Paradise Lost,*" *PMLA* 57 (1942): 698.

church government. On the same page, Milton, alluding to Uzzah (2 Samuel 6), who was struck dead for presuming to steady the ark of the covenant, asks darkly, "who is he *so arrogant so presumptuous* that durst dispose and guide the living arke of the holy Ghost . . . , *without the conscious warrant of some high calling*" (my emphasis).[13] Later, in the long autobiographical digression, Milton will claim the prophetic warrant all but explicitly for himself. Milton is clearly aware of the danger of prophetic claims. Without inspiration, one is presumptuous and arrogant, and claims to inspiration may themselves be invented for rhetorical purposes; if one is not a Moses, one might be one "with authority anough . . . [to] give it out to be so." In identifying a strategy he might be thought to follow himself, Milton exposes the springs of an anxiety that threatens his self-construction.

That anxiety marks Milton's concentrated autobiographical digression in the Preface to Book Two, which would be remarkable for its length if nothing else. Milton concludes the preface to the entire work with something like an apology for its diffuseness: "having now prefac'd enough, I shall no longer deferre" (*YP* 1:750). But that preface is only two pages long, and makes up only 7 percent of the first book. The autobiographical preface, nine pages long, takes up 27 percent of Book Two, and 14 percent of the work as a whole. Although acknowledging the digressive and untimely way in which he interpolates himself, he proceeds nonetheless. Announcing that he has no time to digress, he digresses (*YP* 1:812). The strain of the digression reveals itself, as elsewhere, in tortuous sentence construction: "And though I shall be foolish in saying more to this purpose, yet since it will be such a folly, as wisest men going about to commit, have only confest and so committed, I may trust with more reason, because with more folly to have courteous pardon" (*YP* 1:808). While the general drift is clear enough, it is hard to pin down precisely what this means.

Milton's nervousness about the digression's apparent irrelevance and self-serving nature is as revealing as the autobiographical narrative itself. The passage that introduces his life narrative, a third of the way into the preface, epitomizes the imperatives and anxiety surrounding that narrative:

> Concerning therefore this wayward subject against prelaty, the touching whereof is so distastfull and disquietous to a number of men, as by what hath been said I may deserve of charitable readers to be credited, that neither envy nor gall hath enterd me upon this controversy, but the enforcement of conscience only, and a preventive fear least the omitting of this duty should be against me when I would store up to my

---

13. Milton will invoke the prophets again at the beginning of chapter 2.

self the good provision of peacefull hours, So lest it should be still imputed to me, as I have found it hath bin, that some self-pleasing humor of vain-glory hath incited me to contest with men of high estimation, now while green yeers are upon my head, from this needlesse surmisall I shall hope to disswade the intelligent and equal auditor, if I can but say successfully that which in this exigent behoovs me, although I would be heard only, if it might be, by the elegant & learned reader, to whom principally for a while I shal beg leav I may address my selfe. (*YP* 1:806–7)

As in the previous tract, Milton employs the reflexive construction that carries a suggestion of an objectified self ("I shal beg leav I may address my selfe"), almost as if the "intelligent and equal auditor" whom Milton addresses is Milton himself. The disadvantage of writing while young, "while green yeers are upon my head," is neutralized by the proleptic view of the time when he will look back upon the present debate. He employs an economic metaphor ("store up to my self the good provision of peacefull hours") just as he had several pages earlier ("to lay up as the best treasure . . . of a good old age, . . . the honest liberty of free speech from my youth" [1:804]). If current words and actions compose the fund of virtuous experience that itself will give authority to age, then Milton in a sense is earning the authority of age with every word.[14] This makes the choice to speak not only defensible but inevitable, although on another level it is not a choice at all. Behind the decision to write is the "enforcement of conscience."

The public and the private are intertwined in this passage, as Milton justifies himself as much to himself as to us. In imagining what it would mean to be silent now, in the light of his duty to God and England, Milton comes as close as he ever does to an examination of conscience, but he is unwilling to entertain seriously the possibility of his own moral error; instead he considers what such an error might involve. The interplay of the intimate and the public is written into the subtle modulation of audience in the quoted passage. Milton refers first to "charitable *readers*," who will not assume the worst of him for entering debate. This is a wide circle, as compared for example with the case in *Of Reformation,* which is ostensibly addressed to "a friend." But Milton has turned to the public, as it turns out, after unhappy experience with a more intimate circle. He is worried that his activity will be "imputed"

---

14. In the preface to the first book, Milton is less dramatic, citing the reasonableness of his argument as a justification for speaking out while young, as opposed to the demands of conscience or the promise of future greatness: "if any man incline to thinke I undertake a taske too difficult for my yeares, I trust through the supreme inlightning assistance farre otherwise; for my yeares, be they few or many, what imports it? so they bring reason, let that be lookt on" (*YP* 1:749).

to "some self-pleasing humor of "vain-glory," "*as I have found it hath bin*" (*YP* 1.806). Given the scarcity of published response to his arguments by the date of publication of *The Reason of Church-Government*, it is at least likely that the imputation reached Milton by word of mouth. Accordingly, Milton turns to the "intelligent and equal *auditor*," adding that "I would be *heard* only, if it might be, by the elegant & learned *reader*" (my emphasis). Milton imagines himself in a more intimate setting, heard by a discerning audience, responding orally to misunderstandings. At the moment in his published text when he will defend himself by speaking of his life, he specifies a small group of qualified auditor-readers.

Milton opens the preface lamenting that knowledge, which should be "the best and lightsomest possession of the mind," is a sore burden (*YP* 1:801). This knowledge, like the talents of the parable, must be multiplied and accounted for. While Milton will "lay up" for himself the "treasure" of the exercise of "free speech" and the "good provision" of fulfilled duty (*YP* 1:804,806), the knowledge is not his own but the possession of the poor to whom he must distribute it. Corrupt teachers, who fear that the truth will drive down the market price of their lies, obstruct this work of disinterested benevolence. Milton immunizes himself against attacks on his motives and his qualifications by way of a claim bordering on what he had earlier termed arrogance and presumption:

> though they cannot but testify of Truth and the excellence of that heavenly traffick which they bring against what opposition, or danger soever, yet needs must it sit heavily upon their spirits, that being in Gods prime intention and their own, selected heralds of peace, and dispensers of treasure inestimable without price to them that have no pence, they finde in the discharge of their commission that they are made the greatest variance and offence, a very sword and fire both in house and City over the whole earth. (*YP* 1:802)

Attacks on Milton, having been predicted, can in the future be cited as evidence of a prophetic status that, despite his disclaimers, he embraces. Milton makes a show of reluctance, claiming that "when God commands to take the trumpet and blow a dolorous or a jarring blast, it lies not in mans will what he shall say, or what he shall conceal" (*YP* 1:803), but the group he moves to join has taken up its role "in Gods prime intention *and their own.*"[15]

---

15. Although William Kerrigan argues that the *Second Defence* differs from *The Reason of Church-Government* in leaving behind the tone or sense of "regret" and dwelling on "his special power as a zealous warrior" (*Prophetic Milton* [Charlottesville: University Press of Virginia, 1974], pp. 165, 175), Milton already embraces his prophetic status in the earlier work.

Having grasped the prophetic trumpet, defended again his use of vehement language, and pledged his diligent employment of free speech in defense of the church, Milton falls into a revealing non sequitur: "For if I be either by disposition, or what other cause too inquisitive, or suspitious of my self and mine own doings, who can help it?" (*YP* 1:804). As in the passage in the "Letter to a Friend" (*YP* 1:320) that it echoes, Milton might be said to be too little suspicious of himself. His recorded introspection, unlike that of his Puritan contemporaries, contains no misgivings concerning his righteousness, to say nothing of any authentic conviction of error. Milton does imagine two futures in which he does not answer the divine call: in one the church is defeated, and he is condemned for failing to help save her; in another the church is victorious, and he is excluded from the victory celebrations for the same reason. But these two futures are dismissed as counterfactual: "But now by this litle diligence [in writing the *Reason*], mark what a privilege I have gain'd" (*YP* 1:805).

Despite this confidence, some concern about timeliness lies behind Milton's repetition that his subject is not calculated for popularity or for leisurely composition. By early 1642, when the work was published, the bishops were in full retreat, barely hanging on to their places in the House of Lords. The Earl of Strafford was dead, and Archbishop Laud's power undone. In a real sense Milton was late in his attacks on episcopacy, an unattractive option that he had a moment before dismissed in prospect. It is not his books against the bishops that come before their time, but the embedded literary life story, "pluckt from me by an abortive and foredated discovery" (*YP* 1:820)

Milton is now ready to embark on a condensed autobiography, a task that elicits another defensive set of prefatory remarks:

> I should not chuse this manner of writing wherin knowing my self inferior to my self, led by the genial power of nature to another task, I have the use, as I may account it, but of my left hand. And though I shall be foolish in saying more to this purpose, yet since it will be such a folly, as wisest men going about to commit, have only confest and so committed, I may trust with more reason, because with more folly to have courteous pardon. For although a Poet soaring in the high region of his fancies with his garland and singing robes about him might without apology speak more of himself then I mean to do, yet for me sitting here below in the cool element of prose, a mortall thing among many readers of no Empyreall conceit, to venture and divulge unusual things of my selfe, I shall petition to the gentler sort, it may not be envy to me. (*YP* 1:808).

I noted above the tortuousness of the second sentence, which links two of the more familiar and self-revelatory sentences in all of Milton's prose works. The first exemplifies Milton's habit in these prose works of objectifying himself.

There is in this case a self and another self, the one natural ("the genial power of nature") and the other forced. When he comments that in writing prose "I have the use, as *I* may account it, but of my left hand" (my emphasis), the second "I" is, in the construction of self-representation, the deeper or more natural "poetic" self, for it offers a metaphor for the action of the first, prose writing, "I." In this passage self-representation appears as an art in itself. In splitting "I" and "I" Milton inevitably unsettles the illusion of immediacy that the sentence otherwise fosters. The third sentence similarly divides the self. The soaring poet, despite being presented in the third person, seems to be Milton's deeper or "natural" self. This self speaks of himself without apology, as opposed to the speaker of the digression, who speaks about himself with profuse apology. The self writing now ("for me sitting here below") is a "mortall thing" bared before vulgar readers, "of no Empyreall conceit," divulging "things of my selfe." As in the beginning of this passage, we find both an "I" ostensibly not writing but who dresses the text (and himself) in poetic figures and an "I" ostensibly writing who is as often as not treated as an object rather than a subject of contemplation. When Milton appeals to "the gentler sort," in contrast with the vulgar readers of prose, that his self-revelation "may not be envy to me," it is difficult to discern who this "me" is—the poet, the prose writer, or Milton himself behind the poses.

For the rest of the preface, Milton alternates between writing literary autobiography and nervously defending his doing so. The excellence of his style having been recognized by all competent judges, he began "thus farre to assent both to them and divers of my friends here at home, and not lesse to an inward prompting which now grew daily upon me, that by labour and intent study (which I take to be my portion in this life) joyn'd with the strong propensity of nature, I might perhaps leave something so written to aftertimes, as they should not willingly let it die" (*YP* 1:810). Where before the selected heralds are chosen by God's intention and their own, here Milton assents to both the urging of others and his own "inward prompting" (though the latter, understood as divine inspiration, also comes from outside). The pattern of complementarity continues with the convergence of "intent study" and "propensity of nature," which together prepare him poetic fame and prophetic election. He will devote his poetry to "the honour and instruction of my country" (*YP* 1:810), becoming "an interpreter & relater of the best and sagest things among mine own Citizens," that is, in the vernacular (*YP* 1:811–12). These rhetorical pairings underline Milton's implicit argument that, at least in his own work, artistic excellence and truth are inseparable. This is the burden of his famous pledge "That what the greatest and choycest wits of *Athens, Rome,* or modern *Italy,* and those Hebrews of old did for their country, I in my proportion with this over and above of being a Christian, might doe for mine" (*YP* 1:812). Milton can match the great poets (or nearly, he suggests with unusual but tactful modesty) in what he calls the "critical art of composition" (*YP* 1:816), but he will surpass them inasmuch as he has access to the truth.

Having made this remarkable claim, Milton again pauses to defend his digression: "Time servs not now, and perhaps I might seem too profuse to give any certain account of what the mind at home in the spacious circuits of her musing hath liberty to propose to her self, though of highest hope, and hardest attempting, whether that Epick form whereof the two poems of *Homer,* and those other two of *Virgil* and *Tasso* are a diffuse, and the book of *Job* a brief model . . ." (*YP* 1:812–13). Milton does "seem too profuse" on the subject, especially given the topic of his pamphlet.[16] As in other moments of the anxious framing of self-representation, Milton splits himself, now into the "I," the "mind at home," and that mind's "self." The multiplication of selves highlights the self-dramatization or the mediated nature of the self of the representation. Milton frames and constructs himself before our eyes.

Just as Tasso offered Duke Alfonso II a choice of subjects for his *Gerusalemme Liberata,* Milton imagines himself offering a similar choice: "it haply would be no rashnesse from an equal diligence and inclination to present the like offer in our own ancient stories" (*YP* 1:814). To whom is this offer made? According to William Riley Parker, "Presumably to King Charles."[17] Perhaps, but just as likely to the "elegant & learned reader, to whom principally for a while I shal beg leav I may address my selfe" (*YP* 1:807). If he has not yet concluded, as he does in *Eikonoklastes,* that there is no glory in besting a king in argument, there is no evidence that Milton counted Charles among the knowing readers whom he repeatedly addresses. The most knowing reader, of course, is Milton himself, and as he pondered the choices, of genre, of national models, of subject, it is unlikely that he anticipated anyone lifting the burden of choice from his shoulders.

From this point, Milton turns increasingly to scriptural models. Sophocles and Euripides are measured against the Song of Songs and Revelation, and Pindar and Callimachus against Hebrew lyrics. In preferring the latter not merely for their content but their formal and aesthetic properties, Milton further cements the link between prophetic and poetic vocations. For Milton, the Bible offers not only truth but also the highest models of formal excellence. Poetic ability derives from God, who grants greater shares, not incidentally, to singers of divine truth:

> These abilities . . . are the inspired guift of God rarely bestow'd, but yet to some (though most abuse) in every Nation: and are of power beside

---

16. The Yale editor, Ralph A. Haug, suggests that the outlines for tragedies in the Trinity ms. (*YP* 8:554–60) comprise the "certain account" that Milton forgoes here, but Milton clearly says more than is necessary here about his plans.

17. Parker, *Milton: A Biography,* 2 vols. (Oxford: Clarendon, 1968), 1:210.

> the office of a pulpit, to imbreed and cherish in a great people the seeds of vertu, and publick civility, to allay the perturbations of the mind and set the affections in right tune, to celebrate in glorious and lofty Hymns the throne and equipage of Gods Almightinesse. (*YP* 1:816–17)

Milton reintroduces the moral into the equation here. The poet requires moral purity along with poetic craft and a true subject, as this tale of the loss of inspiration to abuse implies. Abilities are granted to few. This group is further winnowed by abuse of the gift. Those left can boast both a divine gift and acquired merit. If he is among them, Milton joins the great poets mentioned in his preface, much as Dante ranks himself with his great classical predecessors in *Inferno*. But these predecessors drop away as well, as true poets lead their compatriots in celebrating hymns to God and teach them the "holy and sublime" truths of religion, something only Milton, "with this over and above of being a Christian," can do. In a typically Miltonic move, a bid for inclusion in a select group ends in a stringent sorting that leaves, arguably, a set of one.

Nearing the end of his preface, Milton yet again apologizes for dwelling upon himself. He characterizes his self-representation as a premature birth: "The thing which I had to say, and those intentions which have liv'd within me ever since I could conceiv my self any thing worth to my Countrie, I return to crave excuse that urgent reason hath pluckt from me by an abortive and foredated discovery" (*YP* 1:820). The sense is tortured. Returned from whence? Crave excuse from whom? The uncertainty is a measure of anxiety. The language of prematurity answers implicitly the concern with greenness and anonymity. The orthography of "my self" and "any thing" underline the objectification pervasive in Milton's self-representations.[18] If there is a sense of urgency and untimeliness, it is balanced by the measuredness of "reason," which here precipitates the digression. The need to meet the time with a supposedly unpolished work means that the work is both timely and untimely simultaneously. It is appropriate that this passage and a similar one—"Although it nothing content me to have disclos'd thus much before hand" (*YP* 1:821)—frame another promise of prophetic achievement in its proper time:

> Neither doe I think it shame to covnant with any knowing reader, that for some few yeers yet I may go on trust with him toward the payment of what I am now indebted, as being a work not to be rays'd from the heat of youth, or the vapours of wine, like that which flows at wast from the pen of some vulgar Amorist, or the trencher fury of a riming parasite, nor to be obtain'd by the invocation of Dame Memory and her Siren

---

18. The phrase "conceiv my self" carries a hint of self-generation; Milton creates himself as he contemplates and represents himself.

daughters, but by devout prayer to that eternall Spirit who can enrich with all utterance and knowledge, and sends out his Seraphim with the hallow'd fire of his Altar to touch and purify the lips of whom he pleases: to this must be added industrious and select reading, steddy observation, insight into all seemly and generous arts and affaires, till which in some measure be compast, at mine own peril and cost I refuse not to sustain this expectation from as many as are not loath to hazard so much credulity upon the best pledges that I can give them. (*YP* 1:820–21)

If he is late with the bishops, he is before himself in promises of poetic achievement. He borrows from Shakespeare's Sonnet 129 ("The expense of spirit in a waste of shame / Is lust in action") a pun on "waste" to declare that the fury of love will not be his muse. His muse, now as in *Paradise Lost,* is the Spirit of God, who will touch his lips as Isaiah's were touched (Isaiah 6:6–7). As in all the prophetic passages, Milton meets this divine favor halfway, working tirelessly to acquire the learning and skills necessary for the poet-prophet. Despite or perhaps because of this claim to specially elect prophetic status, he ends this brief passage once more with knotted syntax, clotted with negatives and with terms suggesting more diffidence and tenuousness than one might expect from one whose lips are about to kiss the sacred coal.

Milton concludes the digression with another mini-drama of disclosure and reticence. Now that "all men" offer to succor the church (thus belying Milton's claims to have been supporting an unpopular cause), "it were sad for me if I should draw back, for me especially" (*YP* 1:822). He was destined for service to the church "by the intentions of my parents and friends . . . and in mine own resolutions" (*YP* 1:822). His intentions intersect with those of his parents and friends here at the end of the digression as they intersected with God's at the beginning. He cannot be silent now, though he once preferred "a blamelesse silence" before a place in the pulpit "bought . . . with servitude and forswearing" (*YP* 1:823). The silence of having been "thus Church-outed by the Prelats" is his warrant to speak now.

Underlying Milton's brief against the bishops is righteous anger at the usurpation of *his* rights as a Christian, resentment at being treated as one who might profane the sanctuary. The faithful rely not on censorious bishops but on shame to reclaim errant members. In the final body chapter, Milton argues that backsliders can be recalled by "a religious dred of being outcast from the company of Saints" (*YP* 1:841). But for Milton the most important shame culture unfolds within: "But there is yet a more ingenuous and noble degree of honest shame, or call it if you will an esteem, whereby men bear an inward reverence toward their own persons" (*YP* 1:841). Milton is about to deploy for the purposes of the ethical proof a third-person self-representation, complementing a similar moment in the first chapter of the first book. Again the audience for Milton's representation of himself as judicious and pure is not only his readers but himself. The set of knowing readers capable of judging dwindles to the small group of like mind with Milton, and perhaps by extension to a vanishing point of one. As Milton describes this third person, it begins to sound like his represented self:

> And if the love of God as a fire sent from Heaven to be ever kept alive upon the altar of our hearts, be the first principle of all godly and vertuous actions in men, this pious and just honouring of our selves is the second, and may be thought as the radical moisture and fountain head, whence every laudable and worthy enterprize issues forth. And although I have giv'n it the name of a liquid thing, yet is it not incontinent to bound it self, as humid things are, but hath in it a most restraining and powerfull abstinence to start back, and glob it self upward from the mixture of any ungenerous and unbeseeming motion, or any soile wherewith it may peril to stain it self. . . . Nor can he fear so much the offence and reproach of others, as he dreads and would blush at the reflection of his own severe and modest eye upon himselfe, if it should see him doing or imagining that which is sinfull though in the deepest secrecy. (*YP* 1:841–42)

The fire of God recalls the burning coal of Isaiah in the digression, the similarity signaling Milton's familiar conflation of the prophetic office and the greatest moral purity. The ethical proof directed outward is necessary for persuasion; the ethical proof directed inward is necessary for speech itself. The proof here is cast in sexual imagery, and while "not incontinent" and "abstinence" can be glossed, as they are in the Yale edition, in neutral terms, their sexual referents are barely submerged. The link made in *A Mask* between sexual purity and prophetic utterance informs the *Reason* as well. Moral purity fits one to do great things, as for Milton doing and celebrating great deeds are interchangeable: "he that holds himself in reverence and due esteem . . . accounts himselfe both a fit person to do the noblest and godliest deeds, and much better worth then to deject and defile, with such a debasement and such a pollution as sin is, himselfe so highly ransom'd and enobl'd to a new friendship and filiall relation with God" (*YP* 1:842).

The tension between the classical ethical proof and the Christian ethos comes to a head in this passage. Milton recoils from the prospect of finding any sin within, but it is precisely this that all Christians are called to do, as they find that the law, in the words of Michael in *Paradise Lost*, "evince[s] / Their natural pravity" (12.287–88). Milton's contemporaries tirelessly recorded their horrified discoveries of secret sin; Milton finds only blamelessness.

Milton constructs his image in *The Reason of Church-Government* in the manner of a set of nesting boxes. At the heart is a self-representation as a gifted and diligently prepared author, professionally qualified to speak for God. On either side, in the first and last body chapters, Milton presents a more purely ethical version of himself as a prophet whose status is guaranteed by moral virtue. The separation responds to the Christian commonplace, derived from 1 Corinthians 1, that the simple and virtuous can be wiser about God than the proudly learned. But, as we have seen, Milton smuggles the ethical self-image into his literary self-construction. Though recognizing that the two excellences are separate, he represents himself as peculiarly and indivisibly excellent in both ways. And if literary excellence is separable from virtue, he also seems to want to say that the highest literary excellence is reserved for the virtuous Christian.

An Apology for Smectymnuus: "What Helpe but to Turne the Inside Outwards"

Milton interweaves literary and ethical self-representations even more closely in his final anti-prelatical tract, *An Apology for Smectymnuus* (April 1642). Milton's ethico-literary arguments in the *Apology* address questions of self-representation and the textuality of the self in surprisingly modern ways. A curious work, the *Apology*, though anonymous, is occupied centrally with the defense of its author's name. The full title of the work is a better guide to its theme than the conventional one: AN *APOLOGY* Against *a Pamphlet* CALL'D *A Modest Confutation of the Animadversions upon the Remonstrant against* SMECTYMNUUS. The *Modest Confutation* had attacked Milton as author of the *Animadversions,* and Milton counters that attack in the *Apology;* his defense of the Smectymnuans is indirect, incidental even. John Guillory has observed that "The *Apology* is virtually exhausted by . . . self-defense, adding little to the anti-prelatical arguments of its more cautious predecessor."[19] The point-for-point rebuttal of the *Confutation,* itself comprised largely of self-representation and self-defense, follows a concentrated self-representation and defense that takes up the opening third of the work. The Confuter had attacked his opponent's character and his learning; Milton's responses to the two attacks converge in revealing ways.

The autobiographical sections of the *Apology* are the most intimate that Milton wrote. Milton promises his readers "the discovery of my inmost thoughts" (*YP* 1:889); as will become clear, the unavoidable if unintended ambiguity of "discovery" governs Milton's self-representation. He again writes of his literary education and aspirations, but more personally and less programmatically

---

19. John Guillory, *Poetic Authority: Spenser, Milton, and Literary History* (New York: Columbia University Press, 1983), p. 97. Guillory also discusses the significance of Milton's refusal to give his name in the work (pp. 94–103).

than he had in the preceding tract. He calls to witness the high regard he earned from his university teachers, his present ideals of chastity and honor, and his future aims. He gives an intimate if brief account of his daily habits. He is "up, and stirring, in winter often ere the sound of any bell awake men to labour, or to devotion; in Summer as oft with the Bird that first rouses, or not much tardier" (*YP* 1:885); the qualification "or not much tardier" adds a note not merely of modesty (itself at issue in this work) but also of verisimilitude. We learn of his breeding in comfort though not luxury, the amplitude of his education, and his preference for "a virgin of mean fortunes honestly bred, before the wealthiest widow" (*YP* 1:929). His self-disclosure is provoked by the hostile representation of the Confuter, who portrays the author of the *Animadversions* as unlearned, delinquent, profligate, and unaccomplished. Despite the fact that Milton can console himself that his acquaintances know the absurdity of the Confuter's charges (*YP* 1:870,882), and despite the fact that he published both the *Animadversions* and the *Apology* anonymously, Milton is clearly stung by the charges. The Confuter, as Milton accurately claims, "blunders" and "flings out stray crimes at a venture" (*YP* 1:882), but he knows enough of Milton from his earlier pamphlet to fling such charges that would rankle most.

As before, Milton's turn to autobiography elicits anxious and self-conscious justifications. Already on the first two pages, Milton is tangled in his own syntax:

> if I have done well either to be confident of the truth, whose force is best seene against the ablest resistance, or to be jealous and tender of the hurt that might be done among the weaker by the intrapping autority of great names titl'd to false opinions, or that it be lawfull to attribute somewhat to guifts of Gods imparting, which I boast not, but thankfully acknowledge, and feare also lest at my certaine account they be reckon'd to me many rather then few, or if lastly it be but justice not to defraud of due esteeme the wearisome labours and studious watchings, wherein I have spent and tir'd out almost a whole youth, I shall not distrust to be acquitted of presumption. (*YP* 1:869)

The hypertrophied suspension, with its concatenation of uncertainly related clauses, and its puzzling equivocation on God's gifts (can one mention them? will I be taken to be claiming too great a share of them?), issues finally in a main clause that in its small compass recapitulates the tense emotional rhythm of the sentence, "I shall not distrust to be acquitted of presumption." The negative does not entirely dispel the effect of "distrust." Acquittal is the hope of the accused, and the sentence ends on the charge of presumption to which Milton finds himself to be vulnerable.

A moment later, Milton explicitly acknowledges the uneasiness that comes with self-praise and that accounts, I believe, for his tangled prose:

> I must be forc't to proceed from the unfained and diligent inquiry of mine owne conscience at home (for better way I know not, Readers) to give a more true account of my selfe abroad. . . . Albeit that in doing this I shall be sensible of two things which to me will be nothing pleasant; the one is, that not unlikely I shall be thought too much a party in mine owne cause, and therein to see least; the other, that I shall be put unwillingly to molest the publick view with the vindication of a private name; as if it were worth the while that the people should care whether such a one were thus, or thus. (*YP* 1:869–70)

Milton laments his awkward position. How can he appear unbiased when defending himself, and how can he avoid the charge of naive egocentrism? The Confuter has charged him with sins "perhaps not without some suttlety to cast me into envie, by bringing on me a necessity to enter into mine own praises. In which argument I know every wise man is more unwillingly drawne to speak, then the most repining eare can be averse to heare" (*YP* 1:883). Milton wrestles nervously with the question of whether to defend himself: God has warned the just that they will not be praised; he senses God coming to his aid; he could defer self-defense. There are at least as many reasons to forbear as to counter slander, reasons that, as we saw in chapter 2, led Thomas Edwards to a conclusion Milton consistently rejects: "conceiving the danger of this way in comparing with the Apologists, least I might become a foole in glorying, . . . I resolved to forbeare all those comparisons and vindications of my selfe, and to refer all to God."[20] Milton concludes, nevertheless, that failure to defend himself might harm the cause of truth.

Milton continues, even now at the biblically significant age of thirty-three, to assert pugnaciously his right to challenge older and apparently more distinguished opponents. He is still, and somewhat anomalously, the youth: "lest any one should be inquisitive wherefore this or that man is forwarder then others, let him know that this office goes not by age, or youth, but to whomsoever God shall give apparently the will, the Spirit, and the utterance" (*YP* 1:875). Milton here reiterates a sentiment already found in the opening paragraph of the work: "it were but hard measure now, if the freedome of any *timely spirit* should be opprest meerely by the big and blunted fame of his elder adversary; and that his sufficiency must be now sentenc't, not by pondering the reason he shewes, but by calculating

---

20. Thomas Edwards, *Antapologia* (London, 1644), A1ʳ.

the yeares he brings" (*YP* 1:869; my emphasis). As he had a decade before in Sonnet 7, Milton claims "inward ripeness," but now instead of contrasting himself with "more timely-happy spirits," he asserts that reason and God's choice have made *him* the "timely spirit." The timeliness and forwardness that he claims serve as counterweights against worries about belatedness as a literary figure and as an opponent of bishops.

Answering the Confuter, Milton is as upset by the charge of being unlearned as he is by the charge of being a haunter of brothels. He reacts to the "conceit that all who are not Prelaticall, are grosse-headed, thick witted, illiterat, shallow." "Can nothing then," an exasperated Milton asks, "but Episcopacy teach men to speak good English, to pick & order a set of words judiciously?" (*YP* 1:873). The Confuter has insulted Milton where he lives. Three hundred years before, Petrarch had been offended by young friends who had discounted his learning. The contrast is instructive, for Petrarch's ironic strategy was to acknowledge the justice of their opinion, and to claim that it is more important to him to be good than to be learned.[21] Milton constructs his own image to demonstrate that he is both good and learned, suggesting, as he had in *The Reason of Church-Government*, that goodness and learning, as manifest in eloquence, are inseparable:

> I rather encline, as I have heard it observ'd, that a Jesuits Italian when he writes, is ever naught, though he be borne and bred a *Florentine,* so to thinke that from like causes we may go neere to observe the same in the stile of a Prelat. For doubtlesse that indeed according to art is most eloquent, which returnes and approaches neerest to nature from whence it came; and they express nature best, who in their lives least wander from her safe leading, which may be call'd regenerate reason. So that how he should be truly eloquent who is not withall a good man, I see not. (*YP* 1:874)

The pure Florentine dialect, the language of poets and scholars, is debased in the Jesuit's mouth, as is eloquence in a bishop's. Without goodness, one might command what Socrates in the *Phaedrus* calls a mere empirical knack, a technique without soul, but not the eloquence of true rhetoric.[22] Despite his theoretical confidence that goodness, like murder, will out, Milton must

---

21. In *On His Own Ignorance and That of Many Others* (1366), Petrarch writes, "Most gladly should I divide between me and these brothers of mine the inheritance of Mother Nature and heavenly Grace, so that they would all be men of letters and I a good man. I should wish to know nothing of letters or just so much as would be expedient for the daily praise of God" (in *The Renaissance Philosophy of Man*, ed. Ernst Cassirer, Paul Oskar Kristeller, and John Herman Randall Jr. [Chicago: University of Chicago Press, 1948], p. 54).

22. See Plato, *Phaedrus* (261a and 270b).

convince his readers that his self-representation is not debased eloquence, a morally dubious, false exterior covering a spotted interior. Will readers take his self-justification, in short, as one more strategy of a crafty speaker, or as an organic outgrowth of a virtuous speaker?[23]

The pose of seamless continuity between the moral agent and his writing is complicated by Milton's recounting of his internal monologues. The literary may emerge from and reveal the man, but the literary goes all the way down. The self is, ineluctably, constructed. The Confuter, observing that he knows no more of the author of *Animadversions* that what he had said about himself in that work, proceeds as a literary critic, interpreting a life from the text: "and therefore, as our industrious Criticks for want of clearer evidence concerning the life and manners of some revived Authours, [I] must fetch his character from some scattered passages in his own writings."[24] Milton replies that the resulting hostile portrait derives not from his own words but "from some penurious Book of Characters" (*YP* 1:883).[25] Despite their opposition, the antagonists agree that the Confuter has gathered the character from a text rather than from direct observation of a life. And while Milton will point to his life as a reply to the Confuter's textual fantasy, he writes as if the "self" is a textual production. He claims that "I conceav'd my selfe to be now not as mine own person, but as a member incorporate into that truth whereof I was perswaded, and whereof I had declar'd openly to be a partaker" (*YP* 1:871). "Conceives" looks in two directions; Milton both understands himself and creates himself, and that self is inseparable not only from the truth, but from the texts in which that truth is proclaimed, the truth as he has openly advocated it in his earlier works. Milton moves from observation of himself at home to an account of himself abroad (*YP* 1:869–70), or from a self as he observes it to such a one as might be observed by others. But, as this passage demonstrates, that objective, external portrait is both different from and generated by the subjective portrait. Milton again "conceives himself."

The person that Milton introduces is familiar: a prodigy of learning and a hero of virtue, particularly chastity. Milton backs into praise of his performance at Cambridge, suggesting that to minimize his accomplishments would libel the reverend teachers who spoke highly of him. He handles the distressing charge that he was "vomited" from the university, a charge apparently "flung out at a venture" that came uncomfortably close to his experience

---

23. See Joseph Shub, "Milton's Prose Exordia and the Persuasion through Character," *Prose Studies* 21 (1998):1–31.

24. *A Modest Confutation*, "To the Reader," p. A3ʳ. Reprinted in facsimile in William Riley Parker, *Milton's Contemporary Reputation* (1940; repr. New York: Haskell House, 1971).

25. The Character was a popular mid-seventeenth-century genre, in which Joseph Hall himself had published (thus the gibe) and which Samuel Butler was soon to attempt.

of rustication, in typically convoluted fashion. He denies the charge, points to the high regard his teachers had of him, but then switches course and implies that because the universities have often vomited out the best ("the worser stuffe she strongly keeps in her stomack, but the better she is ever kecking at, and is queasie" [*YP* 1:885]) his being expelled is a sign of his virtue. The argument leaves no room for a negative construction of the author: I was not vomited, but valued; being vomited can be a sign of virtue; if I was vomited, it is a sign of that virtue.

Since leaving the university, he has devoted his life to bodily, mental, and spiritual exercise. After a morning of study, Milton turns to his body: "Then with usefull and generous labours preserving the bodies health, and hardinesse; to render lightsome, cleare, and not lumpish obedience to the minde, to the cause of religion, and our Countries liberty, when it shall require firme hearts in sound bodies to stand and cover their stations" (*YP* 1:885–86). By a seamless extension from body to mind to nation, he is incorporated into England as well as into the truth.

Chastity crowns Milton's bodily, spiritual, and literary labors. He turns against the Confuter his charge that the imagery of *Animadversions* proves its author to be familiar with playhouses and bordellos: if the Confuter traced the images to these places, he himself must be familiar with them. The argument is disingenuous, but no more so than the Confuter's. The charge sends Milton back to his college days, to voice his contempt for the comic plays acted by fellow undergraduates destined for the ministry, in a passage illustrating the "niceness" of nature that will inform the ensuing discussion of reading and chastity: "There while they acted, and overacted, among other young scholars, I was a spectator; they thought themselves gallant men, and I thought them fools, they made sport, and I laught, they mispronounc't and I mislik't, and to make up the *atticisme,* they were out, and I hist" (*YP* 1:887). Not Milton at his most attractive.

Before describing his early reading as a spur to chastity, Milton again interrupts the forward movement with a kind of medial preface of the kind that punctuated his representation of himself in *The Reason of Church-Government.* Then Milton had digressed on his reading as a font of models for his future literary works; now he treats that reading as a preparation for virtuous life or, put another way, as a font of models for himself as a literary work:

> I was confirm'd in this opinion, that he who would not be frustrate of his hope to write well hereafter in laudable things, *ought him selfe to bee a true Poem,* that is, *a composition,* and patterne of the best and honourablest things; not presuming to sing high praises of heroick men, or famous Cities, unlesse he have in himselfe the experience and the practice of all that which is praise-worthy. (*YP* 1:890; my emphasis)

Skeptical that autobiographical writings can give us access to unmediated selves, we remind ourselves that they are artifacts. Milton, as in so much else, has been there ahead of us, and he has gone further. The self, even before making its mediated way into writing, is already textual; Milton sees himself as composing himself even before taking up his pen. The image of the self as an extraliterary composition emerges, however, embedded in a literary text, and this results in an infinite regress.

Reading the best authors has inspired Milton to emulate the poetry and the virtues celebrated (*YP* 1:889–90); given his identification of poet and poem they amount to the same thing. He singles out Dante and Petrarch, "the two famous renowners of *Beatrice* and *Laura*," for their sublimity and purity (*YP* 1:890). Milton does acknowledge briefly that poetic gifts can be divorced from virtue: "if I found those authors any where speaking unworthy things of themselves; or unchaste of those names which before they had extoll'd, this effect it wrought with me, from that time forward *their art I still applauded, but the men I deplor'd*" (*YP* 1:890; my emphasis). But the argument of the book runs counter to this acknowledgment; the work is framed at the beginning by the claim, noted above, that only a good man can be eloquent, and the parallel assertion at the end that "true eloquence I find to be none, but the serious and hearty love of truth" (*YP* 1:874,949). It is a short step from the claim that only the good can be eloquent to its reciprocal: only the eloquent can be good. Milton views purity in action and in language as inseparable in his own case, and apparently as inseparable in principle.

Milton's aspiration to be a great poet and a true poem depends on sexual purity. The purity of virgin lady, chaste reader, and honorable author animate one another. Milton celebrates, chiastically, tales of "the honour and chastity of Virgin or Matron" (*YP* 1:891); one can imagine the virginal Lady of Christ's, who would soon marry, casting himself as the subject as well as the teller of such tales. He goes on to suggest that unchastity is a graver sin in a man, the "image and glory of God," than in a woman, the "glory of man." If romances have led others to "loose living," they entice Milton to virtue. Against the Circean "thick intoxicating potion" of debased living and literature Milton opposes the "charming cup" of virtue, available in "the divine volumes of *Plato*, and his equall *Xenophon*," that is given "to those who are worthy" (*YP* 1:891–92). No longer committed to virginity, Milton dwells at length on his continued commitment to chastity. He recalls the reward given "to those who were not defil'd with women" in Revelation, with which he ended his elegy to Diodati, but insists here that defilement "doubtlesse meanes fornication: For mariage must not be call'd a defilement" (*YP* 1:892–93).

Even granting the pressure of the rhetorical situation and the requirements of the ethical proof, Milton's claims to purity are hyperbolic. They are, moreover, in tension with the Christian doctrine of inherited moral weakness.

Despite his claim to have conducted an "unfained and diligent inquiry of mine owne conscience at home" (*YP* 1:869), his examination of conscience unearths no sins. Milton articulates his ethic of chastity and literary excellence, moreover, in secular terms. Christianity, in which he was "not . . . negligently train'd," enters as an afterthought. Although stipulating that he mentions training in Christian precepts last "as perfection is last" (*YP* 1:892), he implies that literary training and natural disposition are sufficient for chastity: "This that I have hitherto related, hath bin to shew, that though Christianity had bin but slightly taught me, yet a certain reserv'dnesse of naturall disposition, and morall discipline learnt out of the noblest Philosophy was anough to keep me in disdain of farre lesse incontinences then this of the Burdello" (*YP* 1:892). If there is no true learning without goodness, it seems as if good learning, with the possible addition of a promising disposition, can make grace unnecessary.

Milton's description of himself, in other words, implies an exemption from the universal condition of fallenness. He cannot have intended to claim this for himself, as it violates his understanding of the fall, but he omits nonetheless the gestures of conviction that were second nature to his contemporaries. The result is an incoherence or instability at the heart of Milton's representation of himself, which he promptly projects onto the Confuter. Milton counters his opponent's claim "to have affections so equally temper'd, that they neither too hastily adhere to the truth, before it be fully examin'd, nor too lazily afterward," with devastating and doctrinally correct contempt:

> *Which unlesse he only were exempted out of the corrupt masse of Adam, borne without sinne originall, and living without actuall, is impossible* [my emphasis]. . . . [T]his man beyond a *Stoick apathy* sees truth as in a rapture, and cleaves to it. Not as through the dim glasse of his affections which in this frail mansion of flesh are ever unequally temper'd, pushing forward to error, and keeping back from truth oft times the best of men. . . . [I]f ye looke at what he ascribes to himselfe, *that temper of his affections* which cannot any where be but in Paradise, all the judicious *Panegyricks* in any language extant are not halfe so prolixe. (YP 1:909–10)[26]

Milton's *Apology* is itself liable to this criticism. A natural disposition to chastity and to the learning and eloquence that support and crown purity,

---

26. In a related passage Milton will voice a common misrepresentation of Arminianism: "if he be an Arminian and deny originall sinne, all the *etymologies* of his book shall witnesse that his brain is not meanly tainted with that infection" (*YP* 1:917).

along with a reliance on human rather than divine supports, secure Milton on his own account from the degradation that he associates here with the fall. Undermining the coherence and stability of his otherwise orthodox arguments, Milton succumbs to the temptation to claim perfection. Milton examines his conscience and emerges with what looks like an impossible, prelapsarian ideal. This tension between doctrine and self-justification goes far to explain the nervousness and defensiveness that everywhere punctuate Milton's representations of himself in the work.

Defensiveness and claims of purity converge in the middle of the celebration of chastity examined above:

These reasonings, together with a certaine nicenesse of nature, an honest haughtinesse, and self-esteem either of what I was, or what I might be, (which let envie call pride) and lastly that modesty, whereof though not in the Title page yet here I may be excus'd to make some beseeming profession, all these uniting the supply of their naturall aide together, kept me still above those low descents of minde, beneath which he must deject and plunge himself, that can agree to salable and unlawfull prostitutions. (*YP* 1:890).

The equivocation on "modesty" is significant. Earlier Milton had branded as disingenuous and self-contradictory his opponent's labeling his *Confutation* "modest" (*YP* 1:875–76). Now Milton claims modesty for himself, though with a clear hint of anxiety, noting that a profession of modesty is fitting in the body of a work if not in the title page. He attempts to make his own claim of modesty more acceptable by invoking a different sense, that of sexual purity, which does not necessarily clash with egotism. But pride erupts through the surface of the text anyway, though couched as the misconstruction of his motives by hostile observers ("which let envie call pride"). Milton treats the Confuter's claim of modesty as paradoxical evidence of pride. Milton's own immodest claims for his sexual modesty make him vulnerable to the same criticism, which emerges in displaced form in his own text.

Milton's implicit, unacknowledged, and incoherent claims of unfallenness unsettle the text. Images and ideas will not stay still; under the pressure of untenable claims they oscillate and reverse themselves. This is the case in the charged discussion of stained garments, which Milton introduces after his self-designation as "a member incorporate into that truth whereof I was perswaded": "I thought it my duty, if not to my selfe, yet to the religious cause I had in hand, not to leave on my garment the least spot, or blemish in good name so long as God should give me to say that which might wipe it off" (*YP* 1:871). While this blemish recalls the stain of original sin, it differs in two essentials: it is external and removable. But the comforting externality of the stain is less certain when the image reappears later in the text:

> With me it fares now, as with him whose outward garment hath bin injur'd and ill bedighted; for having no other shift,[27] what helpe but to turn the inside outwards, especially if the lining be of the same, or, as it is sometimes, much better. So if my name and outward demeanour be not evident anough to defend me, I must make tryall, if the discovery of my inmost thoughts can. (*YP* 1:888–89).

Milton's meaning is clear. If his public image has been muddied, he will reveal what lies within. Turning what was inside to the outside, he will reveal the unspotted lining of the soiled garment. But the play of inside and outside in the image is itself unstable. The lining, even if normally turned in, is part of a covering. In being turned out, it is now just what the outside of the garment had been, a public face that covers the speaker even as it purports to discover him. Once reversed, the garment more aptly resembles that state of affairs that a garment metaphor might be expected to signify: a spotted inside covered and disguised by "finer" appearance. Secreted in the heart of the very metaphor that Milton invokes to assert the identity between the self and the self as represented in his text is the trace of discontinuity.

In this passage Milton identifies "name and outward demeanour," contrasting both with "the discovery of my inmost thoughts." The *Apology* is repeatedly and, for an anonymous work, paradoxically occupied with the unnamed name of the author. The hostile portrait composed by the Confuter is a "false name . . . invented to wrong" Milton's argument; readers of the *Modest Confutation* have "reade that name, however of small repute, unworthily defam'd"; Milton has "gain'd a name bestuck, or as I may say, bedeckt with the reproaches and reviles of this modest Confuter" (*YP* 1:869, 870, 875). Although Milton says that he follows the Confuter's lead in remaining nameless, in a real sense, indeed in the sense he continually invokes, Milton is already "named" in the *Apology*. The name is the outward face, presented in the earlier works, defamed in the *Confutation,* and reasserted in the *Apology*. It belongs, in Milton's account, to the chaste, knowledgeable, and virtuous self everywhere apparent in the eloquent style of the good and learned man. Milton remarks that "The child doth not more expresly refigure the visage of his Father, then that book resembles the stile of the Remonstrant" (*YP* 1:906). One's style, like one's child, carries one's name. When Milton writes that the Confuter's book is "both namelesse, and full of slanders" (*YP* 1:878), he refers not only to the

---

27. A *shift* is both a strategy or expedient and an undergarment. Milton will appear, figuratively, naked before us.

relative accident of anonymous publication but also to his opponent's essential namelessness. By the figurative logic at work here, there can be no "mute inglorious Miltons." To have a name is to be virtuous, and to be virtuous is to be eloquent.[28]

The logic of self-representation in the *Apology* is continuous with that in the earlier works. While Milton draws virtue and eloquence into a tighter embrace here, he has been moving in that direction all along. Christopher Grose has argued for a departure in the *Apology*, as Milton drops the idea of being split between the willing poet and the grudging, event-driven prose writer. But his key exhibit, offered as signaling the *Apology*'s new direction, is the passage on "radical moisture" taken not from the *Apology*, as Grose mistakenly thinks, but from *The Reason of Church-Government*.[29] The left-handed prose writer is, as Grose suggests, a pose, not an unmediated facsimile of the prose writer. But the *Reason* tells us as much itself, as the rhetorical distinction is introduced by poetic figure (the right hand writing for the left). Already in the *Reason*, Milton presents himself as God's talented and willing spokesperson, the fire of whose prose belies his ostentatiously modest claims for that mode of writing. In the *Apology* as in the earlier works, Milton's language suggests an author standing back and considering himself as an object. But that suggestion is Milton's own, and the self that he purports to find is one that he is in the process of making.

In writing the text, Milton has conceived himself, given birth to himself, and given himself a name. Having a name even while anonymous is a mark of his integrity, virtue, and worth. The *Apology* argues for the continuity between a virtuous interior, a name, and a reliable self-representation. But, as we have seen, this continuity is unsettled by a discontinuity between an unmediated self and a constructed self, between the man and his textual self-representation, a discontinuity that is secreted in the unnamed seam of the garment that Milton invokes to assert the seamless continuity between inner and outer, between self and public self. It is unsettled, in addition, by the hyperbolic and, given his stated understanding of the fall, untenable claims for virtue in his self-representation. The incoherence of these claims will have dramatic effects on the arguments of the prose works of the 1640s.

---

28. Alexander More will turn this logic against Milton in his *Cry of the Royal Blood*, calling him "an unnameable buffoon, [who,] because he cannot acquire a name by virtue, seeks one by crime" (*YP* 4.2:1079).

29. Grose, *Milton and the Sense of Tradition*, 68–69; the misidentified passage from *The Reason of Church-Government* can be found in *YP* 1:841–42.

Chapter 5

"The Spur of Self-Concernment"

The Works on Domestic Liberty

Milton is nowhere more present than he is in his divorce tracts and *Areopagitica*. If they lack the extended autobiographical digressions of *An Apology for Smectymnuus*, *The Reason of Church-Government*, or the *Second Defence*, Milton liberally salts them with laudatory self-representations, as diligent prosecutor of the common good, as prophetic rescuer of God's word and law from monkish misconstruction, as heroic champion of unpopular positions. This chapter explores how Milton writes about himself in the prose works of 1643–45: the divorce tracts, *Of Education*, and *Areopagitica*. Carrying Milton's anxieties and wishes on or near the surface, these works are deeply interested texts. Though arguing on general principles and for the common good, Milton is drawn to adapt his arguments, whether consciously or not, to his own desires and anxieties. The result is significant distortion in the arguments: what is true for the general run of his compatriots might not be true for the virtuous and divinely selected prophet. At the same time, the personal events of the mid-1640s, the failed marriage and the withering response to the divorce tracts, were corrosive to Milton's sense of himself. The mid-1640s were volatile years for Milton, and the effects on his self-understanding and his art would be broad and deep.

The Divorce Tracts

Making a virtue of necessity, Milton acknowledges the role of what he calls in the second edition of the *Doctrine and Discipline of Divorce* "the spurre of self-concernment" (*YP* 2:226). He speaks more truly than perhaps he knew, for the divorce tracts are not merely inspired by personal experience, they are *about* Milton. The imperatives of self-conception and self-representation help to form and ultimately to distort the argument for divorce. The manner in which self-representation drives and then deforms Milton's argument betrays itself in differences between the *Doctrine and Discipline* and *Tetrachordon,* two works that have much in common but whose crucial differences have been glossed over by critics.

The story of Milton's ill-starred first marriage is familiar. In the late spring of 1642, the thirty-three-year-old Milton marries Mary Powell, whom he meets while collecting a debt. A month or two later, she leaves him. The experience contributes to his decision to compose several works advocating divorce for incompatibility, a topic that interested him before his marriage. In both the *Doctrine and Discipline of Divorce* and *Tetrachordon,* Milton argues that divorce was not prohibited by the Gospels, and that the Mosaic law permitting divorce continues to be necessary given the blameless incompatibilities and the infirmities resulting from the fall.

If there is some mystery about the specifics of Milton's courtship and marriage (why did he marry a woman he had known for so short a time, particularly one from a Royalist family? why exactly did Mary Powell leave him? was the marriage consummated before her departure?), there is no doubt that the experience challenged the self-image he had nurtured in the anti-prelatical tracts. For one used to thinking of himself as untouched by frailty and as uniquely virtuous, the experience of arguing for (and in all probability desiring) a remedy that seemed to be expressly prohibited by Christ must have been disorienting. How could a person of virtue and discernment make a catastrophically mistaken marriage choice? How could he now require a remedy suited not to strength but to weakness? Arthur Barker argues that Milton's "self-esteem had suffered a blow of the utmost severity, and he had been forced to recognize his own humanity."[1] This surprised recognition of shared humanity, according to Barker, leads to a revision in the perfectionist thinking that marked the anti-prelatical tracts:

> He has come to recognize that the reformation cannot be sudden; more than that, he has had proof of his own infirmity and imperfection. So far is he from discounting the significance of the Fall that, here at least, the idealist gives place to the realist. The divorce problem and its attendant difficulties not only lead him to remark on the impossibility of Atlantic and Utopian polities, but to justify liberty in terms of fallen nature.[2]

---

1. Barker, *Milton and the Puritan Dilemma, 1641–1660* (Toronto: University of Toronto Press, 1942), p. 66; any discussion of Milton's self-understanding in the works of the mid-1640s is indebted to this work.
2. Ibid., p. 115.

Barker is right to a point—Milton does confront the possibility of his imperfection. Justification comes at the expense of implicating himself in the general weakness of fallen humankind, something he had assiduously avoided in his earlier self-representations. Self-justification and the argument for divorce drive Milton toward inclusion in what he calls the "common lump" of men (*YP* 2:253). As Milton excuses his mistake and acquits himself of sin by reinterpreting Christ's apparent prohibition of divorce in light of the shared weakness of fallen creatures, the problem for the maintenance of his self-understanding is patent. But Milton repudiates the move that Barker describes even as he makes it. Milton's implicit acknowledgment of his own fallen nature triggers a tortuous set of logical moves that ends in the restoration of something like his earlier self-conception.

The result is a succession of self-representations in the divorce tracts, as Milton claims heroic status, obscurely contemplates the possibility of alienation from God, justifies himself by the argument of shared imperfection, and then recoils from inclusion in general infirmity with implicit and ultimately incoherent gestures toward unfallen status. In suggesting that Milton comes to terms with infirmity and imperfection, and makes an accommodation with fallen nature, Barker tells only half the story, eliding, as we shall see, a significant difference between the *Doctrine and Discipline* and *Tetrachordon*. Ernest Sirluck picks up this partial story when he argues that the painful experience of a failed marriage explains why Milton wrote so little poetry in the 1640s. If Milton derived his inspired status from heroic virtue and special election by God, evidence of imperfection shared with others could undermine that status: "Milton's concept of his role as poet developed in such a way as to make the failure of his marriage a direct blow to his poetic inspiration (or, what amounts to the same thing, to his faith in it)."[3] Although Barker and Sirluck recognize ways in which *Tetrachordon* goes beyond or departs from the *Doctrine and Discipline* in argument, they treat the works interchangeably as evidence of Milton's self-conception.[4] Much of the drama of these extraordinary works lies in the progression and variations of Milton's self-representations. The central argument of the divorce tracts exerts real

---

3. Ernest Sirluck, "Milton's Idle Right Hand," *Journal of English and Germanic Philology* 60 (1961): 754.
4. As does Reuben Sánchez, Jr., despite the fact that he writes mainly about *Tetrachordon* (see *Persona and Decorum in Milton's Prose* [Madison, NJ: Fairleigh Dickinson University Press, 1997], pp. 94–96). Much published criticism of the divorce tracts, including my own essay "The Metaphysics of Milton's Divorce Tracts" (in *Politics, Poetics, and Hermeneutics in Milton's Prose*, ed. David Loewenstein and James Grantham Turner [Cambridge: Cambridge University Press, 1990], pp. 69–83), has treated the two works as interchangeable. Lana Cable, for example, subtitles her cogent chapter on the *Doctrine and Discipline* "The Coupling Rhetoric of the Divorce Tracts," despite devoting only a passing reference each to *Tetrachordon* and *Colasterion* (see *Carnal Rhetoric: Milton's Iconoclasm and the Poetics of Desire* [Durham, NC: Duke University Press, 1995], pp. 90–116).

pressure on Milton's familiar self-representation, and in turn the imperatives of self-conception and self-representation, Milton's need to see and present himself as outstanding, exert a very real counterpressure on the argument. Ultimately the counterpressure distorts the argument.

The Doctrine and Discipline of Divorce: *Despair/Dispair/Repair*

The splintering of self-representation that marks the rest of Milton's career begins in the first divorce tract. Milton represents himself as a prophetic restorer of divine mercy, but in a conflicting self-representation he obscurely contemplates the possibility of alienation from God.

In one of the more remarkable self-representations in the first edition, Milton implies that recorded history does not contain a contribution to human good comparable to his own: "he that can but lend us the clue that windes out this labyrinth of servitude to such a reasonable and expedient liberty as this, deserves to be reck'n'd among the publick benefactors of civill and humane life; above the inventors of wine and oyle" (*YP* 2:240). The reading public instead attacked Milton as a promoter of heresy and license.[5] The anonymous author of *An Answer to a Book, Intituled, The Doctrine and Discipline of Divorce* charges that Milton's argument "smels very strongly of little lesse than blasphemie against Christ himself."[6] In a greatly expanded second edition, Milton reacted vigorously to the hostility and ridicule elicited by the first. He assails those of "a waterish and queasy conscience" who "rail and fancy to themselves, that injury and licence is the best of this Book," calling them "the brood of Belial, the draffe of men, to whom no liberty is pleasing" (*YP* 2:225–26).

The self-representation as godly hero is more pronounced in the second edition, as Milton reacts to the abuse that greeted the first. Milton associates himself with heroes of the epic/romance and the biblical traditions.[7] The tract opens, like *The Faerie Queene,* with the defeat of the dragon Error, with Milton replacing Redcrosse Knight as dragon-slayer and romance hero. Milton closes the heroic frame near the end of the second edition, proudly claiming

---

5. See William Riley Parker, *Milton's Contemporary Reputation* (1940; repr. New York: Haskell House, 1971). Parker provides excerpts from contemporary attacks on Milton's divorce tracts.

6. *An Answer* (London, 1640), p. 28. Parker reproduces this entire work in facsimile in *Milton's Contemporary Reputation,* pp. 170–216. One wonders which rankled more, the Answerer's attack on Milton as theologian ("this is a wilde, mad, and frantick divinitie, just like to the opinions of the Maids at Aldgate" [p. 36]) or his dismissal of Milton as stylist ("This frothie discourse . . . sugred over with a little neat language" [p. 41]).

7. For a view of the narrator in the *Doctrine and Discipline* as medieval romance hero, see Charles Hatten, "The Politics of Marital Reform and the Rationalization of Romance in *The Doctrine and Discipline of Divorce,*" *Milton Studies* 27 (1991): 95–113. Hatten's discussion of the historical and sociopolitical context of the tract's insistence on the subordination of women is perceptive; his discussion of the text as representative of elite Puritan cooptation and containment of the radical sects is less persuasive.

the "purity and wisdom" of God's divorcive law as "buckler" and mournfully boasting that it is "a labour of no mean difficulty and envy to defend" the law (*YP* 2:351). The implicit comparison with Hercules here looks forward to an explicit comparison in *Colasterion* for his labor of answering the voluminous but sordid arguments of the Answerer: "Yet *Hercules* had the labour once impos'd upon him to carry dung out of the *Augean* stable" (*YP* 2:756). In his last substantial addition to the first edition he ranges himself alongside God and Moses; criticism of his argument "lights not upon this book, but upon that which I engage against them, the book of God, and of *Moses*" (*YP* 2:354).

Claiming roles borrowed from the heroes of classical myth and the "sage and serious Spenser," Milton seems immune to weakness and doubt. But countercurrents of anxiety and doubt, perhaps stronger for their being unconscious, emerge particularly at moments of most heroic self-representation. Even the opening Spenserian allegory of Error and Custom, with Milton as Redcrosse Knight, is subject to counterpressures. The allegory opens with a surprising analogy between Custom's book of knowledge and the prophetic scroll in Ezekiel: "her [Custom's] method is so glib and easie, in some manner like to that vision of *Ezekiel,* rowling up her sudden book of implicit knowledge, for him that will, to take and swallow down at pleasure; which proving but of bad nourishment in the concoction, as it was heedlesse in the devouring, puffs up unhealthily, a certaine big face of pretended learning" (*YP* 2:222–23). Milton's opponents swallow Custom's empty confections, but their swallowing is compared with Ezekiel's swallowing of the scroll. Expected roles are reversed, feeding the uncertainty and dis-ease echoed in the murky syntax.[8] Another surprise awaits us at the end of the allegory. In *The Faerie Queene* Error is a grotesquely fecund mother; in the *Doctrine and Discipline* Truth is the mother: "Error and Custome . . . with the numerous and vulgar train of their followers, make it their chiefe designe to envie and cry-down the industry of free reasoning, under the terms of humor, and innovation; as if the womb of teeming Truth were to be clos'd up, if shee presume to bring forth ought, that sorts not with their unchew'd notions and suppositions" (*YP* 2:224). Milton as mother/father of teeming truth (the gender confusion surrounding the metaphor of birth is so common as to be a signature of Milton's) is uncomfortably close to Error the mother of her swarming and devouring litter.[9] Having placed

---

8. I note the paradoxical relation of this passage to the passage in *The Reason of Church-Government* in which Milton compares himself to the evangelist John eating the book of Revelation (Rev. 10:9–10) in "Intention and Its Limits in *Paradise Lost*," in *Literary Milton*, ed. Diana Treviño Benet and Michael Lieb (Pittsburgh: Duquesne University Press, 1994), pp. 168–69.

9. On the metaphor of birth and Milton's appropriation of both gender roles, see chap. 5, "The Art of Generation," in John Rumrich's *Milton Unbound* (Cambridge: Cambridge University Press, 1996).

himself metaphorically as mother and father, Milton in the next breath positions himself as the paradoxically unique culmination of a teeming brood: "now the duty and the right of an instructed Christian cals me through the chance of good or evill report, to be the sole advocate of a discount'nanc't truth: a high enterprise Lords and Commons, a high enterprise and a hard, and such as every seventh Son of a seventh Son does not venture on" (*YP* 2:224). Out of miraculous and prodigious fertility comes not the promiscuous spawn of Error, but the unprecedented and unparalleled chosen son.[10]

The anxiety finds more direct expression. Already forming in the first edition and fully developed in the second is a pattern that will mark the rest of Milton's works. Veering between antithetical extremes, he will claim heroic stature, grounded in a virtue improbable in fallen creatures, even as he contemplates behind veils the possibility of mortal error. Annabel Patterson has deciphered the working of encoded autobiographical micronarratives in the *Doctrine and Discipline,* which allow Milton to ponder obscurely that which he cannot or will not confront openly, the possibility of guilt and failure.[11] We recognize Milton in the third-person description of those "soberest and best govern'd men" who, because they "have spent their youth chastly" and "are lest practiz'd in these affairs," are liable to innocent error in choice of a marriage partner (*YP* 2:249). When this happens, the natural burning for companionship is frustrated, giving rise to an innocent hate, "not that Hate that sins" (*YP* 2:253). The paradox suggests that the blamelessness of Milton's veiled self-representation is sustained tenuously at best. He proceeds nonetheless, suggesting that this natural hate, like the natural loneliness that gives rise to it, "hath not the least grain of a sin in it, *if he be worthy to understand himself*" (*YP* 2:253; my emphasis). However much Milton attempts to assert this other self's blameless purity, by the next page he/it teeters at the edge of a chasm:

> though he be almost the strongest Christian, he will be ready to *dispair* in vertue, and mutin against divine providence: and this doubtles is the reason of those lapses and that melancholy despair which we see in many wedded persons, *though they understand it not,* . . . and is of extreme danger; therefore when human frailty surcharg'd, is at such a

---

10. In the Bible the parenting of seven sons appears to be a token of rare good fortune (see Ruth 4:15, where Ruth is more precious than seven sons, and Job 1:2, where having seven sons is the first and highest sign of Job's wealth and good fortune). Admittedly, being one of the seven does not guarantee special favor or sanctity, as witness Acts 19:14, where an evil spirit rebukes the seven sons of a priest for their attempt at exorcism. I am not aware of any passage in the Bible in which the rarity of seven sons is squared to the seventh son of a seventh son.

11. Patterson, "No Meer Amatorious Novel," in *Politics, Poetics, and Hermeneutics in Milton's Prose,* ed. David Loewenstein and James Grantham Turner (Cambridge: Cambridge University Press, 1990), pp. 88–95.

losse, charity ought to venture much, and use bold physick, lest an over-tost faith endanger to shipwrack. (*YP* 2:254; my emphasis)

Both passages raise the question of self-understanding; significantly, the positive statement is conditional ("if he be worthy to understand himself"). Self-understanding and the self-representation built on that understanding are crucially important to Milton; the displaced uncertainty glimpsed here threatens his authority as a writer and his sense of himself. The struggle for equilibrium marking the tract is played out here in small compass. I am the strongest Christian, Milton seems to say, and I am ready to divorce virtuously, or to "dis-pair in vertue"; though the strongest Christian, owing to an intolerable law I am in danger of despair, loss of faith, and mutiny against God.[12] What is missing is the third term: I am a reasonably virtuous and conscientious Christian, struggling to understand and follow God's will.

As was evident in the allegory of Custom and Error, anxiety emerges especially in moments when Milton is being self-assertive, as in a passage recalling the *Apology*'s declarations of heroic virtue and spotless probity:

> hee who shall indeavour the amendment of any old neglected grievance in Church or State, or in the daily course of life, if he be gifted with abilities of mind that may raise him to so high an undertaking, I grant he hath already much whereof not to repent him; yet let me arreed him, not to be the foreman of any mis-judgd opinion, unlesse his resolutions be firmly seated in a square and constant mind, not conscious to it self of any deserved blame, and regardles of ungrounded suspicions. (*YP* 2:224)

Milton again distances himself from any spot or blame, and derives his authority from his purity. Examinations of conscience yield assurance rather than conviction. But, as things now are, of how many actions can it be said, as Milton said of the natural hatred of ill-yoked spouses (his own experience, as is palpable in the tract), that it "hath not the least grain of a sin in it" (*YP* 2:253)? The psychological and theological pressures attending a claim of freedom from "any deserved blame" are substantial.

The resulting pressures inevitably betray themselves. The other self who would amend old grievances is one who will be the "foreman of any mis-judgd opinion." While Milton clearly means that one's true opinion may be

---

12. The punning spelling *dispair* in this passage is not unique, but it is unusual, with variants employed once in *The Reason of Church-Government* and one other time in the *Doctrine and Discipline* (*YP* 1:847 and 2:339). Variants beginning *des*, on the other hand, appear thirteen times in Milton's prose published before his blindness. For additional gestures toward despair, see *YP* 2:259–60, 273, 275.

misjudged as false, the syntax invites a reading of misjudgment on the part of the "foreman." What if the tract's rereading of Christ's apparent proscription of divorce in Matthew 19 and its opposition to a settled majority opinion is the result of improper judgment? What if the same faulty judgment errs in failing to recognize "deserved blame"? When Milton offers one of his typical, and typically nervous, knotted negatives, "he hath already much whereof not to repent him," the cumbersome construction evokes precisely what Milton means to exorcize, the taint of guilt.

Given that Milton's unhappy marital situation made him an interested participant in the controversy, the traces of anxiety are not surprising. In one of the most revealing moments of the tract, Milton wrestles with the demon of "self-concernment," running the phrase through hoops to make it work for rather than against him, deflecting it from self-servingness toward disinterested service to God and country. His critics blaspheme in their arguments against divorce, reproaching God

> whom they doe not deny to have belawgiv'n his owne sacred people with this very allowance, which they now call injury and licence, and dare cry shame on, and will doe yet a while, till they get a little cordiall sobriety to settle their qualming zeale. *But this question concerns not us perhaps:* Indeed mans disposition though prone to search after vain curiosities, yet when points of difficulty are to be discusst, appertaining to the removall of unreasonable wrong and burden from the perplext life of our brother, it is incredible how cold, how dull, and farre from all fellow feeling we are, without *the spurre of self-concernment.* Yet if the wisdome, the justice, the purity of God be to be cleer'd from foulest imputations which are not yet avoided, if charity be not to be degraded and trodd'n down under a civil Ordinance, if Matrimony be not to be advanc't like that exalted perdition, writt'n of to the *Thessalonians, above all that is called God* [Milton's emphasis], or goodnesse, nay, against them both, then I dare affirm there will be found in the Contents of this Booke, that which *may concern us all. You it concerns chiefly,* Worthies in Parliament, on whom, as on our deliverers, all our grievances and cares, by the merit of your eminence and fortitude are devolv'd: *Me it concerns next,* having with much labour and faithfull diligence first found out, or at least with a fearlesse and communicative candor first publisht to the manifest good of Christendome, that which calling to witnesse every thing mortall and immortall, I beleeve unfainedly to be true. Let not other men thinke their conscience bound to search continually after truth, to pray for enlightning from above, to publish what they think they have so obtain'd, & debarr me from conceiving my self ty'd by the same duties. (*YP* 2:226; my emphasis)

In the middle we hear the unmistakable cry of outraged suffering: those not spurred by self-concernment are blind and deaf to the burden and perplexity caused by the prohibition of divorce. But in short order self-concernment is transmuted into disinterested service. His attackers are actually God's attackers, and they need "a little cordiall sobriety to settle their qualming zeale." How they will reach this sobriety is not specified; instead Milton adds, "this question concerns not us perhaps." But after the intervening admission of self-concernment, it turns out that punishing the scoffers will in fact concern Milton, not as one suffering burden and perplexity but as one selflessly fighting God's (and Parliament's) battles. Milton moves quickly from the hint that God's action will repay the scoffers to the conclusion that Milton will repay them. Along the way, the notion of self-concernment is transformed; if it is the concern of everyone that God's justice be vindicated, it is the special concern of Parliament, the guardians of the nation, and of Milton, the searcher after truth. Milton is self-concerned now not as a suffering husband but as a godly interpreter facing ignorant opposition and calumny.

In arguing for a relaxation of divorce laws, then, Milton not only claims his birthright as a son of God, he engages in theodicy. He does so from above and from below. Milton speaks as if alongside God and above the frailties of human beings, as if untouched by human misery (except as a compassionate observer) and as if free from sin. Unconscious of any blame, shoulder to shoulder with God and Moses, Milton is a superhuman benefactor. At the same time, Milton speaks from below, out of painful, fallen experience. He demonstrates that divine law concerning marriage and divorce is properly adapted to the weakness of fallen human beings, to those who are not "heroically vertuous" but belong to "the common lump of men" (*YP* 2:253). If it were not so adapted, a person of good will saddled with the blameless hatred that is not sin would be led to despair, the sin against the Holy Spirit: "the whole worship of a Christian mans life should languish and fade away beneath the weight of an immeasurable grief and discouragement" until he (as opposed to she) is driven "at last through murmuring and despair to thoughts of Atheism" (*YP* 2:259–60). Even if a bad marriage does not damn him, it can kill him: "they ofttimes resent one anothers mistake so deeply, that long it is not ere grief end one of them" (*YP* 2:273). The third-person portrait that culminates in this language of despair is at the outset indistinguishable from Milton himself. This language of despair, heavy with the weight of anguished experience, contributes to a self-construction more disguised but no less authentic than the more familiar heroic one.

The tension between the explicit self-representation as heroically virtuous, divinely chosen, and untouched by fallen frailty and the implicit self-representation as potentially alienated from God is highlighted by the fact that the argument of the *Doctrine and Discipline* invokes the distinction between what is appropriate before and after the fall.[13] The fall ushered in not only sin but also sinless imperfection, the human equivalent of natural as opposed to moral evil. Nature and natures change with the fall; from that date planets meet in "synod unbenign" and sinless animals make mutual war (*PL* 10.661,710). Analogously, sinless people cannot live together in harmony if their natural tempers clash. A theory of natural, sinless antipathy serves Milton's psychological purposes; he would not be eager to assign his need for divorce to his sin. Repeatedly in this text Milton argues that natural incompatibility is free of sin.[14] Considering his own case as he explores the biblical warrant for divorce as accommodation to the fallen, Milton redefines the fall to allow for weakened but sinless individuals.

But the admission of imperfection, even morally blameless imperfection, entailed in the argument runs counter to Milton's former practice and his deep inclination. He argues that blameless thralldom in an unfit marriage can lead to neglect of duty toward God, "if there be not a miracle of vertue on either side" (*YP* 2:260). But Milton has consistently represented himself as miraculously virtuous, as uniquely worthy of blessing. In a revealing moment, Milton argues that divorce is necessary for the man (such as himself) who finds himself in an unhappy marriage, "unlesse he be a thing heroically vertuous, and that are not the common lump of men for whom chiefly Laws ought to be made, though not to their sins, yet to their unsinning weaknesses" (*YP* 2:253–54). Within ten lines of implicitly associating himself with the "common lump of men," Milton externalizes and neutralizes this admission by describing the wife as "an image of earth and fleam [i.e., phlegm]" (*YP* 2:254). His self-representations as imperfect are unstable, in part because Milton cannot for long think of himself as common and in part because he has difficulty keeping culpable and nonculpable imperfection separate.[15]

The difficulty of keeping morally neutral and morally suspect weaknesses separate is evident in the opening lines of the *Doctrine and Discipline*. The second edition begins with the fall: "whether it be the secret of divine will, or the originall blindnesse we are born in, so it happ'ns for the most part, that Custome still is silently receiv'd for the best instructer." The result is "counterfeit knowledge" that "depress[es] the high and Heaven-born spirit of Man, farre beneath the condition wherein either God created him, or sin hath sunke him" (*YP* 2:222–23). Is the following of custom natural, as inevitable as bad weather,

---

13. For the relation of prelapsarian to postlapsarian states in the divorce tracts, see James Grantham Turner's *One Flesh: Paradisal Marriage and Sexual Relations in the Age of Milton* (Oxford: Clarendon, 1987), chap. 6.

14. See *YP* 2:235–37, 249, 253, 260, 272, 328, 342, 345, 346, 355.

15. Compare Samson's dismissal of Dalila's appeal to her weakness, "All wickedness is weakness" (*SA* 834). While Milton wants to argue in the *Doctrine and Discipline* that this formula is not reversible, he seems to be unable to avoid reversing it.

or is it morally culpable? It seems to be a general failing, but it turns out that some are exempt.[16] In refusing the easy teaching of custom, Milton implies that he is, in that respect at least, not subject as are others to "the originall blindnesse we are born in," to say nothing of the "condition wherein . . . sin hath sunke" man. Milton's rhetoric holds out the possibility not only of resisting the teaching of custom, but in doing so of not sinking below the created condition. Milton seems to exempt himself not merely from moral weakness but from the blameless imperfection attendant on the fall. If there are inconveniences in the postlapsarian state (north winds, dropsies, blindness, susceptibility to custom, inability to predict natural incompatibility?), some few seem to be untouched even by blameless weakness.

The acknowledgment of imperfection that Barker identified in the *Doctrine and Discipline* triggers a volatile, double reaction. Unable or unwilling to maintain the distinction of culpable and blameless weakness on which his own argument depends, Milton contemplates despair and alienation, a typical Puritan experience most familiar to us perhaps in Bunyan. And immediately, in a counterreaction, Milton reasserts his freedom from all varieties of imperfection, and thus implicitly dissociates himself from the fall.[17] This claim must remain implicit, to Milton as well as to the reader, for it is incompatible with his Augustinian belief in the universality of the fall. This unacknowledgeable claim nevertheless betrays itself as Milton introduces a line of argument placing the injured husband in a position that precisely foreshadows the unfallen Adam's in *Paradise Lost*.[18] In the epic, after the fallen Eve has decided that, if she must die, she will take Adam with her, Adam throws in his lot with his spouse:

> Some cursèd fraud
> Of Enemy hath beguiled thee, yet unknown,

---

16. The psychological and rhetorical situation requires that Milton not be alone in exemption from what otherwise appears the universal lot of fallen humanity. If the many are deluded by Custom and the empty shows of human authority, he will depend on the wise and knowing few, an increasingly familiar audience: "the wise and right understanding handfull of men" and "the choisest and the learnedest, who have this high gift of wisdom to answer solidly, or to be convinc't" (*YP* 2:232, 233). Milton's heroic task is to bring truth to a world from which it has fled, and the likelihood of a hostile reception is a measure of his singularity and his courage.

17. In a private communication, Jason Rosenblatt suggests that the *Doctrine and Discipline*'s Hebraic teaching that "the law incarnates deity" might help to account for Milton's implicit pretensions to unfallenness, inasmuch as a "corollary of the Hebraic emphasis on law would be an absence of reference to original sin." For a penetrating discussion of the Law and Gospel in the divorce tracts, see Rosenblatt's *Torah and Law in "Paradise Lost"* (Princeton: Princeton University Press, 1994).

18. On the relevance of the divorce tracts to the situation of Adam after Eve's fall, see Rosenblatt, *Torah and Law*, pp. 196–203; as Rosenblatt observes, "Adam speaks to Eve fatalistically, 'Submitting to what seem'd remediless' (*PL* 9, 919), and all four tracts offer divorce as the remedy of a sick marriage" (196). On the *Doctrine and Discipline* as prophetic of *Paradise Lost*, see Barker, *Milton and the Puritan Dilemma*, p. 98.

> And me with thee hath ruined, for with thee
> Certain my resolution is to die;
> How can I live without thee, how forgo
> Thy sweet converse and love so dearly joined,
> To live again in these wild woods forlorn?
> (*PL* 9.904–10)

While Adam does not consider divorce, the *Doctrine and Discipline* offers one of the only ways (if not the only way) for him to avoid falling, in its proposing divorce when one's spouse conspires against one's life, whether physical or spiritual. This reason for separation is recognized even in canon law, otherwise so cold to the plight of the unhappily married:

> The Canon Law and Divines consent, that if either party be found contriving against the others life, they may be sever'd by divorce; for a sin against the life of mariage is greater then a sin against the bed: the one destroys, the other but defiles it. The same may be said touching those persons who beeing of a pensive nature and cours of life, have summ'd up all their solace in that free and lightsom conversation which God & man intends in mariage: wherof when they see themselves depriv'd by meeting an unsociable consort, they ofttimes resent one anothers mistake so deeply, that long it is not ere grief end one of them. When therfore this danger is foreseen that the life is in perill by living together, what matter is it whether helples greef, or wilfull practice be the cause? This is certain that the preservation of life is more worth then the compulsory keeping of mariage. (*YP* 2:273–74)

In *Paradise Lost* we find both "helples greef" and "wilfull practice," the former proleptically in Adam's fear of being deprived of "sweet Converse" ("lightsom conversation") and the latter in Eve's fallen design ("Confirm'd then I resolve; / *Adam* shall share with me in bliss or woe" [9.830–31]). Curiously, the disappointed (as opposed to the warring) spouses in the *Doctrine and Discipline* "resent one anothers mistake" rather than their own; even in this moment of apparent mutuality, fingers are pointed. In the interval between Eve's fall and Adam's, Adam could legitimately absolve himself and resent Eve for her mistake; he chose a spouse wisely, but she is no longer what she was. The discursive gap between mutual blamelessness and the guilt of the woman, which will widen in *Tetrachordon,* is mediated by the example of Adam and Eve, never far from the surface in texts built on the tension between prelapsarian and postlapsarian marriage. In his increasing emphasis on the innocence of the man facing a guilty, idolatrous, and dangerous woman, Milton returns to a moment when a recuperation of the original fall of man can be enacted.[19]

Tetrachordon: *"temtation eevn in the faultles person"*

The *Doctrine and Discipline* reveals that Milton's experience of marriage caused him to recognize and acknowledge his imperfection. His swift and paradoxical reaction to this recognition, in the form of implicit gestures toward unfallenness, is already present in the *Doctrine and Discipline,* particularly in the second edition, but it dominates the self-representations of *Tetrachordon*. In the *Doctrine and Discipline* Milton emphasizes natural incompatibility and a kind of "no fault divorce" for unfortunate couples who cannot love one another. But in *Tetrachordon,* despite a new reading of Matthew 19 that should promote the language of mutual blamelessness, Milton exchanges that language for another, bewailing the plight of the innocent party shackled to a faithless or sinning partner. The veiled self-representations of a man in despair are replaced by equally veiled self-representations of one who has escaped or undone the fall.

Tetrachordon, like the 1644 *Doctrine and Discipline,* begins with a heroic self-representation. Thanking Parliament for refusing to censure or censor him, Milton hints at the value of his gratitude: "such thanks perhaps they may live to be, as shall more then whisper to the next ages" (*YP* 2:579).[20] If he is no less confident than he was in first setting out his arguments in 1643, he is now embittered by what he views as ignorant attacks on the *Doctrine and Discipline*. He invokes two heroic predecessors.[21] He compares himself to Socrates, who was accused of making the worse appear the better

---

19. The situation in the *Doctrine and Discipline* foreshadows *Samson Agonistes* as well, but with a difference. Samson reacts to Dalila by divorcing the woman he sees as a mortal threat. On the other hand, he neither is nor sees himself as blameless. When Dalila appeals to common weakness, he replies: "I gave, thou say'st, th' example, / I led the way; bitter reproach, but true, / I to myself was false ere thou to me: / Such pardon therefore as I give my folly, / Take to thy wicked deed" (*SA* 822–26).

20. Milton echoes the pledge in *The Reason of Church-Government* to "leave something so written to aftertimes, as they should not willingly let it die" (*YP* 1:810), and he anticipates the pose adopted a decade later in the *Defensio Secunda,* when he represents himself as a worthy singer of heroic deeds and by extension a hero himself (*YP* 4.1:553–55).

21. Between the *Doctrine and Discipline* and *Tetrachordon,* Milton invokes a more recent predecessor, a Reformation hero who had anticipated his divorce argument. In his signed address "To the Parliament" prefaced to the *Judgement of Martin Bucer,* Milton is caught on the horns of a dilemma, claiming on the one hand originality and on the other the authorizing precedent of Bucer. He recounts the story of finding Bucer's similar arguments only after he had published the *Doctrine and Discipline,* and concludes, "I may justly gratulat mine own mind, with due acknowledgement of assistance from above, which led me, not as a lerner, but as a collateral teacher, to a sympathy of judgment with no lesse a man then *Martin Bucer*" (*YP* 2:435–36).

reason (*YP* 2:583), and he assumes a role later claimed by his Samson: "if men want manlinesse to expostulate the right of their due ransom, and to second their own occasions, they may sit hereafter and bemoan themselves to have neglected through faintnesse the onely remedy of their sufferings, which a seasonable and well grounded speaking might have purchas'd them" (*YP* 2:585).[22] Having experienced the treachery of those he has sought to help, Milton characteristically invokes classical and biblical predecessors.

An argument new to *Tetrachordon* has implications for Milton's self-construction. Milton revisits Christ's answer to the Pharisees, "Moses because of the hardness of your hearts suffered you to put away your wives: but from the beginning it was not so" (Matt. 19:8). Earlier Milton, taking hard-heartedness as characterizing a subset of the Jews, argued that God allowed divorce for the relief of the conscientious despite knowing that the hard-hearted—such as the questioning Pharisees—would abuse the law by divorcing for trivial reasons. Now finding in hard-heartedness two senses, the conscious sinfulness of the few invoked earlier ("a stubborne resolution to doe evil" [*YP* 2:662]) and the imperfection or weakness among even the good after the fall ("infirmity, and imperfection, which was in all the Apostles" [*YP* 2:661]), Milton assigns the innocuous meaning to Matthew 19:8. In doing so, he salvages for virtuous Christians the Mosaic permission of divorce as glossed by Christ, without having to evoke a complex and ironic interpretive setting. This reinterpretation, that is, has the virtue of allowing Milton to read Matthew 19:8 as spoken directly to all, and not obliquely as a coded teaching for the Pharisees.[23] The new definition of hard-heartedness and re-reading of the verse nevertheless dovetails with the argument in the *Doctrine and Discipline* that, had we remained in paradise, we would not need permission to divorce, for in the perfect state we would be perfect mates for each other. All are weakened at the fall, and all are subject to blameless error in marriage choices. But if the overarching argument remains the same, Milton now has Christ speaking directly in its support.

---

22. See *Samson Agonistes* 1211–16:

    I was no private but a person raised
    With strength sufficient and command from Heav'n
    To free my country; if their servile minds
    Me their Deliverer sent would not receive,
    But to their masters gave me up for naught,
    Th'unworthier they; whence to this day they serve.

23. This paragraph follows Ernest Sirluck's introduction to the divorce tracts, *YP* 2:153–58. Sirluck notes a second major change in the later tract: a far-reaching discussion of the primary and secondary laws of nature, with the secondary law fitted to our fallen condition and providing a basis for the law of nations.

The newly interpreted sense of Christ on "hardness of heart" seems to promise a firmer foundation for the argument for no-fault divorce advanced in the *Doctrine and Discipline*. It is curious, then, that this argument all but disappears from *Tetrachordon*. The generous recognition that both parties might be blameless for the failure of a marriage, that incompatibility can be traceable to immutable and involuntary differences in temperament, is frequent in the *Doctrine and Discipline*. Milton writes, for example, that "ofttimes the causes of seeking divorce reside . . . deeply in the radical and innocent affections of nature" or in "the guiltles instinct of nature" (*YP* 2:345, 346). Some marriages fail through no one's fault but because of "natures unalterable working" (*YP* 2:249).[24] These gestures toward mutual blamelessness, despite the new and innocent meaning of "hardness of heart," disappear from *Tetrachordon*. In the first description of a failed marriage in *Tetrachordon* there is no question of a blameless, natural, and mutual antipathy:

> seeing woman was purposely made for man, and he her head, it cannot stand before the breath of this divine utterance, that man the portraiture of God, joyning to himself for his intended good and solace an inferiour sexe, should so becom her thrall, whose wilfulnes or inability to be a wife frustrates the occasionall end of her creation, but that he may acquitt himself to freedom by his naturall birthright, and that indeleble character of priority which God crown'd him with. If it be urg'd that sin hath lost him this, the answer is not far to seek, that from her the sin first proceeded, which keeps her justly in the same proportion still beneath. She is not to gain by being first in the transgression, that man should furder loose to her, because already he hath lost by her means. (*YP* 2:589–90)[25]

There is a trace of blamelessness in the "inability to be a wife," but the remainder of the passage tips the scales toward the other alternative, the wife's "wilfulness." Carried away as he imagines objections to his argument, Milton invokes Eve's transgression and imagines that women's aim is to enthrall husbands and "to gain by being first in the transgression."

This passage sets the tone for the rest of the work. Where in the *Doctrine and Discipline* Milton suggests that contrariety of natural tempers lies behind the failure of at least some marriages, in *Tetrachordon* the cause again and again comes down to the wife's willfulness and hostility.[26] Men look for

---

24. For additional passages in which Milton argues for no-fault divorce based on immutable differences in temperament, see note 14 above.

25. In an illustration of the psychological complexity of the divorce tracts, a moment earlier Milton had acknowledged that the woman should rule the husband "if she exceed her husband in prudence and dexterity."

26. Previous commentators have not seen the difference between the tracts that I discuss here. Barker, for example, curiously elides the distinction between culpable hostility and blameless

helpmeets when they take wives, he argues, but if wives are "neither fit helps, nor tolerable society, what thing more natural, more original and first in nature then to depart from that which is irksom, greevous, *actively hateful*, and *injurious eevn to hostility*, especially in a conjugal respect, wherin antipathies are invincible, and wher the forc't abiding of the one, can bee no true good, no real comfort to the other" (*YP* 2:621–22; my emphasis). This passage, like the one examined a moment ago, looks in two directions. Hatefulness and hostile injuriousness point toward willfulness; such wives are active in their opposition to their husbands. Invincible antipathies, on the other hand, recall the blameless natural tempers invoked repeatedly in the *Doctrine and Discipline*. But now Milton treats invincible antipathies as interchangeable with hatefulness and injury. In the following sentences, Milton seems to return to natural and blameless dislike, only to conclude with a distinction between guiltless and guilty: "For if hee find no contentment from the other, how can he return it from himself, or no acceptance, how can hee mutually accept? what more equal, more pious then to untie a civil knot for a natural enmity held by violence from parting, to dissolv an accidental conjunction of this or that man & woman, for the most natural and most necessary disagreement of meet from unmeet, guilty from guiltles, contrary from contrary?" Milton discusses invincible antipathy in both works; the difference is that in the *Doctrine and Discipline* these discussions are accompanied by reminders that they can arise from what he calls "the faultles proprieties of nature" (*YP* 2:237), while in the later work they are accompanied by reminders of the woman's guilt and the man's innocence. The emphasis on guilt informs the remarkable anatomy of ill-yoked marriages near the conclusion of *Tetrachordon*'s section on Deuteronomy:

> And what confusion els can ther bee in separation, to separat, upon extrem urgency, the Religious from the irreligious, the fit from the unfit, the willing from the wilfull, the abus'd from the abuser, such a separation is quite contrary to confusion. But to binde and mixe together

---

incompatibility of temper. In his discussion of the divorce tracts, he offers a passage from the *Defensio Secunda* as an example of temperamental incompatibility:

> a consideration of divorce was particularly necessary "when man and wife were often the fiercest enemies, he being at home with his children, while she, the mother of the family, was in the camp of the enemy, threatening slaughter and destruction to her husband." The consistent argument of the divorce tracts is *therefore* that "indisposition, unfitness, or contrariety of mind, arising from a cause in nature unchangeable," provide a sounder reason for divorce than frigidity or adultery. [*Milton and the Puritan Dilemma*, pp. 66–67]

(Barker quotes the *Second Defense* from *The Works of John Milton*, 20 vols., ed. F. A. Patterson et al. [New York, 1931–40], 8:133; the passage from the *Doctrine and Discipline* can be found in *YP* 2:242). Milton presumably thought that one's choice of sides in the Civil War was a matter of principle rather than temperament.

holy with Atheist, hevnly with hellish, fitnes with unfitnes, light with darknes, antipathy with antipathy, the injur'd with the injurer, and force them into the most inward neernes of a detested union, this doubtles is the most horrid, the most unnatural mixture, the greatest confusion that can be confus'd! (*YP* 2:635)

The anguished tone of the passage points to its roots in painful experience. The lone phrase to suggest mutuality and perhaps blamelessness, "antipathy with antipathy," is overwhelmed by a tide of anger, injury, and accusation.

The distance between the two works can be gauged by juxtaposing two related passages:

> there is indeed a twofold Seminary or stock in nature, from whence are deriv'd the issues of love and hatred distinctly flowing through the whole masse of created things, and that Gods doing ever is to bring the due likenesses and harmonies of his workes together, except when out of two contraries met to their own destruction, he moulds a third existence, and that it is error, or some evil Angel which either blindly or maliciously hath drawn together in two persons ill imbarkt in wedlock the sleeping discords and enmities of nature lull'd on purpose with some false bait, that they may wake to agony and strife. (*DDD, YP* 2:272)

> besides the singular and substantial differences of every Soul, there is an intimat quality of good or evil, through the whol progeny of *Adam*, which like a radical heat, or mortal chilnes joyns them, or disjoyns them irresistibly. (*Tetra., YP* 2:606)

The earlier passage is complex to the point of obscurity. Is it that some things come from the seminary of love and others from the seminary of hate? The opening seems to admit that reading, but the rest of the passage suggests the reading that hatred arises from the mixing of things from different seminaries. In any event, the agent of the ill-yoked marriage here is neither spouse but "error, or some evil Angel."[27] The spouses seem to be hapless and blameless victims of an accident or cosmic joke. The later passage parallels the first, and Milton seems to have the same phenomenon in mind, but now in place of a two-fold seminary one finds "an intimat quality of good or evil." The new terms epitomize the perspective of *Tetrachordon* as it diverges from the *Doctrine and Discipline*. Despite a new definition of hardness of heart as a kind of

---

27. In describing the agent as acting "either blindly or maliciously," Milton translates to the abstract or supernatural realm the causes elsewhere ascribed to the wife's failure to be a fit help: inability or willfulness.

blameless imperfection shared by all fallen creatures, Milton cannot seem to pass by any discussion of incompatibility without asserting blame or evil on one side and innocence on the other. Blameless error is repeatedly transmuted into the woman's blamable and "most unnatural fraud" (*YP* 2:626); mutual blamelessness is replaced by "anothers fault against him" (*YP* 2:625). At one point even "inability" becomes culpable:

> I argue, that man or wife who hates in wedloc, is perpetually unsociable, unpeacefull, or unduteous, either not being able, or not willing to performe what the maine ends of mariage demand in helpe and solace, cannot bee said to care for who should bee dearest in the house; therefore is worse then an infidel . . . ; either in undertaking a duty which he cannot performe, to the undeserved and unspeakable injury of the other party so defrauded and betrai'd, or not performing what he hath undertaken, . . . to the perjury of himselfe more irreligious then heathenisme. (*YP* 2:691)

The inability to love, formerly a tragic but blameless result of fallen nature, is evidence of deception and breach of promise. Although Milton includes man as well as woman as potentially guilty here, the larger context firmly ties to the woman the refrain of inability to be a spouse.

Tetrachordon comes closest to echoing the *Doctrine and Discipline* on mutual blamelessness when Milton writes of the innocence of the man "who puts away by mutuall consent" with love and gentleness (*YP* 2:669). A moment after this interlude of tender concern for the woman and acknowledgment of mutual blamelessness, however, Milton refers to the poorly matched wife as "a helpelesse, unaffectionate and sullen masse" (*YP* 2:670), in a reprise of the *Doctrine and Discipline*'s "image of earth and fleam."

How does one account for the all but complete disappearance of the argument of mutual blamelessness from *Tetrachordon?* The answer cannot lie simply in *Tetrachordon*'s insistent patriarchalism, for it shares that characteristic with the *Doctrine and Discipline*.[28] While the *Doctrine and Discipline* makes a case for mutual blamelessness, it does not argue for equality (though it does gesture now and then in that direction); Milton presents instead the possibility of two unequal partners being equally blameless along with the possibility of the unfit woman's stubborn refusal to be a wife. In *Tetrachordon,* the first possibility is elided, even though the new reading of "hardness of heart" would seem to invite it.

---

28. See, e.g., the earlier work's claim that "the freedom and eminence of mans creation gives him to be a Law in this matter to himself, beeing the head of the other sex which was made for him" (*YP* 2:347).

If not patriarchalism, what? I suggest that the change springs from Milton's need to represent himself to himself and to us as heroic, as chosen because of eminent virtue. He can argue for a universal yet not necessarily sinful hardness of heart after the fall, but ultimately he does not want to count himself among the herd, even when the herd is blameless. Sirluck is right to see that "hardness of heart" in *Tetrachordon* becomes "a description of the fallen condition of man" (*YP* 2:154), but Milton disowns this as a self-description as soon as he offers it. Yes, Moses allows divorce because of the imperfection after the fall of even the virtuous, and, yes, Christ seconds this permission, but Milton cannot reconcile himself to owning to that imperfection. James Turner rightly identifies Milton's distinction between intention and practice, between "pursu[ing] the full Edenic ideal" and "fight[ing] for such regulations 'as reason and present nature can bear.'"[29] But the disappearance from *Tetrachordon* of veiled representations of himself as despairing or even imperfect reveals Milton's deep reluctance to apply the universally applicable to his own case. The reading of "hardness of heart" as blameless natural imperfection evokes the same ambivalence and tension as the claim in the *Doctrine and Discipline* that a law the author contemplates availing himself of is made not for the "heroically vertuous" but for the "common lump of men" (*YP* 2:253). Milton scrambles on a precipice between two slippery slopes: either acknowledgment of shared weakness will undermine his self-representation as heroically virtuous, or disavowal of weakness will involve him in untenable claims of unfallenness (and eviscerate his argument for divorce). The tendency to slip into the claim of unfallenness is on display in a passage introduced earlier:

> If it be urg'd that sin hath lost him this [his birthright and priority], the answer is not far to seek, that from her the sin first proceeded, which keeps her justly in the same proportion still beneath. She is not to gain by being first in the transgression, that man should furder loose to her, because already he hath lost by her means. Oft it happens that in this matter he is without fault; so that his punishment herein is causeles. (*YP* 2:590)

The primary meaning of "this matter [in which] he is without fault" is the unhappy marriage. But the immediate allusive context is that of the fall, in which Eve is "first in the transgression." If the man (or Milton) loses "by her means," he nevertheless remains "without fault," in the first instance in the marriage but by allusion in the fall.

Milton argues that divine permission to divorce accommodates not our sinfulness (God does not accommodate and thus abet sin) but what he had called in the earlier tract our "unsinning weaknesses." But as he projects

---

29. Turner, *One Flesh*, p. 193, quoting *Tetrachordon* (*YP* 2:666).

himself onto the schema that he has articulated, he redefines and distorts the schema to fit his self-construction. Milton begins to undo the new signification of "hardness of heart" even before he has finished articulating it. He pivots on the term "weakness," which signifies both an effect of original sin and an innocent source of error. The ambiguity allows Milton to shift from weakness as the effect of sin first to innocent weakness and then to entire innocence. The passage, noted above, in which he defines "hardness of heart" illustrates the complexity of the relationships among sin, weakness, and innocence in Milton's conception of the effects of the fall:

> hardnesse of heart hath a twofould acception in the Gospel. One, when it is in a good man taken for infirmity, and imperfection, which was in all the Apostles, whose weaknesse only, not utter want of beleef is call'd hardnes of heart, *Marke* 16. partly for this hardness of heart, the imperfection and decay of man from original righteousnesse, it was that God suffer'd not divorce onely, but all that which by Civilians is term'd the *secondary law of nature and of nations* [Milton's emphasis]. . . . [H]ee suffer'd divorce as well as mariage, our imperfet and degenerat condition of necessity requiring this law among the rest, as a remedy against intolerable wrong and servitude above the patience of man to beare. Nor was it giv'n only because our infirmity, or *if it must be so called,* hardnesse of heart could not endure all things, but because the *hardnes of anothers heart might not inflict all things upon an innocent person,* whom far other ends brought into a league of love and not of bondage and indignity. . . .
> In a second signification hardnes of heart is tak'n for a stubborne resolution to doe evil. (*YP* 2:661–62; my emphasis)

Milton's first examples of hardness of heart are the Apostles, who betray moments of weak faith but do not fall into faithlessness. Hardness of heart in this sense is not sinfulness revealed in breaking the law, but the weakness or frailty that makes law necessary. But even in the middle of the passage introducing this sinless hardness, Milton begins to speak of injury inflicted by the hardness of one on the *innocence* of another; one might not think from the clause "if it must be so called" that it was Milton himself who made the identification of "hardness of heart" with general infirmity the moment before; as he contemplates membership in this universal set, he can only grudgingly accept the label of hardness of heart with respect to himself. He immediately begins to distinguish the innocent from the guilty or hard-hearted; now it is "anothers heart" that is hardened, and this hardness inflicts injury on "an innocent person." This distinction might seem to fit more logically under the discussion of the second meaning of hardness of heart, a "stubborne resolution to doe evil," which governed the interpretation of the *Doctrine and Discipline*. No sooner does Milton name a category in which he fits with all others, than he begins to divide and distinguish, to open a gap between himself and the imputation of imperfection, even from an imperfection derived from the universally shared guilt of original sin.[30] Imperfection may enter Milton's self-representation, but when it goes again it leaves no spot or blame behind.

Having established the man's innocence, Milton claims a special perfection for the divorcer:

> Him I hold *more in the way to perfection* who forgoes an unfit ungodly & discordant wedloc, to live according to peace & love, & Gods institution in a fitter chois, then he who debarrs himself the happy experience of all godly, which is peaceful conversation in his family, to live a contentious, and unchristian life not to be avoided, in temptations not to be liv'd in, only for the fals keeping of a most unreal nullity, . . . the remedy wherof God in his law voutsafes us. Which not to dare use, he warranting, is not our perfection, is our infirmity, our little faith, our timorous and low conceit of charity: and in them who force us, it is their masking pride and vanity, to seem holier & more circumspect then God. *So far is it that we need impute to him infirmity,* who thus divorces: since the rule of perfection is not so much that which was don in the beginning, as that which now is nearest to the rule of charity. This is the greatest, the perfetest, the highest commandment. (*YP* 2:666–67; my emphasis).

Milton writes that one should not impute "infirmity" to the one who divorces, but this is precisely the characteristic that provides the gloss for hardness of heart and that makes the divine permission to divorce not only merciful but just. Within several pages Milton has insulated the innocent party to divorce, and by extension himself, from just these properties. While the language of "greater perfection" need not be more than relative, in a context where the fall and its effects are central it calls to mind Edenic perfection. While Milton at one point gestures toward celibacy as proper to and possible only for the "supernaturally gifted," he seems more in character when he claims, on several occasions, greater perfection for one like himself: "Men of most renowned vertu have sometimes by transgressing, most truly kept the

---

30. Sánchez argues that in *Tetrachordon* Milton finds a middle way: "Milton will have it both ways by placing himself somewhere in the middle, between the two extremes of *altogether* good and *altogether* evil" (*Persona and Decorum*, p. 89). While such a placement is plausible given the argument of the *Doctrine and Discipline* and the premises of *Tetrachordon,* Milton reacts in *Tetrachordon* against such a placement.

law" (*YP* 2:588).³¹ The greater perfection refers literally to the action of the man who dissolves an unfit marriage relative to that of the man who suffers in one, but again Milton's language seems to point beyond the local meaning to a greater perfection absolutely conceived. The language of "greater perfection" in *Tetrachordon* marks a step beyond the language of "lesse evil and lesse in scandal" with which he makes the same point in the *Doctrine and Discipline* (*YP* 2:328).

To explain how someone neither imperfect nor infirm could make a poor marriage choice, as Milton believed he had done, Milton relies on the Uriel defense: the unavoidability and moral neutrality of intellectual/perceptual error.³² Milton argues that one's life should not be ruined "meerly for a most incident error which no warines can certainly shun" or for "the most irreprehensible mistake in choosing" (*YP* 2:601). The analogy to Uriel is apt not only for the innocence of the error, but for its arising from fraud. For the unfortunate husband as for the angel, "goodness thinks no ill / Where no ill seems," and the husband, like the angel later, is thus unable to see through a "fraudulent impostor" (*PL* 3.688–89, 692). Those who would forbid divorce say that the unfortunate husband should have discerned potential adultery in the woman he chooses, in "every glaunce of her eye, every step of her gate" (*YP* 2:629). But the unfortunate husband has been defrauded by a trickster, who can disguise her bad faith and unsuitability. Milton asks, "Why should his own error bind him, rather then *the others fraud* acquit him? . . . [I]t is not equal that error and fraud should be linkt in the same degree of forfeture, but rather that error should be acquitted, and fraud bereav'd his morsel" (*YP* 2:630; my emphasis).³³

Tetrachordon at this point foreshadows the route of *Paradise Lost* from Uriel on the sun to Adam in Eden; once again the paradoxical position Milton carves out for himself in *Tetrachordon* resembles Adam's just before his fall. If one finds oneself in an unfit marriage, "Then follows dissimulation, suspicion, fals colours, fals pretences, and wors then these, disturbance, annoyance, vexation, sorrow, *temtation eevn in the faultles person,* weary of himself, and of all action public or domestic; then comes disorder, neglect, hatred, and perpetual strife,

---

31. The mention of celibacy occurs in a passage in which Milton attacks as Romanizing any tampering with divine law (*YP* 2:595).
32. See Barker, *Milton and the Puritan Dilemma*, p. 113, on the substitution of intellectual for moral error.
33. For fraud in the tract, see also *YP* 2:626. In the passage concerning hard-heartedness discussed above, we saw that Milton only grudgingly admits a sense he has just himself invoked ("our infirmity, or if it must be so call'd, hardnesse of heart" [*YP* 2:661–62]); the same gesture of reluctance appears in his discussion of error in judgment: "With great reason therfore and mercy doth it heer not torment an error, *if it be so,* with the endurance of a whole life lost to all houshold comfort and society" (*YP* 2:629; my emphasis).

all these the enemies of holines and christianity" (*YP* 2:631; my emphasis). This catalogue looks forward to the effects of the fall in *Paradise Lost*,[34] but the italicized phrase pushes us back figuratively before the fall. The driving apart of the guilty and the innocent, along with the figuring of the prelude to an ill marriage as a successful seduction of one who expects no ill, suggests once again the position of Adam before his fall and after Eve's, only now perhaps a greater Adam who would not fall if not deceived. Milton's argument depends for its plausibility on general weakness, but inasmuch as he identifies with the wronged husband he drives the woman toward the seductress in the Garden and the man toward the still innocent Adam. Divorce, then, holds out the promise of a return to Eden, an undoing of the fatal error in Eden. Here is a way to recapture the pristine state and to make metaphoric sense of oneself as unfallen, and this I conclude is perhaps what Milton, despite his theological beliefs, most wants to do.

Colasterion: *"this fleamy clodd of an Antagonist"*

In *Colasterion* (March 1645), the response to the anonymous Answerer of the *Doctrine and Discipline,* Milton places himself and his antagonist in the roles of the wronged husband and the unfit wife. Where the unfit wife had been an "image of earth and fleam," the Answerer is "this fleamy clodd of an *Antagonist*" (*YP* 2:254,740). Having anticipated rational conversation about marriage and divorce, he finds his book yoked to "an illiterat, and arrogant presumer in that which hee understands not" (*YP* 2:724). The Answerer, lacking the learned languages to which he pretends, is in a sense mute, like the "mute and spiritles mate" of the *Doctrine and Discipline* (*YP* 2:251); he is a grunting "Barrow," or castrated boar (*YP* 2:725,747); the grotesque sexual reference is apt in context. Milton is outraged to be reduced to answering a servingman (*YP* 2:726,741). Eager to cast himself into the kind of grave and stately role available in tragedy, Milton is dismayed to find himself pulled into the low world of comedy. He disowns the low form of his own reply, ascribing it to his vulgar adversary: "If they can afford mee none but a ridiculous adversary, the blame belongs not to mee, though the whole Dispute bee strew'd and scatter'd with ridiculous" (*YP* 2:757). If the proper response of a man whose spouse is unfit for conversation in marriage is divorce, so Milton's response to the disappointment of his hope to find a fit interlocutor is to divorce the Answerer, to refuse to be yoked in debate with him: "I mean not to dispute Philosophy with this Pork, who never read any" (*YP* 2:737). In the end, he dismisses him much as a man dismisses his wife under Mosaic law: "Thus much to this *Nuisance*" (*YP* 2:757).

---

34. This is true both in general of Books 9–12 and in particular of passages such as 9.1121–31.

The Tracts on Education and Freedom of the Press

Of Education: *"to repair the ruins of our first parents"*

Of Education, like *Of Reformation,* is an anonymous work addressed to a friend, though now the friend is neither anonymous and fictitious, but the reformer Samuel Hartlib.[35] From the beginning, Milton portrays himself as a grave, learned, and selfless advocate of God's will and human good. He writes that he considered declining Hartlib's request to write of education, "one of the greatest and noblest designes, that can be thought on, and for the want whereof this nation perishes" (*YP* 2:363), because more pressing issues occupied him. He submits to Hartlib's urging because of his worth:

> Nor should the lawes of any private friendship have prevail'd with me to divide thus, or transpose my former thoughts, but that I see those aims, those actions which have won you with me the esteem of a person sent hither by some good providence from a farre country to be the occasion and the incitement of great good to this Iland. (*YP* 2:363)

Hartlib works for the common good "either by the definite will of God so ruling, or the peculiar sway of nature, which also is Gods working" (*YP* 2:363). Milton praises Hartlib in terms he usually reserves for himself: God has chosen Hartlib (like Milton) for important work, for which he (like Milton) is suited by nature.

While associating himself with Hartlib, Milton contrasts himself with the mercenary products of a corrupt educational system, who "grow into hatred and contempt of learning" and hurry

> either to an ambitious and mercenary, or ignorantly zealous Divinity; Some allur'd to the trade of Law, grounding their purposes not on the prudent, and heavenly contemplation of justice and equity which was never taught them, but on the promising and pleasing thoughts of litigious terms, fat contentions, and flowing fees; others betake them to State affairs, with souls so unprincipl'd in vertue . . . that flattery, and court shifts and tyrannous aphorismes appear to them the highest points of wisdom. . . . Others lastly of a more delicious and airie spirit, retire themselves knowing no better, to the enjoyments of ease and luxury. (*YP* 2:375–76)

---

35. What Marin Mersenne was to physical science in the mid-seventeenth century, Samuel Hartlib was to social science. Both were tireless correspondents and intellectual matchmakers, with ties to the most prominent intellectuals of the age. See G. H. Turnbull, *Hartlib, Dury and Comenius* (London: Hodder & Stoughton, 1947).

In this vignette we see everything he does not want to be, and by contrast how he wishes to be perceived himself.[36]

While Milton indicates that he would not be a greedy lawyer, an unprincipled politician, or an idle dandy, he omits to mention what he is and has been, a teacher. He does, however, offer a portrait of the heroic teacher, who resembles the author's image in the anti-prelatical tracts. By art, eloquence, mild persuasion, and discipline, "*but chiefly by his own example,* [the teacher] might in a short space gain them [his students] to an *incredible diligence and courage:* infusing into their young brests such an ingenuous and noble ardor, as would not fail to make many of them renowned and matchlesse men" (*YP* 2:385; my emphasis). Just as the writer is not a mere chronicler of heroic deeds, but one who shares the heroism of those whose acts he records, so the teacher exemplifies the heroic virtues that he instills in his pupils. It is not often that teachers are credited, even by themselves, with "incredible . . . courage."

The poet described in *The Reason of Church-Government* was a teacher of the nation (*YP* 1:815); the prominent place assigned to poetry in *Of Education* implies that this teacher is a poet. Whereas poetry normally came first, as an element of the grammatical and philological foundation of learning, Milton gives it pride of place at the end, crowning a curriculum devoted to grammar, natural philosophy, moral philosophy, politics, theology and church history, history, tragedy, drama, and rhetoric:

> To which Poetry would be made subsequent, or indeed rather precedent, as being lesse suttle and fine, but more simple, sensuous and passionate. I mean not here the prosody of a verse, which they could not but have hit on before among the rudiments of grammar; but that sublime art which in *Aristotles poetics,* in *Horace,* and the *Italian* commentaries of *Castelvetro, Tasso, Mazzoni,* and others, teaches what the laws are of a true *Epic* poem, what of a *Dramatic,* what of a *Lyric,* what decorum is, which is the grand master peece to observe. This would make them soon perceive what despicable creatures our common rimers and play-writes be, and shew them, what Religious, what glorious and magnificent use might be made of Poetry both in divine and humane things. (*YP* 2:403–6)

As crown of the arts, poetry is both subsequent and precedent, first in importance but last in sequence given the knowledge needed for its composition and comprehension. The interplay of subsequence and precedence is deeper, however, as the list of studies preceding the passage suggests, for Milton had

---

36. Elsewhere in the essay we see Milton the meritocrat, characteristically bridling at respect based on hereditary nobility rather than merit (*YP* 2:406).

already included epic poetry and Greek drama under the study of history, and Hesiod, Lucretius, and Virgil under natural and practical philosophy (*YP* 2:400–1,394–96). Though reserving the final place for poetry, he cannot resist making it precedent in more than one sense; it comes first, middle, and last in Milton's plan. The prominence given to poetry, with the students not only as readers but as composers "fraught with an universall insight into things" (*YP* 2:406), reveals the author's own ambitions.[37]

Milton promises extraordinary results for his educational plan, a generation of poets and heroes. A true son of the seventeenth century, Milton seems, like Bacon or Descartes, to have unlimited confidence in method. But at the same time we catch glimpses of the Milton who insists on thinking of himself as singular and inimitable. At the end of the pamphlet, having laid out a path for education that would be "laborious indeed at the first ascent, but else so smooth, so green, so full of goodly prospect, and melodious sounds on every side, that the harp of *Orpheus* was not more charming" (*YP* 2:376), he seems to dissuade any teacher less than heroic from following the method.[38] His method will be easy to follow "*if* God have so decreed, and this age have spirit and capacity anough to apprehend" (*YP* 2:415; my emphasis). An intervening caveat suggests that this "if" is not merely rhetorical: "Only I believe that this is not a bow for every man to shoot in that counts himselfe a teacher; but will require sinews almost equall to those which Homer gave Ulysses."[39] Even allowing for rhetorical emphasis, this is a remarkable statement. Teachers not only can but must be heroes. Milton had confided his desire to be teacher to the nation; his picture of the teacher in *Of Education* fits that heroic ambition.

The first word on teaching, after the induction, is more arresting than the last: "The end then of learning is to repair the ruins of our first parents by regaining to know God aright, and out of that knowledge to love him, to imitate him, to be like him, as we may the neerest by possessing our souls of true vertue, which being united to the heavenly grace of faith makes up the highest perfection" (*YP* 2:366–67). In implying education's potential to undo in part the effects of the fall, Milton does more than give a conventionally pious nod to the religious roots and aims of learning. The passage does mention grace and faith, but it is unclear whether these lead to virtue or are combined with

---

37. In his last word on the attainments of the students of his proposed academy, Milton points to his own signal achievement, already a matter of public record in *The Reason of Church-Government* and soon to be in *Areopagitica:* "if they desire to see other countries at three or four and twenty yeers of age, not to learn principles, but to enlarge experience, and make wise observation, they will by that time be such as shall deserve the regard and honour of all men where they passe, and the society and friendship of those in all places who are best and most eminent" (*YP* 2:414).

38. There is already a warning, perhaps, in the allusion to Orpheus, whose ability to charm is a divine gift.

39. Milton refers to Homer's *Odyssey* 21.393–423.

a virtue already attained, though the latter and unorthodox reading seems to be the primary one. Milton's Baconian inheritance plays a role here; Bacon believed that method could unlock the secrets of nature, allowing us to tame what had been rebellious since the fall. But Milton refers to education's effect on the moral nature. If Milton treats himself almost as if immune from the effects of the fall in the *Apology*, here he seems to treat the effects of the fall as easily ameliorable, and by means other than those prescribed in Scripture. The late anti-prelatical tracts revealed in Milton a nascent and inchoate strain of perfectionism. He does not repudiate the doctrine of depravity and grace in *Of Education*, but he writes around them.

Areopagitica: *"the disburdning of a particular fancie"*?

Areopagitica (November 1644) contains some brief, explicitly autobiographical passages, but they are eclipsed in significance by what, following Patterson, I have been calling displaced third-person or "he who" self-representation. As in *Tetrachordon*, the pressure of self-reference leads to a distortion in the reasoning. Even as Milton builds an ostensibly disinterested argument, his reaction to the prospect of being silenced himself unsettles the logic of his proposal.

By displaying his name with unusual prominence on the title page and labeling his work a "speech . . . to the Parlament of England," Milton calls attention to himself as vividly present, as he does with his narrative of his Italian experience and his account of his motivations and intentions. In these openly autobiographical moments he compares himself to heroic and outspoken figures present and past. He also warns that if the Licensing Order of 1643, the occasion of Milton's tract, is not rescinded, Parliament will be numbered among the enemies of liberty, including the Inquisition, which silenced Galileo:

> And lest som should perswade ye, Lord and Commons, that these arguments of lerned mens discouragement at this your order, are meer flourishes, and not reall, I could recount what I have seen and heard in other Countries, where this kind of inquisition tyrannizes; when I have sat among their lerned men, for that honor I had, and bin counted happy to be born in such a place of *Philosophic* freedom, as they suppos'd England was, while themselvs did nothing but bemoan the servil condition into which lerning amongst them was brought; that this was it which had dampt the glory of Italian wits; that nothing had bin there writt'n now these many years but flattery and fustian. There it was that I found and visited the famous *Galileo* grown old, a prisner to the Inquisition, for thinking in Astronomy otherwise then the Franciscan and Dominican licencers thought. And though I knew that England then was groaning loudest under the Prelaticall yoak, nevertheless I took it as a

pledge of future happines, that other Nations were so perswaded of her liberty. (*YP* 2:537–38)

Milton contrasts English liberty with Italian and Spanish oppression, and allies himself with Galileo, hero of free thought in the service of truth. In his tacit reservations concerning liberty under the bishops, Milton implies that Parliament would be both backsliding and Romanizing to maintain its oppressive licensing law. His access to Galileo illustrates his acceptance among the learned of cultured lands, an attainment he holds as a goal for students in *Of Education* (*YP* 2:414). In the next breath after the implicit self-comparison with Galileo, Milton compares himself with Cicero:

> it was as little in my fear, that what words of complaint I heard among lerned men of other parts utter'd against the Inquisition, the same I should hear by as lerned men at home utterd in time of Parliament against an order of licensing; and that so generally, that when I had disclos'd my self a companion of their discontent, I might say, if without envy, that he whom an honest *quaestorship* had indear'd to the *Sicilians,* was not more by them importun'd against *Verres,* then the favourable opinion which I had among many who honour ye, and are known and respected by ye, loaded me with entreaties and perswasions; that I would not despair to lay together that which just reason should bring into my mind, toward the removal of an undeserved thraldom upon lerning. (*YP* 2:539)

As in the passage on Galileo, Milton subtly threatens Parliament. Listen to me or be branded as Romanizing censors; listen to me or be driven from power, as Verres was driven into exile by Cicero's rhetoric. At this stage, still relatively young, Milton invokes Cicero to purchase authority, but given his growing body of eloquent writings the comparison to Cicero is not altogether fanciful. As in *Of Education,* Milton is exhorted by the mature and learned for his powers of mind and expression.

Milton continues in an equally revealing manner: "That this is not therefore the disburdning of a particular fancie, but the common grievance of all those who had prepar'd their minds and studies above the vulgar pitch to advance truth in others, and from others to entertain it, thus much may satisfie" (*YP* 2:539). That others have urged him to write confirms that Milton is not focused on a "particular fancie." Milton's defense focuses attention on the implied accusation. The language of the tract uncovers a private grievance, a spur of self-concernment, which, along with his disinterested concern, motivates Milton. Milton takes the licensing order personally. The righteous indignation of the potentially thwarted author lurks just below and sometimes erupts through the surface of the text. Given his outspoken temperament and sometimes unorthodox ideas, Milton stood to lose by the enforcement of the Licensing Order of 1643, a fact confirmed by Herbert Palmer's denunciation of the *Doctrine and Discipline* as "a *wicked booke* . . . abroad and *uncensured,* though *deserving to be burnt.*"[40]

In part to deflect the accusation of self-concern, Milton turns again to veiled, third-person self-representation. Imagining the effects of the licensing order, Milton limns a figure resembling his representations of himself. "God," we learn, "sure esteems the growth and compleating of one vertuous person, more then the restraint of ten vitious" (*YP* 2:528). As elsewhere, Milton the layman reminds readers that virtue and learning, far from being restricted to the clergy, are more common among lay Christians: "I never found cause to think that the tenth part of learning stood or fell with the Clergy" (*YP* 2:531). As Milton contemplates the plight of the imagined author facing the restrictions of the licensing act, his passion betrays his personal investment and suggests that he is writing about himself:

> If therefore ye be loath to dishearten utterly and discontent, not the mercenary crew of false pretenders to learning, but the free and ingenuous sort of such as evidently were born to study, and love lerning for it self, not for lucre, or any other end, but the service of God and of truth, and perhaps that lasting fame and perpetuity of praise which God and good men have consented shall be the reward of those whose publisht labours advance the good of mankind, then know, that so far to distrust the judgement & the honesty of one who hath but a common repute in learning, and never yet offended, as not to count him fit to print his mind without a tutor and examiner, lest he should drop a scism, or something of corruption, is the greatest displeasure and indignity to a free and knowing spirit that can be put upon him. (*YP* 2:531)

The next several pages comprise the moment of greatest passion in this passionate work, all devoted to an indignant reaction to potential insult. In the opposition between the vicious and miscellaneous "they" or "the mercenary crew" on the one hand and the "free and knowing spirit" on the other, we see a version of Milton's self-reflexive single champion. In the middle of a passionate (self-)defense of the diligent seeker after truth against the forces of conformity and repression comes a passage worth quoting in full for the insight it offers into Milton's understanding of the act of composition:

> When a man writes to the world, he summons up all his reason and deliberation to assist him; he searches, meditats, is industrious, and likely

---

40. Palmer, *The Glasse of Gods Providence towards His Faithfull Ones* (London, 1644), excerpted in Parker, *Milton's Contemporary Reputation,* pp. 73–74.

consults and conferrs with his judicious friends; after all which done he takes himself to be inform'd in what he writes, as well as any that writ before him; if in this the most consummat act of his fidelity and ripenesse, no years, no industry, no former proof of his abilities can bring him to that state of maturity, as not to be still mistrusted and suspected, unlesse he carry all his considerat diligence, all his midnight watchings, and expence of *Palladian* oyl, to the hasty view of an unleasur'd licencer, perhaps much his younger, perhaps far his inferiour in judgement, perhaps one who never knew the labour of book-writing, and if he be not repulst, or slighted, must appear in Print like a punie with his guardian, and his censors hand on the back of his title to be his bayl and surety, that he is no idiot, or seducer, it cannot be but a dishonor and derogation to the author, to the book, to the priviledge and dignity of Learning. And what if the author shall be one so copious of fancie, as to have many things well worth the adding, come into his mind after licencing, while the book is yet under the Presse, which not seldom happ'ns to the best and diligentest writers; and that perhaps a dozen times in one book. The Printer dares not go beyond his licenc't copy; so often then must the author trudge to his leav-giver, that those his new insertions may be viewd; and many a jaunt will be made, ere that licencer, for it must be the same man, can either be found, or found at leisure; mean while either the Presse must stand still, which is no small damage, or the author loose his accuratest thoughts, & send the book forth wors then he had made it, which to a diligent writer is the greatest melancholy and vexation that can befall. (*YP* 2:532)

Milton describes the process of publication from beginning to end. With one significant exception, the passage might represent his own experience with *Areopagitica*. The author who "writes to the world" recalls the Milton of the opening who joins the number of those "who to States and Governours of the Commonwealth direct their Speech" (*YP* 2:486). Milton stresses the author's "industry" and "diligence" in consulting both contemporaries and "any that writ before him," industry and diligence on ample display in the erudition of his own text, with its historical sweep and careful reading of precedents for both liberty of the press and press censorship. The reference to the "best and diligentest writers" makes it likely that Milton is thinking of himself.[41] His horrified reaction to the possibility that someone such as himself would be subject to the vividly evoked inconvenience of licensing, with

---

41. Milton later in the tract offers another vignette of the diligent and judicious author, "labouring the hardest labour in the deep mines of knowledge" (*YP* 2:562). In this passage, the mining metaphor gives way to a military one, where licensers are shameless and shameful layers of ambush ranged against the frank and open champion of truth.

its repeated trips to the licenser for vetting of revisions and additions, to say nothing of the possible mutilation of the text by ignorant licensers, points to the significant exception noted above. Milton did not submit *Areopagitica* for licensing, and his book, bearing neither license nor publisher's name, is a singularly graphic defiance of the Licensing Order. Milton's stance amounts to civil antinomianism. He argues for a higher moral imperative that dwarfs civil law, which may in conscience be ignored. Given that *Areopagitica* supports the sects both implicitly and explicitly, the book's enactment of a secular version of antinomianism is fitting.

In the anti-prelatical tracts, the relatively young and unknown author argued for the irrelevance of reputation and age. Two years in the rough and tumble of anti-prelatical polemic, along with the fame (or notoriety) purchased with two editions of the *Doctrine and Discipline of Divorce*, have had their effect. Whether he actually sees himself as substantially older or more mature, or whether he finds it advantageous to present himself now in this way, Milton claims authority based on a body of works that have given him a name. He bridles at submitting to a licenser not merely "inferiour in judgement" but "perhaps much his younger." Milton expresses his authority in an image drawn from his daily experience as a schoolmaster: "How can a man teach with autority, which is the life of teaching, how can he be a Doctor in his book as he ought to be . . . , whenas all he teaches, all he delivers, is but under the tuition, under the correction of his patriarchal licencer. . . . I hate a pupil teacher" (*YP* 2:532–33).[42]

By adding to his account of the author under licensing a lament for the plight of the prophet, Milton reasserts his familiar claim to prophetic status. Licensers will be disposed to approve conventional wisdom rather than prophetic words and to censor any "sentence of a ventrous edge, utter'd in the height of zeal, and who knows whether it might not be the dictat of a divine Spirit, yet not suiting with every low decrepit humor of their own, though it were *Knox* himself, the Reformer of a Kingdom that spake it" (*YP* 2:534). Milton's concern that the wisdom of an author "shall to all posterity be lost" is self-regarding as well. He fears the "homicide," "martyrdome," and "massacre" of his own "elementall life, . . . that ethereall and fift essence, the breath of reason it selfe" (*YP* 2:493).

The threat to Milton is also a threat to God's people, the English. Milton calls England a "Nation of Prophets," adding that the time seems at hand for the fulfillment of Moses' wish (Numbers 11:29) that "all the Lords people are become Prophets" (*YP* 2:554,556). But alongside this egalitarian and

---

42. When Milton laments that England, once leader of reformation, now lags behind other reformed nations, he chooses the same image: "we are become hitherto the latest and the backwardest Schollers, of whom God offer'd to have made us the teachers" (*YP* 2:553).

optimistic vision of national inspiration is another, more familiar, vision of the specially elect spokesperson of unusual aptitude and heroic preparation. In times of upheaval, "God then raises to his own work men of rare abilities, and more then common industry not only to look back and revise what hath bin taught heretofore, but to gain furder and goe on, some new enlightn'd steps in the discovery of truth" (*YP* 2:566). These prophets, according to the church-outed Milton, should not be looked for among the clergy, for "God hath fitted for the speciall use of these times [individuals] with eminent and ample gifts, and those perhaps neither among the Priests, nor among the Pharisees" (*YP* 2:567).

The resemblance between the heroic, inspired author wronged or thwarted under a regime of licensing and Milton's acknowledged self-representations suggests that despite his denials the argument of *Areopagitica* is in part "the disburdning of a particular fancie" (*YP* 2:539). This helps to account for the choppy nervousness of the opening of the work, where he projects the experience of a private man addressing the public good:

> I suppose them as at the beginning of no meane endeavour, not a little alter'd and mov'd inwardly in their mindes: Some with doubt of what will be the successe, others with feare of what will be the censure; some with hope, others with confidence of what they have to speake. And me perhaps each of these dispositions, as the subject was whereon I enter'd, may have at other times variously affected; and likely might in these formost expressions now also disclose which of them sway'd most, but that the very attempt of this address thus made, and the thought of whom it hath recourse to, hath got the power within me to a passion, farre more welcome then incidentall to a Preface. Which though I stay not to confesse ere any aske, I shall be blamelesse, if it be no other, then the joy and gratulation which it brings to all who wish and promote their Countries liberty; whereof this whole Discourse propos'd will be a certaine testimony, if not a Trophey. (*YP* 2:486–87)

The picture of wavering and competing passions is unusually frank. A potential loss of control is figured in the syntactic suspension and inversion of the second sentence, as the speaker becomes the object of the action of competing dispositions. The straining of syntax is the prelude to the near disintegration of sense that follows. Passion may be more welcome than incidental to a preface, but it is difficult to sort out the alternation of confession and blamelessness that follows. Who would ask for a confession, and of what sort? Why would the joy of others make him blameless, and what is the referent of "it" in "if it be no other"? Far from requiring confession, the discourse quickly becomes a trophy.

Anxiety ramifies in the ensuing defense against the potential charge that he flatters Parliament, which he refutes by claiming that (1) he praises praiseworthy qualities, (2) these qualities are in those praised for them, and (3) he has reason to believe so. The last criterion is the most subjective, and Milton acknowledges that the proof that he sincerely finds in Parliament heroic qualities "belong[s] chiefly to mine own acquittall" (*YP* 2:488). Confession, defense, acquittal: these terms suggest that Milton views his position as open to question. He ends his defense with an oddly solipsistic argument: "I might defend my selfe with ease, if any should accuse me of being new or insolent, did they but know how much better I find ye esteem it to imitate the old and elegant humanity of Greece, then the barbarick pride of a *Hunnish* and *Norwegian* statelines" (*YP* 2:489). Those who would accuse the author of *Areopagitica* might be expected to care very little for how that author views the Parliament's tolerance. If Milton meant to tell his Parliamentary audience that they are more tolerant than any backbiters, he could have found a more direct expression.

In the vitalist theory of *Areopagitica*, a book does not merely represent its author, it distills its author's essence. This extraordinarily close identification of book and author complements Milton's repeated recourse to self-representation. In the celebrated passage on books as "not absolutely dead things," Milton plays variations on his vitalist vision (*YP* 2:492–93). A book is "reason it selfe, . . . the Image of God, as it were in the eye," and "a good Booke is the pretious life-blood of a master spirit, imbalm'd and treasur'd up on purpose to a life beyond life." An additional image in this vitalist catalogue resonates throughout not only this text but almost all of Milton's representations of himself as author: books "contain a potencie of life in them to be as active as that soule was whose progeny they are; nay they do preserve as in a violl the purest efficacie and extraction of that living intellect that bred them" (*YP* 2:492). This Platonic notion of intellectual works as the children of their creators is common enough, but Milton is unusual in the frequency and vividness of his birth imagery and in the interchanging of gender roles. The male author, not coincidentally constructed on the experience of the "Lady of Christ's," takes over the functions, and as we shall see in a moment, the organs of the woman. Before the Inquisition, Milton writes, "Books were ever as freely admitted into the World as any other birth; the issue of the brain was no more stifl'd then the issue of the womb: no envious *Juno* sate crosleg'd over the nativity of any mans intellectuall off spring" (*YP* 2:505). The female goddess thwarts the male birth. This closing, delay, and frustration are contrasted with the irresistibly forward movement of Milton's argument; when he gets ahead of himself, he remarks, "See the ingenuity of Truth, who when she gets a free and willing hand, opens her self faster, then the pace of method and discours can overtake her" (*YP* 2:521). If Milton is earlier a birthing mother, here Truth, encountering the true lover, opens herself to his advances, and if anything exceeds his passion. Thus Milton is both the male lover and the female mother of truth.[43]

The confusion, or appropriation, of gender roles informs one of the most arresting images in all of Milton's prose, which records Milton's fear that his books—and by extension Milton himself—will be eviscerated by the licensers. The Council of Trent and the Spanish Inquisition "engendring together brought forth, or perfeted those Catalogues, and expurging Indexes that rake through the entralls of many an old good Author, with a violation wors then any could be offer'd to his tomb" (*YP* 2:503). The proximity of the term "engendring," the context of books as intellectual children or offspring, and the anatomically graphic image of raking through entrails together evoke abortion.[44] The violation is offered, in terms of Milton's vitalist and reproductive metaphorization of writing, not only to the author's tomb but also to his *womb*.[45] Elsewhere, Milton's dark imagining of dismemberment and evisceration inhabits images of Orpheus, notably in "Lycidas." Now the evisceration is practiced on the female body of the author. When Milton refers to the "torn body of our martyr'd Saint" (*YP* 2:550), he echoes his image of the censoring of books as a "martyrdome" of the "season'd life of man" (*YP* 2:493).

Under many forms and through all the arguments of *Areopagitica* Milton writes about himself. The persistent self-regard and self-representation help to account for a striking gap in the argument of the tract.[46] The question involves whether books should be subject to any control. *Areopagitica* acknowledges at the outset, just before the passage on the life of books, that books can err, and that "it is of greatest concernment in the Church and Commonwealth, to have a vigilant eye how Bookes demeane themselves, as well as men; and thereafter to confine, imprison, and do sharpest justice on them as malefactors" (*YP* 2:492). Already in this articulation there is a false note, as the church is supposed to have punitive power, something Milton nowhere else endorses. As the argument proceeds, moreover, the rationale for "sharpest justice," except in the case of libel, dissolves. Even bad books, he writes, can serve good ends.

---

43. The intermixing of male and female roles is repeated in the gender-mixing metaphor of feminine England as Samson: "Methinks I see in my mind a noble and puissant Nation rousing herself like a strong man after sleep, and shaking her invincible locks" (*YP* 2:557–58).

44. In this passage Milton is also negotiating his relationship with his predecessor and teacher Spenser, whose episode of the Dragon Error in *Faerie Queen* 1.1 lies behind Milton's image.

45. Michael Lieb, in *Milton and the Culture of Violence* (Ithaca, Cornell University Press, 1994), has written of Milton's fear of dismemberment as ironically proleptic of the violation of his tomb in the late eighteenth century. For the convergence of "tomb" and "womb," see Shakespeare's Sonnet 86, "That did my ripe thoughts in my brain inhearse, / Making their tomb the womb wherein they grew," and Milton's description of Chaos in *Paradise Lost* as "the womb of Nature and perhaps her grave" (2.911).

46. For incoherencies in *Areopagitica*, see Thomas N. Corns, *Uncloistered Virtue: English Political Literature, 1640–1660* (Oxford: Clarendon, 1992), p. 57.

A good reader can read even the worst book with profit, and a vicious reader will suck only poison even from a good book.[47] It is not clear that Milton's argument would not extend even to libelous works, and if his own practice is any indication, Milton would give a wide latitude for character assassination. Michael Wilding has argued that Milton's early and ostensible endorsement of punishment for bad books is, with deliberate irony, undercut by the imagery of mutilation, borrowed from scenes of the savage repression of Puritan free speech, with which Milton associates the disciplining and censoring of books.[48] New discoveries under licensing will be subject, like the Presbyterian William Prynne's ears, to "cropping" (*YP* 2:492). The bishops have been in the business of tearing bodies, and to meddle with books is to tear the internal bodies of their authors. Milton may have thought that some books required disciplining, but as he develops his argument he cannot or will not break out of the charmed circle of his own experience and plans. Books may need watching, but Milton refuses to countenance having his own books watched.[49]

Milton's puzzling reference to Arminius opens another gap in the argument. Despite his later clear Arminianism, and despite the Arminian-leaning passage on free will in *Areopagitica* itself ("when God gave him reason, he gave him freedom to choose, for reason is but choosing" [*YP* 2:527]), Milton offers Arminius as an example of the corruption of the learned and the good by books: "It is not forgot, since the acute and distinct *Arminius* was perverted meerly by the perusing of a namelesse discours writt'n at *Delf*, which at first he took in hand to confute" (*YP* 2:519–20). Milton may be guilty of ad hoc argument. Earlier in the tract he wrote that good readers cannot be corrupted by bad books; now he observes that the "acute and distinct *Arminius*" was so corrupted. At the moment he is intent on showing that dangerous books on religion will not corrupt an honest layperson unless sponsored by a learned cleric such as Arminius. (That Arminius inhabits an ambiguous no-man's land, as a figure whose corruption consists in a stance Milton is in the process of adopting, makes the reference all the more anomalous.) But given the clear

---

47. "Wholesome meats to a vitiated stomack differ little or nothing from unwholesome; and best books to a naughty mind are not unappliable to occasions of evill. Bad meats will scarce breed good nourishment in the healthiest concoction; but herein the difference is of bad books, that they to a discreet and judicious Reader serve in many respects to discover, to confute, to forewarn, and to illustrate" (*YP* 2:512–13). On the paradox of books as being finally indifferent, see Corns, *Uncloistered Virtue*, 57–58, and Stanley Fish, "Driving from the Letter: Truth and Indeterminacy in Milton's *Areopagitica*," in *Re-Membering Milton: Essays on the Texts and Traditions*, ed. Mary Nyquist and Margaret W. Ferguson (New York: Methuen, 1987), p. 238.

48. See Michael Wilding, "Milton's *Areopagitica:* Liberty for the Sects," *Prose Studies* 9 (1986): 12.

49. Corns offers an alternative reason for the gap in the text's logic: Milton may have included the section on punishing books to reassure his Parliamentary audience that tolerance of independence would lead to no restrictions and thus to anarchy (*Uncloistered Virtue*, pp. 58–59).

self-investment in the tract, the motivation for the anomalous Arminius passage may lie once again in Milton's reading the issue through the lens of his own experience and self-understanding: some of the learned may be vulnerable, but Milton is not.

In *Areopagitica,* as in the divorce tracts, Milton's self-construction does more than attempt to purchase authority; it inflects his argument. The acknowledgment that some books might deserve punishment is swamped by Milton's assertive confidence that he as a reader can turn *all* books to good use and by his horror that his own books might be altered or punished. Given human weakness, and tendency to vice, there is reason to beware of and regulate vicious books, but Milton is outraged that any press restrictions or penalties might be applied to the godly, especially to that shrinking set of the godly that funnels down to and centers on Milton himself. In *Tetrachordon* a plausible and sympathetic argument that inherited human weakness makes unfit marriage likely and divorces necessary is overwhelmed by an argument, based in Milton's own unhappy marital experience, that divorces are necessary because woman, made to serve the man, willfully breaks marital concord. The intimation, even the self-generated intimation, that Milton shares common human weakness, evokes a visceral, implicit, and ultimately incoherent claim for his own perfection and innocence.

In this chapter, perhaps more than in any other, my song is partial. It is because I am interested in this book in Milton's self-representations and their implications and effects that I have highlighted what I see as local distortions in works that I admire deeply. *Areopagitica* in particular vigorously, nobly, and effectively advances high ideals of freedom of expression, and the divorce tracts at their best offer a vision of marriage significantly ahead of their time. A complete reading of any of these works would register much left out here. It is possible, however, to recognize the gravitational pull of Milton's self-regard while continuing to recognize his genius and the nobility of his achievement.

Interlude

Interregnum Poetry

While Milton wrote mostly prose during two tumultuous decades of polemics and government service, he did write lyric poetry sporadically through the decade and a half following *Poems 1645*. Inspired by the harsh reaction to his divorce tracts, by the Civil War and its Parliamentary heroes, by friendship, by the vogue for psalm translation, and by the onset of blindness,[1] he wrote a remarkable series of sonnets. With the notable exception of the sonnets in praise of Parliamentary Civil War heroes, the poems became part of Milton's poetic self-presentation in the *1673 Poems*.

In several of the poems, Milton defends himself, sets himself apart from the vulgar, and laments his blindness. The poems share with the works following the divorce tracts awareness of fallibility and intimations of danger. In two sonnets, Milton reacts viscerally to the harsh reception of his divorce tracts. In Sonnet 11, "A book was writ," by mocking an unreceptive audience unable to get their mouths around the Greek title *Tetrachordon,* Milton portrays himself as one of the cultured few among the barbarian many. In the earlier Sonnet 12, "I did but prompt the age," that stance is transposed to a moral register. His argument for liberty has been either embraced or rejected as an argument for licence.[2] Milton presents himself in terms that recall *A Mask:*

> straight a barbarous noise environs me
> Of owls and cuckoos, asses, apes and dogs.

---

1. Milton's eyesight deteriorated from the middle of the 1640s; by February of 1652 he was totally blind.
2. N. H. Henry argues that Milton attacks sectarians who embraced *Tetrachordon* for the wrong reasons ("Who Meant Licence When They Cried Liberty?," *MLN* 66 [1951]: 509–13);

> As when those hinds that were transformed to frogs
> Railed at Latona's twin-born progeny
> Which after held the sun and moon in fee.

The inarticulateness satirized in Sonnet 11 can be traced to the Circean transformation of his controversial opponents in Sonnet 12; in the terms of the simile, Milton replaces Apollo and Diana and thus becomes a figure of poetic power and chastity. As if to cast off the ignominy of association with lower-class libertinism, Milton stresses in these sonnets his learning and elegance. The effect is underlined by the sonnet that follows these two (both chronologically and in the pages of the *1673 Poems*), in which Henry Lawes plays Casella to Milton's Dante. In the Latin poem to John Rous of the following year, Milton again separates himself from the vulgar many, placing a copy of his *Poems 1645* under the protection of the Bodleian librarian, where they will be safe from the "unruly tongue of the mob [*lingua procax vulgi*]" and the "degenerate crowd of readers [*Turba legentum prava*]" (79, 80).

These poems of the mid-1640s continue the self-conscious effort of *Poems 1645* to present the author as a cultured literary figure, above the rough and tumble of political conflict.[3] Milton's notoriety as a prose controversialist suggests the need for this tactic. Milton would not have wanted the wrangling of *Animadversions* and *Colasterion* in particular to define the high-minded poet with epic ambitions. By 1652, another potential threat to that persona had emerged. Milton's blindness would become a table on which his opponents could write a story of divine retribution. Milton attempts to prevent them by writing his own story on the tabula rasa of his lost eyesight. While David's eye grows "weak" in Psalm 6, in Milton's 1653 translation David's eye "is waxen old and *dark*" (14; my emphasis). Blindness is the central theme of three of the eight sonnets that Milton wrote in the 1650s. "When I consider how my light is spent" presses the question of the sonnet "How soon hath time" inscribed nearly two decades earlier in the 1633 "Letter to a Friend": What has Milton to show for his time? As in that letter, Milton invokes the

---

according to Barbara Lewalski, Milton's target is Presbyterians who fail to recognize true liberty (*The Life of John Milton,* [Oxford: Blackwell, 2000], pp. 203–4).

3. Thomas N. Corns examines *Poems 1645* as a contribution to Milton's assertion of his social, cultural, and scholarly status ("Milton's Quest for Respectability," *Modern Language Review* 77 [1982]: 769–79). For other illuminating discussions of *Poems 1645* as self-presentation, see Stella Revard, *Milton and the Tangles of Neaera's Hair: The Making of the 1645 "Poems"* (Columbia: University of Missouri Press, 1997); Louis Martz, *Poet of Exile: A Study of Milton's Poetry,* 2nd ed. (New Haven: Yale University Press, 1986), pp. 31–59; Corns, "Ideology in the *Poemata* (1645)," *Milton Studies* 19 (1984): 195–203; Ann Baynes Coiro, "Milton and Class Identity: The Publication of *Areopagitica* and the *1645 Poems,*" *Journal of Medieval and Renaissance Studies* 22 (1992): 261–89; and John K. Hale, "Milton's Self-Presentation in *Poems . . . 1645,*" *Milton Quarterly* 25 (1991): 37–48. Hale describes the volume's arrangement as "a major personal statement" (41) and argues that "the self and its presentation are not separable, not even distinguishable" (45).

parable of the talents, fearing that with the onset of blindness the one talent will be "Lodged with me useless." The anxiety in the poem is both urgent and short-lived. A tumble of truncated clauses runs up to the danger that God will "chide" him, only to have the line that we expect to be devoted to God's chiding taken over by Milton's own plaintive question, "Doth God exact day labor, light denied?" In a virtuoso reversal of the familiar pace of sonnet structure, the resolution is articulated by "patience" in an unhurried manner, an effect made possible by Milton's having moved the turn up to the eighth line, scarcely more than halfway through the poem. In the 1633 "Letter" Milton had deflected fears of divine punishment for hiding the talent by making a virtue of belatedness, redescribed as patient preparation. Now he strikes the same pose to deflect the charge that his blindness is itself a punishment for political sin.[4]

Milton wrestled again with his blindness in a 1655 sonnet to Cyriack Skinner. Echoing his comment in the 1654 *Defensio Secunda* that his eyes "are as clear and bright, without a cloud, as the eyes of men who see most keenly" (*YP* 4.1:583), Milton writes now that his eyes are "clear / To outward view, of blemish or of spot." His complaint, "Nor to their idle orbs doth sight appear / Of sun or moon or star throughout the year, / Or man or woman," will be expanded into the plaintive lament in the invocation to Book 3:

> Thus with the year
> Seasons return, but not to me returns
> Day, or the sweet approach of ev'n or morn,
> Or sight of vernal bloom, or summer's rose,
> Or flocks, or herds, or human face divine.
> (3.40–44)

Both the sonnet and the invocation record the anguish of the blind author, even as that blindness is deployed in self-authorizing narratives. In the sonnet Milton immediately turns from anguish to righteous resolution: "Yet I argue not / Against Heaven's hand or will." This declaration in the sixth line signals a turn in this Petrarchan sonnet even earlier than the turn in the previous sonnet on his blindness. It is as if the tension that conventionally fills the Petrarchan sestet is resolved with heroic ease, leaving the final two thirds of

---

4. Noting the manner in which the voice of Patience takes control of the poem's sestet and concludes with an allusion to the parable of the workers in the vineyard ("They also serve who only stand and wait"), David Urban argues persuasively that the emphasis on divine generosity in the vineyard parable counterbalances the self-regarding emphasis on merit in the octet's speaker's allusion to the parable of the talents ("The Talented Mr. Milton: A Parabolic Laborer and His Identity," *Milton Studies* 43 [2004]: 18).

the poem for calm enjoyment of a clean conscience. Milton is buoyed by the realization that he lost his sight "In liberty's defense, my noble task, / Of which all Europe talks from side to side." The reference to his writings for Cromwell's government probably explains why this sonnet, along with those to Vane, Fairfax, and Cromwell, was omitted from the *1673 Poems.*

Milton's final sonnet, and the last lyric poem that he left, is an even more plaintive self-representation by the blind poet, "Methought I saw my late espousèd saint" (Sonnet 23). With the caveat that any emotion in a poem is mediated by form and technique, and with the added caveat that Milton is one of the most self-conscious of poets, this final sonnet seems as close as we come in Milton to direct representation of felt experience. While Milton carefully juxtaposes classical, Judaic, and Christian elements with calculated effect, for once he is not the hero of his poem. He plays Admetus to the poem's Hercules; in each of the poem's three registers he is the passive husband receiving his wife as a gift. Significantly, given the previous sonnets' pressing back the Petrarchan turn earlier in the poem, "Methought I saw," while Petrarchan in rhyme scheme, is Shakespearean in its disposition of elements into a 4–4–4–2, with its startling and desolating reversal in the final two lines: "But O as to embrace me she inclined, / I waked, she fled, and day brought back my night." We see the pain and raw vulnerability patent in these lines only once elsewhere, in the *Pro Se Defensio (Defence of Himself)*, where, as we will see below, he laments his failing health, deaths in his family, and the loss of his sight. Milton drops at these moments his lifelong labor of building a heroic and self-authorizing image; in the sonnet he still is using his powers to craft an image, but the image now seems a privileged glimpse at the private man.

Chapter 6

"It Was I and No Other"

Interregnum Prose

The process of self-representation in the prose of 1649–1655, the first years of the Interregnum, is complicated by the fact that Milton now speaks explicitly for Cromwell's party, the party in power. The result is a sparer, more restrained, and more impersonal style, at least until the violent attack in the *Clamor* goads Milton into the extravagant prose and the familiar self-representation in the *Defensio Secunda* of 1654. Thomas N. Corns persuasively traces the controlled tone and the relative impersonality of the *Tenure of Kings and Magistrates* and *Eikonoklastes* to the fact that "Milton is acting on behalf of an organization to whom he owes both corporate allegiance and discipline."[1] It can be more exhilarating to rail from the wilderness than to speak for and from authority. At the same time, a deep irony invests the transition from prophetic outsider to palace spokesperson; it is in 1649 and afterward that Milton fulfills the heroic stance he claims for himself in the antiprelatical tracts, of speaking courageously for a minority position. Milton's self-representations are inflected as much by the rigors of countering popular opinion, and particularly deeply ingrained reverence for monarchs, as they are by his emerging status as official spokesperson. As the 1650s ended, in the final years of the Interregnum and amid the ruins of England's republican experiment, Milton resumes what is paradoxically his most congenial stance: the lone voice of truth in a world of error.

---

1. Corns, *Uncloistered Virtue: English Political Literature, 1640–1660* (Oxford: Clarendon, 1992), p. 217. See also Corns's excellent *The Development of Milton's Prose Style* (Oxford: Clarendon, 1982).

Repudiating Monarchy and the King's Image after the Execution of Charles I

On January 30, 1649, in a public relations debacle from which Cromwell's republican party never fully recovered, Charles I was beheaded at Whitehall. Milton responded to the event swiftly. Within two weeks, he published *The Tenure of Kings and Magistrates,* a work that attracted the attention of England's new rulers, who then commissioned Milton to respond to the wildly popular *Eikon Basilike* (or "image of the king"), which appeared in London on the day of the execution. In these two works Milton established himself in England as spokesperson for Cromwell's party and as antagonist of kings, roles he would develop through the 1650s.

The Tenure of Kings and Magistrates: *"the soule of that enterprise"*

Looking back in the *Defensio Secunda,* Milton describes *The Tenure of Kings and Magistrates* as a response to the hypocrisy of the Presbyterian ministers, who, having contended against Charles in print and on the battlefield, now argued that all Protestant churches opposed judicial proceedings against kings:

> I concluded that I must openly oppose so open a lie. Not even then, however, did I write or advise anything concerning Charles, but demonstrated what was in general permissible against tyrants, adducing not a few testimonies from the foremost theologians. And I attacked, almost as if I were haranguing an assembly, the pre-eminent ignorance or insolence of these ministers, who had given promise of better things. This book did not appear until after the death of the king, having been written to reconcile men's minds, rather than to determine anything about Charles (which was not my affair, but that of the magistrates, and which had by then been effected). (*YP* 4.1:626–27)

Milton's stance of disinterested principle accurately reflects the *Tenure*. Arguing from natural law, Milton claims that kings and magistrates receive their power by contract from the people and that when rulers violate the spirit of this contract they can and should be deposed and disciplined.

Milton lays out the origins of kingship in a contract designed for the common good, defines the tyrant as one who rules for himself, offers classical and biblical warrant and precedent for tyrannicide, and warns the Presbyterians that their rediscovered allegiance to Charles is both hypocritical and ill-calculated to achieve its mercenary aim of averting royal wrath at their role in recent events.[2] As in *Eikonoklastes,* there is relatively little explicit self-representation. Milton no longer speaks as the singular and prophetic voice. Instead, he includes himself in the body of the virtuous and godly who won the war and brought the king to justice.

Milton's emphasis on the band of heroes who fearlessly liberated England underlines a poignant irony: the revolutionaries, inspired by republican principles, lack majority support, a fact illustrated and exacerbated by Charles's execution. If his claims in the anti-prelatical tracts of championing of an unpopular position were belated and tenuous, he now finds himself speaking for a position at once ascendant and unpopular. In *The Reason of Church-Government,* he had cast himself as a disinterested champion of minority opinion: "if I were wise only to mine own ends, I would certainly take such a subject as of it self might catch applause, whereas this hath all the disadvantages on the contrary" (*YP* 1:807). But Milton is in a smaller minority defending the execution of a king in 1649 than he was supporting an end to episcopacy in 1642. His sense of the unpopularity of his position is evident in the addition to the second edition of a set of supporting arguments drawn from leading Reformers, a strategy he had used in the *Judgement of Martin Bucer* in response to the chorus of hostile abuse that met the *Doctrine and Discipline of Divorce.* Another sign is the argument, also added in the second edition, that truth "among mortal men is alwaies in her progress" and consequently under attack from the slaves to custom and to self-interest (*YP* 3:256). This argument resembles those surrounding Milton's introduction of new ideas in the divorce tracts and in *De Doctrina Christiana.* The ironies of his position color his representation of himself as an individual and as a member of a group in the *Tenure.*

If the bishops were the enemy in the early 1640s, now it is the vulgar and ungodly majority. Already at the inception of the Commonwealth, Milton, unable to claim clear majority support, falls back on the warrant of military victory. The people owe allegiance "to the present Parliament & Army, in the glorious way wherin Justice and Victory hath set them; the only warrants through all ages, next under immediat Revelation, to exercise supream power" (*YP* 3:194). While he targets the Presbyterians specifically, in the opening lines he distinguishes between bad men in general, who love servitude, and the heroic men who have carried out God's will. Of the former he writes,

> being slaves within doors, no wonder that they strive so much to have the public State conformably govern'd to the inward vitious rule, by which they govern themselves. For indeed none can love freedom heartilie, but good men; the rest love not freedom, but licence; which

---

2. Milton nakedly threatens the backsliding Presbyterians. See *YP* 3:192,195,239.

never hath more scope or more indulgence then under Tyrants. (*YP* 3:190)

Against these, Milton arrays the godly minority, among whom he counts himself by the act of writing: "others for the deliverance of thir Countrie, endu'd with fortitude and Heroick vertue to feare nothing but the curse writt'n against those *That doe the worke of the Lord negligently,* . . . goe on to remove, not only the calamities and thraldoms of a People, but the roots and causes whence they spring" (*YP* 3:191). These godly heroes, the "soule of that enterprize," must "be swett and labour'd out amidst the throng and noises of Vulgar and irrational men" (*YP* 3:192). As he will increasingly as the Interregnum experiment falters, Milton identifies with the "uprighter sort . . . , though in number less by many, in whom faction least hath prevaild above the Law of nature and right reason" (*YP* 3:197).

Milton does refer to himself briefly on two occasions early in the *Tenure*. To the backsliding Presbyterians, he offers himself as teacher: "To these I wish better instruction, and vertue equal to thir calling; the former of which, that is to say Instruction, I shall indeavour, as my dutie is, to bestow on them" (*YP* 3:194). And he asserts the merit of the virtuous middle-class man, soon to be a staple figure in Milton's self-representations:

> surely no Christian Prince, not drunk with high mind, and prouder then those Pagan *Cæsars* that deifi'd themselves, would arrogate so unreasonably above human condition, or derogate so basely from a whole Nation of men his Brethren, as if for him only subsisting, and to serve his glory; valuing them in comparison of his owne brute will and pleasure, no more then so many beasts, or vermin under his Feet, not to be reason'd with, but to be trod on; among whom there might be found so many thousand Men for wisdom, vertue, nobleness of mind, and all other respects, but the fortune of his dignity, farr above him. (*YP* 3:204–5)

The affront to the dignity of the middle class is a personal affront, to which Milton reacts bitterly.

Despite these widely spaced passages of individual self-reference, the usual strategy is to represent the group of the godly. Milton's new strategy is driven as much by the approach of his enemies as by his new role as spokesperson. As Don M. Wolfe argues, Milton's foray into the ethical proof is modest in comparison to that of the Presbyterian authors of *A Serious and Faithful Representation of Ministers of the Gospel,* to which Milton responds in the *Tenure*. The authors label themselves "Ambassadors of Christ,"[3] the kind of

---

3. Quoted in Don M. Wolfe's introduction to vol. 3 of the *Yale Prose (YP),* p. 108.

title of which Milton was fond but which he eschews in the *Tenure*. Milton is perhaps prevented from praising himself as much by the counterexample of his opponents as by his role of spokesperson for a group. This is evident in *Eikonoklastes,* in which Milton is faced with the example of the fulsome self-representations of Charles I.

Eikonoklastes: *"not less than Kings"*

Copies of *Eikon Basilike,* composed ostensibly by Charles I but mainly by John Gauden, were already published by January 30, 1649, the day of the king's execution, circulating the image of Charles as martyred saint rather than punished tyrant.[4] The nascent Commonwealth government's Council of State directed Milton to answer this wildly popular book.[5] Reading the *Eikon* is an uncanny experience for the student of Milton's self-representations, and it must have been doubly so for Milton, as his characteristic strategies of self-representation are inflected through the voice of Charles. Where Milton had deployed his own image to underwrite and authorize his arguments in the past, now the practice of circulating the image itself comes under suspicion.[6] The *Eikon* reads like a digest of Milton's strategies of self-representation: the speaker as upholder of conscience; the speaker as prophet, eager or reluctant; the speaker as preternaturally free from sin or error. As an ironic but inevitable result, the *Eikonoklastes* avoids those strategies; Milton has been preempted, and he spends his time now castigating moves that he has made repeatedly and that he will make again.

Like Milton, Charles invokes his conscience. When he traces his rejection of the nineteen propositions of June 1642 to his willingness to give away all but "the incommunicable jewel of my conscience,"[7] Milton responds contemptuously:

> But the *incommunicable Jewell of his conscience* he will not give, *but reserve to himself.* It seemes that his conscience was none of the Crown Jewels; for those we know were, in *Holland,* not incommunicable to buy Armes against his Subjects. Being therfore but a privat Jewel, he could not have don a greater pleasure to the Kingdom then by reserving it to himself. But he, contrary to what is heer profess'd, would have

---

4. Editor's Introduction, in *Eikon Basilike: The Portraiture of His Sacred Majesty in His Solitudes and Sufferings,* ed. Philip A. Knachel (Ithaca: Cornell University Press, 1966), p. xi.

5. The *Eikon Basilike* went through sixty editions in the first year (*YP* 3:150).

6. Reuben Sánchez, Jr., notes that Milton in *Eikonoklastes* "responds to what he considers the inappropriateness, the violation of decorum, of Charles I's self-presentation" (*Persona and Decorum in Milton's Prose* [Madison, NJ: Fairleigh Dickinson University Press, 1997], p. 118).

7. *Eikon Basilike,* p. 53.

his conscience not an incommunicable, but a universal conscience, the whole Kingdoms conscience. (*YP* 3:459)

Charles sold the crown jewels, held in trust for his people, as if they were private property. Piling error on error, he did so to buy weapons to harm the jewels' true owners. Milton suggests that he would have done a greater service had he kept to himself the private jewel of his conscience. But his claiming to retain it is a cover for his dispersing it among the people he has swindled. Now the king's private conscience is made the conscience of the people. Milton makes the same point when dismissing Charles's agonies of conscience for his handing over the Earl of Strafford to certain execution. That execution was just, Milton says, "But his sole conscience thought the contrary. And thus was the welfare, the safety, and within a little, the unanimous demand of three populous Nations to have attended still on the singularity of one mans opinionated conscience" (*YP* 3:368). Charles has appropriated one of Milton's favorite roles: the one just man in the face of universal opposition. Ironically, given the highly questionable claim that the death of Strafford was, "within a little, the unanimous demand of three populous Nations," a claim that would have surprised and angered Charles's supporters, Milton does more to place Charles in that distinctive position than Charles himself had done. But now, the opposition of one conscience to the voice of the many is not heroic but palpably misguided. Caught in the uncomfortable position of damning Charles for a stance that he has praised in himself, Milton resorts to a rationalization. Charles had no right to make his conscience determinative for his people: "For certainly a privat conscience sorts not with a public Calling; but declares that Person rather meant by nature for a privat fortune" (*YP* 3:369). The tenuousness of the rationalization is all the more apparent when one notes that Charles in this case had not imposed the dictates of his conscience on the people, though he might well have had he been able. Milton thus attacks Charles for doing something that he has not done, but that Milton has presented himself as doing. Milton recasts Charles in his own image, and then attacks that projected image. Charles, on the other hand, has done something Milton scrupulously avoids: admit a grievous sin and error.

In attacking the *Eikon*'s use of the ethical proof, Milton attacks a strategy that he himself had often used and would use again. Milton replies, for example, to Charles's claims of heroic patience at the 1642 siege of Hull:

> he againe relapses into the praise of his patience at *Hull*, and by his overtalking of it, seems to doubt either his own conscience, or the hardness of other mens beleif. *To me, the more he praises it in himself, the more he*

seems to suspect that in very deed it was not in him [my emphasis]; and that the lookers on so likewise thought. (*YP* 3:428)

At the end of the book Milton attacks Charles's claim to a forgiving nature in the same manner: "Wise men would sooner have beleev'd him had he not so oft'n told us so. But he hopes to erect *the Trophies of his charity over us*" (*YP* 3:600–1).[8] Charles, though, would be hard-pressed to exceed the standard of self-praise set by Milton himself. To Charles's claim that "the straitness of my conscience will not give me leave to swallow down such camels as others do of sacrilege and injustice both to God and man,"[9] Milton responds derisively with a charge that fits his own practice: "This is the Pharisee up and down, *I am not as other men are*" (*YP* 3:469). Readers of *An Apology* or *The Reason of Church-Government* might find Milton's abuse of Charles ironic. Milton had built his authority on being not as other men were, and nowhere in the works is there anything like Charles I's at least token acknowledgment of sin.[10]

The *Eikon*'s insistence on Charles's singular virtue helps explain Milton's uncharacteristic reticence about his own singularity in *Eikonoklastes*. He says on the first page that his intention in writing the work is not "fond ambition, or the vanity to get a Name, present, or with Posterity, by writing against a King: I never was so thirsty after Fame, nor so destitute of other hopes and means, better and more certaine to attaine it" (*YP* 3:337). I will return to those means, presumably poetic, in a moment. As in the *Tenure*, Milton celebrates the virtuous few in whom the fate of England rests. A drama unfolds as the phalanx of liberty's heroes confronts the disordered ranks of the slavish:

> Certainly, if ignorance and perversness will needs be national and universal, then they who adhere to wisdom and to truth, are not therfore to be blam'd, for beeing so few as to seem a sect or faction. But in my opinion *it goes not ill with that people where these vertues grow so numerous and well joyn'd together,* as to resist and make head against the rage and torrent of that boistrous folly and superstition that possesses and hurries on the vulgar sort. This therfore we may conclude to be a high honour don us from God, and a speciall mark of his favor, *whom he*

---

8. Despite his scornful dismissal here, Milton had earlier erected his own trophy, in *Areopagitica*, which he describes as a "Trophey" of either English liberty or his own wish to promote that liberty (*YP* 2:487).

9. *Eikon Basilike*, p. 59 (p. 74 of first edition).

10. See especially the prayers at the end of each chapter and the self-flagellating chapter on the Earl of Strafford's death.

hath selected as the sole remainder . . . to stand upright and stedfast in his cause. (*YP* 3:348; my emphasis)

If he was once a single prophetic voice, he now is honored to be included among the godly few, though uneasily aware that his party lacked majority support. The small number of the republican faithful, which might make them seem a "faction," instead mark them as God's "sole remainder." Their minority status is reversed by the number of their virtues, the compact body of which is ranged against "the rage and torrent" of "folly and superstition," in which individual members or qualities are indistinguishable and thus uncountable. The suffrage of virtues is thus unanimous for Milton's party, and he can claim majority status as well as membership in the godly few. His discourse can then be addressed to the "best-affected People" (*YP* 3:512):

> The happiness of a Nation consists in true Religion, Piety, Justice, Prudence, Temperance, Fortitude, and the contempt of Avarice and Ambition. They in whomsoever these vertues dwell eminently, need not Kings to make them happy, but are the architects of thir own happiness; and whether to themselves or others are not less than Kings. (*YP* 3:542)

Milton's party wins by the suffrage of virtues. The slavish, on the other hand, who foolishly venerate the name of king, are susceptible not to argument but are "like men inchanted with the *Circæan* cup of servitude" (*YP* 3:488). Indistinguishable from each other, they are, by Milton's figurative logic, not worth counting. They are a "race of Idiots" and "an inconstant, irrational, and Image-doting rabble" (*YP* 3:542,601).

Milton does not derive his authority in *Eikonoklastes,* as he had in the earlier tracts, from prophetic status or conscience.[11] Both forms of authorization come under suspicion and attack because of their use by Charles/Gauden in the *Eikon.* Milton writes now as servant of godly leaders ("I take it on me as a work assign'd rather, then by me chosen or affected" [*YP* 3:339]), and castigates Charles for the pose of prophetic spokesperson that Milton himself had earlier made his own:

> No evil can befall the Parlament or Citty, but he positively interprets it a judgement upon them for his sake; *as if the very manuscript of Gods*

---

11. For the process of self-authorization in *The Reason of Church-Government* by a conscience at once an internal and earned possession and an external and divine guide, see Amy R. McCready, "The Ethical Individual: An Historical Alternative to Contemporary Conceptions of the Self," *American Political Science Review* 90 (1996): 90–102.

judgements had bin deliverd to his custody and exposition. But his reading declares it well to be a fals copy which he uses; dispensing oft'n to his own bad deeds and successes the testimony of Divine favour, and to the good deeds and successes of other men, Divine wrath and vengeance. *But to counterfet the hand of God is the boldest of all Forgery:* And he, who without warrant but his own fantastic surmise, takes upon him perpetually to unfold the secret and unsearchable Mysteries of high Providence, is likely for the most part to mistake and slander them; and *approaches the madness of those reprobate thoughts,* that would wrest the Sword of Justice out of Gods own hand, and imploy it more justly in thir own conceit. (*YP* 3:563–64; my emphasis)

The prophetic Milton, who has not been reticent, most notably at the end of *Of Reformation,* to assume the authority of divine judgment, would seem vulnerable to his own warnings and denunciations here. The passage highlights the narrow margin separating appropriate claims of prophetic status from damnable presumption. Milton's measured stance in *Eikonoklastes* may betray an awareness of the danger in his own practice that he confronts in the image of Charles. If Milton has been "counterfet[ing] the hand of God," he may be near to the "madness of reprobate thoughts." He takes the reality of prophecy too seriously to contemplate without some anxiety the possibility of his own error. As in the *Doctrine and Discipline,* this anxiety emerges in the contemplation of reprobation, displaced there onto a third-person self-portrait and here onto his opponent.

One can empathize with Milton's disorientation and frustration as he answers the *Eikon Basilike.* The king had co-opted his self-representational gestures and models, and Milton faced the prospect of attacking what looked like an image of himself (or an image of his self-image). With the strategies by which Milton had earlier defined himself contaminated by Charles, Milton falls back on what distinguishes him from Charles. He is a writer and an intellectual. Condescension punctuates *Eikonoklastes.* On the first page Milton notes sardonically that few have gained honor by debating with kings: "no man ever gain'd much honour by writing against a King, as not usually meeting with that force of Argument in such Courtly *Antagonists,* which to convince might add to his reputation" (*YP* 3:337).[12] Milton is if anything more caustic in dispatching Charles's claim that he had the support of men "*both learned and Religious above the ordinary size*": "if his great Seal without the Parlament were not sufficient to create Lords, his Parole must needs be farr more unable to create learned and religious men,

---

12. See also *YP* 3:393, 409.

and who shall authorize his unlerned judgement to point them out?" (*YP* 3:499). What allows one to authorize is having the learnedness of an author. Milton claims in the *Eikonoklastes* that the *Eikon Basilike* lacks authority because Charles is not an author. Milton slyly remarks that it is not clear whether he should address "the King, or his Houshold *Rhetorician*" (*YP* 3:383). Arguing on both sides, Milton suggests that both the strengths and the weaknesses of the *Eikon*'s style show the work to be by a hand other than Charles's. It is too high to be the king's: "tis beleev'd this wording was above his known stile and Orthographie, and accuses the whole composure to be conscious of som other Author" (*YP* 3:393). And it is sufficiently wooden and conventional to betray the hand of a particular kind of author: "These petty glosses and conceits on the high and secret judgements of God . . . are so weake and shallow, and so like the quibbl's of a Court Sermon, that we may safely reck'n them either fetcht from such a pattern, or that the hand of some houshold priest foisted them in" (*YP* 3:430). The ethical proof, the claims of prophetic status, and the insistence on the priority of conscience will all become hollow if the text, which depends for its force on a royal author, is shown to be ghostwritten.

If Charles has authored any of the text, Milton derides his writing as debased poetry. Because of what Milton sees as the fictional nature of the narration of events, the *Eikon* might be called "a peece of Poetrie" (*YP* 3:406). Milton seems to assume that Charles has written of the virtues of his wife, but he does so "in straines that come almost to Sonnetting" (*YP* 3:420–21). Charles is as bad a poet as he is a king, and like bad poets, bad kings "sit and starve themselves with a delusive hope to win immortality" (*YP* 3:502). The *Eikonoklastes,* on the other hand, will immortalize its author. As he concludes his long work, Milton reasserts the inseparability of his heroism and his authorship, after attempting to dismantle that combination in Charles by disputing his heroism and denying his authorship. Milton claims for himself the immortality of the heroic author:

> And if by sentence thus writt'n it were my happiness to set free the minds of English men from longing to returne poorly under that Captivity of Kings, from which the strength and supreme Sword of Justice hath delivered them, I shall have don a work not much inferior to that of *Zorobabel:* who by well praising and extolling the force of Truth, . . . freed his Countrey, and the people of God from the Captivity of *Babylon.* (*YP* 3:585)

Milton has recovered. Having dispatched Charles, he is able to resume the rhetoric of extraordinary merit and special election. He has wrestled, or attempted to wrestle, the prophetic mantle from the hated king, and he now takes his place at the head of his countrymen.

"Milton, twice great, for the people": The *Defences*

The three Latin *Defences* of the early 1650s allow Milton once again to write about himself. He must establish his credibility with a new European audience as a worthy respondent to the eminent French scholar Claudius Salmasius, whose 1649 *Defensio Regia pro Carolo I* upheld the divine right of kings and deplored Charles' execution. Making the character of the author central to his argument, Milton compares his role as defender of the Commonwealth to the role of national epic poet (*Defensio Secunda; YP* 4:685). With each successive work, self-representation and self-defense occupy more space. If in the *Pro Populo Anglicano Defensio (Defence of the English People)* of 1651 he justifies the actions of his country and party before the court of European opinion, in the *Pro Populo Anglicano Defensio Secunda (Second Defence of the English People)* of 1654 he devotes a great deal of attention to countering the personal attacks occasioned by the earlier work. By the time of the 1655 *Pro Se Defensio (Defence of Himself)*, the defense of his party is completely displaced by a response to attacks on his character.[13] The series of titles, from the *Defence of the English People* to the *Defence of Himself,* concisely describes the trajectory of the works.[14]

In 1657, with his service as defender/historian of the revolution and republic behind him, Milton would write to Henry de Brass in terms reminiscent of the *Apology:* "he who would write worthily of worthy deeds ought to write with no less largeness of spirit and experience of the world than he who did them, so that he can comprehend and judge as an equal even the greatest, and, having comprehended, can narrate them gravely and clearly in plain

---

13. I refer to the first two Latin Defences by their short titles: the *Defensio* and the *Defensio Secunda*. The *Defensio Secunda* features an attack on Alexander More, whom Milton named as the author of the anonymous response to the *Defensio*, the *Regii Sanguinis Clamor* (*The Cry of the King's Blood*). The *Pro Se Defensio* parries the attack of More, who in the *Fides Publica* (*Public Faith*) accurately denies his authorship of the *Clamor* and accuses Milton, perhaps fairly, of making a consciously false attribution (the *Clamor* was written by Peter du Moulin).

14. A similar trajectory informs the anti-prelatical tracts: the dense arguments of *Of Reformation* and *Of Prelatical Episcopacy* are replaced by the ad hominem attacks and personal defenses of *Animadversions* and the *Apology for Smectymnuus*. Between the latter two works *The Reason of Church-Government* sandwiches the longest and most elaborate defense and autobiography between ecclesiological and biblical argument. The progression is more rapid in these works, which are all published within a year, between May 1641 and April 1642. The divorce tracts of 1643–1645 exhibit a similar pattern, with the crude and savage polemics replacing the more reasoned and conciliatory stance of the *Doctrine and Discipline of Divorce*.

and temperate language" (*YP* 7:501). This passage illustrates a move often repeated in Milton's Interregnum prose. The status of the writer is initially secondary to the status of those about whom he writes. This is the conventionally modest but atypical Milton whom we see, for example, in this passage from the *Defensio Secunda:* "Indeed, in the degree that the distinguished orators of ancient times undoubtedly surpass me, both in their eloquence and in their style (especially in a foreign tongue, which I must of necessity use, and often to my own dissatisfaction), in that same degree shall I outstrip all the orators of every age in the grandeur of my subject and my theme" (*YP* 4.1:554).[15] Here Milton borrows glory from his subjects, the heroes of the republic. But in the letter to de Brass, as in the *Apology,* he makes a larger claim. The writer must equal those subjects not only in "largeness of spirit" but also "experience of the world"; in doing so, he can "judge as an equal even the greatest." Given that he is in addition able to compose events "gravely and clearly in plain and temperate language" (*YP* 7:501), the writer arguably surpasses the actors whose deeds he records.

Repeatedly, Milton sets up and then collapses binary pairings of actor/recorder or hero/writer, subsuming the heroic into the literary and the literary into the heroic. The collapsing of these pairs exerts an intolerable pressure on the self-representing author, and not merely because the writer with the literary talent to record great deeds must also "comprehend and judge as an equal" the great actors on the historical stage. The greater pressure comes with the self-imposed requirement that the writer embody the ideal that, according to Sir Philip Sidney, can be embodied only in fictional characters, precisely because they are fictional.[16] The gap between the conventional modesty topos illustrated a moment ago from the *Defensio Secunda* and the claims of heroic status echoed in the letter to de Brass is measured and betrayed by moments of anxiety, in which Milton projects onto others his own propensity for self-serving self-representation.

Alexander More, whom Milton lampoons mercilessly in the *Defensio Secunda,* proves, political and personal bias notwithstanding, to be a shrewd literary critic of Milton. In the *Fides Publica,* he writes that Milton's *Defensio* is "a windy panegyric delivered by yourself upon yourself." In the *Defensio Secunda,* according to More, "the people is a mere appendage. In this very

---

15. This is the secular version of his promise in *The Reason of Church-Government* to surpass ancient epic poets because of his Christian theme (*YP* 1:812).

16. Echoing Aristotle's *Poetics,* Sidney asserts that it is fictionality that allows a literary character to be a pattern of virtue. While the historian is restricted to "what men have done," the poet is able "not only to make a Cyrus, which had been but a particular excellency, as nature might have done, but to bestow a Cyrus upon the world, to make many Cyruses, if they will learn aright why and how that maker made him" (*An Apology for Poetry,* in *Critical Theory since Plato,* ed. Hazard Adams [New York: Harcourt Brace, 1971], pp. 157–58).

Second Defence of yourself or the people, as often as you speak for the people your language grows weak, becomes feeble, lies more frigid than Gallic snow; as often as you speak for yourself, which you do oftener than not, the whole thing swells up, ignites, burns."[17] Milton bridles at this, but, as we shall see, even his rebuttal illustrates the charge.

The Interregnum prose echoes the anti-prelatical prose in its insistence on Milton's status as one of what *The Reason of Church-Government* calls God's "selected heralds" (*YP* 1:802). Milton brackets the *Defensio* (1651) with claims of divine inspiration. At the outset he suggests that it would be impossible to compose the work "if I were to rely on my diligence alone, whatever it may be, and my strength alone." Having finished, he asserts that if the establishment of civil freedom

> was not successfully undertaken and completed without divine inspiration [*sine divino instinctu*], there is good reason for us to suppose that the same assistance and guidance led to its being recorded and defended by my words of praise. So I would have all men believe, rather than attribute to me any degree of talent or wisdom or industry [*id quod ab omnibus multo malim existimari, quàm aliam quamvis felicitatem vel ingenii vel judicii vel diligentiæ mihi tribui*] (*YP* 4.1:305, 536; *Works* 7:556).[18]

As he sums up in the *Defensio Secunda* his recent career of advocacy for the Commonwealth, he glories in having been "aided and enriched by the favor and assistance of God" (*divino favore & auxilio adjutum atque auctum*) (*YP* 4.1:558; *Works* 8:18). In the *Pro Se Defensio* (*Defence of Himself*) of 1655 he boasts, "Singular indeed is the favor of God toward me [*Singulare quidem in me divini numinis beneficium*]" (*YP* 4.2:735; *Works* 9:86). Milton argues in the *Defensio* that those who have freed the English from royal tyranny are themselves prophets (*YP* 4.1.346).

The 1651 Defensio: *"by his efforts alone"*

While the trajectory of the *Defences* is toward greater and greater valorization of the heroic writer, Milton begins his flight in the first *Defensio* from an already exalted position. At the outset, the heroic labor of freeing the English is ascribed directly to God. Because God "overthrow[s] haughty and unruly kings," "We followed him as our leader," and the "wonderful deeds [were]

---

17. *The Public Faith of Alexander More*, quoted from selections reprinted in *YP* 4.2:1097,1106.
18. Here and elsewhere, I take Milton's Latin from *The Works of John Milton*, 20 vols., ed. F. A. Patterson et al. (New York, 1931–40), cited in my text as *Works*.

performed evidently by almighty God himself rather than by mortal men" (*YP* 4.1:305). The only labor for men involves recording divine feats, and that labor is reserved for one in a million: "What elevated and splendid discourse, what outstanding talent [*excellens ingenium*], could be capable of sustaining such a burden?—especially when in all the centuries hardly one person can be discovered able to write with distinction [*vix reperiatur tot seculis qui luculentè possit scribere*] about the deeds of famous men or states" (*YP* 4.1:305; *Works* 7:6). In this manner Milton repositions himself, from one who humbly follows others as scribe, writing down *their* heroic deeds, to one who is God's rarely discovered right-hand man. Others are ushered off the historical stage, leaving only Milton and God. Milton acknowledges a moment later that his duty is "second in importance" to that of the leaders of the state, but when he adds that his task is "one in which the sword and implements of war are of no avail, but which requires other weapons" he may be implying, as he argues elsewhere, that the word and reason are the noblest and most effective weapons.

In the *Defensio* Milton again claims that he has written a work that will live, and that the work of other writers will live only by association with his own. He predicts that Salmasius's fame will be ephemeral:

> You dull, stupid, ranting, wrangling advocate, born only to pull apart or copy good writers, did you really think you could create anything which would live? You whom the next generation will seize and hurl to oblivion, you may be sure, along with all your worthless works. It may be, though, that this royal defence will draw some life from my reply, and will be read again after long-neglected obsolescence. (*YP* 4.1:324)

The placement of this passage at the end of the Preface to the *Defensio* suggests its centrality for Milton; however egotistical the claim might be, history has proved Milton right. At the end of the work he returns to the subject of his own heroism and the immortality of his writing. "[W]ith God's help," he claims, he has, like an Odysseus facing Scylla or a Theseus facing the Minotaur, calmed "the jealous rage and madness" of his enemy, by writing a work that, "I see, will not easily perish" (*video . . . non facile interiturum*) (*YP* 4.1:535,536; *Works* 7:554). His final comparison is not with Samson or Achilles or another figure of Bible or myth, but with the writer and statesman Cicero:

> as the great Roman consul, when retiring from office, swore in the assembly of the people that by his efforts alone he had saved the state and the city, so I too, as for the last time I devote myself to this work, may venture this assertion at least, calling on God and men as my witnesses. (*YP* 4.1:536)

Milton rounds to a conclusion by promising his receptive audience, at home and abroad, that he is "at this time hoping and planning still greater things, if these be possible for me, as with God's help they will" (*YP* 4.1.537). The defense of the English people begins to resemble a defense, or assertion, of Milton. With the *Defensio Secunda* the scale will tip ever farther.

Defensio Secunda: *"praises that will never die"*

Defensio Secunda (1654) contains the longest and most systematic of Milton's autobiographical set pieces.[19] The passage has been mined exhaustively for biographical information and for clues to Milton's personality and psychology. The story is familiar to all students of Milton. In response to ad hominem attacks by the author of *The Cry of the Royal Blood,* Milton lays out his life for his readers, beginning with his upbringing by virtuous parents and his extraordinary and precocious studiousness. In relating his career at the university, in private study afterward, on his Grand Tour, and back in England both as a private citizen and as an unremunerated servant of the public, Milton emphasizes the high regard in which he was held by cultured men. At Cambridge, "untouched by any reproach," he enjoyed "the good graces of all upright men" (*procul omni flagitio, bonis omnibus probatus*) and departed "to the regret of most of the fellows of the college"; Sir Henry Wotton, "a most distinguished gentleman, . . . gave signal proof of his esteem for me" as Milton prepared to leave for the Continent, and in Florence he "at once became the friend of many gentlemen eminent in rank and learning" (*multorum & nobilium sanè doctorum hominum*) (*YP* 4.1:613,614,615; *Works* 8:120,122). He seems particularly proud of the regard shown him by Tasso's patron, Giovanni Battista Manso, Marquis of Villa, a "man of high rank and influence," who befriended Milton and would have shown him even more favor had Milton been more circumspect concerning religion (*YP* 4.1:618). Looking back on his life, Milton claims a place in the aristocracy of merit, a place recognized by the aristocracy of blood. However much Milton had insisted, in *Eikonoklastes* and the *Defensio,* on the virtue and even the superiority of the middle class that produced him, he is anxious, as he was in publishing *Poems 1645,* to establish that he has passed muster with the class thought to be the most discerning judges of literary merit.

Milton is anxious as well to establish his unspotted virtue. In Italy one can test oneself against not only the most discerning judges of literature and manners but also the most alluring temptations to sensuality. He calls "God to witness that in all these places, where so much licence exists, I lived free and untouched by the slightest sin or reproach [*ab omni flagitio ac probro*

---

19. *YP* 4.1:610–29.

integrum atque intactum vixisse], reflecting constantly that although I might hide from the gaze of men, I could not elude the sight of God" (*YP* 4.1:620; *Works* 8:126). His virtue finds expression also in an unbending Protestantism that, while not curtailing his enthusiastic interaction with his Roman Catholic hosts, including clergy, led him to speak openly of his allegiance to the Reformation. His outspokenness even in Rome, "the very stronghold of the Pope," led, he claims, to a plot against his life by English Jesuits (*YP* 4.1:619).

In this autobiographical excursion Milton attempts to lay to rest charges that have dogged him. That he was expelled from Cambridge for moral turpitude. That he wrote on divorce out of a libertine disposition and history. That he was politically incendiary and irresponsible. Stung by the response to the divorce tracts, he takes pains to address the question not once but twice, at the beginning and middle of the excursion. He "wrote nothing different from what [the reputable reformer Martin] Bucer had written before me—and copiously," as had Fagius and Erasmus. "No one," he observes plaintively, "blamed them for so doing, and I fail to understand why it should be to me above all a source of reproach" (*YP* 4.1:609). Twelve pages later he returns to the propriety and Protestant orthodoxy of his arguments for divorce, citing the law of Moses and the precedent of John Selden's *Hebrew Wife,* and indirectly addressing what he had labeled earlier the "spurre of self-concernment":

> in vain does he prattle about liberty in assembly and market-place who at home endures the slavery most unworthy of man, slavery to an inferior. Concerning this matter then I published several books, at the very time when man and wife were often bitter foes, he dwelling at home with their children, she, the mother of the family, in the camp of the enemy, threatening her husband with death and disaster. (*YP* 4.1:625)

Donald Roberts hears a dissonance with the pose of objectivity that Milton has been cultivating a moment before: "he spoke of his divorce tracts as part of a large plan, objectively conceived, for the liberation of men in various areas of life. Here, however, he seems to consider them topical works designed to meet a wartime situation."[20] Roberts is right to observe that the situation here is not identical to that of the childless Milton in 1643, but it is not clear that, as he argues, "the personal application should be resisted." Milton and his wife were in enemy camps prior to reconciling, and the advocacy of divorce as self-defense recalls the argument of the divorce tracts that a mismatched wife could be the death of a man. The dissonance that Roberts observes points to the personal application that he resists.

20. Annotation in *YP* 4.1:625.

Throughout the *Defensio Secunda,* self-representation and defense are never far from the surface of the text. Nearly as revealing as the autobiographical digression itself are the nervous justifications with which Milton brackets it. The author of the *Cry* probed a sore spot when he labeled Milton a poor and unknown antagonist for Salmasius. The concern about belatedness marking many of Milton's works erupts in his reply:

> I carried silently in my breast that which, if I had then wished to publish it, would long since have made me as famous as I am today. But I was not greedy for fame, whose gait is slow [*eàque in sinu gestabam tacitus, quæ si tum proferre libuisset, æquè ac nunc, inclaruisse jamdudum poteram: sed cunctantis famæ avidus non eram*], nor did I ever intend to publish even this, unless a fitting opportunity presented itself. It made no difference to me even if others did not realize that I knew whatever I knew, for it was not fame, but the opportune moment for each thing that I awaited. Hence it happened that I was known to a good many, long before Salmasius was known to himself. (*YP* 4.1:608; *Works* 8:112)

Milton was more than forty years old when he wrote the *Defensio,* and it is natural that he would be more uneasy about the appearance of belatedness than he had been earlier. On the other hand, he had made a name for himself with *Poems 1645* and his prose tracts in the 1640s. Here he acknowledges his relative anonymity, but he turns defense into offense and ends by suggesting that, unlike Salmasius, he knows himself. The stance of being unknown to others justifies the autobiographical digression. In response to the libels of the *Cry,* he is compelled to make his life an open book or run the risk that his cause will be tainted by association with him. As he comes to the end of the digression, he returns to the idea:

> I have given an account of myself to this extent in order to stop your mouth, More, and refute your lies, chiefly for the sake of those good men who otherwise would know me not. Do you then, I bid you, unclean More, be silent. Hold your tongue, I say! For the more you abuse me, the more copiously will you compel me to account for my conduct. From such accounting you can gain nothing save the reproach, already most severe, of telling lies, while for me you open the door to still higher praise of my own integrity [*mihi ad integritatis commendationem eo latiùs viam aperias*]. (*YP* 4.1:628–9; *Works* 8:138)

He suggests later that heaven has blessed him with attackers like the corrupt author of the *Cry* (*YP* 4.1:659–60), and the blessing at least in part lies in the opportunity to celebrate himself in self-defense.

The other half of the two-handed engine of Milton's self-defense is his lurid description of Alexander More's profligacy. The image of More's sexual corruption and avaricious opportunism serves as a kind of photographic negative of the image of the sexually pure and disinterested Milton; the poet and his antagonist assume the roles of Lady and Comus in *A Mask*.[21] Salmasius also comes in for sexual dissection; sexually ambiguous, "Salmasia" is henpecked by his wife (*YP* 4.1:556). If More helps Milton to exorcize accusations of sexual impurity,[22] Salmasius helps him exorcize the uncharitable reading of his Christ's College nickname of Lady.

Befitting the scrivener's son, Milton repeatedly weighs himself in a ledger against allies and opponents, heroes and villains. He is a member of the virtuous middle class, which produces more men than the desiccated aristocracy; he is a refined and cultured man who is appreciated by the discerning aristocracy. He is the dutiful servant of the heroes of the fight against tyranny; he is the true hero of that fight. His own relative merit among republicans occupies Milton as much as the relative merit of republicans and kings. Blind and below middle stature, Milton is careful to stress his one-time proficiency with the sword (*Defensio Secunda, YP* 4.1:583). But like others who have not been combatants, he is defensive about having missed military service: "it is easy to defend myself from the charge of timidity or cowardice, should such a charge be leveled. For I did not avoid the toils and dangers of military service without rendering to my fellow citizens another kind of service that was much more useful and no less perilous [*multò utiliorem, nec minore cum periculo meis civibus navârim*]" (*YP* 4.1:552; *Works* 8:8).[23] If he has not fought with the sword, he has done his part with the pen. He is relatively weak of body and strong of mind, and so he serves where he is most needed and most valuable. His labor seems compensatory and secondary at first. But a moment later, he turns the tables. God wished Cromwell and the other soldiers to "achieve . . . noble deeds," and God wished further

> that truth defended by arms be also defended by reason [*defensam armis veritatem, ratione etiam*]—the only defence ["*præsidium*," a term meaning "garrison"] truly appropriate to man. Hence it is that while I admire the heroes victorious in battle, I nevertheless do not complain about my own role. Indeed I congratulate myself and once again offer most fervent thanks to the heavenly bestower of gifts that such a lot has befallen

---

21. I owe this observation to John Rumrich, in a private communication.
22. His possession of sexual purity (*YP* 4.1:620), noted above, sets him apart from his antagonists.
23. Whatever the validity of this claim, Milton surely earns his spurs in 1660 with the courageous if not foolhardy *The Readie and Easie Way*.

me—a lot that seems much more a source of envy to others than of regret to myself [*aliis invidenda multò magìs, quàm mihi ullo modo pœnitenda videatur*]. (*YP* 4.1:553; *Works* 8:10)

The envy and regret from which Milton distances himself by the end of this passage follow hard upon the defensiveness with which the passage begins. Through the alchemy of rhetoric, Milton's own service as wielder of words takes precedence over the deeds that he records. Milton's role foreshadows Abdiel's, as one who prevails in reason rather than in arms. The recorder of heroic history and glorious military exploits himself contends on "another field, as it were" (*iterum quasi campum*) (*Works* 8:215,214).[24] And if the pen is mightier, and more noble, than the sword, Milton is not content to be the victor in the higher realm of reason only; he leaves more than arguments and reputations in his wake. He hints, citing with scarcely restrained pride the observation of others, that he has killed Salmasius: "with Salmasius, since he is dead, I think my war is over. How he died, I shall not say, for I shall not impute his death as a crime to him, as he imputed my blindness to me [*non enim ut ille mihi cæcitatem, sic ego illi mortem vitio vertam*]. Yet there are those who even place the responsibility for his death on me and on those barbs of mine, too keenly sharpened" (*YP* 4.1:559; *Works* 8:20). He uses the pen rather than the sword, but the pen turns out to be a sword after all: "I met him in single combat and plunged into his reviling throat this pen [*adacto convitiantis in jugulum hoc stylo*], the weapon of his own choice" (*YP* 4.1:556; *Works* 8:14).[25] Belated in service to the republic as he has been belated as a writer, Milton has not taken part on the field of battle, but once again he turns potential embarrassment into virtue. From diffident beginnings, offering excuses for avoiding combat, he gradually reconstructs himself as a central hero, and almost even the martial hero, of the republic; by the *Pro Se Defensio* he compares himself to Scipio Africanus (*YP* 4.2.700).[26]

Beginning from the relatively humble position as the literary servant of England's leaders, Milton assumes the role of pan-European hero:

> I do not now feel that I am surrounded, in the Forum or on the Rostra, by one people alone, whether Roman or Athenian, but that, with virtu-

---

24. I use the Columbia translation, so as not to stack the deck with the freer Yale translation, "a second battlefield, so to speak" (*YP* 4.1:668).

25. The Latin term *stylo*, translated here as "pen," refers literally to a long, pointed metal instrument for cutting letters into wax tablets; in Italian, as Milton knew, it also meant "dagger."

26. For Milton's use of military metaphors to characterize his service to his party, see Robert Thomas Fallon, *Captain or Colonel: The Soldier in Milton's Life and Art* (Columbia: University of Missouri Press, 1984), pp. 125–26.

ally all of Europe attentive, in session, and passing judgment, I have in the *First Defence* spoken out and shall in the *Second* speak again to the entire assembly and council of all the most influential men, cities, and nations everywhere. I seem now to have embarked on a journey and to be surveying from on high far-flung regions and territories across the sea, faces numberless and unknown, sentiments in complete agreement with mine [*Jam videor mihi, ingressus iter, transmarinos tractus & porrectas latè regiones, sublimis perlustrare; vultus innumeros atque ignotos, animi sensus mecum conjunctissimos*]. Here the manly strength of the Germans, hostile to slavery, meets my eye; there the lively and generous ardor of the Franks, worthy of their name; here the well-considered courage of the Spaniards; there the serene and self-controlled magnanimity of the Italians. Wherever liberal sentiment, wherever freedom, or wherever magnanimity either prudently conceals or openly proclaims itself, there some in silence approve, others openly cast their votes, some make haste to applaud, others, conquered at last by the truth, acknowledge themselves my captives [*Quicquid uspiam liberorum pectorum, quicquid ingenui, quicquid magnanimi aut prudens latet, aut se palàm profitetur, alii tacitè favere, alii apertè suffragari, accurrere alii & plausu accipere, alii tandem vero victi, dedititios se tradere*]. (*YP* 4.1:554–5; *Works* 8:12–14)

Milton holds all these nations as his captives, becoming a modern-day Alexander.[27] But instead of enslaving them he shows them the way to liberty. As England in the anti-prelatical tracts was the cradle of the Reformation and religious freedom, making all the more galling its failure to throw off episcopacy, now England, through Milton, becomes the source and giver of political and secular freedom.

While ostensibly subordinate to his superiors in England, Milton oscillates between self and world, figuring himself as hero and liberator on the world stage. His labors, aided by God, will be of greatest use as he addresses "the entire human race against the foes of human liberty, amid the common and well-frequented assembly (so to speak) of all nations. . . . Anything greater or more glorious than this I neither can, nor wish to, claim [*quo ego majus aut gloriosius quicquam mihi tribuere, neque possim ullo tempore neque cupiam*]" (*YP* 4.1:558; *Works* 8:18). The pressure of these lofty claims agitates the surface of the text. Shortly before the last cited passage, the pressure is revealed in one of Milton's knotted double negatives: "But not entirely unknown, nor perhaps unwelcome, shall I return [*Sed nec ignotus planè, nec fortasse non gratus rursum advenero*] if I am he who disposed of the contentious satellite of

---

27. Near the end of the work, Milton again imagines pan-European admiration, particularly among each nation's choicest spirits (*YP* 4.1:654–5).

tyrants, hitherto deemed unconquerable, both in the view of most men and in his own opinion" (*YP* 4.1:556; *Works* 8:14).

As in the anti-prelatical tracts, Milton represents himself as enabled by a lifetime of achieved moral virtue to bear a prophetic burden. The examination of conscience that laid vice bare for his contemporaries renewed in Milton a sense of blamelessness. Assertions of extraordinary virtue and innocence underwrite claims of the author's heroic status, as in this passage in which the formula of conviction seems stillborn:

> For my part, I call upon Thee, my God, who knowest my inmost mind and all my thoughts, to witness that (although I have repeatedly examined myself on this point [the cause of his blindness] as earnestly as I could, and have searched all the corners of my life [*recessus vitæ omnes excussi*]) I am conscious of nothing, or of no deed, either recent or remote, whose wickedness could justly occasion or invite upon me this supreme misfortune [blindness]. As for what I have at any time written (since the royalists think that I am now undergoing this suffering as a penance, and they accordingly rejoice), I likewise call God to witness that I have written nothing of such kind that I was not then and am not now convinced that it was right and true and pleasing to God [*me nihil istiusmodi scripsisse, quod non rectum & verum, Deóque gratum esse*]. (*YP* 4.1:587; *Works* 8:66)

Unspotted virtue and unblemished conscience fit Milton to be God's spokesperson. He claims that "I and my interests are . . . under the protection of God" (*YP* 4.1:557). As he does with the heroes of his poetry, Milton constructs his self-image from classical as well as biblical elements. He represents himself as facing a version of the choice of Achilles. Recalling the advice of doctors that he would risk losing his eyesight if he labored on works defending the English, he dramatizes his situation:

> Either I must necessarily endure the loss of my eyes, or I must abandon my most solemn duty. And there came into my mind those two fates which, the son of Thetis relates, his mother brought back from Delphi [death with an immortality of fame or long life with obscurity]. . . . Then I reflected that many men have bought with greater evil smaller good; with death, glory. To me, on the contrary, was offered a greater good at the price of a smaller evil: that I could at the cost of blindness alone fulfill the most honorable requirement of my duty. (*YP* 4.1:588)

He is able to make this choice, he says, because of "the sound of a certain more divine monitor within" (*YP* 4.1:588), not Thetis now but God. Milton claims a heroism at first equal to and then greater than the heroism of a leading figure in classical epic. And the Christian God rewards his champion by making good out of the evil of his sacrifice and bringing strength out of his chosen weakness. Achilles, speaking to Odysseus in the underworld, complains bitterly of the death he has chosen; Milton celebrates his blindness, which steals from him only the surfaces of things, while "What is true and essential . . . is not lost to my intellectual vision" (*YP* 4.1:589). In ranging Milton with the afflicted, the blindness moreover earns him the "mercy and protection" of God. This protection clothes the blind prophet in invincibility: "Woe to him who mocks us, woe to him who injures us. He deserves to be cursed with a public malediction. Divine law and divine favor have rendered us not only safe from the injuries of men, but almost sacred [*nos ab injuriis hominum non modò incolumes, sed penè sacros, divina lex reddidit, divinus favor*], nor do these shadows around us seem to have been created so much by the dullness of our eyes as by the shade of angels' wings" (*YP* 4.1:590; *Works* 8:72). The Christian paradox of the emergence of strength from weakness here is a strange bedfellow with Milton's failure to find blame within and tendency to turn criticism into praise.

The pervasiveness of self-representation in the *Defensio Secunda*, apart from the famous autobiographical set piece, lends credence to More's hostile observation that Milton's first two *Defences* were more defenses of Milton than of the English people. In his advice to the Protectorate's Council of State at the end of the *Defensio Secunda*, Milton, as he had in *Areopagitica*, writes from a keen sense of personal grievance and personal prerogative. They "should keep only those laws that are essential and pass others—not such as subject good men with bad to the same yoke, nor, while they take precautions against the wiles of the wicked, forbid also that which should be free for good men" (*YP* 4.1:678–9). The problems of governing all the people take second place to the needs and freedoms of the choicest spirits. The subject of the ringing peroration of one of Milton's greatest prose works is Milton and not the English people. He returns to the central points of his self-representation: that the service of his pen more than compensates for his absence from the literal battles, that he is the one faithful one amid the backsliders, that he has the special protection of God. As optimism wanes with the passing of the 1650s, Milton sets himself against the rest: "If the most recent deeds of my fellow countrymen should not correspond sufficiently to their earliest, let them look to it themselves. I have borne witness, I might almost say I have erected a monument that will not soon pass away" (*YP* 4.1:685). The monument, he makes explicit in the next moment, is the equivalent of an epic poem, and thus he claims for himself the highest literary position. He is alone there, as he was alone in his continued faithfulness to the Good Old Cause of antiroyalist and tolerationist republicanism in the work's final words:

> It will seem to posterity that a mighty harvest of glory was at hand, together with the opportunity for doing the greatest deeds, but that to this opportunity men were wanting. Yet there was not wanting one

who could rightly counsel [*non defuisse qui monere recta*], encourage, and inspire, who could honor both the noble deeds and those who had done them, and make both deeds and doers illustrious with praises that will never die [*victuris in omne ævum celebrare laudibus potuerit*]. (*YP* 4.1:685–6; *Works* 8:254)

This is Milton in his most comfortable, uncomfortable role: as successor to and precursor of Abdiel. In his last prose work of the tumultuous decade Milton would again claim the dangerous but exalted privilege of being the one faithful man among the faithless.

Pro Se Defensio: *"I have never praised myself"*

Despite Alexander More's skill in probing Milton's sore spots, writing the *Pro Se Defensio* (1655) must have been something of a relief. Here, as he responds to a concentrated attack on himself as opposed to an attack on his party, Milton does not need to justify writing about himself.

Before More, who compares him to a "late-sprung mushroom," Milton, long concerned about belatedness, draws himself up: "You err, More, and know not me. To me it was always preferable to grow slowly, and as if by the silent lapse of time" (*Erras, More, & me non nosti: mihi lentè crescere, & velut occulto ævo satius semper fuit*) (*Yale* 4.2:819; *Works* 9:280). This evocative image contributes to a powerful self-dramatization, one that again turns a perceived weakness into a strength. More himself is the mushroom, who as young man "suddenly came forth as a professor of Greek." Milton ties More's incontinent haste in his career to his sexual incontinence (and contrasts both with his own chastity and timely growth): "Soon among the mushrooms, and the cabbage, and the kitchen vegetables, the mushroom *being newly tumescent* [*mox inter fungos, & olera, & armamenta olitoria, fungo* recens tuberante], you did not indeed destroy Claudius [Salmasius], but you laid Claudia [Pelletta] on her back" (*YP* 4.2:819; *Works* 9:280; my emphasis).

In a passage that More dissects as symptomatic of a habit of self-directed panegyric, Milton writes in the *Defensio Secunda* that "He alone is to be called great who either performs or teaches or worthily records great things [*Is solus magnus est appellandus, qui res magnas aut gerit, aut docet, aut dignè scribit*]" (*YP* 4.1:601; *Works* 8:94). These criteria at least appear self-serving for a writer who attempts in his works to be "doctrinal to a nation" and who has been given the task of recording the heroic deeds of his countrymen. It is hard to disagree with More's analysis:

> To him [Cromwell] you grant arms and empire; for yourself you lay claim to genius and the toga. "He alone is to be called great," you say, "who

either does great things," as Cromwell does, "or teaches them," as does Milton about divorce, "or writes about them suitably," as does Milton, twice great, for the people. . . . [F]rom the beginning of your book this arrogance of yours and Thrasonic haughtiness, which you have woven, as did the Pharisee in the Gospel, from the showy action of charms, perpetually increase to unmentioned abundance, like the crocodile, which, they say, grows in its whole life until it comes to its full growth at the end, until, *more poetically than prophetically,* you boast that you "celebrate your citizens in praises that will endure forever."[28]

As he had with the charge of belatedness, More strikes home with this charge of self-promotion, despite the fact that Milton, as it has turned out, was prophetic about the afterlife of his works. (Milton's extraordinary genius and achievements underwrite many of the claims he makes about himself. What would be conceited posturing from a lesser writer is often in Milton's case accurate self-assessment.) When he comes to answer this passage in the *Defence of Himself* (*YP* 4.2:774–75), Milton has little to say. Instead, he again condemns More as a fornicator.

More's scornful assertion that Milton's claims for the literary afterlife of his writings in defense of the English people are more *poetic* than *prophetic* is, if not merely a shot in the dark, particularly astute. Milton in *Eikonoklastes* had levied against Charles I the same charge of peddling morally suspect fictions in the guise of prophetic utterance. As Milton predicted of Charles then, so More predicts now that Milton's pretensions to immortality are hollow. What More says of Milton in the *Fides Publica,* Milton says of Charles in the *Eikonoklastes:* rather than testifying to moral authority, self-praise exposes hypocrisy and egotism. "This," Milton writes, "is the Pharisee up and down, *I am not as other men are*" (*YP* 3:469). The convergence of More's charge against Milton, Milton's against Charles, and Milton's own practice and stance is arresting. More would apply Milton's charge to Milton himself: "glorious deeds don to ambitious ends, find reward answerable, not to thir outward seeming, but to thir inward ambition" (*YP* 3:429–30). *Fides Publica* echoes *Eikonoklastes,* and one can imagine Milton's fury as he read his diagnosis of Charles I mirrored in More's attack on him. This fury fuels the *Pro Se Defensio,* which returns to the model of the *Animadversions* and *Colasterion* of point-for-point rebuttal and abuse.

Annabel Patterson has suggested that Milton's dogged reiteration in the *Pro Se Defensio* of *Defensio Secunda*'s mistaken attribution of the *Regii Sanguinis Clamor* to More, even after it became clear that More was not the author, shook Milton's idealized self-image of invariable rectitude. Patterson finds a parallel

---

28. *Fides Publica,* excerpted in *YP* 4.2.1109–10 (my emphasis).

in Milton's unhappy marriage and the resulting strained arguments of the divorce tracts a decade earlier.[29] One of the compelling dramas of the *Pro Se Defensio* is the gradual, grudging, and oblique admission of error by an author who has placed great stock in the rectitude of his life and the inerrancy of his writings. Milton even contemplates publicly the possibility of his having lied, before blurring that possibility in a conditional clause: "not from my mendacity, *if such there be*, but from your own veracity, if there be aught, should you take your strength [*non meo,* siquod fuit, *mendacio, sed tuâ te veritate, siqua fuit, munire debuisti*]" (*YP* 4.2:755; *Works* 9:132; my emphasis). By the end of the work he is rapidly backpedaling, and his language, marked by the same conditional grammatical construction, betrays surprising vulnerability: "This [the mistaken attribution], therefore, *if it be not true,* is also most trivial; and concerning it I ought not exert myself in the least, and you ought not exult [*Hoc igitur* si verum non sit, *est quoque levissimum; de quo & ego minimè laborare, & tu minimè exultare debeas*]" (*YP* 4.2:811; *Works* 9:260; my emphasis).

The problem Milton confronts in 1655, however, is bigger or less localized than one of mistaken attribution. It is the gap between a modest self-representation as servant of the republic and a grandiose and egocentric self-representation, diagnosed by More, as preeminent hero. With the melancholy but self-aggrandizing last words of the *Defensio Secunda,* quoted earlier, Milton casts himself prospectively as a lone remnant, the only one remaining faithful to the republic when the rest will have fallen away. Not merely a participant in a heroic struggle, he is the lone heroic figure left. By setting so rarefied a mark, impossible for any human being to reach, Milton inevitably purchases anxiety, which marks the *Pro Se Defensio* in moments of surprising candor, vulnerability, and even querulousness. He describes his pitiable state as he set about replying to the *Clamor:* "at that time especially, infirm health, distress over two deaths in my family [his wife, Mary, and daughter, Deborah, in May 1652], and the complete failure of my sight beset me with troubles of a far different kind" (*YP* 4.2:703). Challenged by More as to why he had not answered all of his detractors, Milton replies in some anguish, "Will you have more reasons? Because I am my own master; because I had not leisure; in fine, because I am a man, possessed of a human nature, not an iron one, though you may be an Alexander of brass [*Vis plura? quia liberum erat; quia non vacabat; quia denique homo sum, humana mihi latera sunt, non ferrea, tu licet Alexander ærarius sis*]" (*YP* 4.2:768; *Works 9:166*).[30]

These uncharacteristically frank admissions of weakness provide indirect evidence of More's deftness as a reader of Milton. More lays bare what Milton

---

29. Annabel Patterson, "The Civic Hero in Milton's Prose," *Milton Studies* 8 (1975): 71–101.

30. For further glimpses of a vulnerable and anxious Milton, see the letters of July and September 1654 to Henry Oldenburg and Leonard Philaras respectively (*YP* 4.2:866,868).

has labored mightily to conceal from himself—the self-serving exaggeration that mars Milton's exercise in ethical proof. Milton has been challenged on his claims to be extraordinarily virtuous and chosen by God. It is an index of the depth of the impulse registered by More to see Milton turning to self-praise even as he disputes More's claim:

> What if, as you object, in a brief digression, I had praised myself? Who would not admit that often there are those times and occasions when appropriate praises are not indecorous, even to the most saintly and modest men [*sanctissimis modestissimísque viris*], nor have ever been? If I should wish to illustrate this topic by a copious supply of examples, I might, indeed, easily prove myself to all men, and you would be struck dumb. *But I have never praised myself;* nor, as you charge, will you ever find a panegyric pronounced by me upon myself. *Singular indeed is the favor of God toward me* [Sed me nusquam laudavi; *nec, quod criminaris, Panegyricum à me mihimet dictum usquam invenies.* Singulare quidem in me divini numinis beneficium], that He has called me above all others to the defence of liberty. (*YP* 4.2:735; *Works* 9:84–86; my emphasis)

There is no shame in praising oneself in such a digression as the *Defensio Secunda* undoubtedly (and fortunately) contains, and to have composed such a digression is to join the company of the "most saintly." But, Milton goes on, he has not praised himself, nor will he ever, for it would not be fitting for one specially chosen by God for an extraordinary purpose, chosen, we know from elsewhere, by merit of his singular virtue for a difficult task that he has triumphantly completed. We are whipsawed here. If I did it, I did it with the saintly; I didn't do it; I'm doing it again.

In response to More's dissection of his claim to heroic virtue, Milton reiterates the claim in revealing language: "whatever your rumor-mongers may mutter or speak about me, I am singularly secure [*unicè securus*]. You will learn that there is within me that moral consciousness, that I have that credit among good men" (*YP* 4.2:767; *Works* 9:162). The word "secure" is a double-edged sword in Milton. The Father in *Paradise Lost* charges Raphael with warning Adam "to beware / He swerve not too secure" (5.237–38). Adam was rudely awakened from complacency.

Milton attempts to turn the tables on More, accusing him of hyperbolic magnificence and presumption in his praise of Queen Christina of Sweden, which, as it happens, parallels Milton's own enthusiastic praise of Christina. Milton seems to shadowbox; More takes on the outlines of the image that Milton projects, and Milton strikes at that image. Milton says derisively, "It does not please me, I confess, to soar so high; for from such a height I should inevitably either tumble down ridiculously or freeze among the clouds [*Mihi, fateor, non placet sic altè insurgere; unde statim necesse erit, vel ridiculè ruam, vel inter nubes frigescam*]" (*YP* 4.2:770; *Works* 9:170). But More could be excused for thinking that in his *Defences* Milton soars far above middle flight in his representation of himself as a singular hero, equal or superior in courage and liberating efficacy to those whom he ostensibly defends and celebrates. The image he chooses here foreshadows the cautionary simile of Bellerophon (discussed in chapter 8), which haunts the self-referential invocation to Book 7 of *Paradise Lost*. Milton gambles in the *Defences* as in *Paradise Lost*. If he is God's "selected herald," and if he is a singularly heroic figure, all is well. But if he is, as More mocks, arrogant, haughty, and Pharisaical, then Milton has less between him and the earth than did the presumptuous Bellerophon. The exercises in Latin prose epic share with his verse epic shadows of anxiety: if all is Milton's, and not God's, then in the *Defences*, as in *Paradise Lost*, he has much for which to answer.

1659–1660: The Restoration Approaches

In 1659 and 1660, Milton turned again to self-generated polemic in three works, *A Treatise of Civil Power in Ecclesiastical Causes* (1659; *Civil Power*), *Considerations Touching the Likeliest Means to Remove Hirelings from the Church* (1659; *Hirelings*), and, in two editions, *The Readie and Easie Way to Establish a Free Commonwealth* (1660; *The Readie and Easie Way*). After a decade as official spokesperson for his party, he was, I will argue, freed by the disintegration of the Good Old Cause. *Eikonoklastes* and the first two *Defences* had been imposed labors; however much Milton welcomed the confidence of his masters and gloried in his role as spokesperson of England and liberty, the works had taken a toll on him. The burden of writing for his party could only have become heavier with the failure of the Interregnum governments to make good on the promise of full toleration and the separation of church and state, and with the failure of the English people to support republican government. As the restoration of monarchy approached, Milton was freed to adopt once again his favorite pose: the lone prophetic voice crying out in a faithless world.

Civil Power *and* Hirelings: *"the event will bear me witnes"*

Civil Power is a straightforward and, for Milton, impersonal work. At the end Milton remarks that "Pomp and ostentation of reading is admir'd among the vulgar: but doubtless in matters of religion he is learnedest who is planest," adding that he chose "not to make much ado where less may serve" (*YP* 7.272). *Civil Power* is one of the few works by Milton of which this is true. This modesty seems to be on display when he remarks earlier that "no man can know [divine illumination] at all times to be in himself" (*YP* 7.242), although here Milton employs the argument to deflate the pretensions of those who would prescribe religious practice to others.

After the impersonality of *Civil Power,* Milton begins *Hirelings* by writing about himself:

> Owing to your protection, supream Senat, this libertie of writing which I have us'd these 18 years on all occasions to assert the just rights and freedoms both of church and state, and so far approv'd, as to have bin trusted with the representment and defence of your actions to all Christendom against an adversarie of no mean repute, to whom should I address what I still publish on the same argument, but to you. (*YP* 7:274)

Milton recalls for his readers his nearly two decades of polemical engagement, beginning with the *Of Reformation* of 1641. He highlights, as he has often done, his vanquishing of Salmasius, the "adversarie of no mean repute." The defeat of Salmasius has become a central pillar of Milton's image, the validation of his claim that his service in the liberation of England has been not merely heroic but martial. Milton ends the pamphlet as he had begun, by referring to his service as an especially worthy witness. He does so in a manner that looks forward to the ringing peroration of *The Readie and Easie Way:* "If I be not heard nor beleevd, the event will bear me witnes to have spoken truth: and I in the mean while have borne my witnes not out of season to the church and to my countrey" (*YP* 7:321). The external confidence with which Milton began his eighteen years of polemic, that his arguments will effect political change, has waned, but his self-confidence seems intact. And, paradoxically, pessimism regarding the result seems to invigorate Milton, as he positions himself as Old Testament prophet, the one righteous man warning a backsliding people.

We hear the personal and self-revelatory note in *Hirelings* most clearly when Milton, echoing *The Reason of Church-Government,* complains bitterly about the monopoly of an educated but ignorant clergy. They "claim . . . by divine right and freehold the tenth of our estates, to monopolize the ministry as their peculiar, which is free and open to all able Christians, elected by any church" (*YP* 7:320). Perceiving himself shouldered aside by a mercenary professional class, Milton reacts bitterly.

The Readie and Easie Way: *"the best affected . . . and best principl'd of the people"*

The Readie and Easie Way, because of its appearance in two editions in rapid succession during a critical moment in the life (and death throes) of the Good Old Cause, provides a valuable window into Milton's unfolding self-representation. In both editions Milton expresses the familiar outrage of injured merit when he attacks a king's audacity to "lord over his brethren, whom he cannot but know, whether as men or Christians, to be for the most part every way equal or superiour to himself" (*YP* 7:364;429).[31] He employs his common tactic of bland assertion of the provocative and controversial when he adds, "I doubt not but all ingenuous and knowing men will easily agree with me, that a free Commonwealth without single person or house of lords, is by far the best government" (*YP* 7:364–5;429). Both editions end with an assertion of the author's heroism and singularity:

> wth all hazard I have ventur'd what I thought my dutie, to speak in season, & to forewarn my country in time: wherin I doubt not but there be many wise men in all places and degrees, but am sorrie the effects of wisdom are so little seen among us. . . . [T]her will want at no time who are good at circumstances, but men who set thir mindes on main matters and sufficiently urge them, in these most difficult times I finde not many. What I have spoken, is the language of the good old cause: if it seem strange to any, it will not seem more strange, I hope, then convincing to backsliders. (*YP* 7:387–88;462)

In the ringing peroration from which this passage is taken, Milton figures himself as a new Jeremiah.[32] Unencumbered by the responsibility of speaking for superiors, he no longer needs to justify questionable policies or actions. And he again emerges as the one speaking in opposition, faithful to God and willing to risk opprobrium. The stance of the one just man in a hostile world had long been his most congenial one. In the dire circumstances of 1660 Milton recovers this paradoxically liberating stance.

In several additions to the revised edition of *The Readie and Easie Way* Milton advances an argument for rule by an enlightened minority. The rhetoric here reflects his self-construction. Whatever the lack of support for republican government, a lack of support requiring the purging of Parliament, the "best affected also and best principl'd of the people, stood not numbring or computing on which side were most voices in Parlament, but on which side appeerd to them most reason, most safetie" (*YP* 7:414). The appeal to right over numbers to establish the legitimacy of a republican government is a precarious one. Milton is forced to argue that the "greatest part" of his countrymen "have

---

31. In citing passages contained in both editions, I quote the version in the first edition and indicate the location of passages that contain minor variations in spelling and pointing in the second edition.

32. Laura Lunger Knoppers, "Milton's *The Readie and Easie Way* and the English Jeremiad," in *Politics, Poetics, and Hermeneutics in Milton's Prose,* ed. David Loewenstein and James Grantham Turner (Cambridge: Cambridge University Press, 1990), pp. 213–25.

both in reason and the trial of just battel, lost the right of their election what the government shall be" (*YP* 7:455). The only solution is the addition of might to right, as the minority must force the majority to be free rather than allow themselves to be enslaved by the majority.[33]

In these arguments, Milton applies to the political arena arguments honed in theological and ecclesiastical debates, which is not surprising given that his ideal is a republic ruled by godly men. As the voice of the individual led by the Spirit trumps centuries of tradition, imposed church doctrine, and any other measure, so Milton's godly minority should trump any appeal to the ballot box. The obvious difficulty is that in the purely religious argument each individual, according to a Protestant principle tirelessly invoked by Milton, is responsible for his or her own interpretation of Scripture and relationship with God. Politics, however, is a corporate undertaking, which makes the appeal to the authority of the right affected both tenuous and dangerous. In any event, Milton as political thinker like Milton as religious thinker builds a great deal on his self-construction as one of the few, or perhaps the one, able to see truth in a world going astray.

The self-regarding nature of Milton's political argument is most on display in his strikingly impractical proposal for elections passing through progressively finer sieves (*YP* 7:442–43). Candidates for the Council of State are to be nominated only by those not disqualified (by, presumably, support for a king or a House of Lords). A more select group of worthies will further winnow the candidates. The remaining candidates are then sifted a third and fourth time by judges even more select. The logical culmination of the direction of the proposal would seem to be final approval of a slate of members by a very small group. Milton's proposal for the selection of a supposedly republican government resembles his description of the emergence of the heroic writer. Milton had often written of the winnowing of candidates able to write in defense of the Good Old Cause, or of candidates able to write the great Christian epic, in each case ending with someone looking very much like Milton himself. By extension, the goal of Milton's election procedure seems to be the selection of a small body of men resembling Milton. The impossibility of his proposal here, however framed as "ready" and "easy," is a vivid sign of Milton's difficult position, with darkness and with dangers compassed round.

---

33. Not surprisingly, Milton's opinion of the common people grew more pessimistic as they failed to rally around the Good Old Cause. He is more consistent in his high valuation of his own class, the middle class. In *Eikonoklastes* (1649), Milton alternates between castigating the common people for their susceptibility to monarchic show and praising them as the Talus who drove out the bishops (*YP* 3:344,390–91,601). In the *Defensio* Milton argues that "More often far more of the commoners surpass the lords in character and intellect" (*YP* 4.1:470); these commoners are the gentry and middle class, as becomes clear in the reference a page later to "the middle class, which produces the greatest number of men of good sense and knowledge of affairs."

Those dangers leave their mark on the text of the second edition, and Milton is keenly aware of them as, in darkening circumstances, he begins work. The additions to the prefatory paragraph, for example, reveal pessimism and anxiety: "I never read of any State, scarce of any tyrant grown so incurable, as to refuse counsel from any in a time of public deliberation; much less to be offended. If thir absolute determination be to enthrall us, before so long a Lent of Servitude, they may permitt us a little Shroving-time first, wherin to speak freely, and take our leaves of Libertie" (*YP* 7:408–9). The nervousness betrays itself in Milton's effort to prevent Parliament from taking offense (or worse) at his words. At the end of the text he will make clear that he knows the cause is lost, and that he writes to bear witness to a truth that the multitude has spurned. Here at the opening he acknowledges the potential cost of that witness, a cost that underwrites his claims to heroism. As a testimony to that heroism added in the second edition, Milton once again recalls his victory over Salmasius:

> Nor was the heroic cause unsuccesfully defended to all Christendom against the tongue of a famous and thought invincible adversarie; nor the constancie and fortitude that so nobly vindicated our liberty, our victory at once against two the most prevailing usurpers over mankinde, superstition and tyrannie unpraisd or uncelebrated in a written monument, likely to outlive detraction, as it hath hitherto convinc'd or silenc'd not a few of our detractors, especially in parts abroad. (*YP* 7:420–1)

Milton subdues an invincible adversary and leaves behind him a work that the world will not willingly let die. His reputation is universal. However weak and endangered his position at home, he is remembered as a doughty warrior "in parts abroad." As elsewhere in his self-representations, Milton's efforts with his pen are hard to distinguish from the efforts that he celebrates, and questions of priority are overturned or at least blurred.

At the end of the day, he is the last Englishman left standing. In the additions to his peroration in the second edition, Milton presents himself in terms like those with which he will present Abdiel in Satan's camp at the end of Book 5 of *Paradise Lost*. He asks his compatriots to "bethink themselves a little and consider whether they are rushing" before they allow "the deluge of this epidemic madness" to push them over "a precipice of destruction" (*YP* 7:463). Milton repeats the self-regarding allusion to Jeremiah (Jer. 22:24–29) from the first edition: "Thus much I should perhaps have said though I were sure I should have spoken only to trees and stones; and had none to cry to, but with the Prophet, *O earth, earth, earth!*" (*YP* 7:462). But he changes the next line, dropping "to tell the verie soil it self what God hath determined of *Coniah* and his seed for ever" (*YP* 7:388), with its allusion to Charles I and his cursed seed, and adding "to tell the very soil it self, what her perverse inhabitants are deaf to" (*YP* 7:462–63), which turns its focus to his foolish countrymen. He then adds, "Nay though what I have spoke, should happ'n (which Thou suffer not, who didst create mankinde free; nor Thou next, who didst redeem us from being servants of men!) to be the last words of our expiring libertie." Despite the optimism implied by the prayer to creator and redeemer, the speech reads more like the testimony of the last witness than the prelude to the multiplication of the faithful. The prayer, like the allusion to Jeremiah, cements Milton's prophetic status as the one faithful man in a welter of faithlessness. It is a role that Milton appears to relish, as is evidenced by the feeling with which he writes about Abdiel, his alter ego:

> Among the faithless, faithful only he;
> Among innumerable false, unmoved,
> Unshaken, unseduced, unterrified,
> His loyalty he kept, his love, his zeal;
> Nor number, nor example with him wrought
> To swerve from truth, or change his constant mind
> Though single.
> (*PL* 5.897–903)

In the final lines of *The Readie and Easie Way*, one can hear the "retorted scorn" with which Abdiel turns his back on "those proud towers to swift destruction doomed" (5.906–7), the scorn that Milton, the prophet and the one just man, has always turned on the many who fail to see the truth. After the restraint of the *Tenure of Kings and Magistrates* and *Eikonoklastes*, Milton has returned to his element.

Chapter 7

"Elect above the Rest"

De Doctrina Christiana and *Paradise Lost*

In a prefatory letter to a heavily revised and layered Latin manuscript that would languish forgotten and unpublished for 150 years after his death, Milton wrote that "with feelings of universal brotherhood and good will . . . I am sharing . . . my dearest and best possession with as many people as possible" (*YP* 6:121). Anticipating a harsh reaction to his *De Doctrina Christiana,* he asks his readers to be sympathetic and patient and to avoid "prejudice and malice, even though they see at once that many of the views I have published are at odds with certain conventional opinions." The prefatory letter, like the brief preface to the heretical fifth chapter on the Son of God, bristles with Milton's familiar belligerent defensiveness.[1] Whatever one might expect from a systematic theological treatise, *De Doctrina* carries on between its lines the work of self-justification and self-representation central to Milton's other works. Moreover, tensions within the treatise concerning merit and election, which carry implications for Milton's heroic self-construction, help isolate and highlight similar tensions in his epic. This chapter examines *De Doctrina* and *Paradise Lost* together, not so much

---

1. For what I view as the fundamentally unconvincing case against Milton's authorship, see William Hunter, "The Provenance of the *Christian Doctrine,*" *Studies in English Literature,* 32 (1992): 129–42; "The Provenance of the *Christian Doctrine: Addenda from the Bishop of Salisbury,*" *Studies in English Literature* 33 (1993): 191–207; and "Animadversions upon the Remonstrants' Defenses against Burgess and Hunter," *Studies in English Literature* 34 (1994): 195–203. Hunter's arguments are gathered in his *Visitation Unimplor'd: Milton and the Authorship of De Doctrina Christiana* (Pittsburgh: Duquesne University Press, 1998). See also Paul Sellin, "John Milton's *Paradise Lost* and *De Doctrina Christiana* on Predestination," *Milton Studies* 34 (1996): 45–60. Hunter's 1992 *SEL* article is followed by a "Forum" with critiques by Barbara Lewalski (143–54) and John Shawcross (155–62) and a response by Hunter (163–66). The 1994 article is itself a response to a second "Forum" with contributions by Maurice Kelley, "The Provenance of John Milton's *Christian*

using treatise as a gloss upon the epic (as Maurice Kelley does in his landmark study of the works),[2] but using a famous crux in the epic as a lens to focus elements of the author's self-representation in the treatise.

Chosen by Peculiar Grace?

In 1619, the Synod of Dort, defending orthodox Calvinist teaching on predestination and election, warned against "curiously scrutinizing the deep and mysterious things of God."[3] That same year, the ten-year-old John Milton sat for a portrait, his closely cropped hair a visible sign of the influence, his widow would tell John Aubrey years later, of his Puritan teacher, perhaps the Calvinist Thomas Young.[4] Whatever the principles instilled by Young, Milton by the time of *De Doctrina* had become the kind of curious scrutinizer rebuked by the Synod, echoing the Arminian or Remonstrant doctrines of universal and sufficient grace that the Synod condemned. Impatient with mystery,[5] he would not balk at skeptically probing divine justice; instead he would reject the Calvinist claim that divine justice is inscrutable and unquestionable.[6] God's actions are subject to rational scrutiny and approval because they conform to accessible standards of reason. Freed from its equivocating context, Milton would subscribe to the aphorism he authors upon Satan, "Not just, not God" (*PL*

Doctrine: A Reply to William B. Hunter" (153–63) and Christopher Hill, "Professor William B. Hunter, Bishop Burgess, and John Milton" (165–93). (Hill's contribution contains an impressive appendix listing parallels between *De Doctrina* and twenty of Milton's prose works as well as four of his sonnets.) See also my essay "Milton's Arminianism and the Authorship of *De doctrina Christiana,*" *Texas Studies in Literature and Language* 41 (1999): 103–27. A working group of Gordon Campbell, Thomas N. Corns, John K. Hale, David I. Holmes, and Fiona J. Tweedie convened to sift evidence of authorship; their conclusions in their interim report ("The Provenance of *De Doctrina Christiana,*" *Milton Quarterly* 31 [1997]: 67–117) were tentative. Their report at the International Milton Symposium in Grenoble in June 2005 came down firmly on the side of Milton's authorship.

2. Maurice Kelley, *This Great Argument: A Study of Milton's "De Doctrina Christiana" as a Gloss upon "Paradise Lost"* (Princeton: Princeton University Press, 1941).

3. "Of the Doctrine of Divine Predestination," art. 12, quoted from *The Articles of the Synod of Dort,* trans. Thomas Scott (Philadelphia: Presbyterian Board of Publication, 1841), p. 266. Further quotations from the *Articles* will be taken from this edition.

4. William Riley Parker, *Milton: A Biography,* 2 vols. (Oxford: Clarendon, 1968), 1:8, 2:701–2. For Elizabeth Milton's comment, see *Aubrey's Brief Lives,* ed. Oliver Lawson Dick (1949; repr. Ann Arbor: University of Michigan Press, 1957), p. 200.

5. Witness his rejection of the Trinity in *De Doctrina* (three is three and one is one). There are mysteries in *Paradise Lost;* why, e.g., would one occupying Satan's position conceive sin? But the mysteries cluster around events and characters before creation, as Milton, as much as one writing a universal epic can, remains true to the position of *De Doctrina* (1.7): "Anyone who asks what God did before the creation of the world is a fool; and anyone who answers him is not much wiser" (*YP* 6:299).

6. John Stachniewski suggests that Milton's project of "justifying" God is a reaction against Calvinist insistence, in response to attacks on the doctrine of predestination, that "God should not be brought to the bar of human justice" (*The Persecutory Imagination: English Puritanism and the Literature of Religious Despair* [Oxford: Oxford University Press, 1991], p. 333).

9.701). Though Calvinists denounced as sinfully presumptuous attempts to subject God's justice to rational evaluation, Milton was confident that, aided by the Spirit, he could draw out this leviathan with the hook of his reason.[7]

Given Milton's eagerness to rationalize the myth and the doctrines of fall and salvation, it is all the more surprising that there remains in *Paradise Lost* one crucial passage that resists this rationalizing urge. When the Father describes the economy of salvation in Book 3, an apparent residue of Calvinist teaching on election disturbs the otherwise Arminian and libertarian doctrine of the mature Milton, resulting in a tension between claims for different and incompatible forms of distinction. The unresolved tension in the Father's speech helps bring to light a similar tension in *De Doctrina*. Not surprisingly, given the demands of the genre, the conflicting forces left unresolved in *Paradise Lost* are resolved in the treatise. But the mere presence of the conflicting forces in the treatise betrays the degree to which *De Doctrina*, despite the appearance of impersonality required by its genre, shares with Milton's other works a project of self-justification. Through epic and treatise run fault lines in Milton's self-conception and self-representation.[8]

---

7. Readers from his time to ours have agreed that Milton attempts to recast the biblical story of sin and salvation on rational lines; on his success, though, at least in *Paradise Lost*, there is no consensus. Andrew Marvell recognized the implications of Milton's great argument, worried that Milton would "ruin . . . / The sacred Truths," but concluded by endorsing his friend and colleague's claim of prophetic status ("On Mr. Milton's *Paradise Lost*" [7–8, 43–44], in *The Poems and Letters of Andrew Marvell*, ed. H. M. Margoliouth, 2nd ed., 2 vols. [Oxford: Clarendon, 1952], 1:131–32). Alexander Pope, whose concern is more exclusively literary than Marvell's, famously reproaches Milton for having his epic God argue like a "school divine" (*Imitations of Horace*, "Epistle to Augustus," 99–102). More recently, the success of Milton's rational exploration of divine justice in *Paradise Lost* has been claimed explicitly by Dennis Burden and implicitly by Dennis Danielson (Burden, *The Logical Epic: A Study of the Argument of Paradise Lost* [Cambridge, MA: Harvard University Press, 1967]; Danielson, *Milton's Good God: A Study in Literary Theodicy* [Cambridge: Cambridge University Press, 1982]). But even that most ardent of admirers of Milton's rationalist redaction of Scriptural myth, Philip Gallagher, wonders uneasily if Milton's lust for order has flattened some salutary mysteries in the Bible (*Milton, the Bible, and Misogyny* [Columbia: University of Missouri Press, 1990], p. 48).

8. For more on my use of the terms "Calvinist" and "Arminian," see the essay from which this discussion is adapted, "'Elect above the Rest': Theology as Self-representation in Milton" (in *Milton and Heresy*, ed. Stephen Dobranski and John Rumrich [Cambridge: Cambridge University Press, 1998], pp. 94–95). In brief, I employ the term *Arminian* as it was employed in the seventeenth century, to label (and often to condemn) the belief in conditional predestination to salvation, contingent on an individual's choice to accept or reject universal and resistible grace. That is to say, I am not using the term "Arminian" as defined by Nicholas Tyacke in his *Anti-Calvinists*, according to which Milton must be counted in some ways not merely not Arminian but positively anti-Arminian (*Anti-Calvinists: The Rise of English Arminianism c. 1590–1640* [Oxford: Oxford University Press, 1987]). Unlike Tyacke's "English Arminians," for example, Milton denied that sacraments conferred grace (to say nothing of his opposition to the High Church "Arminian" politics and ceremonialism of William Laud). These and other "English Arminian" positions are

In Book 3, the Father reads a lecture on the economy of salvation:

> Some I have chosen of peculiar grace
> Elect above the rest; so is my will:
> The rest shall hear me call, and oft be warned   185
> Their sinful state, and to appease betimes
> Th' incensèd Deity, while offered grace
> Invites; for I will clear their senses dark,
> What may suffice, and soften stony hearts
> To pray, repent, and bring obedience due.   190
> To prayer, repentance, and obedience due,
> Though but endeavored with sincere intent,
> Mine ear shall not be slow, mine eye not shut.
> And I will place within them as a guide
> My umpire conscience, whom if they will hear,   195
> Light after light well-used they shall attain,
> And to the end persisting, safe arrive.
> This my long sufferance and my day of grace
> They who neglect and scorn, shall never taste;
> But hard be hardened, blind be blinded more,   200
> That they may stumble on, and deeper fall.
> (*PL* 3.183–201)

The division of souls here is trifold: those elect by special grace, those who with the aid of general grace accept God's call to salvation, and those who reject this general grace and who are thus damned. Each of the relevant theological contexts, on the other hand, disposes souls into two categories. Calvinists divide persons into the elect and the reprobate. In terms of the passage itself, the Calvinist elect are those "chosen of peculiar grace," and the reprobate are those who, though hearing God call, "neglect and scorn" it; there are none who respond properly to the call without being specially elect.[9] The Arminian twofold distinction, again in the terms of the passage, falls *within*

---

not found in Arminius himself. In using the label "Arminian" to designate Milton's acceptance of Arminius's anti-Calvinist doctrines of conditional election, unlimited atonement, and resistible grace, I am following the lead not only of Maurice Kelley, Don M. Wolfe, and Arthur Barker but also of seventeenth-century polemical writers, including Milton himself, who uses the term in this way in the 1644 *Doctrine and Discipline of Divorce* and the 1673 *Of True Religion* (*YP* 2:293, 8:425).

9. For a poetic expression of Calvinist binarism, see Michael Wigglesworth's *The Day of Doom* (the first of several American editions appeared in 1662, and the first [pirated] London edition

the category of the "rest" who "hear [God] call"; in the Arminian view, there are none chosen for salvation by special grace. Milton seems for the moment to equivocate. In the first four lines of the passage, Milton sounds a Calvinist note. The elect are set off against the "sinful" rest. But as the speech unfolds that "rest" turn out not to be the reprobate, but the elect (who choose to accept grace) and the reprobate (who choose not to).

The opening and body of the passage compete for control of lines 185–86 ("The rest shall hear me call, and oft be warn'd / Their sinful state"). The lines' meaning changes, depending on whether they are viewed from the perspective of the preceding two lines or the succeeding fifteen. The apparently Calvinist perspective of lines 183–86 is contextualized and corrected by the straight Arminianism of lines 185–202.[10] It is wrong to read the opening of this speech as evidence of Milton's unreconstructed Calvinism, but not simply wrong. If the evocation of a Calvinist-style elect in the opening lines is tightly circumscribed by the Arminian discourse that follows, at the same time it encodes the author's characteristic self-understanding as elect prophet, a self-understanding acquired at the expense of his otherwise consistent soteriology. The Father draws an either/or distinction between "some" (183) and "the rest" (185), but in the theology of salvation as articulated by Arminius and in Milton's *De Doctrina* the handful of those "elect above the rest" are subject to the same conditions of salvation applicable in the Father's speech to "the rest." The first category is reassimilated into the second in the treatise if not in the poem.

The problem with God's speech is that the Calvinist and Arminian perspectives coexist no more peacefully here than they did at the Synod of Dort. The conflicting perspectives in God's speech and their place in Milton's self-construction are thrown into relief by a comparison of *De Doctrina* and *Paradise Lost*. The comparison reveals the manner in which the treatise repeatedly approaches and then explicitly neutralizes or domesticates the quasi-Calvinist position of 3.183–84 ("Some I have chosen of peculiar grace/Elect above the rest"). It is a commonplace to point out the perils of treating the poem as if it

---

in 1666), especially stanzas 40–47, 144–63. The distance between Wigglesworth and Milton is measured by the distance between Milton's Arminian formula, the "free / *Acceptance* of large grace" (*PL* 12:304–5; my emphasis) and Wigglesworth's Calvinist insistence on *God's* freedom in dispensing grace: "Else should my Grace cease to be Grace; / For it should not be free, / If to release whom I should please, / I have no libertee" (st. 177), in *The Poems of Michael Wigglesworth*, ed. Ronald A. Bosco (Lanham, MD: University Press of America, 1989), p. 55; see also stanzas 163 and 179. I would like to thank John Shawcross for bringing this poem to my attention.

10. The concluding lines, on God's hardening of sinners, may strike the modern reader as Calvinist, but Arminius agrees that God hardens those who have freely chosen to reject sufficient grace. See, e.g., "Review of Perkins," *The Writings of James Arminius*, trans. James Nichols and W. R. Bagnall, 3 vols. (Grand Rapids: Baker Book House, 1956), 3:329–30.

were a treatise; it is no safer to treat the treatise as a poem. Juxtaposition of the Father's speech and the several related passages in *De Doctrina* demonstrates how the demands of treatise do not allow Milton the kind of equivocation that marks *Paradise Lost*.

It is not surprising, given the irresolvable tensions of the Father's speech, that Maurice Kelley and Dennis Danielson, the two best guides to the embodiment in *Paradise Lost* of the theology of *De Doctrina*, are uncharacteristically inadequate here. Kelley quotes 3.183–84, without elaboration, as an item in a list of otherwise univocally Arminian passages from the treatise and *Paradise Lost* 3.173–202.[11] Danielson demonstrates that Kelley's reading of these lines as Arminian is untenable.[12] He suggests instead that "Milton is attempting a sort of compromise solution.... Perhaps Milton... posits some kind of 'super-elect' (*PL* 3.183–84), and then a generality who receive sufficient grace (3.189), some of these availing themselves of it (3.195–97), some neglecting and scorning the offer (3.198 ff.).... Milton's 'elect above the rest' can reasonably be seen as a category with which he complements an otherwise generally Arminian position."[13] Scholars like the middle ground, but by having recourse to the terms "compromise" and "complement," Danielson risks obscuring or minimizing the great divide on predestination that separated orthodox Calvinism and its repudiated stepchild Arminianism.[14] The untenability of compromise between them is illustrated by the fact that Milton, working under the logical imperative of discursive theological prose, resolves the tension left standing in the Father's speech. He does so not by finding a middle ground between Calvin and Arminius, but by qualifying the suggestion of a super-elect so drastically that it becomes a fully Arminian position. The conflicting imperatives that dwell incongruously and uneasily together in the Father's speech clash at several moments in the treatise before being resolved as they never are in the poem. The speech discloses Milton's incompatible desires to be both among a special super-elect, marked out by a kind of birthright, and among

---

11. Kelley, *This Great Argument*, p. 17.
12. Danielson, *Milton's Good God*, pp. 82–83; Danielson cites not *This Great Argument* but Kelley's "The Theological Drama of *Paradise Lost*, III, 173–202," *PMLA* 52 (1937): 75–79.
13. Danielson, *Milton's Good God*, p. 83.
14. In my view John Shawcross does obscure the divide between Calvinist and Arminian conceptions of predestination in his *John Milton: The Self and the World* (Lexington: University of Kentucky Press, 1993), pp. 138–40. Shawcross writes that "some Calvinists seem to have believed in a strict doctrine of election and thus of absolute grace, others in varying ways and degrees held that . . . election included both those elect from the beginning of time and those who gained salvation through obedience and faith" (138). The latter position, compatible with Arminius's, is anathema to Calvin and is expressly repudiated by the Synod of Dort. While Shawcross is correct that Arminius "staunchly argued his Calvinist orthodoxy" (139), one should note that Arminius attacks Calvin's version of predestination for "mak[ing] God the author of sin [*Deum peccati auctorem facis*]" (*Writings* 3:363; see also 1:228, 3:44).

those who are elect by virtue of their free choices; in a word, he wishes to be elect by both birthright and merit.[15] The Father's speech in the epic begins and ends in a discursive moment that recurs but that is repeatedly mediated and rationalized in the treatise. Intimations of a super-elect are admitted and then overturned in a recurring drama evoked but not completed in the poem.

Theology as Self-Representation in *De Doctrina*

The subtle self-referentiality of *De Doctrina,* uncharacteristic of a normally abstract and impersonal genre but highly characteristic of Milton, constitutes strong if circumstantial evidence of Milton's authorship. Barker argued that Milton's "real concern is not with men in general but with good men."[16] I will press Barker's point and suggest that Milton's real concern is not with men in general but with men like Milton, and that the set is sufficiently small that it seems at times as if Milton is writing for himself. This is true of his theological as well as his political discourse.

In the anatomy of the self-regarding and social virtues in the second book of *De Doctrina,* Milton follows John Wolleb's *Compendium Theologiae Christianae* (1642) so closely that his additions are revealing. Milton, for example, approaches paraphrase of Wolleb in his discussion of "contentment," "frugality," and "industry," but he adds "lautitia," which Sumner translates as "liberality" and Carey as "elegance," or "the discriminating enjoyment of food, clothing and all the civilized refinements of life [*omnemque vitæ cultum*]" (*YP* 6:732; *Works* 17:232). This virtue sits strangely among modesty, decency, contentment, industry, frugality, humility, and high-mindedness, but it does reflect Milton's refined taste and his hostility to asceticism. Milton echoes Wolleb on "urbanity," but he adds an extra-ethical dimension to Wolleb's definition. For Wolleb, "urbanity" is "the virtue by which conversation is carried on with good humor and good taste, suited to the circumstances, as required by manners and ethics."[17] Milton writes, "URBANITY entails not only elegance and wit (of a decent kind) in conversation, *but also the ability to discourse and to reply in an acute and apposite way* [sed etiam qua aliquid acute atque apposite dicitur aut respon-

---

15. Strictly speaking, Arminius agrees with Calvin that the merit of election is God's rather than ours, but Calvinists charged Arminians with claiming for themselves the glory and merit of God in their insistence on human freedom to accept or reject saving grace.

16. *Milton and the Puritan Dilemma, 1641–1660* (Toronto: University of Toronto Press, 1942), p. 313.

17. *Compendium* II.xiii, in *Reformed Dogmatics: J. Wollebius, G. Voetius, F. Turretin,* trans. John W. Beardslee III (New York: Oxford University Press, 1965), p. 255. Further references to Wolleb in translation are from this edition and cited by section and page number in the text.

detur]" (*YP* 6:769–70; *Works* 17:322; my emphasis). This is the Milton who impressed the academies of Florence, the Milton who would himself be a "true Poem" (*YP* 1:890). We hear the Miltonic voice as well in the discussion of modesty. From Wolleb Milton takes his definition, "abstinence from obscene words and suggestive behavior," but he adds his idiosyncratic flourish, "and, in fact, from anything which fails to conform with the strictest standards of personal or sexual conduct" (*YP* 6:727).[18]

Perhaps the most revealing self-referential addition to Wolleb occurs in the discussion of the lawfulness of usury. Milton follows Wolleb point for point, citation for citation, but then goes on to make two additions in the concluding discussion. Wolleb writes,

> That interest is not condemned absolutely and in itself is obvious because (1) if it were wicked under all circumstances, God would not have permitted loans to be made at interest to the foreigner (Deut. 23:20); (2) if land, house, horse, and other goods may be let out at interest, so also can money. God did not want profit to be received from interest in the land of Canaan for reasons connected with the ceremonial law, just as he did not allow land there to be sold in perpetuity (Lev. 25:23). (II. xii.2; p. 249)
>
> *Usuram per se ac simpliciter improbandam non esse, patet: I. Quia si simpliciter turpis esset non concessisset Deus, ut extraneo in usuram daretur,* Deut. 23:20. *II. Quia si fundus, demus, equus & similia ad fructum elocari possunt, tum & pecunia. Regionis Cananae fructus deus usuris subjici noluit, sacremoniali significatione: quemadmodum nec agros ejus, lege mancipii vendi voluit,* Levit. 25:23. (1642 ed., pp. 272–73)

The scrivener's son, whose leisure was purchased by the interest earned from his father's loans (and who met his first wife while collecting on one of those loans), elaborates:

> Usury, then, is no more reprehensible in itself than any other kind of lawful commerce. The proof of this is, in the first place, that if it were blameworthy in itself God would not have let the Israelites take interest from foreigners, Deut xxiii.20, *especially as he elsewhere instructs them to do no injury to foreigners but rather to assist them in all kindness, particularly those*

---

18. In this passage as in many others, Milton quotes rather than paraphrases. Compare Wolleb's "*Verecundia est temperantia a verborum obscoenitate, & gestuum lascivia*" (*Compendium* II.xi.2, p. 261) with Milton's "*VERECUNDIA est temperantia a verborum obscœnitate et gestuum lascivia: ab iis denique omnibus quæ ratione sexus aut personæ probatissimis moribus minus conveniunt*" (*Works* 17:220). Like Wolleb, Milton cites Hebrews 12:28 to illustrate his point.

> *in need.* Secondly, if we may make a profit out of cattle, land, houses and the like, why should we not out of money? *When money is borrowed, as it often is, not to relieve hardship but simply for the purpose of gain, it tends to be more profitable to the borrower than to the lender.* It is true that God did not wish the Israelites to devote the produce of their land to usury, but this was for purely ceremonial reasons, as was his desire that they should not sell their land permanently, Lev. xxv.23. (*YP* 6:776; my emphases).
>
> *Usuram itaque per se ac simpliciter non magis improbandam esse quam cætera quævis commercii civilis genera, ipsa ratio demonstrat: 1. quia si simpliciter reprehendenda esset, non permisisset Deus ut Israelitæ ab extraneo fœnus acciperent,* Deut xxiii.20. præsertim cum alibi præcipiat ne extraneo iniuriam facerent, sed omni potius humanitate, egenti præsertim, subvenirent: *2. si iumenti, fundi, tecti et similium fructus esse potest, cur non pecuniæ?* quæ cum non inopiæ sublevandæ, sed lucri faciendi causa sæpe mutuo accipiatur, accipienti mutuo quam danti fructuosior esse solet. *Terræ quidem Israeliticæ fructum Deus usuris addictum esse noluit, cæremoniali quadam significatione, quemadmodum et agros mancipio noluit vendi*, Lev. xxv. 23. (*Works*, 17:338–40)

Wolleb's discussion implies that usury, carrying associations of predatoriness, is generally suspect; if not commendable, it is not always wicked, and in some manifestations it can be defended on Scriptural grounds. In Milton's reworking usury is stripped of associations with wickedness; it is simply one more acceptable business strategy. Moreover, in Milton's additions, the defense is transmuted into commendation; far from being a predator, the usurer acts benevolently toward those in need and may even place himself at a disadvantage to help the borrower. In Milton's reworking of Wolleb we witness the manner in which Milton allowed his self-conception and the project of self-justification to play a role in the formation of his theology.

The Domestication of Peculiar Grace

The incoherence of the Father's speech in Book 3 derives from the kind of intrusive self-regard that marks the discussion of usury in *De Doctrina*. The opening lines, with their anomalous intimation of a Calvinist elect in the context of an Arminian argument, tell us more about Milton's self-conception and his need to be outstanding than about his theology. The hesitation between models betrays his desire to be elect by both birthright and merit. Similar intrusions occur and are contained in *De Doctrina,* in which we witness a dialectic of attraction to and repudiation of the idea of a Calvinist elect.

Danielson, as I noted earlier, suggests that Milton proposes in the Father's speech a compromise position; he offers the following passage from Richard Baxter as an analogue:

> The Act of *faith* sometimes followeth this [divine] Impulse through its *invincible force;* And sometime it followeth it through its *sufficient force* . . . And sometimes it followeth it *not at all* . . . And if the question be, Why *sufficient Grace* which is *Effectual ad Posse* is not *effectual ad agere?* It is because (being but *sufficient,*) mans *Indisposition* and *wilful neglect* or *opposition,* maketh him an *unfit Receiver.*[19]

Noting Milton's discussion in *De Doctrina* I.iv (Book 1, chap. 4) of the election of individuals as instruments of God (*YP* 6.172), Danielson suggests that Milton's "categories are not the same as Baxter's, but similar." He concludes that if the two difficult lines in the Father's speech do not mark a "relapse into orthodox Calvinism," they nevertheless "should probably not be squeezed into a tightly Arminian mold."[20] This is an astute conclusion as regards *Paradise Lost* by way of a less astute reading of *De Doctrina.* In the treatise, gestures in the direction of Baxter's first category are reined in and "squeezed into a tightly Arminian mold." On the crucial question of saving faith, Milton's categories in *De Doctrina* are decidedly different from Baxter's; no divine impulse comes with invincible force as far as Milton is concerned.

At three points *De Doctrina* explores individual election. In I.iv, Milton distinguishes the general predestination to salvation of all who freely choose to believe from "the election by which he chooses an individual for some employment . . . ; whence they are sometimes called elect who are superior to the rest for any reason" (*unde electi nonnunquam dicuntur quicunque cæteris re aliqua præstant*) (*YP* 6:172; *Works* 14:98). He also distinguishes his anti-Calvinist general predestination from national election such as that "by which God chose the whole nation of Israel as his own people." A few individuals stand out among others, just as Israel stands out among nations, as specially chosen by God. Are these individuals given special (or Baxter's "invincible") grace? Is there, in other words, an opening for a Calvinist-style elect? If so, Milton quickly closes the opening, arguing from the history of the Israelites that neither individual nor national election supports the doctrine of

---

19. Danielson, *Milton's Good God,* 83, quoting Baxter's *Catholick Theology;* the bracketed word (*divine*) is Danielson's. For reasons to be cautious in using Baxter as analogue for Milton, see John Rumrich, *Milton Unbound: Controversy and Reinterpretation* (Cambridge: Cambridge University Press, 1996), 30–32.

20. Danielson, *Milton's Good God,* p. 83.

irresistible grace, as Calvinists contend.[21] Milton maneuvers the analogy in the opposite direction: just as the Israelites at times refused God's grace, so individuals chosen for special employment can turn against God.

Even the faithful apostles are not given irresistible grace: "Peter is not predestined or elected as Peter, or John as John, but each only insofar as he believes and persists in his belief" (*YP* 6:176). Peter appears again as Milton explores the implications of this firmly Arminian conviction for an understanding of the election of individuals for service:

> Who was more certainly elect than Peter? Yet we find a condition imposed, John xiii.8: *if I do not wash you, you bear no part with me.* What then? Peter willingly complied and bore a part with Christ: had he not complied, he would have borne no part. For Judas bore no part, although it is said not only that he was elected, which may refer to his apostleship, but also that he was given to Christ by the Father. (*YP* 6:179)

The condition imposed on those chosen for individual employment is the same as that imposed on all; those who by free choice believe and persist in belief will be saved (i.e., by virtue of that choice they will be included in God's general and conditional decree of predestination and participate in the merit of Christ's saving act).[22]

The problem with an argument that a Calvinist-leaning conception of a "super-elect" complements or poses a compromise within a generally Arminian framework—universal sufficient grace and general and conditional election of those who freely choose to believe—is that the Calvinist position is repeatedly repudiated in the treatise. From Milton's point of view, any separation of salvation from free human choice to accept sufficient but not invincible grace would throw grave doubt on God's justice and undermine Milton's theodicy. He argues that "by separating election from faith," that is, by supposing that God elects any individuals to salvation without foreknowledge of their free acceptance of grace in choosing to believe, "we become involved in perplexing and, indeed, in repulsive and unreasonable doctrines" (*durioribus doctrinis, immo odiosis et ratione carentibus, implicemur*) (*YP* 6:180; *Works* 14:118).[23]

---

21. See Calvin, *Institutes* (1559) III.xxi.5–7.

22. For further discussion of the conditional nature of general predestination in Milton, see *De Doctrina* I.xxv (*YP* 6:506).

23. The Synod of Dort, in its condemnation of Arminian doctrine, in turn specifically repudiates as an imputation on God's omnipotence any claim that predestination to election is conditional on God's foreknowledge of freely chosen belief (*Articles of the Synod of Dort*, "Of the Doctrine of Divine Predestination," pp. 261, 271, 274–78). For Calvin's denial of the possibility that predestination is based on the foreknown merit of chosen faith, see *Institutes* (1559) III.xxii.1–2, 9.

In this first discussion in *De Doctrina* of the election of individuals, we begin with a parallel to the Father's lines in *Paradise Lost,* "Some I have chosen of peculiar grace / Elect above the rest." But very quickly in the treatise the apparent Calvinism is reined in, and thus prevented from unsettling the otherwise Arminian argument.

Milton returns to the question of specially chosen individuals in the seventeenth chapter of the first book, "Of Renovation and also of Vocation."[24] After discussing general vocation or calling, Milton turns to special calling:

> Special vocation means that God, whenever he chooses, invites certain selected individuals, either from the so-called elect or from the reprobate, more clearly and more insistently than is normal. (*YP* 6:455)
> *Vocatio specialis est qua Deus hos quam illos, sive electos quos vocant sive reprobos, clarius ac sæpius, quandocunque vult invitat.* (*Works* 15:348–50)

Once again it seems that Milton approaches a Calvinist super-elect; his first example is Abraham, the hero of faith. It is not clear at first what Milton means when he says that individuals are chosen "either from the so-called elect [*electos quos vocant*] or from the reprobate."[25] It cannot mean, of course, from among those predestined to salvation or damnation regardless of their choosing whether or not to believe. But does it mean that they are chosen without regard to virtue or other meritorious suitability?

Surprisingly, the biblical passages with which Milton illustrates his conception of special vocation are not of much help in answering this question. They say little or nothing about individuals; instead, they point to God's call to groups who either choose or reject his call to belief or obedience. Indeed, two of the four New Testament passages illustrating the selection of individuals by special vocation, Romans 8:28–30 and 2 Timothy 1:9 (*YP* 6:456), are employed earlier to illustrate arguments on general (i.e., Arminian) predestination (*YP* 6:181,173). The passages illustrating the special vocation of individuals among the reprobate have in common the theme of the rejection of God's call by those to whom grace is offered; it is the groups receiving the call, not the individual carrying the call, who are reprobate.[26] By special vocation,

---

24. For Milton on vocation, see John Spencer Hill, *John Milton: Poet, Priest and Prophet: A Study of Divine Vocation in Milton's Poetry and Prose* (Totowa, NJ: Rowman and Littlefield, 1979).

25. Milton must qualify the "elect" as "the so-called elect" or "those whom they call elect" because an individual's elect status is not logically prior to vocation but depends on one's proper response and continued faithfulness to the call.

26. Isaiah 28:13; Ezekiel 2:4–5 and 3:12; Matthew 10:18, 11:21, 22:8–10, and 23:37; Luke 7:30; and Acts 7:51 and 13:46.

then, Milton seems to mean little more than any message concerning salvation delivered by God directly or through intermediaries. When he speaks of individuals selected from the reprobate, he seems to mean recalcitrant groups chosen to receive special embassies from God's spokespersons.[27]

The discussion of the change wrought (or not wrought) by the divine call follows on the discussion of special vocation, with no hint that we have been returned to the category of general vocation. Milton explains that the proper response to the call is a hearing or listening, and concludes, "What can this mean but that God gives us the power to act freely, which we have not been able to do since the fall unless called and restored? We cannot be given the gift of will unless we are also given freedom of action, because that is what free will means" (*YP* 6:457). The category of special vocation, which seemed to promise high spiritual status to a few chosen spokespersons or heroes of faith, more or less dissolves in front of our eyes in chapter 17. Does it apply to the Abrahams of the world, or to the innumerable who are called? Does it involve some special grace that seals one's status among the elect? Whatever hints that we are being led toward a super-elect are quickly undone, until the category seems to leave us with little more than the general call through which all are given the opportunity to believe.

Any putative category of the super-elect is further undermined by Milton's anti-Calvinist discussion of perseverance. Whereas Calvinists insist on the perseverance of the saints, or the impossibility of the apostasy of the elect faithful,[28] Milton sees the continued faithfulness of the saints as conditional. While Calvinists suggest that the saints may stumble but not fall permanently from grace, Milton argues that "NO POWER OR GUILE OF WORLD OR DEVIL MAKES THEM [the saints] ENTIRELY FALL AWAY, SO LONG AS THEY DO NOT PROVE WANTING IN THEMSELVES, AND SO LONG AS THEY CLING TO FAITH AND CHARITY WITH ALL THEIR MIGHT" (*YP* 6:505). Aware that the conditional clauses will run afoul of Calvinist consensus, Milton defends his opinion as following "the overall tendency of scripture," which affirms the freedom of individuals to accept or reject grace and which makes clear that "*God's seed remains*" in the faithful "only so long as he does not himself extinguish it, for even the spirit can be extinguished" (*YP* 6:506,513). In *De Doctrina*, the assurance of perseverance in faith for the elect (which for Calvin and his followers precedes the beginning of time) comes presumably only with the glorification of saints with the Last Judgment, although even here Milton resists stipulating this assurance.

---

27. For Calvin's very different discussion of special calling, see *Institutes* (1559) III.xxiv.8.

28. See, e.g., Calvin, *Institutes* (1559) III.xxiv.6–11; Wolleb, I.32, in Beardslee, pp. 174 ff.; François Turretin, *Institutio theologiae elencticae,* Locus IV, Q.12, in Beardslee, pp. 383–92; *Articles of the Synod of Dort,* "Concerning the Perseverance of the Saints," pp. 314–22.

In the chapter on predestination as well as in the chapter on vocation, Milton exhibits his characteristic concern for the reasonableness of the plan of salvation and the justice of God's disposition of human beings, a concern articulated by the Father in *Paradise Lost:*

> I made him just and right,
> Sufficient to have stood, though free to fall.
> Such I created *all* th' ethereal Powers
> And spirits, *both them who stood and them who failed;*
> Freely they stood who stood, and fell who fell.
> Not free, what proof could they have giv'n sincere
> Of true allegiance, constant faith or love,
> Where only what they needs must do, appeared,
> Not what they would? What praise could they receive?
> What pleasure I from such obedience paid,
> When will and reason (reason also is choice)
> Useless and vain, of freedom both despoiled,
> Made passive both, had served necessity,
> Not me.
> (*PL* 3.98–111; my emphasis)

Certain individuals may be chosen for special ministries, but Milton repeatedly insists that these individuals are subject to the universal condition for election, the free choice to remain faithful and obedient. The quasi-Calvinist category of those "elect above the rest" articulated by the Father shortly after the speech just quoted is not underwritten by the discussions of election and vocation in *De Doctrina.*

Milton returns to the question of God's selection of individuals in his discussion of "extraordinary ministers" (I.xxix, "Of the Visible Church"). This discussion is far briefer than that in the chapter on vocation, as if Milton is resisting the elaboration of this category of special election and hence its inevitable dissolution by the Arminian solvents of the treatise. Milton writes that

> EXTRAORDINARY MINISTERS are sent and inspired by God to set up or to reform the church by both preaching *and by writing* [*viva voce et scriptus*].
>
> To this class the prophets, apostles, evangelists and others of that kind belong. (*YP* 6:570; *Works* 16:238; my emphasis)

Milton (in the Latin) gives twenty-five words to his discussion of extraordinary ministers (followed by six illustrative biblical verses); Ames devotes to the same topic several pages of *The Marrow of Theology* (Book 1, chap. 33). Milton's own definition follows Ames's closely, but despite its brevity, Milton makes a point of adding that the extraordinary minister works "by preaching *and by writing.*" The author who had added, self-referentially, elegance to his discussion of virtues, along with a defense of usury, the practice by which his own studious leisure was purchased, now adds the medium by which one "Church-outed by the Prelats" carried on his own work in reforming the church "of power beside the office of a pulpit" (*YP* 1:823,816). The discussion of ordinary ministry that follows immediately is, significantly, in large part an attack on the exclusive franchise of the ordained clergy.[29]

In the chapter on vocation, as we saw a moment ago, the discussion of special vocation follows that on general vocation; in the course of this discussion the category of special vocation is domesticated and reassimilated into what we would normally consider general vocation. In the chapter on ministry, the order is reversed and the discussion of the special or "extraordinary" category is foreshortened. The result, whether by design or not, is to spare the category of extraordinary minister the kind of Arminian leveling that takes place elsewhere in the text. In its brevity, the discussion acts as a marker of Milton's desire for a special status for such selected heralds as himself. He can remain the heroic figure who has virtuously achieved salvation by choosing faith and obedience, and he can also for the moment think of himself as standing on a special spiritual plateau, inaccessible to the undifferentiated mass of the faithful.

Milton as Elect by Merit and Birthright

Milton's Arminian economy of salvation parallels his republican distrust of hereditary aristocracy. He favored demonstrated merit over inherited blood as the proper determinant of an individual's position in social and political hierarchies. But however radical Milton's politics may have been, he was no democrat. In *The Readie and Easie Way,* as we saw in chapter 6, he expresses distrust of the mob and imagines elections (without universal suffrage) leading by degrees to the most refined individuals. A similar movement and countermovement mark his theology of salvation. *De Doctrina* most often posits a kind of egalitarianism in the divine plan. There is no designation of a spiritual

---

29. For an alternative but not incompatible view, see William Kerrigan's argument that with the corruption of the institutional church and with the resort of the Spirit to individuals rather than to an ecclesiastical body described in *Paradise Lost* 12.524–40, "the ordinary ministers defined in the *De doctrina christiana* lose their function, which is predicated on a true church externally established in a just society" (*The Prophetic Milton* [Charlottesville: University Press of Virginia, 1974], p. 179).

elite before birth, and even those chosen for special ministry by God are subject to the same conditions for eventual election, what Milton will call in *Paradise Lost* the "free / Acceptance of large grace" (12.304–5). The treatise does, however, allow for different degrees of grace. God

> undoubtedly bestows grace on all, and if not equally upon each, at least sufficient to enable everyone to attain knowledge of the truth and salvation. I say not equally upon each, because he has not distributed grace equally, even among the reprobate, as they are called.... For like anyone else, where his own possessions are concerned, God claims for himself the right of making decrees about them as he thinks fit, without being obliged to give a reason for his decree, though he could give a very good one if he wished. (*YP* 6:192)

In endorsing God's arbitrariness in dealing with "his own possessions," Milton echoes Calvinist defenses of predestination. But if Milton tempers here the egalitarianism of his conception of the providential plan, he insists with Arminius that sufficient, if not equal, grace is universal: "So God does not consider everyone worthy of equal grace, and *the cause of this is his supreme will* [Causa ... est suprema ipsius voluntas]. But he considers all worthy of sufficient grace, and *the cause is his justice* [iustitia eius]" (*YP* 6:193; *Works* 14:146–48).[30] The result is that, despite a reassertion of universal, sufficient grace, Milton leaves an opening for a spiritual aristocracy.[31]

This discussion follows one in which Milton wrestles with a verse that apparently undermines his argument, Acts 13:48: "*when the Gentiles heard this they were glad and glorified the word of the Lord; and as many as were ordained [ordinati] to eternal life, believed*" (*YP* 6:184). First Milton points to ambiguity surrounding the term "ordained" (τεταγμένοι); some interpreters, "more acute" in Milton's view, "consider it equivalent to 'well or moderately disposed or affected,' that is, of a composed, attentive, upright and not disorderly mind"

---

30. For orthodox Calvinists, there is no distinction between God's supreme will and his justice, so that predestination to salvation or reprobation, without reference to foreknowledge of the individual's free choices, is just *because* it arises from God's will.

31. Milton gestures again toward a spiritual aristocracy in his astonishing discussion of implicit faith. In *Areopagitica* he had dismissed contemptuously those who let others perform for them the labor of interpreting Scripture, charging them with laziness and Romanizing idolatry (*YP* 2:544). But in *De Doctrina* he finds a role for implicit faith:

> implicit faith, which blindly accepts and so believes, is not real faith at all. Unless, that is, it is only a temporary state, as in novices and new converts who believe even before

(*YP* 6:185).³² Read thus, the verse suggests not a divine decree of predestination but a disposition Milton often sought in his readers: openness, attentiveness, impartiality.³³

From where would these dispositions come, differentiating those more and less well disposed and affected? Perhaps from variable, inborn shares of the traces of the divine image:

> some traces of the divine image remain in man, and when they combine in an individual he becomes more suitable, and as it were, more properly disposed for the kingdom of God than another. Since we are not mere puppets [*neque enim stipites plane sumus*], some cause at least should be sought in human nature itself why some men embrace and others reject this divine grace. One thing may be established at the outset: . . . some are worse than others. This may be observed every day, in the nature, disposition, and habits of those who are most estranged from God's grace. (*YP* 6.185–86; *Works* 14:128)

Given Milton's general argument concerning the centrality of the free acceptance of grace in election, it would be essential for faith to be freely chosen rather than made inevitable by a divinely given predisposition, for the same reason that any predisposition to sin would compromise the freedom of Adam and Eve in, and hence the theodicy of, *Paradise Lost*. But in this passage Milton flirts with just such inborn predispositions. As inheritors of the original sin we are inheritors of some reduced "traces of the divine image," which presumably would be bestowed at birth. Interestingly, Milton here uses the metaphor of the puppet he had used in *Areopagitica*, but it points now in the opposite direction. In the earlier work Milton wrote that "when God gave him [Adam] reason, he gave him freedom to choose, for reason is but choosing; he had bin else a meer artificiall *Adam*, such an *Adam* as he is in the motions" (*YP* 2:527).

---

they enter upon a course of instruction. . . . It is the case, also, with those who are *dull of understanding and practically unteachable*, but who believe, nevertheless, according to their light and attempt to live by faith, and who are thus acceptable to God. [*YP* 6:472; my emphasis]

The first sentence follows Wolleb closely (*Compendium* I.xxix.9, in Beardslee, p. 163), but Milton adds what follows. The apparent sense of the final sentence is that God will be merciful to the slow-witted, and that he will set the gate lower, so that even a Catholicizing implicit faith will be sufficient. It is not like Milton to be moved solely by tender-heartedness and indulgence toward those with fewer gifts than he. If the "dull of understanding" is a large group, Milton's indulgence toward them could be one more way of setting the few apart from the many.

32. In his annotation, Maurice Kelley suggests that the "more acute" interpreters are Remonstrant or Arminian theologians.

33. On Milton's invocation of "ingenuous" readers and its reformed context, see Dayton Haskin, *Milton's Burden of Interpretation* (Philadelphia: University of Pennsylvania Press, 1994), 242–45.

Without freedom, Milton suggests, Adam would be a marionette pulled by the strings of divine will. In the passage in *De Doctrina,* Milton is seeking a cause for why some respond to grace while others do not, playing with the theodicial fire of sufficient causation for human choices. The logic apparently is that we bring something to God's calling, that we are not merely interchangeable blocks of wood. With the language of "nature," though, Milton is in danger of falling back into the "error" of particular predestination.[34]

Milton has worked himself into a position in which election is tied to what might be an inborn virtue, or at least a healthy allotment of the "traces of the divine image." Anticipating Calvinist citation of verses (Deuteronomy 9:5 and Luke 10:13) indicating that God does not choose according to our merited righteousness, Milton suggests that these verses do not pertain to election to eternal life, but to earthly favors. The more difficult verse is Romans 9:16, *"it does not depend on him that wills or on him that runs but on God who is merciful"* (*YP* 6:187). Roused from an interlude in which he has toyed with quasi-Calvinist predispositions to sin or obedience, Milton reasserts his libertarian, Arminian argument:

> But I reply, I am not talking about anyone willing or running, but about someone being less unwilling, less backward, less opposed, and I grant that God is still merciful, and is, at the same time, supremely wise and just. On the other hand, those that say *it does not depend on him that wills or on him that runs,* do presuppose a man willing and running, only they deny him any praise or merit. However, when God determined to restore mankind, he also decided unquestionably (and what could be more just?) to restore some part at least of man's lost freedom of will. So he gave a greater power of willing or running (that is, of believing) to those whom he saw willing or running already by virtue of the fact that their wills had been freed either before or at the actual time of their call. These, probably [*verisimile*], represent here the "ordained." (*YP* 6:187; *Works* 14:134)

There is drama in the equipoise of "*verisimile*"; the verse from Romans is difficult to assimilate to Milton's argument, and the strain appears in the "probably." But there may be some ambivalence at the domestication of the verse to the Arminian argument, connected to Milton's recurrent yearning for a status "elect above the rest," as in his claim in *The Reason of Church-Government* to be among God's "selected heralds" (*YP* 1:802) and in his comparison of himself

---

34. Milton earlier, in *The Doctrine and Discipline of Divorce,* had written of inborn predispositions or temperaments in a way that uncharacteristically suggested determinism. See chapter 5, note 14.

to Jeremiah, Isaiah, and the evangelist John in the same text and to Ezekiel in the *Doctrine and Discipline of Divorce* (*YP* 1:803, 820–21; 2:222–23).

Milton's ambivalence finds expression in a dialectic that I have been tracing in *De Doctrina*. After setting up a clearly and unequivocally Arminian framework, according to which God shares sufficient grace with all and does not exempt even his chosen instruments from the common test of salvation (free acceptance of grace leading to faith and obedience), Milton on several occasions hints at a special status for the few. When he does so, however, these few are quickly reassimilated into the general condition of humankind. The dialectic reveals two deeply ingrained but incompatible self-representations on Milton's part, both tied to his palpable desire to have his merit recognized. Milton is unwilling or unable to accept that faith might be an unmerited gift of God, not merely because of the imputation on God's justice (on what grounds could God withhold from some what he gives to others?) but also because of the imputation on human, and therefore Milton's, merit (what is the value of saving faith if it is not acquired at least in part by one's own effort and merit?). Milton will not see himself as a "meer artificiall Milton," a puppet of divine providence. In his hostile review of Arminianism in 1643, the Calvinist John Owen, who would be Cromwell's aide and eventually chancellor of Oxford University, suggests that attacks on Calvinist predestination arise from a delusion that one can merit praise and from a desire to be outstanding; Arminians attempt "to vindicate unto themselves a power, and independent abillitie of doing good, of making themselves to differ from all others, of attaining everlasting happinesse, without going one steppe from without themselves."[35] Owen describes here a temptation to which Milton seems to have been particularly prone.

There is a price to pay for claiming the merit of free will, not only in terms of the scorn of Calvinists but also in terms of self-conception and representation. To give up the category of the Calvinist elect is to give up one avenue of conceiving oneself as separate from and above the generality of people. No longer is one born into a spiritual aristocracy; instead one is submerged in, to borrow a phrase from the *Doctrine and Discipline of Divorce,* the "common lump of men" (*YP* 2:253). Arminius himself acknowledges that the Calvinist view offers the elect individual the promise of special distinction:

> You will say that, if he [the elect individual] has apprehended the offered grace by the aid of peculiar grace [*peculiaris gratiæ*], it is, then, evident that God has manifested greater love towards him than towards another

---

35. Owen, *A Display of Arminianisme* (London, 1643), chap. 6, p. 50. The subtitle tells the same story: "Being a Discovery of the old Pelagian *Idol Free-will,* with the new Goddesse *Contingency,* advancing themselves, into the Throne of the God of heaven to the prejudice of his *Grace, Providence,* and *Supreme Dominion* over the children of men."

to whom he has applied only common grace, and has denied peculiar grace. I admit it.³⁶

Having acknowledged this, Arminius continues with a surmise—to the best of my knowledge unique in his writings—in which he hints at the kind of hybrid that Milton toys with in the Father's speech:

> I admit it, and perhaps the theory [Arminius's own theory of general and resistible grace], which you oppose, will not deny it. But it will assert that *peculiar grace* is to be so explained as to be consistent with freewill [*ita peculiarem illam gratiam explicandam esse, vt cum libero arbitrio consistere possit*], and that *common grace* is to be so described, that a man may be held worthy of condemnation by its rejection, and that God may be shown to be free from injustice.

It is not surprising that Arminius does not elaborate on this idea here or elsewhere, for the idea of a peculiar saving grace sits awkwardly in the context of his otherwise consistent insistence on the justice of the universality of saving grace. His nod toward a Calvinist conception of saving grace, even though redefined as resistible, is momentary and anomalous. We view for a brief moment the dueling of imperatives that apparently moved Milton in his composition of the Father's speech. Milton can have either the self-satisfaction of the self-made spiritual man or the self-satisfaction of the one chosen by God in a manner different from that by which others are chosen, but he cannot have both self-satisfactions at once. I've been suggesting that Milton's Arminian position satisfies his concern for theodicy even as it partially satisfies his need to have his merit acknowledged, and that the Calvinist eruptions, reassimilated in *De Doctrina* but not in *Paradise Lost,* point to a need for recognition that the Arminian economy cannot satisfy. The Milton who implausibly adds elegance and conversational wit to Christian virtues will not think of himself as just another interchangeable puppet or block of wood.

What, in the end, can we make of the tensions in the Father's speech in Book 3? Not, I have argued, that Milton as theologian (or as theological poet) is undecided between Calvin and Arminius. And not even that he is trying to find a compromise or hybrid form, to become the Tycho Brahe of the motions of faith. Instead, *De Doctrina* helps us to understand the dialectic that gives rise to the anomaly of placing in an Arminian setting the apparently Calvinist lines "Some I have chosen of peculiar grace / Elect above the rest." This incompletely assimilated gesture responds to the requirements of

---

36. *Review of Perkins,* in *Writings,* 3:481–82; *Iacobi Arminii Opera theologica* (Frankfurt, 1631), p. 591.

Milton's self-construction as a heroic and select servant of God; that is, to Milton's own need to be outstanding in as many ways as possible, or rather in more ways than are possible at once. At the same time the pair of lines helps us to recognize the forces behind the dialectic in the treatise, forces that the treatise, because of its imperative of rational consistency, must domesticate.

In the next chapter I will examine another set of unresolved tensions surrounding Milton's self-construction in *Paradise Lost*. If the tensions examined above result from Milton's reaching for two laudatory but incompatible self-representations, I will turn next to the rift in the epic between a valorizing self-representation and one marked by doubt, anxiety, and the shadow of guilt.

Chapter 8

"If All Be Mine"

Confidence and Anxiety in *Paradise Lost*

From Milton's perspective, self-representation is all but required of the aspiring epic poet. Composing heroic poetry, in his view, requires great moral and intellectual fitness. As early as Elegy 6, as we have seen, Milton insisted that the epic poet must live austerely and labor diligently to merit divine inspiration. To undertake an epic, then, is to make claims about oneself. If the one who wished "to write well hereafter in laudable things, ought him selfe to bee a true Poem, that is, a composition, and patterne of the best and honourablest things" (*YP* 1:890), then Milton needs to compose himself in *Paradise Lost*. He takes on this task primarily in the epic invocations, the only places in the poem where Milton writes of himself in his own person.

Varieties of Milton in the Epic

While Milton speaks of himself in his own voice in the invocations, he also inhabits several of the work's characters. Milton populates *Paradise Lost* as he populated *A Mask,* with versions of himself. Milton's idiosyncratic concerns and preoccupations inform the poem. His longing for companionate marriage, so palpable in the divorce tracts, shapes the early picture of Adam and Eve focused intently on each other amid a wilderness of sweets. The blind man's anguished desire for sight, rendered explicitly in the second and third invocations, lies behind the scene in which Michael removes the film from Adam's eyes and "purged with euphrasy and rue / The visual nerve, for he had much to see" (11.414–15). The opponent of tyrants castigates the archetypal tyrant in the form of Nimrod in the epic. The unbending advocate of freedom of the will places his arguments in the mouth of God.

Most recognizably, perhaps, Abdiel stands in or speaks for the Milton who early and late figured himself as the lone voice of godliness, the lone just man. Abdiel approaches Satan as Milton approaches all those who, in opposing him, oppose God:

> His puissance, trusting in th' Almighty's aid,
> I mean to try, whose reason I have tried
> Unsound and false; nor is it aught but just,
> That he who in debate of truth hath won,
> Should win in arms, in both disputes alike
> Victor; though brutish that contést and foul,
> When reason hath to deal with force, yet so
> Most reason is that reason overcome.
> (6.119–26)

Milton prided himself on his skill with the sword, but once blind he traded his sword for a pen, with which he slew Salmasius and defended the Commonwealth and Protectorate more effectively and courageously than any soldier. Abdiel, like Milton in the fleshpots of Italy, remains pure even while all others succumb to temptation. In describing Abdiel's exhortations to and denunciation of Satan and his followers at the end of Book 5, Milton might as well be describing his own career as he saw it:

> So spake the fervent angel, but his zeal
> None seconded, as out of season judged,
> Or singular and rash. . . .
> . . . .
> Among the faithless, faithful only he;
> Among innumerable false, unmoved,
> Unshaken, unseduced, unterrified,
> His loyalty he kept, his love, his zeal.
> (5.849–51, 897–900)

This portrait of Abdiel draws upon the experience of 1660, when, as the English hastened to welcome the Restoration, Milton saw himself as the lone adherent to the Good Old Cause.[1] Abdiel's physical courage ("nor of violence

---

1. John Guillory argues persuasively for Milton's post-Restoration identification in *Paradise Lost* also with the Galileo recalled in *Areopagitica*, "grown old, a pris'ner to the Inquisition, for thinking in Astronomy otherwise then the Franciscan and Dominican licencers thought" (*YP* 2:538) (*Poetic Authority: Spenser, Milton, and Literary History* [New York: Columbia University Press, 1983], pp.160–61).

feared aught" [5.905]) is more applicable to Milton than to the angel Abdiel, who shares the loyal angels' invulnerability to wounds. The figure of the lone just man, impervious to fear, returns later in the epic, particularly in the figure of Enoch, "so beset/ With foes for daring single to be just" (11.702–3). Like Abdiel's victory in Book 6, Enoch's deathless translation to heaven serves as a kind of wish-fulfillment for the poet who knew intimately the experience of defeat, and who wrote his epic while a stubborn advocate of a defeated party.

The parallels between Abdiel and Milton are patent and unmistakable. More surprising is the pattern of resemblance between Milton and Satan.[2] Satan mendaciously describes the power of the forbidden fruit, which he has not tasted, in terms that describe the Miltonic narrator as well; he is able "to discern / Things in their causes, . . . [and] to trace the ways / Of highest agents, deemed however wise" (9.681–83). A moment before, Milton compares Satan, as he often compares himself, to an ancient orator. Satan's boastful address to the inhabitants of the vast tracts of Hell on his defeat of humankind (10.460–503) recalls Milton's imagined speech on his victory over Salmasius before a concourse of nations in the *Defensio Secunda*. Milton associates Satan with the barbarous and heathenish East, but otherwise Milton's self-representation as heroic champion and savior resembles the image of Satan:

> Now, surrounded by such great throngs, from the Pillars of Hercules all the way to the farthest boundaries of Father Liber, I seem to be leading home again everywhere in the world, after a vast space of time, Liberty herself, so long expelled and exiled. . . . I met him [Salmasius] in single combat. . . . And (unless I wish to reject outright and disparage the views and opinions of so many intelligent readers everywhere, in no way bound or indebted to me) I bore off the spoils of honor. (*YP* 4.1:555–56)

If Milton after heroic toil leads home liberty, Satan will "lead [the devils] forth / Triumphant out of this infernal pit" to "possess, /As lords, a spacious world . . . / . . . by my adventure hard / With peril great achieved" (10.463–69). As Milton has deprived Salmasius of his glory, Satan will deprive the Father of his creation. Satan remarks, "Long were to tell / What I have done," and then, like his literary author, goes on to describe at length what he has

---

2. For penetrating discussions of the convergence of Satan and poet, see William G. Riggs, *The Christian Poet in Paradise Lost* (Berkeley: University of California Press, 1972), pp. 15–45; William Kerrigan, *The Prophetic Milton* (Charlottesville: University Press of Virginia, 1974), pp. 125–87; and Neil Forsythe, *The Satanic Epic* (Princeton: Princeton University Press, 2003), pp. 268–89.

all but promised to leave unspoken. The specter of Satanic pride, given substance by the convergence of Satan's story with Milton's, is the first cause of the anxiety that I will trace in the invocations.

A balanced self-understanding on Milton's part would place him between Abdiel and Satan, neither as heroically virtuous as the one nor as degraded as the other.[3] And, although Milton's temperament seems to lead him more often to extremes than to balance, he places as much of himself in flawed and falling Adam (and Eve) as he does in the faithful and faithless angels. Following the lead of Arthur Barker and Annabel Patterson, I argued in chapter 5 that Milton's experience with marriage and his counterintuitive reading of Matthew in the divorce tracts were pivotal in the development of his self-conception away from an insistence on preternatural virtue. Adam's Book 10 lament on marriage woes closely echoes the Milton of the divorce tracts. Adam complains that his heirs will suffer because of women:

> for either
> He never shall find out fit mate, but such
> As some misfortune brings him, or mistake,
> Or whom he wishes most shall seldom gain
> Through her perverseness, but shall see her gained
> By a far worse, or if she love, withheld
> By parents, or his happiest choice too late
> Shall meet, already linked and wedlock-bound
> To a fell adversary, his hate or shame.
>   (10.898–906)

This is an authentic cry of pain from a man gored by the experience of his first marriage, with its melodrama of rejection, separation, and enforced reunion, or perhaps of his thwarted relationship with Miss Davis in 1645.[4] The drama of the separation scene, as Adam wrestles with the problem of reconciling two potentially conflicting values—marriage as a meeting of equals or near equals in voluntary and free association or marriage as an institution headed by the man—likewise replays the tensions in Milton's view of marriage in the divorce tracts. The War in Heaven in *Paradise Lost* fails, it has been argued, to meet the tragic gravity of the epic genre. The requirements of tragedy are met in moments like this, however, as Milton gives intimate voice to human suffering.

If marital woes are one of the first fruits of the fall in the epic, Milton's own marital woes may have been the shock that awoke him to his fallibility. The traits in Adam and Eve that contribute to their fall resemble Milton's. They share with Milton a potentially transgressive curiosity. Eve's question about the

---

3. Milton's relation to Abdiel and Satan echoes his relation, discussed in chapter 3, to the Attendant Spirit and Comus in *A Mask*.
4. Lewalski, *The Life of John Milton* (Oxford: Blackwell, 2000), pp. 184–85.

heavens in Book 4 ("But wherefore all night long shine these, for whom / This glorious sight, when sleep hath shut all eyes?" [4.657–58]), while seemingly resolved quickly by Adam, resonates and ramifies through the epic's middle books. If "the prime wisdom," as Adam learns from Raphael, concerns what "before us lies in daily life" (8.193–94), then the first pair's, and particularly Adam's, pressing of this inquiry raises the question of overreaching. Overreaching is the central danger for Milton as epic poet. As early as the "Vacation Exercise" verses Milton figured his poetic ambitions as flight to heaven. Eve, in her dream in Book 5 shortly after asking Adam about the heavens, experiences both the rapturous flight to which Milton aspires and the abrupt fall that he fears when he contemplates his career as a prophetic and heroic poet:

> Forthwith up to the clouds
> With him I flew, and underneath beheld
> The Earth outstretched immense, a prospect wide
> And various: wond'ring at my flight and change
> To this high exaltation; suddenly
> My guide was gone, and I, methought, sunk down.
> (5.86–91)

While Eve raises the question and has the dream, Adam exhibits in his conversation with Raphael a potentially transgressive desire for knowledge even more morally problematic than hers. Because so many stars must travel so fast through spaces so vast to serve the Earth, Adam observes, "reasoning I oft admire, / How nature wise and frugal could commit / Such disproportions" (8.25–27). Going beyond curiosity about the heavens, Adam challenges the wisdom of Nature's (read God's) disposition of the heavens. Adam enters dangerous territory, much as, from Calvin's perspective at least, Milton does in taking on the project of theodicy, as will become clear below. God's justice and the heavens are, for Calvin and Raphael respectively, to be praised and admired (in the sense of wondered at) rather than questioned or admired (in the sense of puzzled over). In describing Adam and Eve, Milton, whether intentionally or not, describes the danger that he risks in telling of things invisible to mortal sight and in justifying the ways of God to men.

Adam and Eve negotiate a space in *Paradise Lost* between the moral certainty of Abdiel and the certain depravity of Satan, a space familiar to the poem's readers. The fact that we can debate endlessly whether or not Adam or Eve acts virtuously in the separation scene in Book 9 points to a degree of moral complexity unlike anything surrounding Abdiel or, despite Romantic readings, Satan. The degree to which Milton invests himself in the morally complex characters of Eve and Adam helps account for the paradox at the heart of the poem. Without the supernatural confidence in himself and assurance of direct divine inspiration, it is difficult to see how Milton could have allowed himself to write the epic. At the same time, the intimations of frailty and error written into the voice of the speaker of the invocations make explicable the empathy with which Milton writes of the fallen human experience of Adam and Eve. There is little left of the moral condescension that marks, for example, the digressions in *An Apology for Smectymnuus* or *The Reason of Church-Government* or even the *Defensio Secunda*. However one decides the question of whether Adam's fall is the "illustrious evidence" of "exceeding love," as Eve terms it, or merely the result of culpable uxoriousness, that this is a live question points to Milton's hard won understanding of human frailty.

The paradoxically enabling combination of confidence and self-doubt hinted at in dispersed resemblances between Milton and his characters lies at the heart of his invocations, the sites of Milton's concentrated, and conscious, self-representation in *Paradise Lost*. Andrew Marvell is our best reader of the cross-currents of confidence and anxiety in Milton's epic. He describes the experience of reading the epic:

> At once delight and horrour on us seise,
> Thou singst with so much gravity and ease;
> And above humane flight dost soar aloft
> With Plume so strong, so equal, and so soft.[5]

Marvell contrasts Milton's confident ease with the observers' vertigo. The passage is a study in contrasts. Delight and horror, the observers' vertiginously contrasting emotions, are themselves contrasted with Milton's equable "gravity and ease." He takes his mighty flight on a feather (or pen) "so strong, so equal, and so soft." The first and third terms, so apparently different, are spliced firmly by the intervening "equal."

Marvell knows well that Milton is not as equal or as calm as this passage suggests; at the end of this chapter, I will argue that Marvell's poem encodes in displaced form his recognition of Milton's ambivalence and anxiety. Marvell's picture of Milton's balance and ease at dizzying heights recalls the Son on the pinnacle in *Paradise Regained*. Satan tests the Son's identity, probing what he infers to be the Son's special claim of divine status; Milton in ranging "above human flight" courts the charge of making exalted claims for himself.

Milton's God tasks Raphael with alerting Adam and Eve to the dangers of complacency:

> warn him to beware
> He swerve not too secure: tell him withal
> His danger, and from whom, what enemy

---

5. "On Mr. Milton's *Paradise Lost*," 35–38, in *The Poems and Letters of Andrew Marvell*, ed. H. M. Margoliouth, 2nd ed., 2 vols. (Oxford: Clarendon, 1952), 1:131–32.

> Late fall'n himself from Heav'n, is plotting now
> The fall of others from like state of bliss.
>
> (5.237–41)

The locution "swerve not too secure" is unusual. The general sense is clear enough. Adam should be aware of the dangers of his position; overconfidence can lead to a misstep and a fall. Milton was familiar with the Lucretian "swerve" of free will, the uncaused turn of atoms from their vertical fall through space.[6] Adam and Eve can swerve, but so perhaps can Milton in his superhuman flight. The error or swerve is made more rather than less likely by the confidence that Marvell praises in Milton.

Marvell demonstrates a penetrating sense of Milton when he writes that "delight and horrour on us seise." To be seized or "rapt" is a signature boast *and* fear for Milton. It is the opposite of being "secure," a term Marvell also associates with Milton ("of thy own sense secure" [46]). The terms "secure" and "rapt" dance around each other in the epic. Prophets are "rapt," seized by divine inspiration or the divine hand; when Satan on the bare outside of the universe is tempted by the proximity of heaven, Milton alludes to Elijah "*Rapt* in a chariot drawn by fiery steeds" (3.522; my emphasis). Enoch is rewarded by being seized by God:

> him the Most High
> *Rapt* in a balmy cloud with wingèd steeds
> Did, as thou saw'st, receive, to walk with God
> High in salvation and the climes of bliss,
> Exempt from death; to show thee what reward
> Awaits the good.
>
> (11.705–10; my emphasis)

Enoch is, much as Milton styles himself in the prose, "The only righteous in a world perverse, / And therefore hated" (11.701–2). To be rapt or seized by God is to be rescued from the miscellaneous and hostile crowd, to occupy the position Milton represented himself as occupying. But this exalted singularity comes at a price. Halfway through *Paradise Lost*, as Milton turns from events in Heaven to creation and life in Eden, he sounds relieved: "Standing on earth, not rapt above the pole, / More safe I sing" (7.23–24). Rapture, translation high above the earth, at times a mark of divine favor, is here associated with danger. The song may be dangerous to the singer. Milton associated rapture also with song. The divinely inspired song can seize listeners with ecstasy, a sense Milton employed in the "Nativity Ode": the song of the angels "in blissful rapture took" the souls of the shepherds

---

6. See Lucretius, *De rerum natura* 2.216–93.

in Bethlehem (98). Angelic song leads to rapture several times in *Paradise Lost*.⁷ The poet archetypally associated with this kind of rapture is Orpheus, who sang "In Rhodope, where woods and rocks had ears / To *rapture*, till the savage clamor drowned / Both harp and voice; nor could the muse defend / Her son" (7.35–38; my emphasis). This passage brings together two of the senses of rapture. Orpheus seizes listeners, even inanimate nature, with his song, only to be seized (and dismembered) by frenzied women.

To be "secure" in *Paradise Lost* is to be sheltered from both the exaltation and the danger of rapture. Only God is truly secure. The Son remarks that the Father, under attack by Satan, "secure / Laugh'st at their vain designs and tumults vain" (5.736–37). Beëlzebub, on the other hand, has a vain hope that the devils may live in "some mild zone / . . . not unvisited of Heav'n's fair light / Secure" (2.397–99). Security is more often than not deceptive in *Paradise Lost*.⁸ The ease or security that Marvell sees in Milton, and that Milton sometimes affects, can be a trap. And Milton, as in the prose works, betrays anxiety in the epic even in the midst of his confident assertions of prophetic or elect status. The poem as we have it would not have been possible without the combination of security and anxiety or the related combination of confident virtue and intimations of frailty. If Milton did not think of himself as uniquely gifted with prophecy, he could never have written *Paradise Lost*; if he did not have more empathy for human frailty than he showed earlier in his career, we could not read it.

Milton's Proems

Annotating the opening of Book 9, the eighteenth-century editor Thomas Newton finds Milton's digressions on himself in the proems as welcome as they are unconventional and unexpected:

> These prologues, or prefaces, of Milton to some of his books, speaking of his own person, lamenting his blindness, and preferring his subject to those of Homer and Virgil and the greatest poets before him, are condemned by some criticks: and it must be allowed that we find no such digression in the *Iliad* or *Æneid;* it is a liberty that can be taken only by such a genius as Milton, and I question whether it would have succeeded in any hands but his. As Voltaire says upon the occasion, I cannot but own that an author is generally guilty of an unpardonable self-love, when he lays aside his subject to descant upon his own person: But that human frailty is to be forgiven in Milton; nay, I am pleased

---

7. See 3.369, 5.147.
8. For other significant uses of *secure,* see 1.261, 1.638, 2.359, 4.370, 4.791, 5.638, 6.672, 9.339, 9.348, 9.1175, 11.196, and 11.802.

with it. He gratifies the curiosity he has raised in me about his person; when I admire the author, I desire to know something of the man; and he, whom all readers would be glad to know, is allowed to speak of himself.[9]

While sharing Newton's gratitude, I do not view Milton's "speaking of his own person" in the proems as digressive indulgence to be allowed to genius. The self-referential elements in the proems are integral to Milton's project. In them, Milton stakes a claim for the inspiration and authority essential for the composition of Christian epic. At the same time, the proems register the anxiety that inevitably accompanies such a claim.

The proems recapitulate the stages of Milton's prior career of self-representation, moving from prophetic confidence, reminiscent of the early poetry and the anti-prelatical works, in the invocation to Book 1, toward anxiety and awareness of the possibility of error and alienation, recalling the divorce tracts and the *Pro Se Defensio*, in the invocation to Book 7. In reading these proems, I will trace gaps between assertive ambition and obscure contemplation of failure, and between confidence and anxiety. Both sides of these polarities constitute aspects of Milton's self-representations, I will argue, in contrast to those who interpret the same gaps as evidence of Milton's distancing himself intentionally from the narrator.

John Mulder sees in the proems' "double pattern of affirmation and denial . . . the recantation of an overweening aspiration through the reenactment of that aspiration."[10] For Mulder, the distanced narrator is Milton's strategy for recording a drama in which the poet is "forced by the process of inspiration . . . to submit to the liabilities of human reason . . . ; he is converted from ambition to humility."[11] I fail to find in Milton's proems humility or a relinquishing of the aspiration to a uniquely privileged position as narrator. Instead, I find him veering between confident assertions of inspired status and dark intimations of exclusion and abandonment. Rather than presenting what Mulder describes as a "persona" who is educated, Milton both represents his aspirations and betrays his anxieties. Joseph Wittreich argues that Milton invests himself in characters, including speakers and narrators, only to distance himself from them. Wittreich's Milton "hints at a knit of identity while always maintaining a distinction."[12] I will suggest that Milton is not so

---

9. Newton, as cited in *The Poetical Works of John Milton, with notes of various authors*, ed. Henry J. Todd, 5th ed., 6 vols. (London, 1826), 3:135.
10. Mulder, "The Lyric Dimension of *Paradise Lost*," *Milton Studies* 23 (1987): 147.
11. Ibid., p. 152.
12. Wittreich, "'Reading' Milton: The Death (and Survival) of the Author," in *John Milton: The Writer in His Works*, ed. Albert C. Labriola and Michael Lieb, *Milton Studies* 38 (2000): 13. While I take issue with this point, this wide-ranging essay is subtle and illuminating.

much maintaining distinctions as betraying cracks in his carefully nurtured self-representations.

Milton writes four proems in *Paradise Lost*. Licensed perhaps by Virgil's brief renewed invocation before the descent to the Underworld (*Aeneid* 6.264–67), Milton composes a full-scale invocation with each shift in epic locale, charting his own course in the poem as well as that of the poem itself. There are three or four invocations in *Paradise Lost,* depending on how one counts.[13] Milton invokes divine aid in Book 1 to undertake the poem as a whole, in Book 3 to speak of heaven and its light despite and because of his blindness, and in Book 7 to return safely to earth after the excursion to heaven (and to license his expansion of the Mosaic creation account). In Book 9, switching from the subservient imperative of the speaker of epic invocation, he turns to the hypothetical, embarking on several books on the fallen world if he can "answerable style . . . obtain / Of [his] celestial patroness" (9.20–21). In these proems Milton displays the confidence, pugnacity, and anxiety that mark his self-representations in the prose works.

Book I: "no middle flight"

The peculiar character of Milton's first proem stands out in comparison to the practice of a more conventional poet, Abraham Cowley. Fortunately for us, Cowley annotated *Davideis,* a poem precisely contemporary with *Paradise Lost;* his reflections on the shape and function of the epic invocation and on his own self-representation help us to bring Milton more sharply into focus. In his first annotation, Cowley describes the evolution of the epic invocation:

> The custom of beginning all *Poems,* with a *Proposition* of the whole work, and an *Invocation* of some God for his assistance to go through with it, is so solemnly and religiously observed by all the ancient *Poets,* that though I could have found out a better way, I should not (I think) have ventured upon it. But there can be, I believe, none better: and that part, of the *Invocation,* if it became a *Heathen,* is no less *Necessary* for a *Christian Poet.* A *Jove Principium, Musæ;* and it follows then very naturally, *Jovis omnia plena.* The whole work may reasonably hope to be filled with a *Divine Spirit,* when it begins with a *Prayer* to be so. The *Grecians* built this *Portal* with less state, and made but one of these *Two;* in which, and almost all things else, I prefer the judgment of the *Latins;* though generally they abused the Prayer, by converting it from the

---

13. Stevie Davies and William B. Hunter, "Milton's Urania: The Meaning, Not the Name I Call," *Studies in English Literature* 28 (1988): 95–111.

Deity, to the worst of *Men*, their *Princes:* as *Lucan* addresses it to *Nero*, and *Statius* to *Domitian;* both imitating therein (but not equalling) *Virgil*, who in his *Georgicks* chuses *Augustus* for the *Object* of his *Invocation*, a *God* little superior to the other two.[14]

Cowley's mind is formulaic: here is what has made epic; here is what makes possible the surpassing of earlier epics by more recent ones; and here, by extension, is how Cowley can assure his position among and above earlier epic poets. The imperative, if not the leaden execution, will be familiar to readers of *Paradise Lost*. Cowley shares Milton's ambition to surpass the ancient poets by matching their formal excellence but, "with this over and above of being a Christian," coming closer to the truth.

Cowley argues that Virgil and the other Latin poets divided the Greek invocation into two parts. Homer's proems join invocation and brief statement of the argument: "Anger be now your song, immortal one, / Akhilleus' anger, doomed and ruinous, . . . " and "Sing *in me,* Muse, and *through me* tell the story / of that man skilled in all ways of contending."[15] In the Roman poets the opening becomes a two-room structure, with the introduction of the story separated from the call for divine aid. Virgil outlines his story in the first seven lines of the *Aeneid,* and in lines 8–11 (of the Latin) he calls on the muse to inspire his song and, as will Milton in his poem, raises the question of divine justice:

> Tell me the reason, Muse: what was the wound
> to her divinity, so hurting her
> that she, the queen of gods, compelled a man
> remarkable for goodness to endure
> so many crises, meet so many trials?
> Can such resentment hold the minds of gods?[16]

Cowley's two-roomed structure governed Renaissance epic practice. Tasso, for example, devotes the first stanza of the *Gerusalemme Liberata* to an outline summary of the story and the second stanza to an invocation to the Heavenly as opposed to the Heliconian Muse. Cowley, significantly, devotes more time to the invocation than to the proposition: the opening twelve-line proposition verse paragraph is followed by a second invocation verse paragraph, two

---

14. Abraham Cowley, *Davideis*, in *Poems: Miscellanies, The Mistress, Pindarique Odes, Davideis, Verses Written on Several Occasions,* ed. A. R. Waller (Cambridge: Cambridge University Press, 1905), p. 266.
15. Homer, *Iliad,* trans. Robert Fitzgerald (New York: Anchor, 1974), 1.1; Homer, *Odyssey,* trans. Robert Fitzgerald (1963; repr. New York: Vintage, 1990), 1.1–2.
16. *Aeneid,* trans. Allen Mandelbaum (New York: Bantam, 1980), 1.13–18. Further quotations of the *Aeneid* in English are taken from this translation.

and a half times as long. Milton, as we will see in a moment, rejects this compartmentalization.

I quoted Cowley's annotation at length because he implicitly argues for a taxonomy or hierarchy of virtue. Ancient poets addressed "some God for . . . assistance." If the Greeks were deficient in the stateliness of their epic architecture, at least they addressed a deity of sorts. Roman poets in this respect were degenerate, invoking the assistance not of a deity but "the worst of *Men.*" If Virgil invokes a divine muse in his epic, he invokes Augustus in the *Georgics;* Lucan and Statius decline farther, invoking Nero and Domitian respectively. A descending scale of poets is arrayed under a descending scale of their objects of invocation, as the erudite Lucan descends below the supposedly rustic shepherd Hesiod because of an impious invocation. Milton's concern with the "meaning not the name" of the object of his invocation responds to this measure of the worth of the epic and epic poet. Cowley leaves no ambiguity in his own invocation, naming the Son of God as his muse: "Thou, who didst *Davids* royal stem adorn, / And gav'st him *birth* from whom thy self was't *born*" (*Davideis* 1.13–14). With the highest of invocatees, Cowley makes high claims for himself, as the implicit logic of his annotation plays itself out:

> Guid my bold steps with thine old *trav'lling Flame,*
> In these untrodden paths to *Sacred Fame;*
> Lo, with *pure hands* thy heav'enly *Fires* to take,
> My well-chang'd *Muse* I a chast *Vestal* make!
> From earths vain joys, and loves soft witchcraft free,
> I consecrate my *Magdalene* to Thee!
>
> (1.27–32)

Cowley in one sense walks on well-traveled paths, but, by the logic he shares with Milton, writing a true Christian epic will carry him above and beyond all previous poets. The price for that distinction here, as it has been for Milton, is chaste virtue, not the rage of Dido but the divine rage of the Christian poet. The "Muse" of these lines is partly the object of invocation and partly the poetic craft of the poet himself. Pure poetry both makes the poet pure and can arise only from a pure poet, in a version of the circular paradox of inspiration (if a poem is inspired, the merit is the muse's, not the poet's, but selection by the muse is itself a mark of merit). The choice of the Son of God over a pagan muse changes him and his art.

Cowley contrasts a metaphorical temple to physical temples that are only apparently more durable,

> Lo, this great work, a *Temple* to thy praise,
> On polisht *Pillars* of strong *Verse* I raise!

> A *Temple*, where if *Thou* vouchsafe to dwell,
> It *Solomons*, and *Herods* shall excel.
> Too long the *Muses-Land* have *Heathen* bin;
> Their *Gods* too long were *Dev'ils*, and *Vertues Sin*,

and concludes the invocation with an extraordinary claim for himself:

> But *Thou, Eternal Word*, hast call'd forth *Me*
> Th'*Apostle*, to convert that *World* to *Thee*;
> T'unbind the charms that in slight *Fables* lie,
> And teach that *Truth* is *truest Poesie*.
>   (1.33–42)

This all sounds like Milton, in theme if not in voice. I have made a temple. I will go where none has before. I can be a prophet because I am chosen by God for the purity of my life. What separates Cowley from Milton is his readiness to explain away his claims as examples of literary convention: "I hope that this kind of boast (which I have been taught by almost all the old *Poets*) will not seem immodest; for though some in other Languages have attempted the writing a *Divine Poem;* yet non, that I know of, has in English."[17] Cowley continues the note, citing Virgil, Horace, Lucretius, Nemesianus, and Gratius, thus carefully insulating his boast from the charge of immodesty in nesting layers of literary precedent. It is inconceivable that Milton would contextualize away his own claims for his singularity and prophetic status. The choice to annotate is itself a sign of a different relation to the poem than Milton cultivates. Milton provides expository arguments and the scathing and condescending note on the verse, worlds apart from the pedantic and temporizing comments of Cowley. In his claim of priority, Cowley attempts to come out on top of a literary game; Milton plays that game as well, but his sights are set elsewhere, and higher.

One measure of Milton's sharp difference from the timid assertiveness of Cowley is the manner in which the proem to the first book of *Paradise Lost* weaves together epic proposition with the claim of inspiration. In Cowley's terms, the proem is "built . . . with less state," though not because Milton approaches the terseness of Homer's "sing in me, Muse." Instead, the proem is remarkable for the reoccupation of the position of the epic hero by the epic speaker. The heroism of the Son of God and of Milton as epic speaker share the first of the two extended sentences of the invocation.

---

17. Cowley's third annotation to Book 1 of *Davideis*, in *Poems*, 266–67.

> Of man's first disobedience, and the fruit
> Of that forbidden tree, whose mortal taste
> Brought death into the world, and all our woe,
> With loss of Eden, till one greater man
> Restore us, and regain the blissful seat,
> Sing Heav'nly Muse, that on the secret top
> Of Oreb, or of Sinai, didst inspire
> That shepherd, who first taught the chosen seed,
> In the beginning how the heav'ns and earth
> Rose out of Chaos: or if Sion hill
> Delight thee more, and Siloa's brook that flowed
> Fast by the oracle of God; I thence
> Invoke thy aid to my advent'rous Song,
> That with no middle flight intends to soar
> Above th' Aonian mount, while it pursues
> Things unattempted yet in prose or rhyme.
>   (1.1–16)

Other epics tell of human heroes, who share with the poets divine aid. Even in Cowley's "first" Christian epic, the hero is David. The only room reserved for man other than for Milton in the invocation involves "man's disobedience." The "greater man" of line 4 is the Son of God, and if one looks for another great man here, one finds only Milton. Milton coolly offers to the inspiring God a choice of names, derived as Muses' names traditionally were from locale. God can inspire as Muse of Oreb or Sinai (itself making one into two) or as Muse of Sion and Siloa's brook near Jerusalem. The seamlessness of the opening of the poem, the refusal to insulate the invocation from the proposition, collapses the distance between Milton and epic hero.

The "Say first" of the tradition comes after the invocation apparently ends, and it is limited to the revolt of Satan, not to the action of the "one greater man." The activity in the opening verse paragraph is God's and Milton's alone. If Achilles, Odysseus, Aeneas, Godfrey, and David pursued adventures in earlier epics, Milton is now the adventurer: "I thence / Invoke thy aid to my advent'rous song, / That with no middle flight intends to soar / Above th' Aonian mount, while it pursues / Things unattempted yet in prose or rhyme." Even as Milton lifts the last line from Ariosto,[18] he changes the context. Ariosto promises to relate Roland's adventures, not his own. Milton devotes to himself invocation

---

18. "*Cosa non detta in prosa mai, né in rima,*" Ludovico Ariosto, *Orlando Furioso,* 1.ii; inevitably, the nineteenth-century translator Gilbert Stuart Rose used Milton's line, "Things unattempted yet in prose or rhyme," to translate Ariosto's.

space traditionally devoted to the hero. Cowley, as we have seen, anticipates Milton here, but his assertion is hedged by apology and qualification.

The temple of Cowley's invocation is the poem; the temple of Milton's is Milton himself:

> And chiefly thou O Spirit, that dost prefer
> Before all temples th' upright heart and pure,
> Instruct me, for thou know'st; thou from the first
> Wast present, and with mighty wings outspread
> Dove-like sat'st brooding on the vast abyss
> And mad'st it pregnant: what in me is dark
> Illumine, what is low raise and support;
> That to the highth of this great argument
> I may assert eternal providence,
> And justify the ways of God to men.
>
> (1.17–26)

Milton speaks out of a sense of entitlement. Because the divine spirit values "th' upright heart and pure," he should instruct Milton. The impregnation of the waters parallels the inspiration of the poet. Milton's audacity lies partly in his grasping in two hands and without apology the prophetic mantle, and partly in the project of justifying the ways of God to man. For Calvin and Milton's mainly Calvinist contemporaries, the project of theodicy, or the defense of divine justice, is itself suspect.[19] The assertion of eternal providence is obligatory in religious works of Milton's time, but by claiming that he will justify God's ways, Milton throws down a gauntlet. Theodicy was explicitly attacked by Calvin as presumptuous, because divine justice cannot be grasped by limited human reason. Where, to lift from the Book of Job, was Milton when God laid the foundations of the earth? Can Milton draw out Leviathan with a hook (Job 38:4, 41:1)? Calvin, quoting Romans 9:20 ("Who are you, O man, to argue with God? Does the molded object say to its molder, 'Why have you fashioned me thus?' "), sternly comments that "such depth underlies God's judgments that all men's minds would be swallowed up if they tried to penetrate it. . . . Monstrous indeed is the madness of men, who desire thus to subject the immeasurable to the puny measure of their own reason" (*Institutes* [1559], III.xxiii.4).[20] The "assertion" behind Milton's project is as much an

---

19. The following discussion is taken from my essay "*Paradise Lost* in Intellectual History," in *A Companion to Milton*, ed. Thomas N. Corns (Oxford: Blackwell, 2001), pp. 330–31.
20. Calvin, *Institutes of the Christian Religion* (1559), ed. John T. McNeill and trans. Ford Lewis Battles, Library of Christian Classics 20–21 (Philadelphia: Westminster Press, 1960), 21:952. References to the *Institutes* will be taken from this edition and identified by section number.

assertion of human reason, and of Milton as reasoner, as it is an assertion of God's justice.

The anti-Calvinist (and Arminian) stance on theodicy is characteristic of Milton in two ways, which taken together are paradoxical. First, it minimizes a gap between divine and human reason that most saw as nearly infinite. Milton in *Paradise Lost* repeatedly collapses hierarchical distinctions and figurative distances, between heaven and earth, between angels and human beings, and—more fitfully—between man and woman. Second, the stance foregrounds Milton's singularity, his assertive and unique self: "what in *me* is dark / Illumine"; "That . . . / *I* may assert"). Milton assumes the mantle of prophet, the lone just man and visionary. Milton the collapser of hierarchical distances confronts Milton the man who stands out from the crowd. The poet, in a paradox that replays his career as a political theorist, is a leveler of hierarchies who needs to think of himself as uncommon, as gifted and blessed above his peers. The tension generated by this paradox will lead to a sharp recoil in the epic, as the specter of alienation and distance haunts the poet-narrator.

In standing out from the crowd, and in making prominent claims for his prophetic status, Milton must guard against Satan's primal sin, the subject of the second verse paragraph:

> pride
> Had cast him out from Heav'n, with all his host
> Of rebel angels, by whose aid aspiring
> To set himself in glory above his peers,
> He trusted to have equaled the Most High,
> If he opposed.
>
> (1.36–41)

Milton skirts an abyss of pride at the threshold of his poem. Like all epic poets, he tries to "set himself in glory above his peers," but without the safety nets of mediation (my poem is great, not I) or generic imperative (I have to claim this, though I don't really mean it). In displacing the Son of God, the briefly named hero of the introductory summary, he also flirts with the danger of attempting to "equal the Most High."

Book 3: "may I express thee unblamed?"

Though mindful that the darkness within must be illumined, the voice of the first invocation is calm and confident. If there is a foreboding of falling off from flight, it is in the evocation of the Grand Parents and the Serpent that immediately follows. Milton's epic narrator will continue to soar while others fall. The invocation to Book 3 is less settled. Emerging into light from the darkness of transgression and its punishment, Milton trails behind him traces of transgressive anxiety: "Hail holy light, offspring of Heav'n first-born, / Or of th' Eternal co-eternal beam / May I express thee unblamed?" (3.1–3). The meaning of the syntactically ambiguous third line is finally indeterminate. Does the question refer only to the second line, the attempt to describe the Son's light as co-eternal with the Father's? Or does it refer to the entire enterprise of expressing God at all? Many editors from the Jonathan Richardsons, father and son, in 1734 and Thomas Newton in 1749 through John Leonard, one of the most recent editors, choose the former alternative, suggesting that the speaker alludes to the blame that might follow an erroneous ascription of co-eternity to the Son.[21] Patrick Hume in 1695 dismisses the anxiety in a paraphrase of 3.3–6 that suggests that Milton immediately resolves the question of blame: "Blameless may I declare thee, because God himself is Light, and from Eternity in amazing brightness, disdaining all approach of Human Eyes, dwelt from Eternity, dwelt then in the [sic], bright Emanation of the brightest being."[22] The editors discount the fear of transgression. Louis Martz also domesticates the passage, which for him illustrates the "modesty and humility of th[e] bard's approach to the divine."[23] But one could turn Martz around. The poet sings of supernatural secrets, and the invocation might record the anxiety of one who is the opposite of humble and modest, one who realizes the gravity of his prophetic claim and the implications if he is in error. He seeks to neutralize the danger of the vertical movement to Heaven, a movement figured later in the Bellerophon allusion of Book 7, by juxtaposing it with the danger he has just eluded when he "Escaped the Stygian Pool" (3.14), an escape made possible, ironically, by his singing "With other notes than to th' *Orphean* lyre" (3.17). Resembling Orpheus, who in his "Hymn to Night" journeys through darkness, Milton also differs from Orpheus in being inspired by the true, heavenly muse. Even at this moment of confidence within this invocation Milton turns to Orpheus, whose myth, Alastair Fowler comments, "focused deep fears in Milton."[24]

---

21. See the notes to this passage in the Richardsons' *Explanatory Notes and Remarks on Milton's "Paradise Lost"* (London, 1734); in Thomas Newton's edition of *Paradise Lost* (London, 1749); and in John Leonard's excellent edition of the *Complete Poems* (Harmondsworth: Penguin, 1998).
22. Patrick Hume, *Annotations on Milton's Paradise Lost* (London, 1695), p. 96.
23. Louis Martz, *Milton: Poet of Exile*, 2nd ed. (New Haven: Yale University Press, 1986), p. 97.
24. Alastair Fowler, ed., *Paradise Lost*, 2nd ed. (Harlow: Longman, 1998), p. 391 (annotation to 7.32–38).

Having compared himself to Orpheus, Milton now compares himself to Aeneas. He has been "Taught by the Heav'nly Muse to venture down / The dark descent, and up to reascend, / Though hard and rare" (3.19–21). Patrick Hume is the first of many to trace this passage to the Sybil's warning to Aeneas: "*facilis descensus Averno* / . . . / *Sed revocare gradus, superasque evadere ad auras / Hoc opus, hic labor est* [easy / the way that leads into Avernus: . . . / But to recall your steps, to rise again / into the upper air: that is the labor; / that is the task]" (*Aeneid* 6.126–29). The Richardsons annotate 3.19–21 tersely: "*though hard and rare* Difficult, and not Commonly done, as only by *Hercules, Orpheus, Ulysses,* &c." Through this allusion, Milton claims kinship with Virgil's hero at the point in the epic when he receives the prophecy of Rome's future greatness, at the moment, in other words, when he combines the functions of visionary and hero to which Milton aspires.

It is at this moment in the invocation that Milton refers first to his blindness:

> thee I revisit safe,
> And feel thy sov'reign vital lamp; but thou
> Revisit'st not these eyes, that roll in vain
> To find thy piercing ray, and find no dawn;
> So thick a drop serene hath quenched their orbs,
> Or dim suffusion veiled.
> (3.21–26)

Milton both has and lacks the union with the divine that he seeks. He feels the lamp, but for the blind Milton its light is indistinguishable from the "universal blank" (or "blanc") of line 48, the white field that was all Milton could "see." Given the palpable anguish of this passage, the blank is uncomfortably close to the "darkness visible" of hell. Milton revisits the divine light, but it does not revisit him. The asymmetry suggests a tantalizing communion that cannot free him from isolation.

Answering in the *Defensio Secunda* the charge that his blindness was a divine punishment, Milton claimed that it placed him in the line of prophets (*YP* 4.1:584). Here in Book 3 of *Paradise Lost* the appearance of blindness shortly after the question of whether his narrative and prayer can be expressed without blame raises again the question of punishment. The anguished description of blindness is followed by a reassertion of poetic power, "Yet not the more / Cease I to wander where the Muses haunt," but the confidence of the assertion is undercut by the tortuous syntax. "Yet I still wander" would be more direct. Even "Yet no less do I wander" would be idiomatic. But the foreignness and strangeness of Milton's construction ("Yet not the more cease I") belies the confident pose, as does the loaded term "wander," associated elsewhere with malign rovings of the Sons of Belial, the futility of the devils' philosophizing, and the sad fate of Bellerophon.[25] The level of ambiguity rises as Milton explains his refusal to leave the muses; he is "Smit with the love of sacred song" (3.29). Milton has been struck by, he has become enamored of, sacred song. Having approached the divine chorus, he can't tear himself away. Or he has been struck *because of* his love of sacred song. His desire to sing of things invisible to mortal sight has been answered with blindness and wandering. The ensuing gesture toward fellowship with prophets and prophetic poets participates in the same dialectic of assertion and anxiety as the statement of steadfastness in dedication to the muses. "[B]ut chief / Thee Sion," he writes,

> Nightly I visit: nor sometimes forget
> Those other two equaled with me in fate,
> So were I equaled with them in renown,
> Blind Thamyris and blind Maeonides,
> And Tiresias and Phineus prophets old.
>
> (3.32–36)

"Nor sometimes forget" is as difficult to untangle as "yet not the more cease I" several lines earlier. While there are ways to explain away how the "other two" become four, with poets and prophets doubled, the effect is unsettling. Milton like the first two is a poet, and a blind poet. The second pair are prophets, each of whom was struck blind for seeing too far into divine affairs. Milton, the poet-prophet flying above the Aonian mount, aspires to the fame of Thamyris and Homer (Maeonides). He does not state clearly a desire to be equal to Tiresias and Phineus, and the omission points to an unspoken fear, that his similarity to them may lie in blindness as divine punishment.

The blindness of all four figures, however different in cause, is tied to their visionary powers, to which Milton lays claim. Milton's song is like the nightingale's, who "in shadiest covert hid / Tunes her nocturnal note" (3.39–40). The light of the mundane sun, the loss of which Milton in part bitterly regrets, might frustrate the song and its attendant vision, so blindness is more

---

25. See 1.501, 2.561, 7.20. John Guillory attributes the grammatical tortuousness of these lines to the "ambivalence of the poet-prophet" (*Poetic Authority,* pp. 124–25). Guillory describes a psychodrama in which Milton must separate himself from Satan as figure of the imagination and archetype of the poet and align himself with the Son.

enabling than disabling.[26] But at this point, when the agony of blindness seems to have been laid to rest, it returns in a recoil of pathos and bitterness:[27]

> Thus with the year
> Seasons return, but not to me returns
> Day, or the sweet approach of ev'n or morn,
> Or sight of vernal bloom, or summer's rose,
> Or flocks, or herds, or human face divine;
> But clouds instead, and ever-during dark
> Surrounds me, from the cheerful ways of men
> Cut off, and for the book of knowledge fair
> Presented with a universal blank
> Of Nature's works to me expunged and razed,
> And wisdom at one entrance quite shut out.
> (3.40–50)

The invocation ends with the claim of the divine gift of internal vision, but this reiterates a claim already made in the passage on the classical poets and prophets. The double recoil on blindness opens the way for a third or fourth, destabilizing the invocation's apparent resolution. Milton's God tells Raphael to warn Adam and Eve that they should be careful to "swerve not too secure" (5.238). Milton has seemed aware of the danger of complacency, of swerving because imagining himself secure, particularly at moments such as the invocation of Book 3 when he is making salient claims for his vision. The danger, though, in the recoiling of the passages on blindness seems to be the opposite. Milton swerves so quickly from anguish to reassurance and back that security seems elusive.

Book 7: "I have presumed / An earthly quest"

The third invocation, in Book 7, contains the most complex of Milton's self-representations in *Paradise Lost*. It is built around a simile in which Milton

---

26. Ernest Sirluck argued that, after a failure of chastity (which Sirluck reads as a breaking of a vow of celibacy), Milton adopts blindness as the "new symbol of poetic inspiration" ("Milton's Idle Right Hand," *Journal of English and Germanic Philology* 60 [1961]: 771). While suggesting that a vow of celibacy would be out of character for Milton, E. R. Gregory has added his voice to those who see blindness at the heart of the inspiration of the late poems (*Milton and the Muses* [Tuscaloosa: University of Alabama Press, 1989], pp. 84–89). I agree with William Kerrigan that blindness is the punishment that precedes and authorizes the transgression of writing the epic (*The Sacred Complex: On the Psychogenesis of Paradise Lost* [Cambridge, MA: Harvard University Press, 1983], p. 190).

27. Guillory (*Poetic Authority*, pp. 126–27) reads these lines differently, seeing in them the ratifying and welcome blindness of the literally inspired prophet.

compares himself to Bellerophon. The multiple strands of the Bellerophon myth allow the simile to signify in more ways than Milton may have intended. Bellerophon is yoked in the invocation with Orpheus, another figure who in some versions of his myth comes to a bad end as a result of his relations with women. Milton desires to be like Orpheus and Bellerophon in some respects, but to avoid their tragic ends. While Orpheus appears throughout Milton's works as an alter ego for the poet, Bellerophon appears only twice in Milton's works, first at the beginning of the writer's career and next near the end. But this central invocation is structured around the comparatively rare figure, as is evidenced by the appearance of his horse, Pegasus, in line 4, long before the simile begins.

The order of Bellerophon's appearances in Milton's works reflects the shape of his story and the lineaments of Milton's own. We find Bellerophon triumphant in the Sixth Prolusion, where as part of an elaborate and facetious compliment to Milton's auditors he slays the Chimera. We leave him here in the invocation to Book 7 of *Paradise Lost,* wandering on the Aleian Field, a self-cautionary tale for the audacious poet. In the Bellerophon allusion we can witness the precision and control of Milton the craftsperson, who, like Michelangelo painting the Sistine ceiling, labored over details likely to be overlooked by those gazing from below. But we also witness the process by which this careful control is ruptured and overwhelmed. The sparsity of Milton's allusions to Bellerophon compared with the profusion of Orpheus's appearances tells us something important about Milton; it may be easier to contemplate the external threat of being savaged by an ignorant audience than the internal threat of foolish presumption. Like a prism, Bellerophon refracts the light of Milton's self-representation in an unanticipated, surprising, and, for Milton, disturbing direction.

As Book 7 begins, and as Milton is about to turn from heaven to earth, his narrator addresses Urania:

> Up led by thee
> Into the Heav'n of heav'ns I have presumed,
> An earthly guest, and drawn empyreal air,
> Thy temp'ring; with like safety guided down
> Return me to my native element:
> Lest from this flying steed unreined, (as once
> Bellerophon, though from a lower clime)
> Dismounted, on th' Aleian field I fall
> Erroneous there to wander and forlorn.
> (7.12–20)

The general sense here is clear: writing of heaven, Milton has courted presumption. Even without a gloss, the reader sees in the Bellerophon myth a family resemblance to the familiar myths of Phaeton and Icarus. Editors' glosses establish more fully the aptness of the allusion: the name for the "Aleian" plain of Lycia comes from the Greek word for "wandering," and Bellerophon like Milton spent his final years blind.

To pursue the strands of the Bellerophon myth beyond the common glosses is to glimpse the depth of Milton's conscious control of his poem.[28] Homer's digression on Bellerophon in the *Iliad* (6.155–210) incorporates several aspects of the myth useful to Milton. In Homer the hero falls out with his patron King Proetus of Argos, whose wife Anteia charged Bellerophon with attempted seduction after he rejected her advances. Proetus, loath to kill his guest, sends him with a coded message to Anteia's father, King Iobates of Lycia. Sharing Proetus's scruple against murdering a guest, Iobates orders Bellerophon to complete several tasks, each designed to end in his death. Against all odds, however, Bellerophon kills the Chimera, defeats the Solymians and the Amazons, and, finally, dispatches a select band of Iobates' soldiers lying in ambush for him. At this point Iobates relents and presents Bellerophon with his daughter in marriage. Some time later, perhaps grieving for the death of two children, Bellerophon leaves his home to wander disconsolately on the Aleian plain.

Two elements from this Homeric account stand out as relevant to Milton's allusion: the false accusation against Bellerophon's chastity and the superhuman nature of his victories, particularly over the Chimera. These elements are if anything more pronounced in other versions of the myth. Hesiod is the first to place Bellerophon on the back of Pegasus, a story repeated with variations by Pindar, Apollodorus, and Pausanias.[29] In Pindar's version, Pallas Athena gives Bellerophon the golden bridle with which he subdues Pegasus. Plutarch highlights Bellerophon's extraordinary modesty and chastity. In the *Moralia*'s version of the attempted ambush, Bellerophon asks Poseidon to flood the plain behind him as he advances on Iobates' palace. Desperate to stop Bellerophon, the Xanthian women raise their skirts above their waists and run toward him, offering their bodies if he will stop: "And now, when the men . . . laboring to put a stop to Bellerophon, availed nothing at all, the women plucking up their petticoats met him full butt; upon which confounded with shame he turned back again and the flood, as they say, returned

---

28. A useful introduction to the appearances of Bellerophon in classical literature and the appropriation of Bellerophon in the Renaissance can be found in Marianne Shapiro's "Perseus and Bellerophon in *Orlando Furioso*," *Modern Philology* 81 (1983): 109–30.

29. Hesiod, *Theogony*, 319–25; Pindar, *Olympia* 13; Apollodorus, *Library* II.iii.1–2; Pausanias, *Description of Greece* II.iv.1.

with him."[30] Retelling the story of Anteia's false accusations, Horace refers to "chaste Bellerophon" (*casto Bellerophontae*).[31]

In Pindar's Seventh Isthmian Ode, we first hear of the incident at the heart of Milton's Bellerophon allusion, the presumptuous flight to Olympus: "Pegasos, / the winged, cast down / Bellerophon, his master, when he strove to reach / the houses of the sky and the fellowship / of Zeus."[32] In Pindar, Bellerophon falls to his death. Conflating the versions of Homer and Pindar, mythographers would have Bellerophon survive his fall in order to wander on the Aleian plain until his death.[33]

As this survey suggests, Milton inherited the Bellerophon myth in significantly different versions; the plasticity of the myth makes it ideal for Milton's use. In all versions Bellerophon is aided by supernatural powers. In several versions, most notably that of Apollodorus, the story ends triumphantly, with Bellerophon's marriage to Iobates' daughter and prospects for a long and happy life. The version with the happy ending finds its way into the *Ovide moralisé*, where Bellerophon is credited with strength, wisdom, and kindness (as well as beauty).[34] Bellerophon's chastity is underscored by Anteia's false accusation and embodied in his reaction to the genital display of the Xanthian women. On the other hand, Bellerophon becomes a figure of foolishness and immaturity in the disproportionate grief marking the end of Homer's version (a sense picked up in Cicero's *Tusculan Disputations* III.63) and in his ill-fated attempt to fly to Olympus.

The myth's variations resonate in the brief allusion in the invocation to Book 7. The allusion does not merely point to a danger that would be shared by anyone attempting to write a poem both epic and sacred, it becomes an echo chamber for the self-referential dialogue that Milton had been having with himself and with his readers for many years. This dialogue proceeds from an uncomplicated and naïve confidence in divine election as a prophet, an election validated in large part by chastity, to the contemplation of doubts and misgivings potentially damaging to that claim. The narrator in *Paradise Lost* embodies this complex self-conception, and the Bellerophon allusion in the invocation to Book 7 encodes it.

---

30. *Concerning the Virtues of Women* 9, *Plutarch's Morals*, trans. by several hands, ed. William W. Goodwin (London: Atheneum, 1870), p. 351.

31. *Odes* III.vii.15, in *The Third Book of Horace's Odes*, ed. Gordon Williams (Oxford: Clarendon, 1969), p. 68.

32. *The Odes of Pindar*, 2nd ed., trans. Richmond Lattimore (Chicago: University of Chicago Press, 1976), pp. 153–54.

33. See, e.g., the version available to Milton in Natalis Comes, *Mythologiae* (Venice, 1567; facs. repr. New York: Garland, 1976), p. 271 (ix.4).

34. Shapiro, "Perseus and Bellerophon in *Orlando Furioso*," pp. 116–17.

Milton begins by placing himself in the position of Bellerophon just before his fall; with the help of his muse Urania, "above th' Olympian hill I soar, / Above the flight of Pegasean wing" (7.3–4). Or rather he places himself higher, for in his flight he follows the "voice divine" of Urania (7.2). Without the protection of the divine muse, Milton has less between him and the earth than did the presumptuous Bellerophon. The equipoise of confidence and anxiety is captured in a paradoxical claim:

> Up led by thee
> Into the Heav'n of heav'ns I have *presum'd*,
> An earthly *guest*, and drawn empyreal air,
> Thy temp'ring; with like safety guided down
> Return me to my native element.
> (7.12–16; my emphasis)

Milton is a guest who has presumed, one who paradoxically has crashed a party to which he has already been invited. If he is still one of the "selected heralds" of God, he is safe; otherwise he is in grave danger.[35]

The Bellerophon allusion serves to inoculate Milton from the threatened danger. This is true both in a general sense, for Bellerophon shares with Icarus and Phaeton the dubious distinction of presumptuous flight, and in a particular sense, for Bellerophon was viewed as Milton wished to be viewed, as a hero of wisdom and chastity. If Bellerophon gains supernatural powers through heroic chastity, then his career parallels Milton's. Milton can be saved from Bellerophon's subsequent foolish presumptuousness by the inspiration of the true muse.[36]

The closeness of the parallels between Bellerophon and Milton testifies to the subtle control that Milton exerts over his self-representation. It is intriguing to consider the question of control at this point of the poem, as Milton wrestles with the specter of overreaching and presumption. Has he ventured beyond mortal limits, and will his poem suffer the literary and spiritual equivalents of free fall? The Bellerophon allusion, with its masterly precision, represents an attempt to exorcize the demon of presumption. By recognizing the

---

35. For a different view, see Stanley Fish, who sees Milton as implicitly accusing the muse rather than himself: "Nominally, this is the language of courtesy, as when one apologizes for having presumed above one's class; but, as is often the case, courtesy is a mask for darker feelings, and here it masks an accusation: 'You've led me on.' 'Up led by thee' assigns the agency to Urania; the presumption, if there is any, is hers." *How Milton Works* (Cambridge, MA: Harvard University Press, 2001), p. 289. The pattern of anxiety in the proem suggests that if Milton has "darker feelings" in the passage, they are directed toward himself and not toward the divine muse.

36. Christine Hogan has pointed out to me the overtones of the Bellerophon myth in Milton's expansion of Matthew 4:5 and Luke 4:9 when writing of Satan's flight with the Son to the pinnacle in *Paradise Regained*, "without wing / Of hippogriff" (4.541–42).

error of Bellerophon, the hero who most closely prefigures his position, Milton will be able to avoid it. His assertion of control, as opposed to the free fall of Bellerophon, is authenticated by the control demonstrated in the allusion.

Milton is now able to breathe a sigh of relief:

> Half yet remains unsung but narrower bound
> Within the visible diurnal sphere;
> Standing on earth, not rapt above the pole,
> More safe I sing.
> (7.21–25)

But, like the relief from blindness in the invocation to Book 3, the relief from a sense of danger is ephemeral. Precisely at this point, as Milton has erected a wall around himself as a protection from danger, danger floods back into the poem. His voice is unchanged,

> though fall'n on evil days,
> On evil days though fall'n, and evil tongues;
> In darkness, and with dangers compassed round,
> And solitude.
> (7.25–28)[37]

The depth of anxiety here is difficult to overstate, given that Milton chooses language to describe himself that echoes language with which he had had Sin describe herself earlier. Sin has been assigned the role of portress of hell, made

> To sit in hateful office here confined,
> Inhabitant of Heav'n, and heav'nly-born,
> Here in perpetual agony and pain,
> With terrors and with clamors compassed round
> Of mine own brood, that on my bowels feed.
> (2.859–63)

It is a small step from "With terrors and with clamors compassed round" to the metrically identical "In darkness, and with dangers compassed round." And with this short step a new perspective opens, in which Milton's language works in spite of rather than for the author, and in which Milton uncovers to us and to himself what he wishes to remain covered. It seems that Milton is not entirely in control of the subtle dialogue across half of his epic; it is hardly credible that he means to put himself in the place of Sin.

---

37. On the relation between Milton's falling on evil days and the effects of the fall of humankind, see Michael Lieb, *Milton and the Culture of Violence* (Ithaca: Cornell University Press, 1994), p. 69.

The mirroring of lines is only the most salient instance of the presence in the Bellerophon allusion of language associated with Satan and the fallen angels. The author fears for the moment lest "on th' Aleian Field I fall / Erroneous there to wander and forlorn" (7.19–20). After his fall Satan turns to Beëlzebub with a question, "Seest thou yon dreary plain, forlorn and wild"? (1.180). The exploring devils of Book 2 are described as "roving on / In confused march forlorn" (2.614–15). If the Bellerophon allusion had succeeded in quelling the narrator's anxiety, these echoes might pass without comment, for Milton would have separated himself finally from Satanic overreaching. But the echoing of Sin's words in the narrator's own blurs that separation and awakes the ominous echoes in the allusion.

Anxiety and a hint of transgression return at the end of the invocation, in the familiar allusion to Orpheus:

> But drive far off the barbarous dissonance
> Of Bacchus and his revellers, the race
> Of that wild rout that tore the Thracian bard
> In Rhodope, where woods and rocks had ears
> To rapture, till the savage clamor drowned
> Both harp and voice; nor could the muse defend
> Her son. So fail not thou, who thee implores:
> For thou art Heav'nly, she an empty dream.
> (7.32–39)

While Richard DuRocher finds in this allusion simultaneous confidence in inspiration and anxiety about reception,[38] I have traced up to this point substantial anxiety about inspiration. There are different opinions in the tradition concerning the cause of Orpheus's dismemberment by the Bacchantes. Some credited Orpheus with chastity for spurning the Bacchantes.[39] Ovid, on the other hand, implies that Orpheus angered the Bacchantes by his practice and advocacy of sodomy.[40] Some viewed Orpheus's spurning of the women as a refusal to honor the god Dionysius. These interpretations may tinge the Orpheus allusion with some of the internal anxiety that colors the Bellerophon allusion. And one might recall also behind this reading of Orpheus the fate of Pentheus in Euripides' *Bacchae*, who is torn apart by the Bacchantes both for

---

38. DuRocher, *Milton and Ovid* (Ithaca: Cornell University Press, 1985), p. 73.
39. Orpheus had foresworn the love of women after losing Eurydice for the second time. The Richardsons stress Orpheus' chastity; their paratactic account suggests but does not confirm that chastity was the cause of his death: "Orpheus ... lost his Beloved Wife *Eurydice* and was very Chaste, the *Ciconian* Women, mad Worshipers of *Bacchus*, tore him to pieces on the Mountain *Rhodope*" (*Explanatory Notes*, p. 292).
40. Ovid, *Metamorphoses*, 10.84–85 and 11.1–19; I owe this observation to John Rumrich.

refusing to honor the god and proximately for his voyeuristic curiosity as he approaches the Dionysian rites.

A structural parallel connects the invocations in Books 3 and 7. The relation between the Orpheus and Bellerophon allusions reenacts the relationship between the two anguished cries of the blind speaker. The recoil or return, from blindness to blindness and now from Bellerophon to Orpheus, can point as easily toward an unceasing oscillation between despair and confidence as it can to the final laying to rest of doubt. If a second reassurance is needed, why not a third, fourth, fifth, and so on?

A similar double significance marks the lines, noted above, that follow the Bellerophon allusion: "Standing on earth, not rapt above the pole, / More safe I sing with mortal voice, unchanged / To hoarse or mute, though fall'n on evil days …" (7.23–25). The poet stands on earth, upon secure ground, but like his song he is "narrower bound." It may seem comforting to be "not rapt above the pole," but rapture, as we have seen, can be of at least two kinds, the mental imbalance associated with presumptuous flight or the divine madness of inspiration anatomized in Plato's *Phaedrus*. The comparative "more safe" is slippery: it may add to a simple, confident assertion of security, or it may, like many comparative adjectives, weaken the statement. On the one hand the narrator asserts that he is safer than he was in previous books, on the other the calculation of degrees of safety unsettles the security of unqualified safety. The ambiguity is compounded when he adds that the safety depends on his singing "with mortal voice," which is both a voice that prudently recognizes its limits and a voice that participates in frailty.[41] Safety is purchased by the fallen state, and a prudent respect for the danger of soaring is purchased by a loss of rapture. The passage's ambiguity is heightened at the enjambment in "unchanged / To hoarse or mute." Read without a break, the phrase suggests that the voice has not faltered despite adversity, but if we pause for the brief moment we hear that the narrator speaks "with mortal voice, unchanged." The model of inspiration offered by the poem, and throughout Milton's career, is of a mortal voice transformed by divine favor and election.

Bellerophon is more like Milton than we realize at first, and the more we learn the more we can appreciate the precision of the device by which Milton seeks to exorcize the specter of presumption. But, as I have argued, precisely at this moment of exquisite control, meanings apparently unintended by the author flood back into the text. They return in the form of resonances outside the text in alternative readings of the Bellerophon myth and resonances within the text between language with which Milton describes infernal characters and language with which he describes himself.

---

41. See Mulder, "Lyric Dimension," p. 157.

The partial success of Milton's attempt to restrict the Bellerophon allusion to favorable meanings is written into the asymmetrical punctuation of the lines that introduce it:

> Return me to my native element:
> Lest from this flying steed unreined, (as once
> Bellerophon, though from a lower clime)
> Dismounted, on th' Aleian field I fall
> Erroneous there to wander and forlorn.
>
> (7.16–20)

Just as the parenthesis fails to close the reference to Bellerophon, which continues, along with Milton's imagined self-representation, in lines 19 and 20, so Milton fails to close off the unwanted associations of Bellerophon from his own self-representation. In this sense, to take Blake out of context, Milton was "of the Devils party without knowing it." To read these resonances as intentional would be to neglect Milton's history of self-representation; in a lifelong project of ethical proof, Milton establishes himself as a prophet inspired by God as a reward for personal merit and shields himself from his own doubts about his fitness. The allusion yields surplus meanings, which run counter to Milton's intention, but which contribute to the structural intentionality of a work that records Milton's covert doubts as well as his overt confidence.

Book 9: "discourse unblamed?"

In the proem to Book 9, Milton does not invoke the Muse; instead he anxiously considers the authenticity of his inspiration and the possibility of its withdrawal. Just as the language of the proem to Book 1 inserted Milton into the role of hero, so the language here associates his status as singer with the fallen figures about whom he sings:

> No more of talk where God or angel guest
> With man, as with his friend, familiar used
> To sit indulgent, and with him partake
> Rural repast, permitting him the while
> Venial discourse unblamed: I now must change
> Those notes to tragic; foul distrust, and breach
> Disloyal on the part of man, revolt,
> And disobedience; on the part of Heav'n.
> Now alienated, distance and distaste,
> Anger and just rebuke, and judgment giv'n.
>
> (9.1–10)

Bracketing the opening lines, which point back to the middle books, are terms from the two preceding invocations, "guest" and "unblamed." Milton describes himself as having "presumed [as] / An earthly guest" in Heaven in Book 7, where the language of courtesy both covers and discovers the fear of presumption. Milton asks in Book 3 if he can "express" the divine light "unblamed." The easy intercourse of Adam and Raphael parallels the easy intercourse of Milton and the divine Muse; if the former can be lost through overreaching, disobedience, and presumption, why not the latter? In the story of Adam and Eve, "unblamed" is about to give way to "blamed"; Milton's own retrospective discourse might have been blameworthy all along. Adam's discourse with the angel has been "venial," or, as Leonard notes, "blameless." Milton's may turn out to be mortal. The alienation, distance, and distaste of heaven, undergone by the first couple, embodies the fear that Milton expressed in the Bellerophon allusion.

These are all undertones at most. Milton writes of Adam and Eve, not of himself, and when he turns to himself, it is with the familiar confidence. His theme is more heroic than the themes of Homer ("the wrath / Of stern Achilles" and "Neptune's ire" 9.14–15) or of Virgil's (the "rage / Of Turnus for Lavinia disespoused" or "Juno's [ire]" 9.16–18), or of medieval and Renaissance chivalric poetry ("long and tedious havoc [of] fabled knights / In battles feigned" 9.30–31). Leaving no doubt that it is principle rather than ignorance that guides him, Milton devotes ten lines to the details of the chivalric genre that he has rejected.

But the undertones of the opening lines are teased out by the rest of the proem. Milton's relation to the divine muse makes him unique, but that relation is no longer guaranteed; it is governed by an "if" clause. He will not recount the torments of Odysseus or Aeneas ("the Greek and Cytherea's son"),

> *If* answerable style I can obtain
> Of my celestial patroness, who deigns
> Her nightly visitation unimplored,
> And dictates to me slumb'ring, or inspires
> Easy my unpremeditated verse.
> (9.20–24; my emphasis)

His muse is heavenly, not an "empty dream" like Odysseus's divine patroness Athena or Aeneas's divine patroness Venus. Again Milton elides the roles of epic author and epic hero, as he takes the place here not of Homer and Virgil but of their heroes. The "if" can suggest uncertainty, but the following lines describe matter-of-factly the visits of the divine muse at night. The uncertainty seems to surround only the question of answerable style, an art fitting to the high subject of inspiration. Inasmuch, however, as the patroness breathes into him "unpremeditated verse," the question of answerable style becomes puzzling. If the patroness inspires, if the verse is breathed into Milton, why is the style in doubt? The end of the proem revises the confidence in inspiration at the beginning. For Milton

> higher argument
> Remains, sufficient of itself to raise
> That name, *unless* an age too late, or cold
> Climate, or years damp my intended wing
> Depressed, and much they may, *if* all be mine,
> Not hers who brings it nightly to my ear.
> (9.42–47; my emphasis)

"Unless" activates the potential of the earlier "if," and points forward to the following one. Given inspiration, the extrinsic factors of historical or personal age or of northern climate should be no impediment. "Intended" is significantly ambiguous. Does Milton intend to write a great poem, or is it the intention of the divine muse to write through him? The answer must be "yes" to both questions if Milton is not to be convicted of overreaching. The risk is that the poem is "all" his and "not hers." The confidence of the final clause is belied by the "if" of the preceding one. The poem's analogue for a creation that is entirely the creature's is Sin's birth from Satan's head in Book 2. If all is Milton's, then all is corrupt and sinful.[42] On the other hand, Milton's recorded scorn for the "pupil teacher," who teaches only with an authorizing imprimatur, wars with the stance of sponsored singer. Autonomy is his instinctive preference. Perhaps it is awareness of that preference that makes him nervous here. In the proem to Book 9, Milton is poised between assertive confidence and intimations of error and presumption. For Milton this is both an uncomfortable and a familiar position. He is flying or he is descending, his spirits are rapt or disconsolate. The latter alternatives are captured concisely in the polysemic "Depressed" that opens line 46 and that is followed by a caesura. The interpenetration of heroic assertion and intimations of error and alienation has become Milton's signature. The paradox is resolvable, here and elsewhere, by our recognition of what Milton struggles to obscure, that the despair is the inevitable concomitant of the confidence.

---

42. Kerrigan observes that "Milton explores the aesthetic and moral dangers of his 'advent'rous song' by comparing himself to Satan" and notes Milton's anxiety lest "his 'Satan' would be a self-portrait drawn in perfect balance to the hidden image of himself" (*Prophetic Milton,* pp. 147, 187).

Milton's Last Word

The last shall be first. Milton's final word in *Paradise Lost* comes at the beginning, in the material added at the request of his printer, Samuel Simmons. The prose arguments added to individual books offer little in the way of self-representation, though they illuminate Milton's reading of his own work, as does his comment in the Book 5 argument that "God to render man inexcusable sends Raphael" to warn and instruct Adam. But Milton reveals himself abundantly in the final word, described almost as an afterthought in Simmons's brief note: "I have procured [the arguments], and withal a reason of that which stumbled many others, why the Poem Rimes not." Milton writes, contentiously,

> The measure is English heroic verse without rhyme, as that of Homer in Greek, and of Virgil in Latin; rhyme being no necessary adjunct or true ornament of poem or good verse, in longer works especially, but the invention of a barbarous age, to set off wretched matter and lame meter; graced indeed since by the use of some famous modern poets, carried away by custom, but much to their own vexation, hindrance, and constraint to express many things otherwise, and for the most part worse than else they would have expressed them.

This is Milton's typical stance when under attack. Defense quickly turns into offense. Criticized for departing from a norm, he judges that norm not merely nonbinding but "barbarous." Far from blemishing his poem, Milton's choice frees the poem from blemishes that others invite by following the norm; their poems are worse than they otherwise would have been. If Milton's personality shows through even when explaining his decision to employ blank verse, he turns more overtly toward self-representation as the Note rounds to a conclusion. Blank verse is more acceptable to "all judicious ears," the ears of the fit audience that Milton claims as a mark of distinction throughout his career. His attentiveness to this audience, and his refusal to capitulate to fashion, is more evidence of his status as heroic liberator:

> This neglect then of rhyme so little is to be taken for a defect, though it may seem so perhaps to vulgar readers, that it rather is to be esteemed an example set, the first in English, of ancient liberty recovered to heroic poem from the troublesome and modern bondage of rhyming.

It is fashionable now to say that all choices are political. Milton, yet once more, was there first. He thinks of himself, and he repeatedly represents himself, as engaged in the struggle for freedom. The advocate of hard liberty will not relax his vigilance, even when choosing verse forms.

Marvell as Milton's Fit Reader

There is a fleeting moment in the Sixth Prolusion, the one other work in which Milton mentions Bellerophon, that gestures poignantly toward the drama to be played out in the later Milton:

> You see, O my hearers, how far I have been rapt [*me raptat*] and carried away by my excessively violent desire and yearning to please you. Actually it comes over me, quite suddenly, that I have been swept away by a desire that is unholy [*Sacrilegium*] and yet, if the thing be possible, is also pious and righteous [*piam, & honestum*].[43]

Milton is rapt here by a desire to please his audience; his tone is light and humorous. Later, when he claims in all seriousness to be rapt by divine inspiration, he will face in deadly earnest the fine line between the pious and the sacrilegious.

Marvell's reading of Milton in "On Mr. Milton's *Paradise Lost*" is a pregnant case of intertextuality interesting in part for its exploration of this fine line. The commendatory poem has been printed just before the epic in most editions since the second in 1674, and thus it has had the privilege of introducing the poem that it follows. Marvell is equal to the position; his poem displaces onto itself and reenacts the drama of inspiration and presumption at the heart of *Paradise Lost*. In bowing to the sublime authority of the epic, Marvell's poem is a record of a reading that follows Milton's intention. At the same time, its self-questioning imitates the doubts and misgivings that threaten to overwhelm the poet in *Paradise Lost*. Moreover, in the tentativeness and repeated qualifications of his commendation, Marvell raises more directly the question of the degree of mastery asserted by the author over the text.

Confronted with the "great Argument," Marvell fears that Milton "would ruine (for I saw him strong) / The sacred Truths to Fable and old Song" (7–8). In the second verse paragraph, Marvell comes to terms with Milton's ambition:

> Yet as I read, soon growing less severe,
> I liked his Project, the success did fear;
> Through that wide Field how he his way should find
> O'er which lame Faith leads Understanding blind.
>
> (11–14)

Line twelve holds a fine ambiguity. Marvell's primary sense is that, having come to approve Milton's plan, he now feared that he would not be able to

---

43. I have used here the translation in Merritt Hughes's *John Milton: Complete Poems and Major Prose* (New York: Odyssey, 1957), p. 614. The Yale translation loses "rapt" for the less Miltonic "drive." The Latin appears in *Works* 12:212.

fulfill it. But a residue of the mistrust of the plan itself remains in the language ("the success did fear"). The language suggests that Marvell fears both that Milton would not successfully embody his project and that he would. As Marvell continues to reflect on the audacious enterprise in the following couplet, he takes an image from Milton's book, specifically from the Bellerophon allusion. Marvell's "wide Field" responds to Milton's "Aleian" one; Marvell fears that Milton will end up like the author's own Bellerophon, wandering blind on a trackless field.[44]

In the middle section of the poem, Marvell complicates his reflections on Milton's audacity by evoking his own audacity in questioning a poem that he has come to view as inspired ("Pardon me, mighty poet, nor despise / My causeless, yet not impious, surmise" [23–24]).[45] With this displacement, Milton rises above reproach: "And things divine thou treatst of in such state / As them preserves, and thee, inviolate" (33–34). If Milton had to suppress fears that he had violated divine mysteries, Marvell places Milton, now paled around by commas, among those divine things worthy of defense against violation. In a fine and unintended irony, Marvell seems to endorse also the chastity that Milton once relied on for his prophetic vision.

The final verse paragraph of Marvell's poem might seem anticlimactic. A poem that began with a consideration of sacred truths ends with a weighing of Milton's decision to abandon rhyme. Yet here, while speaking of an apparently trivial matter,[46] Marvell continues and brings to fruition his reflections on one of the creative paradoxes of *Paradise Lost*. He notes parenthetically, "I too transported by the Mode offend, / And while I meant to Praise thee must Commend" (51–52). Marvell began his poem with misgivings about Milton's; now, in an ironic tautology generated by witty self-deprecation of his own rhyming, he chides himself for commending when he meant to be praising. It is as if, in the presence of Milton, praise is not praise enough. And Marvell's offense is tied to his (ironic) transportation, to Marvell's being taken out of himself, to his being, as Milton would say, "rapt."

Thus Marvell, even when speaking of rhyme, is engaged in witty but intimate dialogue with the inspired poet of *Paradise Lost*. He reads, displaces to

---

44. In Kenneth Gross's "'Pardon Me, Mighty Poet': Versions of the Bard in Marvell's 'On Mr. Milton's Paradise Lost'" (*Milton Studies* 16 [1982]: 77–96), there is a hint of the connection between Marvell's and Milton's fields. Gross writes that the next line, "Lest he perplext the things he would explain," "deploys the opposed words 'perplext' and 'explain' so that their etymological meanings ('tangle together' and 'smooth out') reinforce the figurative representation of thought and faith in terms of travel and topography, as in Milton's 'on th'*Aleian* Field I fall / *Erroneous* there to wander and forlorne'" (p. 86; emphasis Gross's).

45. On this strategy, see Gross's subtle analysis (ibid., p. 87).

46. My terms are relative here; I do not question the manner in which form fits theme in Milton's poem, a fit in the case of prosody expressed in Milton's note on "The Verse."

himself, adjusts for genre, and rewrites Milton's subtle language of inspiration and transgression. And in the witty self-accusations of his own poem, Marvell hints at the anxious self-representation of Milton in *Paradise Lost*. This anxious self-representation takes the form of an oscillation between confidence and anxiety. One pole of this oscillation is the "authorized" self-representation. The other pole is constructed by the reader who perceives what Milton attempts, with only partial success, to suppress.

Chapter 9

"I as All Others"

Paradise Regained and *Samson Agonistes*

Paradise Regained and *Samson Agonistes,* published together in 1671,[1] offer competing and complementary perspectives on many of Milton's central questions: What is the proper avenue for political action? What is an appropriate model for godly action? How does one know when the time is ripe? How, immersed in daily life and in history, does one recognize God's will? In neither of the works does Milton comment directly on himself, as he does in many of the prose works and, in the invocations, *Paradise Lost*. As befits its brevity and austerity, *Paradise Regained* has only one, short invocation. *Samson Agonistes,* a drama, lacks even this, as Milton speaks not in his own voice but through his characters (although he takes advantage of the opportunity of his prefatory reflections on tragedy).[2] Despite the constraints of its dramatic form, *Samson Agonistes* has long been read as pervasively autobiographical. Samson resembles the historical Milton in several ways. Both are chosen by God for important work; both experience defeat and the disappointment of their hope to lead their compatriots to freedom; at the time of the poem's publication and probable composition, Milton like Samson is blind and under the thumb of triumphal enemies. Samson rails against the faithless Israelites in terms that echo Milton's bitter disappointment at the backsliding of the English into monarchy.

---

1. I believe, on the basis of the manifold parallels between Milton's position and Samson's, of versification, and of publication history, that *Samson Agonistes* is a late work. For the arguments, see Barbara Lewalski, *The Life of John Milton* (Oxford: Blackwell, 2000), 691–92, note 11.

2. *Samson Agonistes* lacks even the kind of author-intermediary present in *A Mask* in the character of the Attendant Spirit.

The parallels between the blind poet and the blind hero of *Samson Agonistes* are familiar and compelling. The parallels between the hero of *Paradise Regained* and the poet are, if less obvious, extensive and significant. Each is "one man" set apart from the many, and each has labored in obscurity during an extended adolescence before appearing on the public stage. The Son's belated public ministry authorizes in retrospect the belatedness that worried the young Milton. The Son's obedience is a defining virtue on the one hand open to Milton's emulation and on the other uncongenial to him. Milton can be obedient, but he is predisposed to be rebellious. But obedience and rebelliousness meet in the Son and in Milton, as adherence to the divine requires repudiation of human standards. Similarities between Milton's description of his own youth in *An Apology* and the autobiographical reflections he places in the Son's mouth suggest that the brief epic participates in Milton's lifelong project of self-representation. Milton represented himself, to us and to himself, through the Son, as he does through Samson. In his paired final poems, Milton replays his career and recapitulates the alternative self-representations that have been in dialectical suspension since the divorce tracts.

In both poems, I will argue, familiar self-regarding themes emerge, particularly the theme of belatedness and obscurity versus worldly accomplishment and fame. *Paradise Regained* centers on identity: the Son works toward an understanding of the relation of prophecy to his own life, Satan tries to ascertain in what sense the hero is the Son of God, and Milton works out the relation between the Son of God and himself. I have argued that Milton's extraordinary claims for his own virtue in his earliest self-representations, and at times in his later ones, imply his exemption from the frailty attendant on the fall. Identification with the Son in the brief epic is the culmination or apotheosis of this strain of self-representation. The situation of *Samson Agonistes* is, if anything, more complex. Here the inconclusiveness of the debate between revisionists and regenerationists is instructive.[3] Milton does identify with Samson, as the regenerationists contend. But the manifest flaws in Samson, taken by

---

3. Michael Krouse argues what has been the majority view that Milton's Samson is a proto-Christian hero who, after a lapse, regains his privileged status as God's champion (*Milton's Samson and the Christian Tradition* [Princeton: Princeton University Press, 1949]). Irene Samuel takes the so-called revisionist position that Samson is a flawed figure whose tragic end reflects his shortcomings and errors ("*Samson Agonistes* as Tragedy," in *Calm of Mind: Tercentenary Essays on "Paradise Regained" and "Samson Agonistes" in Honor of John S. Diekhoff*, ed. Joseph Wittreich [Cleveland: Case Western Reserve University Press, 1971], 235–57). Wittreich advances the revisionist position in *Interpreting Samson Agonistes* (Princeton: Princeton University Press, 1987). His more recent *Shifting Contexts: Reinterpreting Samson Agonistes* (Pittsburgh: Duquesne University Press, 2002) emphasizes the variety of Samsons available for appropriation in the Bible and in seventeenth-century interpretation; Wittreich's current espousal of a "mediating" perspective, which does not insist on either a simply regenerate or a simply culpable Samson (*Shifting Contexts*, p. 200), complements my own reading of the poem.

revisionists as undermining the heroic, autobiographical reading of Samson, can point instead to the anxiety and instability in Milton's own self-conception and self-representation. The yoked errors for which Samson berates himself, bad marriage choice and shameful garrulousness in revealing God's secrets, replay both the pivotal error that destabilized Milton's early heroic self-representation and the danger that haunts *Paradise Lost*. If in *Samson Agonistes* the promise of a surprising but still triumphant end is kept alive, the route leads through the kind of frailty from which the young Milton had tried to distance himself, but which he has come to own. The perfectionist claims of *Paradise Regained,* on the other hand, can reflect more directly the claims in Milton's early self-representations because they are displaced onto the Son of God. Milton's self-image informs his image of the Son, which suggests that his heroic self-construction has in part survived.[4]

Paradise Regained: "one man's firm obedience"

As in *Paradise Lost,* the invocation to *Paradise Regained* shows Milton at his most private and self-representational precisely when he is most closely following public conventions. The poem's opening lines situate Milton in a dense grid of personal, salvation, and epic histories:

> I who erewhile the happy garden sung,
> By one man's disobedience lost, now sing
> Recovered Paradise to all mankind,
> By one man's firm obedience fully tried
> Through all temptation, and the Tempter foiled
> In all his wiles, defeated and repulsed,
> And Eden raised in the waste wilderness.
> (1.1–7)

Paradise, lost by one man's disobedience, is recovered by one man's obedience. Milton sang of the loss and is now singing of the recovery. Others have written epics; Milton is now writing an epic. The skeleton of the passage reveals a characteristic preoccupation with the one versus the many: I . . . sung—one man's disobedience—I now sing—recovered Paradise to all mankind—one man's firm obedience. I sung and I sing. One man's disobedience and one man's obedience. The third line replays the significant ambiguity

---

4. I have found parts of my reading of *Paradise Regained* anticipated in Thomas N. Corns's "'With Unaltered Brow': Milton and the Son of God," *Milton Studies* 42 (2003): 106–21. Corns writes that in the Son "Milton offers a divine figure made in his own image, a daring, almost impudent, *imitatio Miltoni*" (108).

of the end of the first invocation in *Paradise Lost:* "And justify the ways of God *to men.*" Is Milton justifying God's ways to men, or justifying to men God's ways? Is Milton singing how all mankind is redeemed, or singing to all mankind how they are redeemed? How pivotal is his role? And is it his obedience even as it is the obedience of the "one greater man" of *Paradise Lost* 1.4? Milton famously skirts the passion,[5] the locus of Christian redemption, in his poetry, and in so doing collapses the space between what the Son does to regain paradise and what Milton can do. Enfolded in the term "passion" for Christ's last act is an ambiguity between the active and the passive, which resonates with the position of the author. Does he passively transcribe events, or is the writing itself a form of heroic action?

The opening of *Paradise Regained,* as has often been noted, echoes the opening of *The Faerie Queene,* which echoes in turn lines long thought to be Virgil's first in the *Aeneid.* But, as he had with Ariosto in the opening invocation of *Paradise Lost,* Milton inflects his borrowing in new directions. According to the lines considered authentic through the Renaissance, Virgil begins, "I am he who once piped my song on a slender reed, then, leaving the woods, compelled the neighbouring fields to serve the greedy farmer, . . . but now I sing of Mars' bristling."[6] The lines outline the poet's ascent of the genre ladder, from pastoral through georgic to epic. In the opening lines of *The Faerie Queene,* Spenser echoes the self-effacement implicit in his model:

> Lo I the man, whose Muse whilome did maske,
> As time her taught in lowly Shepheards weeds,
> Am now enforst a far vnfitter taske,
> For trumpets sterne to chaunge mine Oaten reeds.[7]

Spenser repeats the move from the humble pastoral to martial epic, and gestures toward his unfitness to pursue the high argument. Milton adopts Spenser's sentence structure, but revises drastically the relation to the genre ladder. If the song is higher, it is because it will center on the action of the divine Son of God. There is no intimation that Milton must strain to reach the higher argument, nor that he is unequal to the task. He has, after all, already written an epic poem. And, as in the earlier epic, the line between what the hero does and what the speaker does is blurred.

---

5. For the first fruits of his work on Milton and the passion, see John Rogers, "Milton's Circumcision," in *Milton and the Grounds of Contention,* ed. Mark R. Kelley, Michael Lieb, and John T. Shawcross (Pittsburgh: Duquesne University Press, 2003), pp. 188–213.

6. I quote John Leonard's translation in his *Milton: The Complete Poems* (Harmondsworth: Penguin, 1998), p. 875.

7. Spenser, *The Faerie Queene,* ed. Thomas P. Roche, Jr. (Harmondsworth: Penguin, 1978), I.Proem.i.1–4.

When, in the second half of the invocation, Milton asks the Spirit to "inspire / As thou art wont, my prompted song else mute" (1.11–12), there is only a hint of the anxiety that marked the later invocations in *Paradise Lost*. Without inspiration, Milton will be mute. But inspiring Milton has become a habit for the Spirit. It is time now

> to tell of deeds
> Above heroic, though in secret done,
> And unrecorded left through many an age,
> Worthy t' have not remained so long unsung.
> (1.14–17)

The deeds will be "Above heroic" in the ironic sense that they are deeds of obedience, patience, and heroic martyrdom, virtues as available to Milton as to martial hero or demigod. The irony is underwritten by the Christian paradox of the strength and heroism of weakness, but it is animated by something potentially at odds with the stance of Christian humility, Milton's special identification with the Son. The end of the passage exhibits the syntactic tortuousness that often marks Milton's self-representing moments. The sense offers itself up only after a strenuous process of sorting out the negatives. The emphasis on the length of time in which the deeds have not been recorded highlights Milton's originality in choosing his theme and contextualizing what has long been a preoccupation for Milton, the problem of belatedness and obscurity.

Ashraf Rushdy has shown that self-representation is a political act in Milton's poems of 1671. Rushdy's Milton is caught "between a faint desire for a community of faith and an unrelenting inability to accept the institutions forming such a community." At moments of crisis, Rushdy argues, Milton emphasizes "the significance of the individual . . . by denouncing the idea of the majority" and "inscribe[s] himself into [his] work as the political model of individual resolve."[8] Self-representation, in this view, is less personal indulgence than engaged action. Milton writes himself into his works because it is the responsibility of the individual actor to effect change. In *Paradise Regained* this takes the form of the convergence of Milton and the Son as central actors.

The Son, as Rushdy demonstrates, parallels Milton in many ways, not merely the generic Christian ones of finding strength in weakness and choosing to submit to the divine will.[9] The Son also reflects and embodies Milton's idiosyncratic characteristics. Each offers a retrospective view of childhood and

---

8. Rushdy, *The Empty Garden: The Subject of Late Milton* (Pittsburgh: Pittsburgh University Press, 1992), p. 381.
9. Ibid., pp. 385–86.

adolescence that, as one would expect from the Son though not from a Puritan author, does not center on temptation, failure, and eventual regeneration. Each articulates the need to lead by persuasive speech rather than by the sword. More significantly, the Son by his belated public ministry authorizes the belatedness that caused the younger Milton considerable anxiety. And finally the Son offers a model of the kind of perfectibility that Milton smuggled into his own self-representation.

In the Son's autobiographical monologue of 1.196–293, Milton adapts from the Gospel of Luke a self-representational model that fills the gap left by the absence of conventional Pauline and Augustinian models in his own self-representations. Choosing, and adapting, the life of Jesus as a model is a canny and audacious (but predictable) move. On the one hand, it is an older story, and its temporal priority is something that Milton would like. If others choose the old story of Augustine, Milton chooses the older one of Jesus, just as he chooses an older and more legitimate form of versification over the apparently time-honored but in fact younger convention of rhyme in heroic poems. Milton's choice also has the advantage and the danger that come with identification with the divine. If it is one's Christian duty to imitate the life of Christ, then parallels between Christ's life and one's own witness one's godliness. If it is presumptuous and blasphemous to imply identity with Christ, then parallels can betray dangerous pride and overreaching. And Milton goes even further. In the *imitatio Christi* tradition, one attempts to pattern one's life after Christ's; Milton has the Son of God describe his own life in ways that imitate Milton's life.

The Son's monologue does not unfold in linear fashion. Milton starts in mid-childhood, with the first event recorded in Luke that the Son might plausibly be thought to remember, continues with a flashback sequence of birth and infancy in the form of a remembered speech of Mary's, moves to the baptism by John and, bringing us to the story's present, concludes with the Spirit-led journey into the wilderness. Milton gains more than verisimilitude by this rearrangement. It places at the beginning and the end, the most prominent positions of the narration, two scenes particularly important for him.

The Son's first memory is of his serious study and his precocious exchange with the doctors at the Temple in Jerusalem. According to the source passage in Luke 2,

> [40] And the child grew, and waxed strong in spirit, filled with wisdom: and the grace of God was upon him. [41] Now his parents went to Jerusalem every year at the feast of the passover. [42] And when he was twelve years old, they went up to Jerusalem after the custom of the feast. [43] And when they had fulfilled the days, as they returned, the child Jesus tarried behind

in Jerusalem; and Joseph and his mother knew not of it. ⁴⁴ But they, supposing him to have been in the company, went a day's journey; and they sought him among their kinsfolk and acquaintance. ⁴⁵ And when they found him not, they turned back again to Jerusalem, seeking him. ⁴⁶ And it came to pass, that after three days they found him in the temple, sitting in the midst of the doctors, both hearing them, and asking them questions. ⁴⁷ And all that heard him were astonished at his understanding and answers. ⁴⁸ And when they saw him, they were amazed: and his mother said unto him, Son, why hast thou thus dealt with us? behold, thy father and I have sought thee sorrowing. ⁴⁹ And he said unto them, How is it that ye sought me? wist ye not that I must be about my Father's business? ⁵⁰ And they understood not the saying which he spake unto them. ⁵¹ And he went down with them, and came to Nazareth, and was subject unto them: but his mother kept all these sayings in her heart. ⁵² And Jesus increased in wisdom and stature, and in favour with God and man.

The Son's memory diverges from Luke's account in significant ways:

> When I was yet a child, no childish play
> To me was pleasing, all my mind was set
> Serious to learn and know, and thence to do
> What might be public good; myself I thought
> Born to that end, born to promote all truth,
> All righteous things: therefore above my years,
> The law of God I read, and found it sweet,
> Made it my whole delight, and in it grew
> To such perfection, that ere yet my age
> Had measured twice six years, at our great feast
> I went into the Temple, there to hear
> The teachers of our Law, and to propose
> What might improve my knowledge or their own;
> And was admired by all.
>   (1.201–14)

The selectivity of the Son's memory is consistent with its having been filtered through Milton's representation of himself. The studious youth recalls no one so much as the young Milton. Luke's Jesus grows in wisdom, but we don't know how. If anything, he seems to be impregnated with the "grace of God"; as Mary conceived him after being covered by the dove, so Jesus waxed strong and wise after the "grace of God was upon him." Milton's Son labors much as Milton did. Recall Milton's *Defensio Secunda:* "My father destined me in early childhood for the study of literature, for which I had so keen an appetite that from my twelfth year scarcely ever did I leave my studies for my bed before the hour of midnight" (*YP* 4.1:612). The choice of the twelfth year here may owe as much to Luke 2 as to any precise or unmediated recollection on Milton's part. Like Luke's Jesus, Milton's Son stands out at twelve; unlike Luke's Jesus but like Milton himself, Milton's Son stands out by virtue of his diligence.

If Milton adds the idea of self-denying studiousness to the Lukan account, he omits the conflict with and eventual submission to parents. The agitation of Mary and Joseph ("Son, why hast thou thus dealt with us? behold, thy father and I have sought thee sorrowing") leaves no trace in the poem, nor does Jesus' submission to his uncomprehending parents ("And he went down with them, and came to Nazareth, and was subject unto them"). The elision of the family drama, like the addition of studiousness, derives from Milton's reading of Luke through the prism of his self-construction. Milton's Son shares Milton's characteristic combination of blamelessness and hesitation to put himself under any authority except God. Even when he comes closest to the idea of obedience to parents in his autobiographical writings, Milton stops well short of endorsing or enacting submission, as in the passage noted above from the *Defensio Secunda:* "My father destined me in early childhood for the study of literature" (*YP* 4.1:612). The father does nothing so mundane as to command; instead Milton writes of a grand destiny communicated abstractly. Earlier, in "Ad Patrem," Milton builds a poem around the conceit that his father has opposed his chosen vocation; the young Milton distracts his father with flattery and the intimation that they are kindred spirits cultivating the complementary arts of music and poetry.

Again like Milton himself, the Son makes great plans, or more precisely he recalls himself making great plans. He will "promote all truth," like the young Milton recalled in the *Apology,* and he will perform "What might be public good," like the younger Milton recalled in *The Reason of Church-Government.* Milton's Son promotes truth and public good in the recalled dialogue with the doctors in a manner that also goes beyond anything found explicitly in Luke. Jesus' asking and answering questions in the gospel account may amount to no more than the interaction of a bright student with his teachers. Milton's Son aims to improve the doctors' knowledge and not merely to improve or prove his own.

The internal monologue traces a trajectory of knowledge. The earnest child studies and then amazes and teaches his putative teachers. The adolescent imagines glorious martial victories before demonstrating self-knowledge in the realization that it is "more humane, more Heavenly first / By winning words to conquer willing hearts, / And make persuasion do the work of fear" (1.221–23). This realization itself triggers the proud mother's intimation of his divine parentage, a communication that dovetails with biblical prophecy, and that prompts the Son to await the "time prefixed" (1.269). With the testimony of John and of the divine voice at the Jordan River, the time, along the Son's self-knowledge, is "Now full" (1.287); it is time, in the words of the narrator before the monologue, to "Publish his Godlike office now mature" (1.188). The Son is standing on the verge of his public career, a position to which Milton, long concerned about belatedness, repeatedly assigned himself. But precisely at this moment of mature office, there is another deferral:

> I no more should live obscure,
> But openly begin, as best becomes
> The authority which I derived from Heaven.
> And now by some strong motion I am led
> Into this wilderness, to what intent
> I learn not yet, perhaps I need not know;
> For what concerns my knowledge God reveals.
> (1.287–93)

The passage builds powerfully, as self-knowledge constitutes the moment as the fullness of time, and the convergence of knowledge and time signals the beginning of public ministry, the first sign of which is a "strong motion" to *retreat to the wilderness,* of all things, and to acknowledge that knowledge is incomplete. Stanley Fish argues that this retreat into inaction, into dependence on God, is not only the action of a Miltonic hero, but is the *only* action of a Miltonic hero.[10] But this does not erase the defining tension in Milton between the advancing of knowledge to greater completion and the final acknowledgment that knowledge is always incomplete. If truth on this earth is always in her progress, then the prophetic voice will always be crossing the frontiers of truth without ever gaining possession of it. The striving is necessary, as is the relinquishment, and in the Son's monologue we see both. The dialectic within the Son between readiness and the need for further preparation recalls a familiar move of the young Milton, who claims that he is ready to do great things, worries about belatedness, and trades on the capital of future achievements.

Milton's Son masters not only sacred but also secular classical writings. The Son's notorious attack on classical learning participates in the learned author's representation of himself, a fact witnessed by the discomfort of critics, who are dismayed not so much that the *Son* dismisses classical literature but that *Milton* apparently does. Milton's Son makes clear that he

---

10. Fish, *How Milton Works* (Cambridge, MA: Harvard University Press, 2001), pp. 307–25.

possesses that learning, but, as he tells Satan, he is no more subservient to that learning than he is to other human goods:

> Think not but that I know these things, or think
> I know them not; not therefore am I short
> Of knowing what I ought: he who receives
> Light from above, from the fountain of light,
> No other doctrine needs, though granted true.
> (4.286–90)

The Son receives light from above, as does the blind Milton. The best clue to the identification here of Milton with the Son lies in the signature tortured syntax of the first line and a half. What do they mean? The general sense is clear enough: do not make the mistake of thinking me ignorant of classical learning. But the modern editors do not even attempt to sort out the clotted syntax. 'Do not think anything except that I know these things,' the first clause indicates. The second clause, which means 'Do not think I don't know them,' should begin, to make clear sense, with "nor," not "or." The multiple negatives, when sorted out, do not add up to Milton's, or the Son's, positive statement. This syntactic knot records a conflict within Milton between deep learnedness and a sense of the superfluousness of learning. The struggle between Milton's love of classical literature and the need to subordinate that literature to Christian truth received eloquent expression, as we saw in Chapter 3, in the ambivalence of the poignantly beautiful rout of the pagan gods in the "Nativity Ode." Like the Son in *Paradise Regained,* Milton wants both to stand out for adherence to God's wisdom only and to leave no doubt of his mastery of classical learning and wisdom.

The permeability of the boundary line between Milton's Son and Milton himself is itself a constituent element of Milton's imagination rather than an isolated and self-aggrandizing gesture. In the Son's autobiographical monologue the boundaries between the Son and Mary and the Son and John the Baptist also blur. The Son recalls his mother's words to him at a crucial time between his visits to Jerusalem and the Jordan. For thirty lines the Son, to whom Milton has ceded his voice, cedes his own voice in turn to Mary (1.229–58). By this device Milton inserts into the Son's autobiographical survey a narrative of events the Son would have been too young to remember. I am interested in the frame of the passage:

> These growing thoughts my mother soon perceiving
> By words at times cast forth inly rejoiced,
> And said to me apart, High are thy thoughts
> O Son, but nourish them and let them soar. . . .
> . . . .

> Just Simeon and prophetic Anna, warned
> By vision, found thee in the Temple, and spake
> Before the altar and the vested priest,
> Like things of thee to all that present stood.
> This having heard, straight I again revolved
> The law and prophets, searching what was writ
> Concerning the Messiah, to our scribes
> Known partly, and soon found of whom they spake
> I am.
>
> (1.227–63)

Mary ends her narration with the recognition of the infant Messiah by Simeon and Anna, who speak of the Son's ancestry. Their speech is heard, but by whom? Line 259, "This having heard, straight I again revolved," seems at first to be spoken by Mary, who has just reported speech. A moment later, however, it becomes clear that the Son resumes speaking in his own person at this line. But the ambiguity appears to be intentional; the shape shifting is highlighted and repeated, again implicitly, in the second phrase, "straight I again revolved." From this vantage point another ambiguity, now a punning one, appears at the other end of the frame: "said to me apart" (*took me aside to say*) or "said to me a part" (*spoke as a part of me*)? Certainly the first meaning is primary. The second meaning hovers in the background, however, as part of a pattern of identity-mixing wordplay.

Milton executes a similar move by different means when the Son recalls his meeting with John the Baptist, who "Straight knew me, and with loudest voice proclaimed / Me him (for it was shown him so from Heaven) / Me him whose harbinger he was" (1.275–77). Milton often employs enjambment and repetition when highlighting suspense concerning, and the resolution of, identity. The effect here is heightened by the suspension introduced by the parenthetical clause. *He proclaimed me him.* The line between John and the Son flickers for the space of a line, to be reestablished when "him" emerges belatedly as the referent of the clause "whose harbinger he was." Several lines later, the Son recalls the Father's voice, which "pronounced me his, / Me his beloved Son, in whom alone / He was well pleased" (1.284–86). The move repeats the earlier one with a crucial difference, with enjambment and repetition suspending identification. Now the Son is *sui generis*, marked off from rather than melting into other servants of God. The "alone" is also ambiguous, referring primarily to the Son's unique status, but also to the Father's: I, alone or isolated, am well pleased.

The language highlights the dual nature of the Son. On the one hand, as the first of creation he is the Son of God in a special way; Milton's Arianism does not level the distinction between the Son of God and sons of God. At the same time, as a man, the Son enters a community in which identities can seem interchangeable, with the lines between himself and his mother or his harbinger tantalizingly permeable. The Son recalls, "*I as all others* to his baptism came, / Which I believed was from above" (1.273–74; my emphasis). The ambiguity and permeability are concentrated in the small word "as." The Son comes as others do, and the Son comes *as* the others. At the many moments when the representation (and indeed the self-representation) of the Son converge with Milton's representation of himself, Milton gestures toward a community, the founding dynamic of which he encodes in the syntactic ambiguity of his poem. But the gesture is not modest, for the named community he joins includes Mary and the Baptist. Like them, he falls into a prophetic line; unlike even them, the details of his autobiography converge closely with the Son's.

In the temptation in the desert that forms the body of *Paradise Regained*, Satan presses just those questions of identity that preoccupy the Son and that Milton explores in rich semantic and syntactic ambiguity (observing that "sons of God both angels are and men," Satan ascribes his temptations to a wish to "try whether in higher sort / Than these thou bear'st that title" [4.197–99]). Milton both follows and alters the Lukan account. The long middle of the brief epic expands Luke's terse account (2:5–8) of the second temptation:

> [5] And the devil, taking him up into an high mountain, shewed unto him all the kingdoms of the world in a moment of time. [6] And the devil said unto him, All this power will I give thee, and the glory of them: for that is delivered unto me; and to whomsoever I will I give it. [7] If thou therefore wilt worship me, all shall be thine. [8] And Jesus answered and said unto him, Get thee behind me, Satan: for it is written, Thou shalt worship the Lord thy God, and him only shalt thou serve.

Into *his* version Milton injects his own visceral concern with belatedness, exorcizing that recurring demon by having Satan champion the value of early and public action. Satan praises the Son's words and his martial potential, but he asks a question that Milton at times had anxiously asked himself:

> These godlike virtues wherefore dost thou hide?
> Affecting private life, or more obscure
> In savage wilderness, wherefore deprive
> All earth her wonder at thy acts, thyself
> The fame and glory, glory the reward
> That sole excites to high attempts the flame
> Of most erected spirits, most tempered pure

> Ethereal, who all pleasures else despise,
> All treasures and all gain esteem as dross,
> And dignities and powers all but the highest?
> Thy years are ripe, and over-ripe.
>
> (3.21–31)

The echoes here reach back through the autobiographical digressions of *An Apology for Smectymnuus* and *The Reason of Church-Government,* through the meditation on fame as "the spur that the clear spirit doth raise / (That last infirmity of noble mind)" of "Lycidas," through the breathless confession in a 1637 letter to Diodati that he seeks, "so help me God, an immortality of fame," all the way to the sonnet on his twenty-third year. High ambitions emerge early, but Milton long remains obscure. As Milton apparently cannot help comparing himself to other, more "timely happy" spirits, Satan presses on the Son a comparison with Alexander the Great, who by the Son's age had already conquered the world. But Satan, while claiming that the desire for fame does not wane with age ("Yet years, and to ripe years judgment mature, / Quench not the thirst of glory, but augment"), holds out a consolation that Milton long clung to: "but thou yet art not too late" (3.37–38,42). The Son responds with a defense of obscurity and patience. Public praise, by definition from the promiscuous crowd, is worthless. True fame is recorded in heaven, and true glory is won by "deeds of peace, by wisdom eminent, / By patience, temperance" (3.91–92). Patience is a virtue that, like temperance, will bring true glory, but it is also the defining virtue of one who does not seek glory for its own sake. Satan is impatient, rushing from place to place, always busy, even insisting, when asked why he pushes toward what must be his own destruction, that he is impatient to be at the worst, for that is his "port." When Satan insists that the Son's patience is irrational, for if a thing obtained is a good, the sooner the better, the Son replies, "All things are best fulfilled in their due time" (3.182). In the brief epic a drama plays out that has been playing itself out at least since the 1633 "Letter to a Friend," where Milton like the Son of *Paradise Regained* turns a defense of obscurity and belatedness into a defiant assertion of virtue and godliness: "this very consideration of that great com̃andment [not to hide the talent] does not presse forward as soone as may be to underg[o] but keeps off wth a sacred reverence & religious advisement how best . . . to undergoe [,] not taking thought of beeing late so it give advantage to be more fit, for those that were latest lost nothing when the maister of the vinyard came to give each one his hire" (*YP* 1:320). Nearly forty years later, Milton is still defending obscurity, and the Son in *Paradise Regained* redeems the convoluted self-exculpatory logic of Milton's youthful letter.

Between the completion of the poem's action and the brief, four line coda, an angelic chorus comments on the epic drama and repeats the temporal paradoxes at the heart of Milton's self-representations as accomplished hero and belated servant. From the angels' perspective the Son's action is both in the recent past ("*now* thou hast avenged / Supplanted Adam, and by vanquishing / Temptation, hast regained lost Paradise" [4.606–8; my emphasis]) and in the future ("*Now* enter, and begin to save mankind" [4.635; my emphasis]). Like Milton, who both stands and waits and who has proved his heroic stature on a pan-European stage, the Son has fulfilled his potential and is poised to exhibit it. The angels insist both that the tempter "never more henceforth will dare set foot / In Paradise to tempt," and that a *future* "time shall be / Of tempter and temptation without fear" (4.610–11,616–17). Milton is of course playing with the ancient Christian theme of the intersection of the timeless with time; if Christ's passion is both a unique event in history and a sacrifice played out at all times since, so is the temptation in the desert. But the repetition is inflected through the imperatives of Milton's self-representation.

Paradise Regained ends with a modest vision of its hero, who has accomplished a greater victory than any other man, as "he unobserved / Home to his mother's house private returned" (4.638–39). Satan is the upstart mushroom, and the Son is like the Milton of the *Defence of Himself,* who responds to Alexander More, "You err, More, and know not me. To me it was always preferable to grow slowly, and as if by the silent lapse of time" (*YP* 4.2:819).

Samson Agonistes: "Proudly secure"

Samson Agonistes complements *Paradise Regained* not by repeating or echoing its themes and dynamics, but by reversing them. The closet drama reflects the other side of Milton's self-representation. *Paradise Regained* echoes the benign tensions of Milton's perfectionist self-conception and self-representation. The pressing concern is whether his unquestioned virtue has yet to manifest itself in decisive action, or whether it is expressed in expectant readiness. This tension is expressed in the temporal dialectic that I have just outlined, between the Son's saving action as already complete or as always in prospect. *Samson Agonistes* explores a darker side of Milton's self-conception and self-representation. A man chosen by God, with the potential to liberate a people also chosen by God, falters. As such, Samson illustrates a principal articulated in *De Doctrina Christiana* and examined in Chapter 7: the freedom of even those specially chosen by God to fall. Milton like his Samson has claimed special election by God. By exploring the ways that Samson has faltered, Milton comes closest to acknowledging the possibility that he has himself faltered.

Samson Agonistes is Milton's most indeterminate poem, the most resistant to critical consensus. As in the brief epic, much of the poem's drama lies in characters' attempts to read the action in which they are embedded. In the companion poem, Satan tries to understand the text of Luke 3:22, with the pronouncement of the Holy Spirit at the Jordan ("Thou art my beloved Son; in thee I am well pleased") by reading the character of the Son. Early in Book 2, the disciples Andrew and Simon Peter, along with Mary, also compare unfolding events with the promise of Scripture. The trajectory from Satan through the disciples through Mary is one of decreasing impatience, culminating in the patient faithfulness of the Son, who, though as intent as the others on understanding the meaning of events, waits for God's time to know:

> And now by some strong motion I am led
> Into this wilderness, to what intent
> I learn not yet, perhaps I need not know;
> For what concerns my knowledge God reveals.
> (*PR* 1.290–93)

Samson Agonistes lacks this limit character; all seem dissatisfied with their knowledge. Manoa and the chorus share the querulousness of disappointed complacency. Why has their hero fallen? Is the fault his or Israel's or God's? Samson oscillates between answers. If the question for the characters is "what does this mean," for us it is "what has this all meant," and not merely because the action is in the historical past. As the poem ends with the Israelites' initial response to the catastrophe, we sense that their interpretation of the event is premature. We are left to sort out elements too quickly labeled and pigeonholed by Manoa and the chorus.

Samson and Manoa and the chorus had been, in words Samson uses to describe himself, "Proudly secure" (55). The premature security of the chorus and Manoa (and Samson himself) inversely mirrors the patience of the Son in the brief epic. It assumes the finality of a present happy state. Just as truth is always in her progress, so a life in a world governed by free will is always in process. In what sense is the Son the Son of God? His refusal to answer Satan's questions or fall into his traps is not merely a case of a cat playing with a mouse. The Son becomes the Son by his choices, his identity achieved by his actions in the epic. He is by merit more than birthright son of God. Milton, likewise, is in process. The pitfall of premature and proud security that threatens in the autobiographical digressions of the anti-prelatical tracts and that Milton obscurely articulates in the self-questioning of the *Defences* is written into *Samson Agonistes*. The ambiguity of this famously indeterminate text signals the provisionality of any uncompleted life.[11]

One can locate the traces of Milton's personal experience in several of the exchanges in *Samson Agonistes*. The exchange with Manoa may reflect both the parental concern that Milton's father lavished on him as well as the failure of the father to understand fully the son's vocation. The confrontation with Harapha may echo Milton's with Salmasius. Milton had taken on a giant of European letters and scholarship in his 1651 *Defensio;* one result of his struggle, at least in his own mind, was his lost eyesight. If this experience finds its way into *Samson Agonistes,* it is in transmuted form, as Samson is already blind when he challenges the giant. In exploring Milton's self-representation in the drama, I will concentrate on Samson's articulation of his blindness and on his encounter with Dalila, an encounter that mirrors Milton's deepest concerns and anxieties.

As *Samson Agonistes* opens, the blind and discredited Samson labors in the mill, having apparently forfeited his ordained role as liberator of his people. The blindness is a punishment that he alternately accepts as his due and curses as an intolerable indignity. Milton writes about the blindness with a visceral poetic power informed by intimate and bitter experience:

> I dark in light exposed
> To daily fraud, contempt, abuse and wrong,
> Within doors, or without, still as a fool,
> In power of others, never in my own;
> Scarce half I seem to live, dead more than half.
> O dark, dark, dark, amid the blaze of noon,
> Irrecoverably dark, total eclipse
> Without all hope of day!
> O first-created beam, and thou great word,
> "Let there be light, and light was over all,"
> Why am I thus bereaved thy prime decree?
> The sun to me is dark
> And silent as the moon,
> When she deserts the night
> Hid in her vacant interlunar cave.
>
> (*SA* 75–89)

In his opening speech Samson bewails his blindness, accepts the justice of this and his other afflictions, bewails his blindness anew, and so repeats the

---

11. Ann Baynes Coiro, in an illuminating essay, calls the poem a "moving and agonized . . . meditation on Milton's poetic career" ("Fable and Old Song: *Samson Agonistes* and the Idea of a Poetic Career," *Milton Studies* 38 [1998]: 123–52; the quotation is from p. 124).

cycle. This pattern recalls the invocation of Book 7, where Milton laments his blindness, finds consolation in inner sight, laments his blindness anew, and again finds consolation. The crucial difference, of course, is that Samson blames himself, something Milton never allows himself to do. *Samson Agonistes* may itself serve that function for Milton.

If blindness is the punishment, what is the sin or transgression? Here the filiations of error in biography, epic, and tragedy are complex and intertwined. The arrestingly crude and dim-witted protagonist of *Samson Agonistes* reflects in surprisingly intimate ways the experience of the refined and sharp-witted author. For each, blindness and political failure trigger introspection and an examination of conscience. For each, again, the punishments are traced with different degrees of obscurity to marital error and to a disobedience embodied in a failure of discretion.

I argued in chapter 5 that the first trace of a serious moral lapse—indeed of any moral lapse at all—in Milton's self-representation appears in the divorce tracts. Milton, unhappily married, does not merely relax the rigorous standard of spotlessness that had hitherto characterized his self-representation and, as far as we can tell, his self-understanding, but appeals to a standard fitted to human weakness. As persuasive as his argument might be on theological and anthropological grounds, it wreaks havoc with prior claims of preternatural virtue. Milton must rely on his rhetorical agility to reassert the special godliness of the divorcer.

A second, potential failing that must be assimilated to Milton's self-construction is the possibly transgressive presumptuousness of his epic narration of things "invisible to mortal sight." The invocations in *Paradise Lost*, as we have seen, record between their lines the anxiety arising from an arguably blasphemous project. A fine line separates prophetic speaker from the self-deluded and self-aggrandizing meddler in divine mystery.

The failings of marital irregularity and presumption that separately and serially threaten Milton's unspotted self-understanding are combined in the conspicuously flawed Samson. Samson, like his creator, marries unwisely. As Manoa bathetically and tactlessly observes, "I cannot praise thy marriage choices, son, / Rather approved them not" (420–21). Samson's first wife, the woman of Timna, betrayed him to her compatriots. The betrayal, significantly, takes the form of the divulging of the answer to a riddle. In a turn of events that would be inexplicable were it not for what Samson himself describes as "impotence of mind, in body strong" (52), Samson makes the same error with his second wife, but now he divulges not a self-generated riddle but a divine secret.

Samson describes his sin as "shameful garrulity":

>   let me here,
> As I deserve, pay on my punishment;

> And expiate, if possible, my crime,
> Shameful garrulity. To have revealed
> Secrets of men, the secrets of a friend,
> How heinous had the fact been, how deserving
> Contempt, and scorn of all, to be excluded
> All friendship, and avoided as a blab,
> The mark of fool set on his front?
> But I God's counsel have not kept, his holy secret
> Presumptuously have published, impiously,
> Weakly at least, and shamefully: a sin
> That Gentiles in their parables condemn
> To their abyss and horrid pains confined.
> (488–501)

Samson explicitly condemns himself for a crime whose shadow hangs over *Paradise Lost*. Even if Milton is inspired by God, is he free to publish what has been disclosed to him? May I express thee unblamed? Milton's ambiguous question acknowledges the danger of divulging divine secrets. As we have seen, Milton comments sternly in *De Doctrina* on those who pry into divine mystery: "Anyone who asks what God did before the creation of the world is a fool; and anyone who answers him is not much wiser" (*YP* 6:299). He is even more pointed in *Tetrachordon:* "in the ecclesiastical stories one demanding how God imploy'd himself before the world was made, had answer; that he was making hel for curious questioners" (*YP* 2:663). In *Paradise Lost* Milton goes well beyond the fool's question, not merely asking what God did before creation but giving an elaborate answer. Milton strides through precincts left mysterious in the Bible, precincts at the entrance of which other poets stopped. Milton is suspended over the hell of curious questioners, an uncomfortable position betrayed by the eruptions of anxiety examined in the last chapter.

If Milton finds in the Samson of Judges a ready-made exemplar of the sin of indiscretion, he must reinvent that Samson to add a parallel to his own marital experience. Samson does not marry Dalila in Judges; Milton invents the brilliant scene of marital recrimination from whole cloth. The changes in Dalila serve in each case to extend the parallel between Milton and Samson. The process of rewriting Samson's erotic history, moreover, starts before the introduction of Dalila. Milton elides entirely the brief episode of the harlot in Judges 16:1–2:

> Then went Samson to Gaza, and saw there an harlot, and went in unto her. And so it was told the Gazites, saying, Samson is come hither. And they compassed him in, and laid wait for him all night in the gate of the city, and were quiet all the night, saying, In the morning, when it is day, we shall kill him.

Milton covers the gap of the missing harlot by splicing the ensuing story of Samson's hoisting of the gate harboring the treacherous Gazites and carrying it to the hill before Hebron (Judges 16:3) to the preceding story of Samson's slaughtering the Philistines with the jawbone of an ass (Judges 15:14–20). A trace of the gap remains, however. In the poem, Samson moves directly from the battle at Lehi to the hoisting of the gate at Gaza. An action motivated in the source text by the story of Samson's visit to the harlot enters without motivation, except for the intratextual motivation of foreshadowing the manhandling of the pillars at the temple of Dagon, into a poem that has excised that story. The barely noticeable disjunction in the text marks the otherwise clean excision of the harlot story.

While Milton's Samson shares some of the limitations of the Samson of Judges, Milton is apparently intent on safeguarding Samson's chastity. That virtue which was the cause and warrant of Milton's own prophetic gift is ascribed, counter to the source text's evidence, to the figure who, like Milton, is the repository of divine secrets. Samson's sexual relationship with the harlot is airbrushed from Milton's text; his sexual relationship with Dalila is legitimized by marriage. In Judges (16:4), Samson "loved a woman in the valley of Sorek, whose name was Dalilah." Milton's Samson convinces himself of the lawfulness of the union by recalling the divine warrant for marriage with the woman of Timna. Samson's self-persuasion is itself open to various interpretations. Is his a reasonable extrapolation, or is it an example of the kind of egocentric willfulness that Samson at times exhibits? Even under the less charitable reading of Samson's motivation, he is still not guilty of conscious violation of chastity. The focus shifts instead to the error of one who has married to his own ruin, a situation resembling the one in which Milton found himself in the 1640s.

As tactless as Manoa's "I cannot praise thy marriage choices" may be, he is right. Samson chooses Dalila too hastily. Like the young man Milton describes (and palpably identifies with) in *The Doctrine and Discipline of Divorce,* Samson is moved by an exterior. To borrow language from *Paradise Lost,* he chooses a "fair appearing good" (9.354). The chorus, right for once, observes, "beauty, though injurious, hath strange power" (1003). Having chosen her, Samson expects her to choose Israel over Palestine. He dismisses her arguments for piety to her gods and civic and family duty ("Being once a wife, for me thou wast to leave / Parents and country" [885–86]). While Samson protests the truth of his love toward his second wife, he exhibits the kind of injured merit and irrational rage that marks the dark alternative to Milton's egalitarian arguments in the divorce tracts. In refusing to choose Israel's God over Dagon, Dalila refuses to be a wife and becomes instead, in the chorus's words, "a thorn / Intestine, far within defensive arms / A cleaving mischief" (1037–39). The language echoes the language of the 1640s. In *Tetrachordon,* the terms "thorn" and "mischief" have already been yoked: "if God took a rib out of his inside, to form of it a double good to him, he would far sooner dis-joyn it from his outside, to prevent a treble *mischief* to him: and far sooner cut it quite off from all relation for his undoubted ease, then nail it into his body again, to stick for ever there a *thorn* in his heart" (*YP* 2:602; my emphasis). Later in the same text Milton asks whether Jesus would have put "this yoke upon a blamelesse person, to league himselfe in chaines with a *begirting mischeif,* not to separat till death?" (*YP* 2:667; my emphasis).

Samson Agonistes exhibits the horror of sexual relations with a mismatched spouse that repeatedly surfaces in the divorce tracts. In the *Doctrine and Discipline,* the unhappy husband, barred from the liberating right of divorce, is left to the "forc't work" of "grind[ing] in the mill of an undelighted and servil copulation" (*YP* 2:258). There is a powerful nexus between marital discord, the plight of Samson, forced labor and "grinding," and sexual slavery, which looks forward to the captive Samson, who must "grind in brazen fetters under task / . . . / Eyeless in Gaza at the mill with slaves" (35, 41).[12] Dalila's offer to have Samson released from prison and to nurse him at home, an offer laden with sensuality ("Life yet hath many solaces, enjoyed / Where other senses want not their delights / At home in leisure and domestic ease" [915–17]), strikes Samson as a slavery more degraded than the one he suffers as a prisoner. This combination of ideas was already in place in 1642 in *The Reason of Church-Government*'s description of Charles seduced by whorish prelates:

> And while he [the king] keeps them ["Temperance and Sobriety"] about him undiminisht and unshorn, he may with the jaw-bone of an Asse, that is, with the word of his meanest officer suppresse and put to confusion thousands of those that rise against his just power. But laying down his head among the strumpet flatteries of Prelats, while he sleeps and thinks no harme, they wickedly shaving off all those bright and waighty tresses of his laws . . . deliver him over to indirect and violent councels, which as those Philistims put out the fair, and farre-sighted eyes of his natural discerning, and make him grinde in the prison house of their sinister ends and practices upon him. (*YP* 1:859)

It is a short step in Milton's imagination from harlot's lap to prison. But Samson, like Milton himself, does not knowingly choose a strumpet or harlot; instead, each is deceived by a woman whom he thought could be a wife, who would be, in the words of *Tetrachordon,* "a meet help, a solace, not a nothing, not an adversary, not a desertrice" (*YP* 2:605).

---

12. See Annabel Patterson, "Milton, Marriage and Divorce" in *A Companion to Milton,* ed. Thomas Corns (Oxford: Blackwell, 2001), p. 292.

The initial use of the term "mischief" in the first edition of Milton's first divorce tract is particularly revealing. The misguided overturning of the Mosaic law of divorce "hath chang'd the blessing of matrimony not seldome into a familiar and co-inhabiting mischiefe; at least into a drooping and disconsolate household captivitie, without refuge or redemption" (*YP* 2:235). Milton writes from painful experience. After years of commitment to chastity, Milton turned to marriage as a necessary blessing, only to find what he came to think of as a household mischief. The reference to "household captivitie, without refuge or redemption" reveals something about the deep springs of the Dalila episode in *Samson Agonistes*. In the extra-biblical episode, Samson must choose between apparent *refuge*, the physical comfort and release from suffering that Dalila offers, to all appearances generously, and the possibility of *redemption* if he remains true to God and hostile to Philistine gods and Philistine hospitality.

Dalila has been "a familiar and co-inhabiting mischiefe" in two senses. She has been intimately familiar with Samson, but the term also suggests a connection to witchcraft. A disillusioned Samson associates Dalila with Circe, with whom Milton often associated dangerous women. Samson makes this connection in the symbolic moment of divorcing Dalila:

> thou and I long since are twain;
> Nor think me so unwary or accursed
> To bring my feet again into the snare
> Where once I have been caught; I know thy trains
> Though dearly to my cost, thy gins, and toils;
> Thy fair enchanted cup, and warbling charms
> No more on me have power, their force is nulled,
> So much of adder's wisdom I have learned
> To fence my ear against thy sorceries.
>
> (929–37)

The charming cup links *A Mask, An Apology for Smectymnuus,* and *Samson Agonistes*. What distinguishes the use early and late is that good men now can fall prey, temporarily, to the charming cup. Milton leaves behind the invincibility claimed in works prior to 1643. Samson has made an error like the one Milton at some level fears that he has made himself. Virtue now involves fighting free of the error rather than remaining exempt from it. Chastity has been breached, and it must be regained.

The chastity to be regained is as much verbal as sexual. Paula Loscocco has demonstrated how Milton's Samson appropriates feminine characteristics.[13]

---

13. Loscocco, "'Not Less Renown'd Than Jael': Heroic Chastity in *Samson Agonistes,*" *Milton Studies* 40 (2002): 181–200.

His sin of "shameful garrulity" is borrowed from the stereotype of the garrulous or indiscreet woman. Conversely, Samson renews himself by appropriating the silence of the Lady of *A Mask,* who could say things to tear down temples but who resists pointed provocation to speak, precisely the test that Samson failed.

It is through his oral promiscuity, along with his failed marriage, that Samson is tied to Milton's own anxieties concerning transgression. If Samson recovers from error in part, as Loscocco contends, by reestablishing his verbal chastity, he does so as well by divorcing himself from the unfit wife. The chorus, in the speech containing the picture of Dalila as "thorn / Intestine," attempts to exonerate Samson by attacking the woman, describing his marital woes in terms that echo the self-referential picture of a failed marriage in the *Doctrine and Discipline:*

> Whate'er it be, to wisest men and best
> Seeming at first all heavenly under virgin veil,
> Soft, modest, meek, demure,
> Once joined, the contrary she proves, a thorn
> Intestine, far within defensive arms
> A cleaving mischief, in his way to virtue
> Adverse and turbulent, or by her charms
> Draws him awry enslaved
> With dotage, and his sense depraved
> To folly and shameful deeds which ruin ends.
> What pilot so expert but needs must wreck
> Embarked with such a steers-mate at the helm?
> (1034–45)

The chorus does for Samson what Milton had done for himself in the divorce tracts. Good men fall prey, blamelessly, to deceptive and *charm*ing women. The chorus must do the rationalizing for two reasons: Samson does not share the young Milton's sense of blamelessness, and Samson is poorly equipped for this kind of mental exercise. To notice this is to notice an anomaly in the chorus's speech. By some criteria, Samson might be called the "best" of men, but it is difficult to imagine in what sense he can be described as among the "wisest." The adjective makes sense only if Samson serves as a (significantly modified) stand-in for Milton. It is easy to see how a hero as intellectually limited as the Samson of Judges might make the mistake that Milton made. As Milton had argued in the mid-1640s, we require the law allowing divorce because of our "unsinning weakness," the limitations of imperfect men. Samson becomes a model of this weakness, but one who at the same time carries the mark of divine favor, the mark that Milton claimed for himself. The irony of the chorus's reference to the "wisest" in relation to Samson points to the true referent of the speech, Milton himself.[14]

The chorus goes on to describe Samson's experience according to a dialectic that Milton had used to describe his thinly veiled alter ego in the divorce tracts:

> Favored of Heav'n who finds
> One virtuous, rarely found,
> That in domestic good combines:
> Happy that house! His way to peace is smooth:
> But virtue which breaks through all opposition,
> And all temptation can remove,
> Most shines and most is acceptable above.
> (1046–52)

A happy marriage is the best state, but one who liberates himself from the prison of a bad marriage is more heroic than one who ignominiously endures. Samson of course has been blinded by his wife and delivered over to his enemies. Milton's heroism, given that it has involved more subtle powers of perception, is all the greater. This is the Milton of *Tetrachordon* (*YP* 2:666–67) who begins by defending the unhappy man (and by extension himself) for requiring the recourse of divorce and ends by asserting the greater perfection of such a man.

Because of his intertwined failures in marriage and in keeping a divine secret, Samson enters his poem in a captivity that vividly illustrates the captivity of his fellow Israelites. His failure leads to blindness and the apparent abdication of his role as deliverer. Milton's poor marriage choice threatened to undermine his carefully nurtured claims to prophetic status, along with his ambition to be a deliverer of the English from ecclesiastical captivity. But Milton had in the divorce tracts recast the "failing" as an opportunity to exhibit heroism, showing his special fidelity to God's will by contemplating divorce (and by championing a repudiated divine law allowing divorce). As for keeping divine secrets, William Kerrigan has argued that Milton's blindness is recast in *Paradise Lost* as a proleptic punishment for the "crime" of prophetic

---

14. Milton had earlier praised Samson's acuity. In a passage from *The Reason of Church-Government* quoted above he had compared Charles to Samson and Charles's prelatical counselors to Philistines: "those Philistims put out the fair, and farre-sighted eyes of his natural discerning." This counterintuitive reading of the Samson of Judges arises from the rhetorical situation: as Milton distinguishes the praiseworthy king from his perfidious advisers, it would be counterproductive to associate Charles with Samson's blockishness.

presumption in the epic.[15] If Milton has already been punished for speaking divine secrets, he is all the more free to assume the prophetic role and press it to its limits.

Milton, as we have seen, turns defense into offense when questions of his rectitude arise. Samson echoes this strategy. He argues, as Milton had in the prose works of the later Interregnum, that a failed deliverance is the responsibility not of the deliverer but of his compatriots. Milton arranges this by grafting a debate about relative responsibility onto the skeletal story from Judges. In the source, in the aftermath of the incident at the wedding with the woman of Timna, the enraged Philistines search out Samson, who is handed over by his countrymen. In Milton's poem, the incident is expanded and debated by Samson and the chorus. The chorus observes, insensitively at least, that despite Samson's strategic marriages with two Philistian women, "Israel still serves with all his sons" (240). Samson immediately transfers the guilt onto "Israel's governors,"

> Who, seeing those great acts which God had done
> Singly by me against their conquerors,
> Acknowledged not, or not at all considered
> Deliverance offered: I on th' other side
> Used no ambition to commend my deeds;
> The deeds themselves, though mute, spoke loud the doer;
> But they persisted deaf.
>
> (242–49)

Had the Israelites followed Samson instead of turning him over, they would by now be free, just as the English would be free had they not persisted on "chusing them a captain back for *Egypt*" (*YP* 7:463). Samson's deeds, he says, "spoke loud the doer," almost as Milton's anonymous 1640s works spoke loud the writer. The claim of modesty, in not commending himself, sounds more like Milton than the blundering and vain Samson of Judges.

Samson concludes this speech in the unmistakable voice of his author, as he washes his hands of the apparent failure of his mission:

> But what more oft in nations grown corrupt,
> And by their vices brought to servitude,
> Than to love bondage more than liberty,
> Bondage with ease than strenuous liberty;
> And to despise, or envy, or suspect
> Whom God hath of his special favor raised
> As their deliverer; if he aught begin,

---

15. Kerrigan, *The Sacred Complex: On the Psychogenesis of Paradise Lost* (Cambridge, MA: Harvard University Press, 1983), pp. 190–92.

> How frequent to desert him, and at last
> To heap ingratitude on worthiest deeds?
> (268–76)

The perceptive reflectiveness of Samson here is not in Judges, and not merely because the sparer narrative leaves no room for dwelling on his thoughts. The Samson of Judges is dull-witted. It is not only the pose of the deliverer failed by his people that is Milton's here, but the intellectual acuity that allows Samson to articulate the pose. Putting words in Samson's mouth allows Milton again to rehearse the role of the one just man, trusted with a sacred office, abandoned by his people. He assigns this familiar and favorite pose to Samson even though Samson's multiple errors make Samson's absolving himself of responsibility all the more tenuous.

Milton also places his signature on Samson in the chorus's comment on Samson's speech. The chorus is reminded of "how ingrateful Ephraim / Had dealt with Jephtha, who by argument, / Not worse than by his shield and spear / Defended Israel" (282–85). The basis in Judges 11 for the chorus's characterization of Jephtha's actions, moreover, is flimsy. According to Newton Jephtha's defense "by argument" is "on account of the message which he sent unto the king of the children of Ammon."[16] The "argument" is brief: "What hast thou to do with me, that thou art come against me to fight in my land?" (Judges 11:12). The picture of Jephtha as fighting with words rather than the sword recalls less the Samson of the source text or even the poem than it does Milton's representation of his service to the commonwealth.

It is fitting that in his last poem Milton wrestles one last time with the anxiety of belatedness and insists on the godliness of patience. Samson was to have accomplished so much, but he now has so little to show. He is tempted by others and by his own ambition to question divine disposition and to think that the time is now past for the heroic actions for which he was born. The chorus, which in the course of the play recommends almost any conceivable attitude and rehearses and condemns the same arguments, comes around to praising patience and urging it on Samson:

> But patience is more oft the exercise
> Of saints, the trial of their fortitude,
> Making them each his own deliverer,
> And victor over all
> That tyranny or fortune can inflict.
> Either of these is in thy lot,
> Samson, with might endued

---

16. Newton's note to *SA* 282, in H. J. Todd, ed., *The Poetical Works of John Milton, with Notes of Various Authors*, 6 vols. (London, 1826), 4:369.

> Above the sons of men; but sight bereaved
> May chance to number thee with those
> Whom patience finally must crown.
>
> (1287–96)

As with Hamlet, Samson's enigmatic final action comes only after he has given up his restless questioning and self-assertion. He emerges victorious, if that is what happens, after he sinks below even the captive but defiant state of the poem's opening. It must seem to the Israelites that the promise of the ascending fire and smoke of the angel's announcement of his birth, mentioned several times in the poem, is extinguished as Samson agrees to a last humiliation, displaying his strength at the festival in honor of Dagon. But that fire returns with Samson's emergence as a phoenix from the ashes:

> So virtue giv'n for lost,
> Depressed, and overthrown, as seemed,
> Like that self-begott'n bird
> In the Arabian woods embossed,
> That no second knows nor third,
> And lay erewhile a holocaust,
> From out her ashy womb now teemed,
> Revives, reflourishes, then vigorous most
> When most unactive deemed,
> And though her body die, her fame survives,
> A secular bird ages of lives.
>
> (1697–1707)

The phoenix, in its immolation and miraculous rebirth, gathers into one image the two Samsons, the failed hero who must suffer and the chosen hero who will live on. Samson must pay a price for sins that resemble Milton's own unacknowledged or half-acknowledged failings. In this way the hero of Milton's last poem resembles that side of Milton's self-representation that emerges only fitfully and incompletely from beneath Milton's self-valorizing. At the same time Samson is the chosen one who achieves a victory over the enemies of God. *Samson Agonistes* draws its strength from the dialectic between Milton's two sets of self-representations, one acknowledged and one unacknowledged. The Samson of the revisionists, with all his faults, is finally no less a stand-in for his author than the Samson of the regenerationist account.

There is a way from weakness to strength. Milton, at the end of his career as at the beginning, when he sat with the angels of the "Nativity Ode" and bided his time in the 1633 "Letter to a Friend," is "vigorous most / When most unactive deemed." Judging himself, Milton has held himself to a high standard. At the same time he has betrayed awareness that the standard is higher than any man might meet. In *Paradise Regained* he had imagined a human being who could meet those standards only because he is in part divine. In *Samson Agonistes* he allows himself to construct a hero out of a frail and fallen man. In building Samson out of elements of his own self-representation, Milton explores the darker sides of his own self-conception, coming closer to the Augustinian autobiographical narrative of conviction and regeneration than he does anywhere else in his writing. This reconstruction is a deeply mature act, and it measures the distance Milton has come from the fantastic and naïve self-constructions of the young man.

Epilogue

Of True Religion, Hæresie, Schism, Toleration, of early 1673, is the last substantial work surviving from Milton's pen.[1] Milton had to argue carefully. He and his contemporaries were asked in effect to support toleration of both Roman Catholics and Dissenters or to support toleration of neither. Some Dissenters were willing to tolerate Catholics as the price of being tolerated themselves. Milton refused either alternative, choosing instead to argue for toleration of Dissenters and the continued prohibition of Roman Catholic practice in England.

But if he refused to compromise either of these constant principles, in *Of True Religion* Milton does make a significant rhetorical compromise. Under the restored Stuart government, Milton can no longer argue effectively for prohibition of a state church. Instead, he argues for toleration of all true Protestants, whether they align themselves with Church of England parishes or dissenting congregations. Earlier he had tarred the established church with the brush of Romanizing coercion, authoritarianism, and idolatry; now he must isolate the Church of Rome as unique in order to argue that Roman Catholics alone should not be tolerated.

He chooses a strategy of disingenuousness, writing of Dissenters and sectarians, whose thinking most closely reflects his own, as sincere if perhaps

---

1. The one later work is a translation of the *Declaration* of the election of Jan Sobieski as King John III of Poland (*YP* 8:445–53). For Milton's translation of the *Declaration* as addressed to the danger of succession by the Roman Catholic heir to the English throne, James II, see Barbara Lewalski, *The Life of John Milton* (Oxford: Blackwell, 2000), pp. 489 and 507.

misguided searchers for Christian truth. His pan-Protestant perspective minimizes differences between competing confessions. As long as all can agree to base their belief on Scripture, sincerely interpreted after imploring the aid of the Spirit, then intolerance has no place among Protestants:

> What Protestant then who himself maintains the same Principles, and disavowes all implicit Faith, would persecute, and not rather charitably tolerate such men as these, unless he mean to abjure the Principles of his own Religion? If it be askt how far they should be tolerated? I answer doubtless equally, as being all Protestants; that is on all occasions to give account of their Faith, either by Arguing, Preaching in their several Assemblies, Publick writing, and the freedom of Printing. (*YP* 8.426)

This follows a remarkable, extended passage in which Milton treats as if interchangeable the beliefs of mainstream "orthodox" branches of Protestantism, presumed heretics, and dissenting sects. "[T]he hottest disputes among Protestants calmly and charitably enquir'd into, will be found," he writes, to involve matters not necessary for salvation:

> The Lutheran holds Consubstantiation; an error indeed, but not mortal. The Calvinist is taxt with Predestination, and to make God the Author of sin; not with any dishonourable thought of God, but it may be over zealously asserting his absolute power, not without plea of Scripture. The Anabaptist is accus'd of Denying Infants their right to Baptism; again they say, they deny nothing but what the Scripture denies them. The Arian and Socinian are charg'd to dispute against the Trinity: they affirm to believe the Father, Son, and Holy Ghost, according to Scripture, and the Apostolic Creed; as for terms of Trinity, Triniunity, Coessentiality, Tripersonality, and the like, they reject them as Scholastic Notions, not to be found in Scripture, which by a general Protestant Maxim is plain and perspicuous abundantly to explain its own meaning in the properest words, belonging to so high a Matter and so necessary to be known; a mystery indeed in their Sophistic Subtilties, but in Scripture a plain Doctrin.... The *Arminian* lastly is condemn'd for setting up free will against free grace; but that Imputation he disclaims in all his writings, and grounds himself largly upon Scripture only. (*YP* 8.424–26)

In this extraordinarily deft passage, Milton assumes a stance above the fray, arguing apparently from no particular Protestant perspective for the inconsequentiality of minor differences, some of which are considered damnable heresies by most Protestants, and some of which define mainstream orthodoxy itself. The master-stroke is the third-person displacement of Milton's own commitments. The displacement is sufficiently effective that at least one recent scholar has read in this passage Milton's disapproval of positions that he has clearly and often advocated.[2] Milton is sympathetic to Socinians, he is himself an anti-Trinitarian, and his position on predestination is Arminian. Far from casting doubt on Arminius, he treats him more sympathetically than he does the Calvinist. The Arminian "ground[s] himself largely upon Scripture only," whereas the Calvinist, on less firm ground, "is not without plea of Scripture," and is saved from the imputation of dishonorableness only by virtue of his overzealousness. The Arian and Socinian turn out to be contradicted not by Scripture but by scholastic gibberish, hand waving, and obfuscation. Later in the text Milton ranges "Anabaptists, Arians, Arminians, & Socinians" (*YP* 8.437) against the Papist. Although the passage seems to move from the authoritative to the marginal, Milton treats sectarian and "heretical" opinions with more respect than he does mainstream ones.

This is not surprising, given that the Olympian perspective is a screen behind which Milton one last time justifies and represents himself. Immediately after his discussion of the Arminian, and not long after the defense of the Arian and Socinian, he writes that "It cannot be deny'd that the Authors or late Revivers of all these Sects or Opinions, were Learned, Worthy, Zealous, and Religious Men, as appears by their lives written, and the same of their many Eminent and Learned followers, perfect and powerful in the Scriptures, holy and unblameable in their lives" (*YP* 8.426). Learned, worthy, zealous, religious, perfect, powerful, holy, above blame: the catalogue of adjectives might as well have been distilled from Milton's self-constructions.

Milton, as he rounds his last text to a close, repeats a gesture he has made many times. How dare anyone silence another who has searched Scripture as diligently and sincerely as the silencer himself? Milton, who had been unable to publish his *De Doctrina* because of the intolerance and restrictions against which he argues in *Of True Religion,* is moved to write once again by the "spur of self-concernment." The one silenced is Milton, and Milton, from the time of *Areopagitica,* has not been able to countenance that: "is it a fair course to assert truth by arrogating to himself the only freedome of speech, and stopping the mouths of others equally gifted?" (*YP* 8.437). Milton has always written of freedom of speech as an achievement, as something earned by exercise, as the "lay[ing] up as the best treasure, and solace of a good old age, . . . the honest liberty of free speech from my youth" (*Reason of Church-Government* [*YP* 1:804]). Now this treasure is in danger of being monopolized by others, and

---

2. Paul Sellin argues that Milton here indicates his disagreement with Arminius ("John Milton's *Paradise Lost* and *De doctrina Christiana* on Predestination," *Milton Studies* 34 [1996]: 59).

Milton fights to retain it. The phrase "equally gifted" is nicely ambiguous. The speaker threatened with silence may be equally gifted with insight into Scripture supplied by the Spirit. He may be the object of a gift given. At the same time, he may be at least equally wise, perspicacious, talented, virtuous. The voice of the Spirit should not be stillborn anywhere. Just as important, men of outstanding merit, such as Milton, should not be relegated to the sidelines, and to silence, by lesser and presumptuous men. We hear the voice, one last time, of injured merit.

As I remarked at the outset, my desire to explore Milton's self-representations was founded on the conviction that he is a figure eminently worth knowing. His accomplishments underwrite claims that would have to be labeled mere arrogance if advanced by a lesser author and man. Milton's works render plausible the assertions of immortality advanced, for example, in *The Reason of Church-Government* and the *Defensio Secunda*. If shining a bright light on Milton's self-representations revealed at times less attractive moments, I can say only that literary scholarship is not hagiography and that Milton is more than great enough to survive criticism. While writing this book, my respect for the man and his art has grown rather than diminished.

Milton's preoccupation with his merit, and his generation of self-representations establishing, defending, and trading on that merit, structure his career in the ways explored by this book. Milton first turns to self-representation to establish the ethical proof. As a relative unknown challenging illustrious opponents in the early polemical prose, Milton purchases authority with autobiographical micronarratives describing his extraordinary virtue. But the resort to the ethical proof is not merely rhetorical; Milton believes in his own heroic virtue. In a manner not adequately explained by differences in rhetorical occasion, Milton does not share with fellow Puritan autobiographers a habit of anxious self-examination. Unlike such contemporaries as John Bunyan and Thomas Shepard, Milton seems oblivious to the possibility of sinfulness, much less reprobation; his early self-representations imply his exemption from the effects of the fall and lay claim to elect, prophetic status. The disjunction between Milton's theology of the fall, obvious not only from *De Doctrina* but also from his two epics, and the absence of any open acknowledgment of sinfulness in his frequent and extensive autobiographical writings, suggests that however much of a theological writer he is, he is not a religious writer. We never see him in his writings, as we see so many of his contemporaries in theirs, wrestling openly with his own *experience* of the doctrines of fall, grace, and regeneration that are central to his theology, indeed to anyone's theology in the seventeenth century.

In the sequence of Milton's self-representations, *The Doctrine and Discipline of Divorce* is a watershed. Milton contends that Christ intended his prohibition of divorce (Matthew 5:31–32) only for the hard of heart and that Christ's intention is to let stand the Mosaic allowance of divorce for the godly. Believing that prophetic power is granted only to those adhering strictly to scriptural norms and that its mark is an inspired reading of the Word, he now finds himself mired in a failing marriage and arguing against the literal sense of the Bible. The prophetic stance cultivated in the tracts of the early 1640s is threatened by the distance between the apparent literal sense of Christ's prohibition and Milton's inventive rereading of it. When Milton suggests in several passages that a literal reading of New Testament proscription of divorce can lead the godly to despair, he betrays a fear that he has been cut off from God.

In the divorce tracts, Milton represents himself in two ways. First, he is the virtuous and thus inexperienced man who through no fault of his own has made a bad marriage choice. Second, he obscurely contemplates the possibility that he may now be separated from the body of Christ. Because self-representation is centrally important in Milton's prose works, the fissures that open give rise to incoherences, as Milton offers prelapsarian solutions to postlapsarian problems. With the fragmentation of the self-representation in the *Doctrine and Discipline,* we enter a new period. Side by side with a continuation of the ethical proof come passages in which Milton obscurely explores, through such veils as third-person displacement and counterfactual proposition, his own possible alienation from God. These competing self-representations, one explicit and one implicit, mark the works of the Interregnum.

The loss of univocity in Milton's self-representations, while it unsettles the author's attempt to set limits on the interpretation of his works, is not to be lamented, for the division of self-representations emerging from the writings on divorce generates much of the creative tension of *Paradise Lost* and *Samson Agonistes.* If the epic's authorial voice retains in places a confidence in special divine appointment reminiscent of the polemical prose, at other times it achieves deep empathy with the fallen Adam and Eve. Milton's narrator both glories in his ability "to see and tell / Of things invisible to mortal sight" and worries that he will fall from this flight and be left "Erroneous there to wander and forlorn." The imagined erroneous wandering points in two directions: (1) toward a feared loss of the special, inspired status that makes *Paradise Lost* possible and (2) toward the mature identification with fallen humanity that makes the poem readable.

Recognition of Milton's divided self-representations and the equivocal voice of *Paradise Lost* provides a key, I have argued, to the most vexed issue in Milton studies, the meaning of *Samson Agonistes.* Is this a comic work in which Samson, the divinely appointed instrument of Israel's liberation, works his way back from sin and alienation to grace and, at the moment of death, redemptive triumph? Many readers see in this Samson's late heroism a self-portrait of Milton. The anti-autobiographical "revisionist" reading suggests that Samson ends the play as he begins it, not reilluminated but destroyed by pride, thirst for vengeance, and suicidal despair. I have argued that a Samson "elect above the rest" who has achieved his end and a Samson profoundly fallen and flawed are equally autobiographical and equally implicated in Milton's lifelong project of self-representation. Such a divided character reflects Milton's profoundly divided representations of himself as they emerge in and shape the course of his career.

Index

1673 Poems, 147
"Ad Patrem," 72–74
ambition: poetic, 7, 48, 52, 65, 76, 135, 207, 213, 234
Ames, William, 195–196
An Answer to a Book, Intituled, the Doctrine and Discipline of Divorce (anonymous), 113, 132
An Apology for Smectymnuus, 2, 5, 30, 41, 53, 63, 88–89, 99–109, 257
Animadversions, 85–88, 100, 103–104
anxiety, 90, 100–101, 208; and assertion, 210–211, 226–228, 236; caused by critics, 141–142; and divorce, 110–111, 117–118; and heroic self-construction, 114–115, 219; literary, 164; moral and religious, 120, 176, 258; and Satan, 206; and syntax, 15, 18, 85, 148, 169, 246
Areopagitica, 6, 136–145, 156n, 198, 267
Ariosto, Ludovico, 216
Aristotle, 39–40
Arminianism, x, 30, 36, 144–145, 184, 184–185n, 186–188, 190–197, 199, 201, 267
Augustine, x, 25, 27–29, 38, 40, 46, 78
authority, 89, 140, 179, 211; and age, 88, 91, 140; and moral purity, 116
autobiography: contemporary, 22, 23, 25–26, 45–46; in Milton's digressions, 2, 3, 88–90, 94–95, 99, 164–166; Puritan, ix–xi, 21, 24, 25, 27–31, 38, 40, 54, 77–78, 242. *See also* Augustine; Calvinism: and spiritual autobiography; Paul

Barker, Arthur, 54, 111–112, 124–125n, 131n, 185n, 188, 206
Barthes, Roland, xi, 5–9
Bastwick, John, 42
Baxter, Richard, 22–23, 28, 35, 36, 191
Beardsley, Monroe C., 7n
belatedness, 2, 14–15, 166, 168, 172, 245, 248, 249, 261
Bellerophon, 176, 223–230, 235
Belsey, Catherine, 9
bishops. *See* episcopacy
Blair, Robert, 28
blindness, 170–171; as punishment, 18, 147–148, 220, 252–253, 259–260; as sign of prophetic power, 220–222, 246, 259
Booy, David, 22n
Browne, Sir Thomas, 22, 41
Bunyan, John, 24, 27, 29, 43
Burden, Dennis, 184n
Burton, Robert, 37–38
Butler, Samuel, 103n

Cable, Lana, 82, 112n
Cadbury, Henry, 36, 37n
Calvin, John, 25–26, 194, 207, 217
Calvinism, 267; and depravity, 30–31; and election, x, 184–188, 190–197, 199–201; and salvation, 36–37; and spiritual autobiography, 23, 25, 41, 61; and theodicy, 183–184, 217–218

Cambridge University, 47–48, 103–104, 164–165
Campbell, Gordon, 50n, 183n
Carey, John, 75–76
Charles I, 151, 154–159, 173, 256
chastity, 53–54, 59–60, 63, 235; Bellerophon and, 224–226; economic, 87; Milton's, defended, 100, 103–104, 107; and opponents' libertinism, 167, 172; Orpheus and, 228; and poetic ambition, 76, 105–106, 147, 214–215; and prophetic power, 98, 225; in *Samson Agonistes*, 257–258. *See also* authority: and moral purity
Cicero, 39–41, 137, 163
Civil Power, A Treatise of, 176–177
Clarkson, Laurence, 32–34
Coiro, Ann Baynes, 147n, 252n
Colasterion, 132
Coleridge, Samuel Taylor, xiii, 1
Coppe, Abiezer, 32–34, 38–39
Coppin, Richard, 32, 36n, 37
Corns, Thomas, 143n, 144nn, 147n, 150, 183n, 239n
Cowley, Abraham, 212–217
Cowper, William, 29
Cromwell, Oliver, 149–151
Crosby, Sara, 73n
The Cry of the Royal Blood (anonymous), 164, 166
Cullen, Patrick, 54

Danielson, Dennis, 30n, 184n, 187, 191
Dante, 96, 105
de Brass, Henry: letter to, 160
De Doctrina Christiana, 182–184, 186–198, 200–202, 250, 254, 267
Defence of the English People. See *Defensio*
Defence of Himself. See *Pro Se Defensio*
Defensio, 3, 160–164, 166, 179n, 252
Defensio Secunda, 2, 148, 151, 160–162, 164–175, 205, 220, 243–244
Delaney, Paul, 22, 28–29, 30n
de Man, Paul, 12, 46
Diekhoff, John, ix–x, 81, 89n
Diodati, Charles, 45, 48, 51, 52, 53, 64, 74
divorce: mutually blameless, 21, 121–127; woman blamed, 121–122, 124–125
Doctrine and Discipline of Divorce, 110–132, 140, 152, 255–256, 258, 268, 269
DuRocher, Richard, 228

Edwards, Thomas, 42–43, 101
Eikon Basilike, 154–159
Eikonoklastes, 95, 150, 154–159, 164, 173, 179n

Elegy 6, 51, 53–54, 70, 203
Elegy 7, 77
Ellwood, Thomas, 32
episcopacy, 85–88, 93, 97, 152
"Epitaphium Damonis," 53, 74–76
ethical proof, x, 39–41, 43, 50, 89, 97, 98, 105, 153, 155, 159, 175, 230, 268–269
Euripides, 62; *The Bacchae*, 228–229; *Medea*, 16n
Evans, J. Martin, 47n, 54, 68–69, 69n
Ezekiel, 114, 200

Fallon, Robert Thomas, 168n
Fish, Stanley, xi, 11–12, 66, 68–69, 144n, 226n, 245
Forsythe, Neil, 205n
Foucault, Michel, 7–8
Fowler, Alastair, 219
Fox, George, 34–36
Fry, Paul, 56
Frye, Northrop, ix

Galilei, Galileo, 136–137
Gallagher, Philip, 184n
Gerard, John, 29–30
Gospel of Luke, 242–244
Gregory, E. R., 222n
Grose, Christopher, 16n, 83n, 109
Gross, Kenneth, 235n
Guillory, John, 3n, 46n, 64, 99, 204n, 221n, 222n

Hale, John K., 147n, 183n
Hall, Bishop Joseph, 85–87, 103n
Halpern, Richard, 47n, 60
Hanford, James Holly, 68–69
Hartlib, Samuel, 133
Haskin, Dayton, 18n, 48n, 198n
Hatten, Charles, 113n
Haug, Ralph A., 95n
Henry, N. H., 147n
Herbert, George, 22
Herman, Peter, xiii, 11n
Hesiod, 214, 224
Heywood, Oliver, 24
Higginson, Francis, 35n
Hill, Christopher, 182n
Hill, John Spencer, 38, 193n
Hogan, Christine, 226n
Holmes, David I., 183n
Homer, 48, 52, 95, 213, 224, 231; Achilles, 170–171
Hume, Patrick, 219–220
Hunter, William, 182 n

Independents, 23, 25
intention: authorial, xi, 5–13, 230; human will, 24; Milton's, 97, 156, 232, 234
introspection, 25–26, 45, 54–55, 93, 253
Isaiah, 38–39, 97–98, 200

Jay, Paul, 45n
Jeremiah, 39, 178, 180, 200
Job, Book of, 95, 217
John, evangelist, 200
Johnson, Samuel, 66
The Judgement of Martin Bucer, 10n, 80, 122n, 152
Judges, Book of, 254–255, 258, 260–261

Keats, John, 58, 65
Keeble, N. H., 21, 22n, 27
Kelley, Maurice, 30n, 182n, 185n, 187, 198n
Kennedy, William J., 72n
Kerrigan, William, xi, 38–39, 49n, 62–63, 92n, 196n, 205n, 222n, 232n, 259–260
Kranidas, Thomas, 79n
Krouse, Michael, 238n

Leonard, John, 219, 231
"Letter to a Friend," 1633, xii, 14–21, 43–44, 46, 60–61, 148, 249, 262
Lewalski, Barbara, 147n, 182n, 237n, 265n
Lieb, Michael, 60n, 143, 227n
Likeliest Means to Remove Hirelings, 176–177
Little, Marguerite, 72n
Loewenstein, David, xiin, 84n
Loscocco, Paula, 257
Lucretius, 209
Luther, Martin, 24–25
Lyas, Colin, 13
"Lycidas," 2, 20, 49, 53, 59, 64–71, 74–76, 80

MacLaren, I. S., 54
Madsen, W. B., 68n
Mallarmé, Stephane, 6, 8
Martz, Louis, 53, 61, 147n, 219
Marvell, Andrew, "On Mr. Milton's *Paradise Lost*," 9–10, 184n, 208–210, 234–235; "To His Coy Mistress," 7
Mascuch, Michael, 22n
A Mask, 53, 62–64, 71, 98, 146, 257
Matthew, Sir Tobie, 29–30
McCready, Amy R., 157
Modest Confutation (anonymous), 99–104, 107, 108
More, Alexander, 43–44, 109n, 160n, 161–162, 167, 171–176
Mueller, Janel, 82–83, 84n
Mulder, John, 3, 211

"Nativity Ode," 53–59, 62, 69, 79–80, 83–84, 246, 262
Nayler, James, 34–36
Newton, Thomas, 210–211, 219, 261
Norwood, Richard, 23–24, 28
Nuttall, Geoffrey R., 21n

Of Education, 110, 133–137, 139
Of Prelatical Episcopacy, 80
Of Reformation, 80–85, 87, 91, 177
Of True Religion, Hæresie, Schism, Toleration, 265–268
Oldenburg, Henry: letter to, 174n
one just man, 155, 178, 181, 204–205, 218, 261. *See also* ethical proof; perfection: Milton's sense of; self-representation: heroic; self-representation: as prophet
Origen, 39
Orlando, Francesco, 13n
Orpheus, 67, 74n, 210, 219, 228, 229
Ovid, 48, 228
Owen, John, 200

Palmer, Herbert, 138
parables, 15–16, 18–20
Paradise Lost, x, 10, 69, 191, 197, 201–203, 208–210, 233–236, 254–255, 269; Abdiel, 4, 168, 172, 180–181, 204–207; Adam, 120–121, 131–132, 175, 198–199, 209; the Father, 184–188; invocations, 176, 211–232, 240, 253; narrator, 2–3, 211; Satan, 204–206, 228
Paradise Regained, x, 4, 32, 43, 208, 237–250, 263
Parker, William Riley, 14n, 32n, 53, 72n, 95, 113n
pastoral poetry, 66, 75
Patterson, Annabel, 115, 136, 173–174, 206, 256n
Paul, 24, 27, 29, 38, 40. *See also* autobiography: Puritan
Pelagianism, 31
perfection: Milton's sense of, 91, 106, 116, 119, 130. *See also* one just man
perfectionism, 31–34, 37, 239
Petrarch, 102, 105
Phaeton, 72–73, 226
Philaras, Leonard, letter to, 174n
Pindar, 62, 224–225
Plato, 51, 65, 78
Poems 1645, 146–147
Pope, Alexander, 184n
Powell, Mary, 111
Powell, Vavasor, 24, 26
Presbyterianism, 22, 23, 42, 153
Prolusions, 45–50
Prometheus, 73

prophets: biblical, 39, 180. *See also* Ezekiel; Isaiah; Jeremiah; self-representation: as prophet; vulgar prophets
Pro Populo Anglicano Defensio. See *Defensio*
Pro Populo Anglicano Defensio Secunda. See *Defensio Secunda*
Pro Se Defensio, 2, 149, 160, 162, 173–174
Prynne, William, 42, 144
Puritanism, 21, 41, 64. *See also* autobiography: Puritan

Quakers, xii, 32, 34–35, 37

Ransom, John Crowe, 67, 69
Ranters, 32–35, 37
The Readie and Easie Way, 176–181, 196
The Reason of Church-Government, 2, 6, 22, 46, 53, 56, 79, 88–92, 94–99, 109, 122n, 134, 152, 162, 256, 267
Richardsons, Jonathan and Jonathan, 219, 220, 228n
Revard, Stella, 2n, 51–52n, 72n, 147n
Riggs, William G., 205n
Roberts, Donald, 165
Rogers, John, 26, 240n
Rose, Gilbert Stuart, 216n
Rosenblatt, Jason, 120n
Rumrich, John, 114n, 167n, 191n, 228n
Rushdy, Ashraf, 241

Salmasius, Claudius, 160, 163, 166–168, 177, 180, 252
Samson Agonistes, 4, 62, 119n, 123, 237–239, 250–260, 262–263, 269–270
Samuel, Irene, 238n
Sánchez, Reuben, Jr., 112n, 130, 154n
Second Defence. See *Defensio Secunda*
self-representation: heroic, 103, 113, 128, 150, 169–170, 174, 178, 196, 205, 233; as prophet, xii, 55–60, 72, 90, 92–93, 95–99, 113, 140–141, 150, 154, 157–159, 160–163, 171, 176–177, 181, 207, 210, 215, 217–221, 225, 230, 245, 248, 253, 259–260, 269; as teacher, 134–135; tensions within, xii, 118–120, 183, 187–188, 202, 211–212, 229–230, 239, 269–270; third-person, 97–98, 136, 138; unintentional, xii, 5, 13, 64, 230. *See also* ethical proof
Sellin, Paul, 182n, 267
Shakespeare, William, ix, 64; sonnets, 7, 67, 97
Shapiro, Marianne, 224n
Shawcross, John, xi, 72n, 182n, 186–187n
Shepard, Thomas, 26–27, 37
Shub, Joseph, 103n
Sidney, Sir Philip, 79, 161
Silver, Victoria, 3n

Simmons, Samuel, 233
Sirluck, Ernest, 112, 123n, 222n
Smith, Nigel, 39
Socrates, 39n, 51, 65, 102, 122–123
Sonnets, Milton's: Sonnet 7, "How soon hath time," 18, 61–62, 147; Sonnet 8, "When the Assault Was Intended to the City," 62; Sonnet 11, "A book was writ," 146–147; Sonnet 12, "I did but prompt the age," 146–147; Sonnet 18, "On the Late Massacre in Piedmont," 7; Sonnet 21, "Cyriack, whose grandsire," 148; Sonnet 23, "Methought I saw my late espousèd saint," 149
Spenser, Edmund, 113, 144, 240
Stachniewski, John, 26n, 183n
Stevens, Paul, 40, 41
Strier, Richard, xn, 30–31
structural intentionality, 12, 230. *See also* intention
Sturrock, John, 45–46
Suh, Hong Won, 18n, 83–84
Sylvester, 49
Synod of Dort, 183, 192n

Tasso, Torquato, 95, 213
Tenure of Kings and Magistrates, 150–153
Tetrachordon, 111–112, 122–132, 145, 254–256, 259
Tillyard, E. M. W., 65–66
Todd, Henry John, 49
Trapnel, Anna, 26, 32, 38
Turner, James Grantham, 88, 119n, 128
Turretin, François, 194n
Tweedie, Fiona, 183n
Tyacke, Nicholas, 184n

Urban, David, 19n, 148n

verse, 233, 235
Virgil, 48, 75–76, 212–214, 231, 240
vulgar prophets, 23, 32, 34

Watkins, Owen, 32
Webber, Joan, 40, 47n, 79n
Weinfield, Henry, 6n
Wigglesworth, Michael, 185n
Wilde, Oscar, 46
Wilding, Michael, 144
Wimsatt, W. K., 12n
Winstanley, Gerrard, 37
Wittreich, Joseph, 3n, 211, 238n
Wolfe, Don M., 153, 185n
Wolleb, John, 188–190, 194n, 198n
Woodhouse, A. S. P., 54

Young, Thomas, 14n

www.ingramcontent.com/pod-product-compliance
Lightning Source LLC
Chambersburg PA
CBHW020642300426
44112CB00007B/214